Further Praise for *In the Presence of Mine Enemies*

"Edward L. Ayers, one of America's leading historians of the South, challenges this understanding of the war's inevitability in his well-researched and fast paced book." —*Raleigh News & Observer*

"A brilliant work . . . a veritable model for how social history should be collected and presented." —*Roanoke Times*

"[A] movingly human chronicle. . . . The transformation by civil war of two groups of Americans makes for fascinating reading and incisive instruction." —*Richmond Times-Dispatch*

"[A] deeply researched and beautifully written study of the early years of the American Civil War." —Wilfred M. McClay, *Chattanooga Times Free Press*

"Ayers breathes life into the way ordinary people experienced the coming and beginning of the war—that is, of history—as everyday life, concerns, and hopes become entangled with events beyond their control." —Alon Confino, *Virginia Quarterly Review*

"As an intimate story of two communities, it is social history at its finest." —*Civil War Times*

"The author's ability to humanize the past . . . makes this volume one of the few Civil War books to truly integrate political, military, and social history." —*America's Civil War*

"A glittering jewel of a book. . . . [Ayers] is a historian of considerable grace, imagination, and power." —*Civil War Book Review*

"Ayers tells his complex story with a master's touch, shifting smoothly between North and South, and between the lesser worlds of his two counties and the wider events of the war that changed them both utterly." —*Publishers Weekly*, starred review

"Original and gracefully written . . . should be required reading for Civil War enthusiasts and scholars alike." —*Library Journal*, starred review

"A penetrating analysis . . . emphasizing the anxiety, excitement, and misery that war provoked." —*Booklist*, starred review

"A first-rate study." —*Kirkus Reviews*, starred review

ALSO BY EDWARD L. AYERS

The Valley of the Shadow: Two Communities in the American Civil War—The Eve of War, CD-ROM and book (coauthor)

American Passages: A History of the United States (coauthor)

The Oxford Book of the American South: Testimony, Memory, and Fiction (coeditor)

All over the Map: Rethinking American Regions (coauthor)

The Promise of the New South: Life after Reconstruction

The Edge of the South: Life in Nineteenth-Century Virginia (coeditor)

Vengeance and Justice: Crime and Punishment in the Nineteenth-Century American South

IN THE PRESENCE OF MINE ENEMIES

WAR IN THE HEART OF AMERICA 1859–1863

EDWARD L. AYERS

W. W. Norton & Company
New York · London

Printed in the United States of America
First published as a Norton paperback 2004

Manufacturing by The Haddon Craftsmen, Inc.
Book design by Chris Welch
Production manager: Julia Druskin

Library of Congress Cataloging-in-Publication Data
Ayers, Edward L., 1953–
In the presence of mine enemies : war in the heart of America, 1859–1863 / Edward L. Ayers. — 1st ed.
p. cm. — (The valley of the shadow project)
Includes bibliographical references and index.
ISBN 0-393-05786-0
1. United States—History—Civil War, 1861–1865. 2. Shenandoah River Valley (Va. and W. Va.)—History—Civil War, 1861–1865. 3. Pennsylvania—History—Civil War, 1861–1865. 4. Virginia—History—Civil War, 1861–1865. 5. Franklin County (Pa.)—History—19th century. 6. Augusta County (Va.)—History—19th century. 7. United States—History—Civil War, 1861–1865—Causes. I. Title. II. Series.
E468 .A98 2003
973.7—dc21

2002015989

ISBN 0-393-32601-2 pbk.

W. W. Norton & Company, Inc., 500 Fifth Avenue, New York, N.Y. 10110
www.wwnorton.com

W. W. Norton & Company Ltd., Castle House, 75/76 Wells Street, London W1T 3QT

3 4 5 6 7 8 9 0

For Will Thomas, Anne Rubin,
and our companions in the Valley of the Shadow

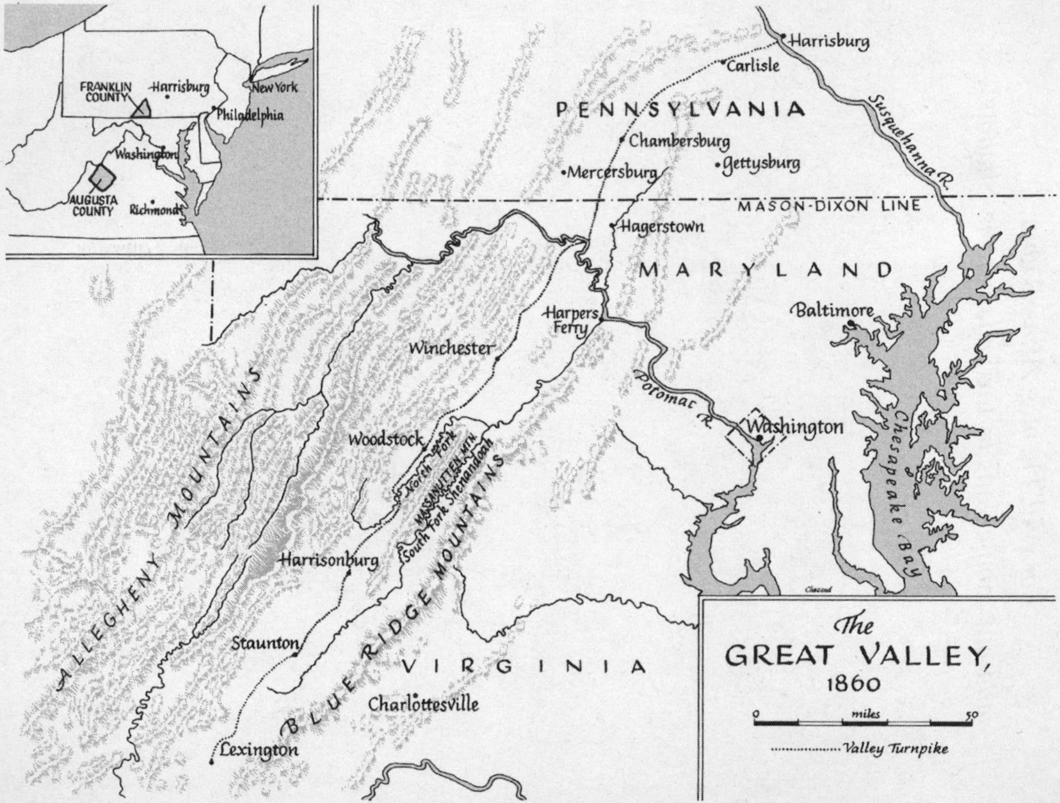
The
GREAT VALLEY,
1860
0
miles
50
Valley Turnpike
PENNSYLVANIA
MARYLAND
VIRGINIA
MASON-DIXON LINE
Harrisburg
Carlisle
Chambersburg
Mercersburg
Gettysburg
Hagerstown
Baltimore
Harpers Ferry
Washington
Winchester
Woodstock
Harrisonburg
Staunton
Charlottesville
Lexington
Susquehanna R.
Potomac R.
Chesapeake Bay
North Fork
South Fork Shenandoah
MASSANUTTEN MTN.
ALLEGHENY MOUNTAINS
BLUE RIDGE MOUNTAINS
FRANKLIN COUNTY
AUGUSTA COUNTY
New York
Philadelphia
Richmond

The EASTERN BORDER IN THE AMERICAN CIVIL WAR
miles
0
50
PENNSYLVANIA
MARYLAND
WEST VIRGINIA (after 1863)
VIRGINIA
Harrisburg
Carlisle
Philadelphia
Chambersburg
Mercersburg
Gettysburg
Hagerstown
CUMBERLAND VALLEY R.R.
Sharpsburg
BALTIMORE & OHIO R.R.
Baltimore
Romney
WINCHESTER & POTOMAC R.R.
Harpers Ferry
Winchester
Kernstown
Manassas Gap
MANASSAS GAP R.R.
Washington
Woodstock
Mount Jackson
Manassas
ORANGE & ALEXANDRIA R.R.
New Market
Chesapeake Bay
Harrisonburg
Monterey
McDowell
Cross Keys
Port Republic
Swift Run Gap
Rapidan R.
Fredericksburg
Brown's Gap
Gordonsville
Potomac R.
Rappahannock R.
Staunton
Waynesboro
Rockfish Gap
Charlottesville
VIRGINIA CENTRAL R.R.
Lexington
James R.
Richmond
Chazaud

THE VALLEY OF THE SHADOW PROJECT

THIS VOLUME IS part of the Valley of the Shadow Project. That project presents, in digital form, thousands of letters, diaries, newspapers, census entries, photographs, maps, and military records for two counties in the Great Valley of the United States, one in Pennsylvania and one in Virginia, throughout the era of the Civil War. Gathered by a team of researchers at the University of Virginia, these sources serve as the basis for a large website and a CD-ROM dedicated to the coming of the war.

Those digital sources provide virtually all the primary sources on which this book is based. Readers can visit the archive of those sources at the Virginia Center for Digital History at http://valley.vcdh.virginia.edu. There, they can explore in greater depth the stories, characters, and analysis of *In the Presence of Mine Enemies* or pursue aspects of life not covered in these pages. Visitors to the archive can also look ahead to the years of war, emanicipation, and the world yet to come to the people of this story.

CONTENTS

LIST OF ILLUSTRATIONS

LIST OF MAPS

PREFACE

AMERICANS COULD NOT have imagined the war they brought on themselves. Though people had long talked of conflict between North and South, no one could have foreseen battlefields stretched across an area the size of continental Europe or the deaths of more than half a million people. No one could have known that the most powerful slave society of the modern world, generations in the making, would be destroyed in a matter of years. No one could have known that a North long complicit in slavery would turn a struggle against disunion into a war against bondage. No one could have known that African Americans could so quickly rise to seize freedom from the turmoil.

Today, of course, we do know these things. Looking back to tell the story to ourselves, we search for opposites and contrasts to explain this overwhelming war, to set abolitionists against secessionists, industry against plantations, future against past. We look for impending crises and turning points, for the reassuring patterns that lead to the end of the story we already know.

This book tells a different kind of story. It offers a history of the Civil War told from the viewpoints of everyday people who could glimpse only parts of the drama they were living, who did not control the history that shaped their lives, who made decisions based on what they could know from local newspapers and from one another. It emphasizes the flux of emotion and belief, the intertwining of reason and feeling, the constant revision of history as people lived within history. It sets aside our knowledge of the war's outcome, starting before war could be envisioned and ending with everything in uncertainty.

The years between 1859 and 1863 saw abrupt transformations in the United States. Political conflict burst into civil war, a reluctant use of state violence turned into furious war making, war making turned into despair. In the North anti-Southernism grew into support for abolitionism that promised revenge and deliverance. In the South passionate loyalty shifted intact from the Union to the states to the Confederacy. Though profound, these transformations were never complete, never certain, and never unchallenged.

Because the Civil War was such a vast and complex event, historians often approach it in the familiar and manageable forms of broad surveys, battle histories, and biographies of generals and presidents. In these accounts, the experiences of the majority of people, soldiers as well as civilians, tend to blur into generalizations, categories, and scattered quotes. It is easy to lose sight of the way the war continually changed its meaning and implications for most Americans.

In pursuit of a more inclusive and more intimate history, this book tells the story of two communities, one Northern and one Southern. Holding a tight focus across the complicated landscape of the Civil War, this book follows the people of Franklin County, Pennsylvania, and Augusta County, Virginia, from peace into the maelstrom of the war. It intertwines the stories of North and South, sometimes using sections in italics, like voice-overs in a film, to comment on the twin narratives. The book follows the cadences of the Twenty-third Psalm, for the Bible's words were a great commonality of the two warring sides.

Augusta and Franklin lay about two hundred miles apart in the Great Valley that stretched across much of the eastern United States, a land of rich farms and pretty towns that found itself at the very center of the Civil War from John Brown's raid to Gettysburg and beyond. These two communities were swept up in nearly all the challenges the nation faced in these years. They played central roles in several episodes of the national drama and their soldiers fought in every major battle in Virginia, Maryland, and Pennsylvania. Augusta and Franklin experienced much of the Civil War in microcosm.

The stories that follow unfold on the borderland these two counties occupied, the borderland that spanned the lower North and the upper South. The people of the border did not start the fight that became the

Civil War. Indeed, they prided themselves on their restraint in the face of what they saw as provocation by extremists above and below them. They weighed the claims of antislavery and proslavery, of Democrats and Republicans, of unionists and secessionists, arguing heatedly with and among themselves, and then they threw themselves into the conflict with a desperate finality. The people of the border contributed far more than their share of critical votes and leaders, more than their share of soldiers, battlefields, and sacrifices. The nation redefined itself on the landscape of the border, the heart of the nation where North and South met.

Conflict based in slavery had divided Americans for generations before the Civil War. Some of the conflict grew from rivalry for power, some from moral outrage, some from memories from past insults, some from new events that inflamed the antagonism. But the unifying forces between the North and South were strong, too. Shared histories, religions, ethnicities, economies, languages, families, and national aspirations made a devastating civil war inconceivable to Americans, no matter what their loyalties.

Although the source of sectional divisions, slavery itself connected the North and South. Its dark threads were woven through Unionism as well as secession, private emotion as well as public policy, the mobile, technological, opportunistic, profit-driven sectors of American life as well as its agrarian and traditional aspects. Slavery relentlessly pulled in white people on both sides of the border who held no obvious stake in the institution, forcing them to take sides. It defined the fears and aspirations of black people no matter where they lived. A war about slavery would be a war that touched everything in America.

Seeing the centrality of slavery to the nation means that we acknowledge great complexity in the coming and fighting of the Civil War. Simple explanations, stark opposites, sweeping generalizations, and unfolding inevitabilities always tempt us, but they miss the essence of the story, an essence found in the deep contingency of history. To emphasize deep contingency is not to emphasize mere chance, all too obvious in a war, but rather the dense and intricate connections in which lives and events are embedded. Because all facets of social life interact, because history is woven throughout people's lives in ways both visible and invisible, all parts of life are contingent on one another, dependent on one another. The brute operations of economy or government continually interacted with the more subtle but no less potent power of culture and ideology. Sometimes people acted from personal or local motivations while at other times distant events drove their actions. A history of the Civil War must comprehend all of these facets of life as they connected in the flow of time.

An interpretation that focuses on deep contingency cuts against the grain of many Americans' understanding of the Civil War. We usually look closer to the surface, seeing the North as a modern society in obvious conflict with an archaic South, the future in conflict with the doomed past. Such a view seems like common sense, for it embodies an understandable and useful desire to see American history as a path, albeit strewn with challenges, to the realization of our best selves. This interpretation of America's great war appears in many forms, from Ken Burns's television epic *The Civil War* to best-selling novels such as Michael Shaara's *The Killer Angels* to influential histories such as James McPherson's *Battle Cry of Freedom*. These works of national affirmation, so beautifully rendered, emphasize the national redemption bought by the war's trial and sacrifice. When these works focus on chance and turning points, they do so to dramatize how things worked out for the best, for freedom, progress, and Union.[1]

Nations need, and crave, such encouraging histories, films, and novels. But nations also need other kinds of stories if they are to use history wisely, if they are to learn all they can from their past. This book dwells on facts that have posed persistent challenges to our understanding of the Civil War. The North and the South, so divided by slavery, also shared a great deal. The South was more economically advanced and the North more racially oppressive than they often seem in retrospect. To many white Southerners slavery seemed safer within the Union than without, so that no simple connection between slaveholding and votes for immediate secession emerged. Most white Southerners did not own slaves and yet supported secession and the Confederacy. The upper South, so strongly Unionist, quickly became devoted to the Confederate cause; the lower North, often sympathetic to the South before the war, threw its allegiance to the Union cause. Both the North and the South faced desperate internal conflict among their citizens, with the North's dissidents more overt and organized than the South's. The North turned against slavery as a military object but many whites, including some among the North's leaders, could not imagine black people as free American citizens. The United States, so overwhelming in its resources, could well have lost, deep into the conflict, much that it went to war to protect from the Confederacy.

Slavery brought war and its own destruction precisely because of these complications, because the war was not a simple and straightforward conflict. And once it began, the Civil War, in all its power, brought changes no one could have foreseen in the quiet and prosperous summer of 1859.

January 2003

The Twenty-third Psalm

1: The LORD is my shepherd; I shall not want.

2: He maketh me to lie down in green pastures: he leadeth me beside the still waters.

3: He restoreth my soul: he leadeth me in the paths of righteousness for his name's sake.

4: Yea, though I walk through the valley of the shadow of death, I will fear no evil: for thou art with me; thy rod and thy staff they comfort me.

5: Thou preparest a table before me in the presence of mine enemies: thou anointest my head with oil; my cup runneth over.

6: Surely goodness and mercy shall follow me all the days of my life: and I will dwell in the house of the LORD for ever.

PART ONE

GREEN PASTURES AND STILL WATERS

FALL 1859 TO FALL 1860

The LORD is my shepherd; I shall not want.
He maketh me to lie down in green pastures: he
leadeth me beside the still waters.

1

THE GREAT VALLEY of the United States cut across the border between the North and South. Walled on both sides by protective mountains twenty miles apart, the Valley stretched from Vermont all the way into Tennessee. Its heart lay in Pennsylvania and Virginia, at the center of the eastern United States.

Five or six generations before the Civil War, white settlers and the slaves they brought with them had flowed into the Valley, a place that seemed naturally made for lush farms and quiet towns. The American Indians had left behind their name for the longest river in the Valley: Shenandoah, Daughter of the Stars. Shenandoah spoke of peace, of time measured on a celestial rather than a human scale.

The terrain of the Great Valley satisfied some human longing for enclosure and protection. Though the Valley had been made by ancient upheavals of land and sea, by convulsions deep enough to create mountains, its appearance now belied its abrupt origins. The limestone beneath the Valley's soil kept the land sweet and bountiful. Dense forests grew on the mountains. Streams and rivers wound through rich farms. Hillsides nestled fine flocks of sheep and herds of cattle. Villages and towns, boasting new railroads, telegraphs, and newspapers, drew the life of the county around them.

A traveler could journey for weeks up or down the Great Valley. The mountains hovered on both the left and the right, their sense of presence shifting with the light. The traveler would notice a fundamental difference between the northern and southern parts of the Valley, however, marked by the place where the Mason-Dixon Line crossed. There slavery began and slavery ended. And slavery shaped everything it touched. Farms arrayed themselves differently on the landscape on either side of that line, towns took different shapes. People understood themselves differently across that border too, calculating their interests and imagining their futures in ways their neighbors across the border could not understand or accept.

VIRGINIA'S AUGUSTA COUNTY gathered in its county seat of Staunton (pronounced "stan'tn") to celebrate the Fourth of July in 1859. "What with the beating of drums, the waving of plumes, the flashing of bayonets, and the flying of colors," a local paper cheerfully reported, "the good old town became so bewildered and unsettled that we verily believe it will take at least a month for it to regain its original natural and dignified appearance." Military units came from surrounding counties, including a set of reenactors "uniformed as the heroes of '76, and commanded by Major Washington—a near relative of the immortal Father of his country." His appearance "irresistibly carried the mind back to those days so dear to every American heart."[1]

Augusta was a proud county, steadfast in its devotion to the Union over the decades since the founding. But for the previous four years the nation, state, and county had witnessed unprecedented bitterness and division. The North and South had warred in Kansas and in Washington, shooting, burning, and slashing each other in the West and assaulting each other in editorials, speeches, sermons, and beatings in the East. In such a time the evocation of Washington and his beloved Union seemed bittersweet.

In Augusta's celebration of its proud history, toasts marched after one another like a long line of troops; a newspaper listed thirteen before it lost count. The words revolved around history, glory, obligation, and memory. "Our ancestors of the revolution," the third toast proclaimed: "immortal for their heroic deeds in the time which tried men's souls—may their descendants ever gratefully cherish in their hearts their memory, and live worthy of such progenitors."[2]

And then, as if the drink had begun to take hold, darker and more contemporary concerns rose to the surface. The toasts became defensive, warnings to one another and to unseen and unspecified foes North and South. The ninth toast pleaded, "May the bonds which make our nation of States one of the greatest of Governments never be weakened by an internal feud." Governor Henry Wise regretted that he could not join his fellow citizens in Staunton, but he did send a toast: "The American

Union: Liberty to all—Equality to all—Protection to all persons and all property everywhere, at home and abroad!"[3] Everyone knew what he meant by "all property everywhere." Enslaved people made up nearly one-fourth of Augusta's population.

FRANKLIN COUNTY, PENNSYLVANIA, displayed itself on the Fourth of July. The county enjoyed a gathering of Sunday school classes, a locomotive covered with flags and evergreen, the firing of artillery and ceremonial muskets, the reading of the Declaration of Independence and inspiring speeches. The bounty of Franklin's rich farms spread out on tables hundreds of feet long. "What a delightful state of society we Americans enjoy!" exulted a local newspaper. "We may quarrel and abuse each other, as much as possible, during political campaigns, and it may be, at other times; but upon the recurrence of our natal day, we drop our weapons of warfare and gather around the festive board, like a band of brothers, not knowing any difference or distinction."[4]

In 1859 Franklin served up an especially exciting spectacle for the Fourth of July: a balloon ascension from the town square, fueled by gas from the new Chambersburg gasworks. The pilot of the balloon, John Light, a twenty-year-old tobacconist, displayed the mastery of machinery so admired in nineteenth-century America. The *Valley Spirit* happily predicted for him "a brilliant career as an Aeronaut." When the pilot jettisoned the bags of ballast, his balloon "shot upwards into the regions above in gallant style. Mr. Light stood up in his car and waved his cap and cheered, seemingly as much delighted as any of the spectators below him, who sent up shouts of applause." The paper judged that the balloon rose a mile before it disappeared behind the clouds.[5]

The young aeronaut reported what he saw as he floated over the Valley: "The diversified scenery of green meadows, fertile fields and clustering woods resembled the rich and gaudy coloring of a map, while the farm houses, towns and villages dotted over the surface of the valley added a deep and enlivening interest to the scene. The view presented the most grand, gratifying and gorgeous spectacle possible for the mind to conceive, and which it is alone the privilege of the Aeronaut to enjoy." He quickly traveled twenty-three miles from Chambersburg to Waynesboro, following the southerly breeze.[6]

Despite the prosperity and excitement of the holiday, the people of Franklin County worried what the next Fourth of July might bring. They had become anxious and agitated, both with themselves and with the people across the border. In July 1859 the Democrats and Republicans prepared for the next election, trying to gauge the direction of the country and their place in it.

People in 1859 could not have known how deeply their lives would change over the next four years, how desperately they would fight for purposes that did not yet exist, how many thousands among them would die. Southerners who hated secession would secede; Northerners who hated Abraham Lincoln would enlist in the Union army. Whites who hated blacks would help end slavery; whites who professed to know and love slaves would fear and distrust them. Black people who had resisted slavery as lonely individuals and desperate families would proudly work to help bring slavery's demise.

Throughout these years words poured out in a flood of diaries, letters, reports, and newspapers. People talked in several conversations at once, explaining themselves, negotiating, rationalizing, making sense of what they found themselves doing. Both sides, certain that God favored their cause, easily invoked His mercy and blessing.

2

FRANKLIN COUNTY LAY suspended in the summer of 1859. The county rested between elections while wheat and corn stood ripening in the hot Valley sun. The *Valley Spirit* and the *Transcript* spent most of their ink on local fairs, accidents, marriages, and obituaries, killing time until the fall elections.

The tedium lifted on Saturday, August 17. That was when Frederick Douglass unexpectedly appeared in Chambersburg and gave a speech in the Town Hall. Douglass, an inexhaustible laborer for freedom in all its forms, a former slave who had become the leading abolitionist in the nation, was one of the most famous people in the United States, certainly the most famous black person. His unannounced arrival in an out-of-the-way town in southern Pennsylvania caused a sensation there. The local papers did not know what to make of the occasion.

The *Valley Spirit*, the Democrats' paper, always quick to turn to crude stereotype and ridicule of black Americans, could not decide exactly how to pitch its account. The paper ran its article under the title of "Fred. Douglas," refusing to complete the famous man's first name or spell his last name correctly. The paper had to admit, however, that "there is no calling in question the extraordinary ability of Mr. Douglass as an Orator. He is an elegant and powerful speaker, and possesses a clear well modulated voice, and a style of elocution unaffected and impressive. His discourse was well received by a large and attentive auditory, and with occasional demonstrations of applause from those who seemed disposed to favor his peculiar doctrine."[7]

That "peculiar doctrine" was "to place the negro on an equality with the white man—to have him eat at the same table, sit in the same pew, and vote at the same ballot box." That was true; Douglass demanded full rights for all Americans, regardless of their skin color. The *Valley Spirit* lectured Douglass for forgetting "altogether that the Creator Himself has made a distinction when he established the great and immovable barrier of color between the races." Douglass attacked churches and ministers for refusing to assail the injustice of slavery and prejudice; the *Valley Spirit* chastised him for "opening his vials of wrath on religion, or by representing our leading divines as monsters of inhumanity. They certainly are as capable of knowing what is right and what is wrong as he is, and may be supposed to be as honest in their views."[8] The criticism was mild indeed, for the acidly racist *Valley Spirit* had just listened to the most important abolitionist in America, and a black man at that, assail slavery only miles from its northern border.

Equally surprising was the version of the speech reported by the Republican paper in town. For the last several months, the *Chambersburg Repository and Transcript* had been reprinting articles from across the North attacking the South. One, drawn from a speech given in the House of Representatives by Congressman Owen Lovejoy from Illinois, ridiculed the white Southern man's supposed abhorrence of "niggers" when in fact that same white man depended on black people for everything from his first nursing until "he invades the nigger quarters, to place himself in the endearing relation of paternity to half niggers."[9] The sarcasm and sexual innuendo had become staples in the Republican attack on slaveholders.

When it came time to report on Frederick Douglass, however, the *Transcript*, like its Democratic rival, warred with itself. The Republican paper echoed the praise of its competitor regarding Douglass's oratorical ability, one of the most highly prized attributes of manliness. Douglass's "theme was, the wrongs of his race. He handled his subject in a style which would have been creditable to many, very many of our white orators. He is, without doubt, an extraordinary man." Douglass "has unlimited command of his voice—which breathes forth betimes the sweetest accents, and again swells to Stentorian volume—and his gestures are graceful; on the whole we do not hesitate about pronouncing him a first class speaker."[10]

But the Republican paper, despite its praise, sought to distance itself from Douglass: "We can easily excuse him—a black man—for advocating the doctrine of immediate and unconditional emancipation; but if such a thing were practicable it would be altogether inexpedient. If slavery was to become rooted out, and the blacks remain among the whites, we honestly believe a war of extermination would soon be the result." The sad fate of the American Indians, the *Transcript* argued, showed "that two distinct races cannot dwell, as equals, in harmony, upon the same soil. If slavery is to be abolished, we must, at the same time, provide for the colonization of the negroes." So much was Republican doctrine; the party hated slavery, detested the slaveholder, yet could not imagine an America where enslaved people became free.[11]

Both Franklin newspapers wondered why "this woolly headed son of Africa . . . dropped so suddenly and unexpectedly into our midst."[12] They accused each other of sponsoring his visit for some unspecified (and unlikely) political gain. They would have been astounded had they known that Douglass came to their town to meet with John Brown.

Frederick Douglass and John Brown had known each other for years. Brown had long been active in the Underground Railroad and had become famous for his violent exploits in the days of Bleeding Kansas three years earlier. He toured the North raising money for the crusade against slavery and basking in the praise of abolitionists. Brown had crossed paths with Douglass several times and had even stayed for a while in the black abolitionist's home in Rochester, New York. He had told Douglass of his plans to launch a rebellion in the mountains of the border South to spark a mass exodus of slaves.

Douglass had no idea that Brown's plans had progressed so far until he received a letter in the summer of 1859, "informing me that a beginning in his work would soon be made, and that before going forward he wanted to see me, and appointed an old stone-quarry near Chambersburg, Penn., as our place of meeting."[13] Such a meeting with a man of Brown's history was not to be taken lightly or without sufficient precaution. Douglass, accompanied by an imposing ally, a former slave named Shields Green, came to the Pennsylvania town by rail. Along the way he went through New York City to raise money for the cause.

John Brown, it turned out, had chosen Chambersburg as a base from which to prepare an attack on the federal arsenal at Harpers Ferry, Virginia. Chambersburg was a convenient staging ground, an outpost of sorts with railroad access to the free states yet just miles from the Mason-

Dixon Line. By the late 1850s Franklin County had more than forty-two thousand residents, four thousand of whom lived in Chambersburg. Built around a square known as the Diamond, Chambersburg prided itself on its gas lights and new buildings of pressed brick and red sandstone. It hoped to get waterworks soon. The town had grown around the river and falls that lay near its center; its grid was interrupted and broken up by the meandering of the waterway, which created lots with shapes that refused to conform to the squares and rectangles of the plan. Stores and houses huddled along the streets, the lots behind them filled with outbuildings, animal pens, and gardens. An imposing courthouse fronted by massive columns overlooked the Diamond. The railroad terminated three blocks from the center of town.

Chambersburg, Pennsylvania

A local paper gushed that "the destiny of Chambersburg, is something beyond the ordinary lot of inland towns, if we are to judge by the piles of brick, lumber &c., with which our streets have been blocked up, since early in the spring, materials for new brick buildings in course of erection. Nor does it appear likely to cease, from the indications we have, until cold weather shall put a stop to the busy hum of the mason hammer and carpenter saw."[14] Some houses had slate roofs, some tin, and some wooden shingles. Some boasted impressive balconies that ran the buildings' length, overlooking the dirt streets and wooden sidewalks of Chambersburg. Houses, stores, shops, and small factories crowded together throughout the small town, for people of all classes walked to work.

Chambersburg had grown steadily throughout the 1850s, pushing out into the countryside, welcoming the train every day into the station in the northern part of town, conducting the legal business of the county on court days, publishing two weekly newspapers, hosting traveling circuses, art shows, and high-wire walkers, watching political rallies and militia marches, offering schools for children of every age, and displaying churches of all the major denominations. Chambersburg was a typical county seat of the border North.

Franklin County distinguished itself mainly by its agricultural wealth: It was the seventh-largest wheat-producing county in the United States in 1859. The rural population had grown steadily for the last twenty years, marked neither by the flight that eroded rural New England nor the flood of newcomers that rushed into western counties. Increasing numbers of people, largely born in the county, filled the 722 square miles of Franklin. Two-thirds of the farmland in the county rested under cultivation; the rest remained in forest to help supply the relentless need for wood. The value of the county's farms increased by nearly five million dollars in the 1850s as the pressure of population on the land drove up prices.

Harpers Ferry lay fifty miles to the south of Chambersburg, at the conjunction of the Potomac and Shenandoah rivers with the Baltimore and Ohio Railroad. Decades earlier the federal government had placed its armory in this inaccessible place to keep it from capture by sea. The small town, like others in the border region, was home for many free black people, who made up nearly half the town's population of twenty-five hundred. John Brown envisioned taking the unguarded arsenal by stealth and then making it the rallying point for slaves in the area, who would flock to Harpers Ferry to begin a rebellion. For his plan to work he had to gather men and resources without attracting attention.

Brown and his allies aroused no suspicion in the summer of 1859 as they took delivery of large wooden boxes at the train station in Chambersburg. From one of Brown's sons in Ohio came fifteen heavy boxes labeled "Hardware"; the boxes contained Sharps rifles and Maynard revolvers. From a foundry in Connecticut came boxes filled with 950 sharp iron pikes to be handed out to the rebellious slaves when they rallied around Brown in Harpers Ferry.

A few people in the town—the trainmen, the grocers, and postmen—noticed the "tall, spare, plainly-clad and heavily-bearded man." The newcomer "engaged boarding with a widow who lived quietly away from the

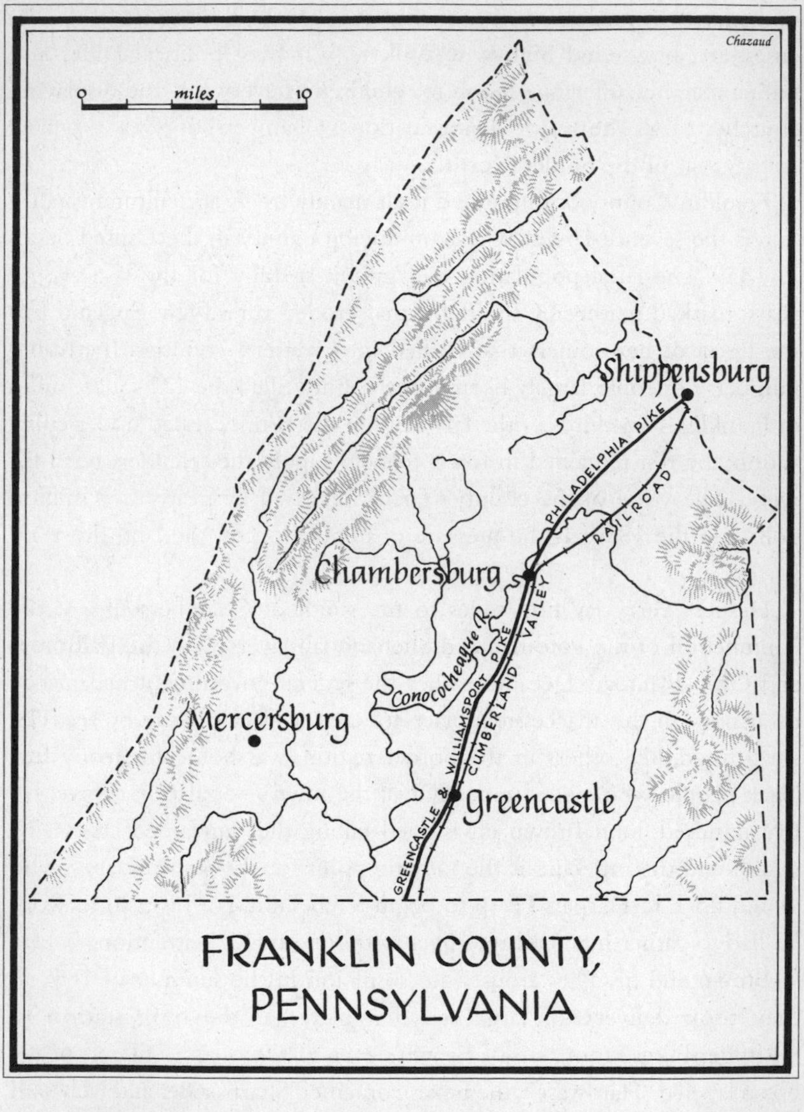

center of the town." The pictures of John Brown of Kansas had shown a clean-shaven man with sharp features; the bearded man in Chambersburg called himself Dr. Isaac Smith and "announced that his purpose was the organization of a considerable force for mining operations in the State of Virginia." The new arrival remained in town for six weeks and "was exceedingly modest in seeking intercourse with those around him." As it

Alexander K. McClure

happened, the most prominent attorney in town, Alexander K. McClure, observed John Brown without knowing it. McClure's office sat next door to the post office in Chambersburg, where the daily papers arrived each day from the East; a crowd of a dozen or more would gather there to wait for the mail. "Smith" was among those who regularly appeared, and McClure chatted with him, "never doubting that he was a quiet business man."[15]

Alexander McClure was a rising figure, not only in Chambersburg and Franklin County but in Pennsylvania and beyond. Though merely in his early thirties, the handsome and self-made McClure had married well and begun a family, built an impressive legal practice, acquired a beautiful farm on the northern outskirts of town, and become well known as the proprietor and editor of the *Chambersburg Repository and Transcript*, one of the earliest Republican newspapers in the state. Owning the paper proved helpful when McClure ran, successfully, for the state legislature in 1857. From his position in the state capital in Harrisburg, McClure had come to know the powerful men who governed Pennsylvania and the growing Republican party of the country. He was back home tending to local business in the summer of 1859—and preparing to run for the state senate that fall, his next move up—when John Brown came to town.

John Brown had become well settled in Chambersburg when Frederick Douglass came to meet him. "When I reached Chambersburg," Douglass reported, "a good deal of surprise was expressed (for I was instantly recognized) that I should come there unannounced, and I was pressed to make a speech to them, with which invitation I readily complied." He would speak that evening. Giving a public talk would be Douglass's best cover.[16]

Douglass met first with Henry Watson, a mulatto barber, forty-eight years old, married but without children, who had about five hundred dollars' worth of property in his shop and home in Chambersburg. Five hundred dollars then would be worth about ten thousand dollars today and made Watson a respectable property holder. Douglass described Watson as "a simple-minded and warm-hearted man, to whom Capt. Brown had imparted the secret of my visit, to show me the road to the appointed rendezvous. Watson was very busy in his barber's shop, but he dropped all and put me on the right track."

Douglass could have found other African American allies in Franklin County. Nearly eighteen hundred people identified in the census as black or of mixed race lived there. Indeed, Franklin held the fifth-highest number of black residents of any county in Pennsylvania. Black families had several reasons for living there. Eight out of ten had been born in Franklin. Slavery had been well established in Pennsylvania in the eighteenth century and had been especially strong in the southern part of the state, where farms differed little from those just across the Maryland border. Several hundred free blacks, moreover, had come from Maryland and Virginia in the decades since.

Most black families lived near one another in small communities and in large households, gathering several generations under the same roof or nearby, seeking security in a threatening world. Many gathered in the southernmost parts of the county, with nearly four hundred in Mercersburg; the other largest group of African Americans in Franklin lived in the South Ward of Chambersburg. They were unwelcome across Market Street in the other ward, where only a few people of color lived. Most black people in Franklin's largest town worked in the same jobs as other black people throughout the North—laborers, porters, waiters, shoeblacks, cooks, and servants—and had just as little to show for it.

Franklin offered a haven for refugee slaves. The mountains that stood on either side of the county held places to hide in their thick trees and rocky outcroppings. Fugitives followed the trails, worn by Indians generations before, into upstate New York and then into Canada. Mercersburg, with its large black population, lay along the Underground Railroad. The small town offered a refuge just over the line from slavery; from there allies worked to spirit slaves into the mountains and along hidden trails farther into freedom. Some called the area Little Africa.

White people from Franklin helped as well. Hiram Wertz of Quincy, on the eastern side of the county, took great risks to aid runaways. A twenty-nine-year-old farmer surrounded by well-to-do kinsmen and aided by his wife, Catherine, Wertz was an "ardent" agent of the Underground Railroad. The Wertz family worked with the neighboring Shockey family, a larger clan with considerably less money, to aid black people fleeing slavery. Both families had been born in Pennsylvania and were well aware of the risks they took. They ushered runaway slaves into the mountains near the Caledonia iron mills.[17]

While Franklin held no open abolitionist meetings and produced no abolitionist newspapers, black and white residents of the border county labored for freedom on slavery's doorstep. Franklin's proximity to the border channeled antislavery feeling into action rather than words, into secret rather than public responses. Precisely because they knew the importance of maintaining a common white front on slavery if North and South were to get along politically, some of the loudest white men in Franklin talked incessantly against abolitionists, parodying them, bullying them. But the friends of slavery could not stop some of their neighbors from aiding the cause of the enslaved.

Frederick Douglass had some idea of what he was getting into when he came to meet Brown: "I approached the old quarry very cautiously, for John Brown was generally well armed, and regarded strangers with suspicion. He was then under the ban of the government, and heavy rewards were offered for his arrest, for offenses said to have been committed in Kansas." Brown sat at the quarry pretending to fish. "He looked every way like a man of the neighborhood, and as much at home as any of the farmers around there," Douglass recalled. "His hat was old and storm-beaten, and his clothing was about the color of the stone quarry itself—his then present dwelling place. His face wore an anxious expression, and he was much worn by thought and exposure."

Douglass and Brown discussed the plan. Brown wanted Douglass to come with him, to help lead the grand emancipation of the slaves of the upper South and perhaps all slaves in the United States. "The taking of Harper's Ferry, of which Captain Brown had merely hinted before, was now declared as his settled purpose," Douglass related, "and he wanted to know what I thought of it. I at once opposed the measure with all the arguments at my command." Douglass argued that any slaves who fled their masters to join Brown would be killed, as would everyone in the party. Such an attack, moreover, would be "an attack upon the Federal government, and would array the whole country against us." Brown "did not at all object to rousing the nation; it seemed to him that something startling was just what the nation needed."

Brown thought his army would be impregnable once they took Harpers Ferry. Douglass fervently argued otherwise, trying to persuade Brown that "he was going into a perfect steel-trap, and that once in he would never get out alive; that he would be surrounded at once and escape would be impossible." Brown listened respectfully but argued that "even if surrounded he would find means for cutting his way out; but that would not be forced upon him; he should, at the start, have a number of the best citizens of the neighborhood as his prisoners and that holding them as hostages he should be able, if worse came to worse, to dictate terms of egress from the town."

Douglass, a man who risked his life every time he spoke, looked at Brown "with some astonishment, that he could rest upon a reed so weak and broken." Douglass told "him that Virginia would blow him and his hostages sky-high, rather than that he should hold Harper's Ferry an hour." Douglass could not dissuade Brown, though the former slave felt certain that his abolitionist ally "was about to rivet the fetters more firmly than ever on the limbs of the enslaved." They talked all day Saturday—before Douglass would speak in Chambersburg's Town Hall that evening—and part of Sunday as well. As he left Brown, Douglass asked Shields Green what he had decided to do, and "was surprised by his coolly saying, in his broken way, 'I b'leve I'll go wid de ole man.' "

John Brown believed his plan would work because he held a special dispensation from God. "Without the shedding of blood," he quoted from the Scriptures, "there is no remission of sins."[18] In his eyes, the Old Testament decreed that violence in the name of the Lord was holy, good, and necessary.

THE WHITE CITIZENS OF AUGUSTA COUNTY, VIRGINIA, admired the beauty and serenity of their locale. Staunton occupied the center of Augusta, and about twenty-five hundred people called the town home. A German painter, Edward Beyer, included Staunton on his itinerary when he traveled through the Shenandoah Valley depicting picturesque scenes. A newspaper reported that the lithograph made from the painting was "universally admired for its accuracy and beauty" and was "richly worth" the five dollars Beyer asked.[19] In the painting, Staunton's main buildings arrayed themselves on the tops of small hills. Churches, seminaries, fine houses, and the courthouse presided over other red-brick and wooden houses spread around them. Hotels stood nearby, ready to provide amenities to the many tourists who passed through on their way to nearby springs and resorts. The railroad depot dominated the front of the painting just as it dominated the trade of the town and county.

Staunton, Virginia

Beyer's portrayal of course did not show the many rickety houses down in the lower areas of Staunton. Those places, where water tended to stand or flood, where privies and animal lots tended to drain, and where houses had neither porticoes nor detached kitchens, contained the homes of the working people, black and white, of Staunton. Their homes mingled among warehouses and workshops, stables and tanneries.

Staunton and Augusta had changed a great deal in the 1850s. "Staunton has become changed from a town to a city—and now rejoices in a Railroad, Telegraph, Gas, and many other wonderful things," a long-time newspaper editor observed.[20] The macadamized Valley turnpike ran through the middle of the county. In the countryside, streams and rivers flowed, driving mills that produced flour valued at half a million dollars per year. Sawmills worked throughout the mountains and along the creeks. Tanneries did the smelly work of turning cowhides into leather. A hundred and fifty blacksmiths worked at crossroads and villages, alongside coopers, wagon makers, shoemakers, and other artisans. The county distilled large quantities of liquor, a specialty of the Valley. Eighteen distilleries employed thirty-seven free men and dozens of slaves, producing nearly 150,000 gallons of whiskey a year.

Augusta's farms, productive and valuable, were worth nearly eleven million dollars, the highest in the state of Virginia. In the 1850s the number of improved acres in the county had jumped by nearly fifty-thousand, and the cash value of farms had grown by nearly four million dollars in that decade. In the late summer of 1859 Augusta was awash with grain of every kind: over a million bushels of corn, wheat, oats, rye, and buckwheat. Farms in the county also produced nearly half a million pounds of butter, seventeen thousand pounds of honey, fifteen thousand pounds of cheese, thirty-six thousand pounds of wool, forty-two thousand bushels of Irish potatoes, and nearly six thousand gallons of molasses. Times had never been better.

None of this would have been possible without the skill and sweat of slaves. Slavery lay at the heart of Augusta County's economy. More than sixteen hundred white households, about a fifth of the white families, owned fifty-five hundred enslaved people. With an average adult slave costing at least twelve hundred dollars in 1860, the slaves of Augusta were worth over six million dollars. Every district of Augusta County depended on slaves for the fundamental work of their households, farms, and industries. With no single staple crop dominating the economy, enslaved people in the countryside did everything from milling wheat to distilling whiskey, from sawing lumber to producing iron, from working in hotels to caring for children.

Slavery had been a fundamental part of Augusta society for generations. While slaveowners acquired new slaves as opportunity or need presented themselves, the number of slaves in the county had remained nearly constant for the last twenty years. About a third of the slaveholders in Augusta possessed only one slave, but two dozen slaveholders each

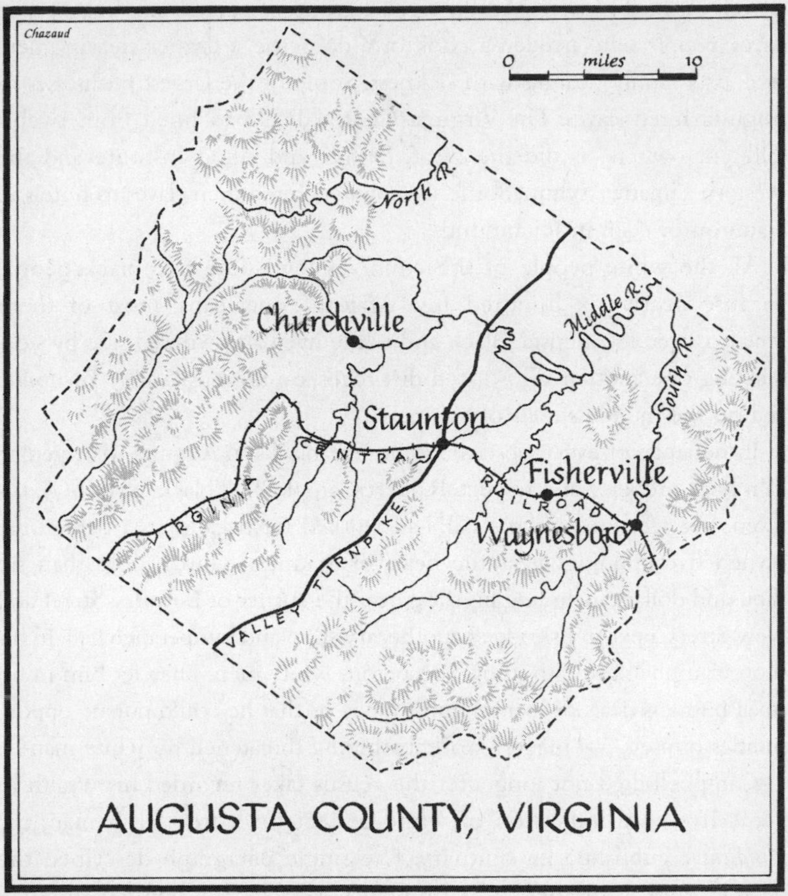

AUGUSTA COUNTY, VIRGINIA

owned more than twenty people. A few plantations held more than forty slaves. The number of male and female slaves had stabilized in about equal proportions. More than a quarter of the enslaved population, fifteen hundred people, bore lighter skin and straighter hair that showed some white ancestry. In Augusta, as in the rest of the South, enslaved people could be borrowed, rented, held as collateral, bartered, and held in escrow. As property slaves represented great flexibility.

About one slave out of ten worked for a white person other than his or her owner. A diverse group of whites hired out their slaves: female heads of households, heirs of estates, trustees, businesses, and corporations as well as small planters. And a diverse group of people employed those slaves: people who needed a cook or a domestic, a farmer clearing new land, or a family dealing with sickness. Some of the largest businesses of Augusta hired slaves. The Virginia Central Railroad hired from twelve different owners, as did the Deaf, Dumb, and Blind Institute and the Western Lunatic Asylum. Some slaveowners hired their slaves to hotels in Staunton or even in Richmond.

All the white people of the county knew some free black people because nearly six hundred free African Americans, most of them mulatto, lived in Augusta. Black and white lived and worked side by side, meeting one another on isolated dirt roads, on the busy Valley Turnpike, and on the muddy streets of Staunton.

In defiance of every obstacle, some free blacks in Augusta managed to gain both property and respect. Robert Campbell, a "black" man of sixty-seven, five feet three inches tall, had worked for decades as a barber. He owned five buildings near the heart of Staunton worth more than six thousand dollars, including his shop near the corner of Beverley Street and New Street, next to Eskridge's apothecary shop and temperance hall. In his shop Campbell came to know prosperous white men. They let him in on small business deals or loaned him money so that he could pursue opportunities himself. As "nigger" work, barbering threatened no white man.

Campbell died not long after the census taker recorded his wealth in 1859. In a rare indication of white respect for a free black man, the *Vindicator* published an obituary. The single paragraph described the sources and strategies of Campbell's success. "Robert Campbell (Colored) one of the oldest inhabitants of Staunton—the pioneer barber, by which he acquired considerable property, dropped dead at his residence on Wednesday last," the article at the bottom of the page briefly noted. The capitalization of "Colored" stood as a subtle, if meaningful, tribute, for editors rarely capitalized the term, as did the acknowledgment of Campbell's property holding. The final sentence too was significant: "'Uncle Bob' was much respected and beliked by all of our citizens." Cultured white Augusta residents prided themselves on their tolerance and affection for such a man, accorded the title Uncle to convey a sort of belittling respect, who somehow managed to build a secure life on the most insecure of foundations.[21]

Most free black people left much briefer records. The county court clerk who registered Augusta's free blacks described each person as he or she came before him. The poverty of the free black people could be read in their very stature. Poor nutrition meant that many, especially women, were barely over five feet tall. Their hands, legs, and feet frequently were crooked, maimed, and crippled. The range of skin shades testified to the complex history of interracial sexual relations in Virginia for many generations. The various white clerks of Augusta strained to find adequate language. Many free blacks seemed simply "dark" or a "bright mulatto," but others elicited greater elaboration. They were very dark, dark mulatto, black, yellow, copper, high mulatto, dark brown, fair, freckled, bright, high bright, light, light brown, and not very black. Sometimes the reason for such a range of colors was made explicit, as in the case of Lange Lambert, who was deemed "of bright mulatto complexion with Roman aqualine nose five feet nine and a half inches high aged about twenty seven years, no marks or scars perceivable and was born free of a white woman in the County of Augusta."[22]

Despite such ambiguities—or perhaps because of them—white people took a great, unexamined, and deep sense of self from their skin shade. They viewed the African American people in their midst, a people of great diversity in appearance as well as every other human attribute, with a mixture of disdain, distrust, affection, resentment, and need. Augusta whites prided themselves on the distinctions they drew among people of color.

Whites told themselves what they wanted to hear about black people. The *Spectator* felt certain that "the intelligent, christian slave-holder at the South is the best friend of the negro. He does not regard his bonds-men as mere chattel property, but as human beings to whom he owes duties." The "Northern Pharisee will not permit a negro to ride on the city railroads," but "Southern gentlemen and ladies are seen every day, side by side, in cars and coaches, with their faithful servants." The paper even insisted that "the honest black man" in Augusta "is not only protected by the laws and public sentiment, but he is respected by the community as truly as if his skin were white. Here there are ties of genuine friendship and affection between whites and blacks, leading to an interchange of all the comities of life." Master and slave cared for each other at times of illness and infirmity; when a slave died, the master and mistress "grieve, not for the loss of so much property, but for the death of a member of the family."[23]

Whatever sentiments whites chose to express about their slaves, they knew that a slave proved an exceedingly good investment in the 1850s. Slave prices had been ballooning for more than a decade and showed no signs of subsiding. The cotton plantations of the states farther south absorbed all the slaves Virginia would export, and Virginia sent tens of thousands every year into that market by foot, rail, and boat. Moreover, railroads, iron furnaces, prosperous farms, and the factories of Richmond and Lynchburg created a consistent demand closer to home. Male slaves increased in value when they learned the skills of blacksmiths, carpenters, and other artisans. Female slaves peaked in value during their childbearing years, but skilled cooks were always in demand.

Slave traders came through Augusta often, and some local citizens eagerly participated in the trade. John B. Smith announced his intentions in the *Staunton Spectator*: "100 Negroes Wanted—I will pay in cash the highest market prices for able bodied young Negroes for the Southern market."[24] The market in slaves was intense, and some wondered if Virginia might be drained of slaves. The *Staunton Vindicator* thought not and offered early reports from the 1860 United States census to prove its case. "Notwithstanding the plaintive appeals of demagogues as to the decrease of slave population in Virginia, here in Augusta county there has been really an increase. We believe, further, that in Western Virginia, notwithstanding the extensive trade in this species of property, the result will exhibit that we have more slaves than in 1850."[25] They were correct, for slavery was expanding in Virginia, especially in the mountains of the southwest. The proportion of the county's population constituted by slaves had remained constant for the last forty years, carefully regulated by ongoing sales, and people did not expect that to change anytime soon. Virginia remained the largest slave state in the Union, just as it had been for decades.

The slave trade stood as a constant threat to African American families. About to be sold to a slave trader, Maria Perkins wrote a desperate letter to her husband in Staunton. She wrote from Charlottesville, about thirty-five miles to the east on the other side of the Blue Ridge, where she was working. She was frantic, for her children were being sold before her eyes:

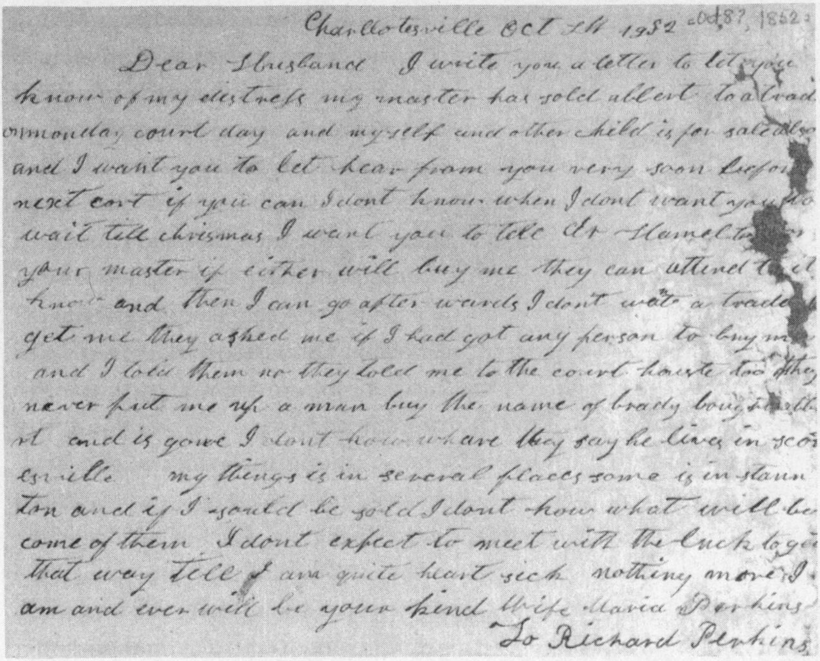

Charlottesville Oct 8th 1852 Oct 8?, 1852
Dear Husband I write you a letter to let you
know of my distress my master has sold albert to a trad
on monday court day and myself and other child is for sale also
and I want you to let hear from you very soon before
next cort if you can I dont know when I dont want you to
wait till christmas I want you to tell Dr Hamelton or
your master if either will buy me they can attend to it
know and then I can go after wards I dont wan a trader to
get me they asked me if I had got any person to buy me
and I told them no they took me to the court house too they
never put me up a man buy the name of brady bought alb
rt and is gone I dont know whare they say he lives in scot
esville my things is in several places some is in staun
ton and if I sould be sold I dont know what will be
come of them I dont expect to meet with the luck to get
that way till I am quite heart sick nothing more I
am and ever will be your kind wife Maria Perkins
To Richard Perkins

Maria Perkins tells her husband of her impending sale

Dear Husband I write you a letter to let you know of my distress. My master has sold Albert to a trader on monday court day and myself and other child is for sale also and I want to let hear from you very soon before next court if you can I don't know when. I don't want you to wait till christmas. I want you to tell Dr Hamilton or your master if either will buy me they can attend to it now and then I can go afterwards. I don't want a trader to get me they asked me if I had got any person to buy me and I told them no. They took me to the court house too if they never put me up. A man by the name of Brady bought Albert and is gone I dont know where. They say he lives in Scottsville. My things is in several places some is in Staunton and if I should be sold I don't know what will become of them. I don't expect to meet with the luck to get that way. Tell I am quite heart sick. Nothing more. I am and ever will be your kind wife, Maria Perkins.[26]

Perkins spoke in a kind of shorthand, knowing that her husband, Richard, also enslaved, would understand. It was traditional for slave sales to take place on court day, when planters and farmers from throughout a county gathered at the county seat. Traders seized that opportunity to buy and sell people like Maria Perkins and her children. Slaves, bought and hired, moved from one place to the next at Christmastime, when contracts began and ended, but Maria Perkins knew that the white men could conduct their business in October and allow her to move later. Perhaps Dr. Hamilton was a former master of Maria's; perhaps Richard's master would want to consolidate a family. She had to tell her husband that one of their children had already been sold away. They might lose their other child as well to the market in slaves.

Enslaved people made distinctions among the white people with whom they lived. Melinda ("Roty") Ruffin, an enslaved woman from Augusta, gave her master credit for not being the worst in the neighborhood, for he "didn't buy nigger, didn't sell nigger." But she recalled the way that another master in Augusta treated her aunt Polly and uncle Bob and Henry: "Whip 'em every morning before they eat mouthful." After the whipping the slaves would "slip over" to Ruffin's mother, who would grease their backs to keep their shirts from sticking to the wounds. Ruffin remembered the ring driven into the whipping post. She remembered Ballard Smith, a seventy-three-year-old farmer with fourteen slaves, who "put her on block" to be sold.[27] Another enslaved woman calculated the benevolence of slaveholders in Augusta this way: "Yes they were good when you could work but when you got sick they sold you."[28]

Augusta's proximity to the border did not dilute slavery. Slavery determined the work slaves did and the place they lived. Slavery determined the white people they had to appease and those they would have to avoid. Slavery decided if they could stay with a husband, wife, or child. Slavery stood as a fundamental fact in the life of the black and white people in Augusta County.

Forward-looking slaveowners carefully calculated the value of slaves as part of a larger portfolio of property. John Imboden, owner of three men and four women in 1859, wrote a friend about his financial thinking: "I have brought 4 young and handsome negroes over from Charlotte [County], and have the offer of any others we may wish. Mary & I dont think we will take but one more, possibly two at Christmas. This will save me a good deal in negro hire."[29]

John Imboden was a man on the make. Only in his late thirties, with dark hair swept back from his forehead and a striking mustache, he had accumulated an impressive set of accomplishments. Coming from a large family of middling wealth, a generation removed from his immigrant German grandparents, he attended Washington College and the Virginia Military Institute in the county south of Augusta. He began his career as a teacher at the Deaf, Dumb, and Blind Institute in Staunton, but though an excellent teacher, Imboden was too restless and ambitious to remain at the school. He read law, worked his way up in the Masons, dealt in real estate, married and began a family, built a home at the top of Market Street in Staunton, and became commissioner of education in Augusta County. His law practice flourished, and he moved into a new office on Lawyer's Row in Staunton. Imboden saw no conflict between owning slaves and his quests for self-improvement and social improvement. To the contrary.

Imboden had long been a political leader in Augusta. He believed in the active role of government in fostering progress and joined the Whig party early in his career. Elected to Virginia's House of Delegates in 1851, Imboden devoted his first two speeches to railroads. He wanted to see Virginia build rail lines to the Ohio River on the northwestern border of the state, and he wanted to see those railroads run through Staunton. Thanks in part to his work, Staunton became a railroad town a few years later, and by the late 1850s the community could hardly imagine what life had been like without that vital connection to the world. Imboden rose to become head of the Census and Statistics Committee of Virginia's General Assembly. With Virginia politics in turmoil over the last few years and the Whig party in decline, Imboden had lost a bid for reelection, but he became county court clerk in 1858, a six-year term and a good place for a young man who wanted to know everything going on in the economic, legal, and political life of Augusta.

In the midst of his success and happiness, Imboden's wife died. The ambitious attorney, politician, militia leader, businessman, and slaveowner was left with three children. He soon remarried, however, and his new wife, Mary, seemed a gift. Eleven years his junior, she stepped into the household with grace. "My children are just as happy as it is possible for children to be," Imboden told his best friend, John McCue. "They almost idolize their new mother. Their home is so much more bright and pleasant now than it has been for months past, that the little things are almost intoxicated with delight at the change." The daughters, Jennie and Russie, "as soon as they are dressed repair to the yard, and each makes a bouquet or weaves a garland of green leaves and gay flowers, with which they voluntarily dress Mary's head when she appears at the breakfast table." And Frank, four years old, "never tires in his little efforts to attract her attention & win an approving smile. All together they are as happy a trio of joyous children as you ever saw." Imboden, happy at home, hoped to make enough money with his clerkship, his law practice, his slaveholding, and his marketing of a railroad coupling device to provide a comfortable setting for his new family.[30]

Like John Imboden, Joseph Waddell enjoyed a prominent position in Augusta. But he was a much quieter man, working behind the scenes rather than in the limelight, contemplative rather than active. The Waddells had been leaders in Virginia for several generations; Waddell's father had studied medicine in Philadelphia with the famous physician Benjamin Rush. Joseph, thirty-nine years old in 1859, ran, with his cousin, the leading newspaper in the county and in the Valley of Virginia, the *Staunton Spectator*. He, like his mother, sisters, and wife, supported the Presbyterian church, local schools, and charitable organizations. Waddell and his wife, Virginia, had no children but took care of others left orphaned, along with female relatives otherwise without a home. Waddell traveled widely in the United States and prided himself on his broad view of public affairs. Neatly bearded and wearing glasses for his extreme nearsightedness, he appeared scholarly and detached. His diary, though, showed that he felt things deeply.

Waddell owned two men and one woman. He confronted a situation all the slaveholders in Augusta confronted in the days of high prices for slaves. "Dr. McGill proposed to buy Selena today, and offered me $1000," he noted in his diary one evening. "I would not have sold her for $20,000, unless she desired to go, or had grossly misbehaved. This thing of speculating in human flesh is utterly horrible to me—the money would cut into my flesh like hot iron." Waddell, obliged to defend slavery in his

Joseph Waddell

paper, admitted in private that "slavery itself is extremely repulsive to my feelings, and I earnestly desire its extinction everywhere, when it can be done judiciously and so as to promote the welfare of both races."[31]

Despite his anxieties about slavery, Waddell insisted to himself, "I am no abolitionist." He believed that "the day for emancipation with us has not come, and we must wait God's time. For the present all that the most philanthropic can do is to endeavor to ameliorate the institution, but it is hard to do this in the midst of the mischievous interference of outside fanatics."[32] In Waddell's estimation, abolitionist "fanatics" prevented the natural and gradual end of slavery and even kept the "most philanthropic" from lessening slavery's burden. He included among the fanatics not only the "Black Republicans" growing in the North but also the fire-eating secessionists farther south and even in Virginia's own Democratic party.

Newcomers to Augusta soon decided where they stood with slavery. In the early 1850s, barely twenty, recently finished with his brief education and in search of adventure, Jedediah Hotchkiss came from his home in upstate New York to take a walking tour of the Cumberland Valley of Pennsylvania and western Virginia. There he met the owner of an iron furnace down in the Shenandoah Valley, who invited Hotchkiss to come to Augusta County to act as a tutor for his brother's children. Hotchkiss was paid three hundred dollars per year, along with room, board, washing, and a horse. Most important, he had plenty of time to hike and read. He taught himself mapmaking and engineering. Several families of the neighborhood, pleased with Hotchkiss's work and on the lookout for a good teacher, raised seven hundred dollars to build Mossy Creek Academy. Hotchkiss oversaw the construction of the school and served as its principal. He soon joined the Mossy Creek Presbyterian Church and began to teach a men's Bible class.

Jed Hotchkiss

In 1853 Hotchkiss went to southern Pennsylvania to marry a young woman he had met there, Sara Ann Comfort, a new wife of education and accomplishment. They returned to Augusta to run the school together and raise a family. They soon had two children, though the birth of their second child, in 1858, damaged Sara's health. Moving closer to the medicinal springs of Augusta, the Hotchkisses sold Mossy Creek Academy. Bathing in the springs helped Sara Hotchkiss recover. Jedediah—Jed, he was called—appeared very much the headmaster, with kind eyes and easy humor. Their little daughters, Nelly and Annie, flourished.

The transplanted Northerners loved Augusta so much that Hotchkiss's brother Nelson moved down from New York in 1859. The brothers went in together to buy a farm near Churchville in northwestern Augusta County and began to build another school, Loch Willow Academy. Nelson, nine years older than Jed, was married and brought five children with him; they all lived on the farm together. The school also housed three other teachers, a young professor from Virginia and two young female teachers from New York. The school and farm were handsome, worth fifteen hundred dollars. The establishment occupied over three hundred acres, two hundred of them improved. Like all their neighbors, the Hotchkisses grew wheat, rye, corn, and potatoes.

Like their other ambitious and well-to-do neighbors, the Hotchkiss brothers bought a slave, a man named Allen. Their mother back in New York was a religious person. While she missed her children and grandchildren, she put their minds to rest on slavery and politics. "You speak of excitement and commotion," she wrote Jed, "but I think you need have no fears from the North. We do not wish to interfere with you on slavery." Mrs. Hotchkiss admitted that "I had rather work myself than have slaves," and she knew there were "some who would like to get up party spirit. But if you at the South feel approved of god to have slaves then all is well. I wish you to have the smiles and approbation of a holy god who does all things right and to whom we must all stand or fall for ourselves." She asked only that her sons "look at the matter candidly and impartially and we can have peace within the storm."[33]

Alansa Rounds moved from rural upstate New York to Augusta to work in her uncle Jed Hotchkiss's school in 1859. "The true, everyday life among the slave owners, where I saw and heard of no cruelty or oppression, and no one servant was overburdened, but each had their respective tasks," she wrote. "I fell in love with dear old Aunt Charity, the cook, and Amanda, the laundress. Then there was a dairymaid, a housemaid, a table waiter and an errand boy, &c. &c." The true glory of the Augusta social order, though, came in the evening, Alansa recalled. "One or more gentlemen were sure to 'drop in.' "The white people played the banjo music and sang "darkey" songs.[34] This is the way whites liked to think of slavery: a collaborative enterprise in which each side played its role and everyone benefited. Whites took on the responsibility for business and direction, they told themselves, while blacks took responsibility for work and cheerfulness.

While slavery had woven its way into the fabric of Augusta society for generations, some aspects of the institution could still divide Augusta's white men in the summer of 1859. A strained debate broke out then over a volatile subject that many had considered long settled, the reopening of the African slave trade. That trade, at least in its legal forms, had been outlawed for half a century. Most white people who had spoken of Africa in the intervening fifty years had dreamed of shipping black people back to that continent, not of bringing more Africans to American shores. But in 1859, with the price of slaves steadily rising and the South never more prosperous, some Southerners in Congress argued that it was time to legalize the slave trade with Africa.

"We have never been able to appreciate the consistency of those who, believing slavery, as it exists in the South, to be morally right, yet denounce the slave trade—the mode in which that existence was created—as an infamous traffic," the *Staunton Vindicator*, the Democrats' paper, agreed. "We have never been able to see anything but nonsense and fallacy in the distinction drawn between the morality of purchasing a slave in Virginia to transport to Alabama, and the morality of buying a slave on the coast of Africa to bring to the United States where he will be better fed, better clothed, and humanized and christianized." Since the Staunton paper "conscientiously and devoutly" believed slavery "the most noble, humane and christian institution with which the creator ever blessed a favored people, we are forced to the logical conclusion, that the slave trade, far from being an infamous traffic, is, on the other hand, all perfectly right, moral and proper."[35] Slavery was God's will, God's way of spreading Christianity, God's way of encouraging progress. Who were mere men to challenge His plan?

A correspondent to Augusta's other paper, Joseph Waddell's paper, countered this argument with a tortured response. The *Spectator* admitted that anyone who challenged the most extreme Southern arguments in 1859 risked being called an abolitionist, but it went on to do just that. "It is a known fact," the anonymous correspondent asserted, "that for every negro imported in the slave ships, ten are slaughtered in Africa, or die of disease in the 'Middle Passage.' " At the time of the Revolution, the author reminded his Virginia audience, revered Virginians had denounced the inhumane slave trade, and "what was murder a hundred years ago we look upon as murder still, and no appeals of ambitious demagogues in other States can make us think otherwise." The paper sneered at the argument that the slave trade would christianize the Africans, denying that "it is christianity to butcher ten men that one may be the recipient of religious instruction."[36]

The *Spectator* argued that the advocates of the African slave trade and the "Black Republicans play into each other's hands, and both are working with all their might for one object, viz: disunion." The paper distrusted both the North and the Cotton South, both Republicans and states' rights Democrats. A new African slave trade would ruin Virginia's economy even without sectional conflict, driving down the price of slaves, estimated by the *Spectator* at, "in round numbers, $500,000,000. We are now as rich in Virginia as any people in the world. Open the slave trade and we should be the poorest; for our property would be a fearful expense to us, and we should have to get rid of it somehow, or run away from our ruin." The Cotton South wanted to abandon the Union and maintain Virginia as a buffer between themselves and the free states. "By thus having no abolitionized border to defend," the *Spectator* bitterly sneered, "they will not be pestered with the Underground Rail Road, and can cultivate cotton in peace."[37]

The white people of Augusta profited from slavery, defended slavery, and believed in slavery. They could not imagine doing without it. But they could see that living on the border of slavery put them at risk.

Despite the two hundred miles and several borders that lay between them, Franklin County and Augusta County shared a great deal. Winter was a little longer and colder in Pennsylvania, summer a little longer and hotter in Virginia, but that mattered little. The people of the two places sought out the same entertainments and read the same books. They bore the same kinds of names and worshiped at the same kinds of churches. The differences were not those that separated city dwellers from rural folk, industrial workers from farmers, Puritans from Cavaliers. The differences were more subtle than that.[38]

One difference could be seen by any visitor. In Franklin County, about fifty-eight people lived on each square mile; in Augusta County, only twenty-six. The density of people on the land in Augusta mirrored, almost precisely, that of Virginia as a whole; the density of Franklin actually registered a bit below the Pennsylvania average of sixty-three. Augusta had larger farms and more unimproved land than Franklin. Small farmers in Augusta, like their more prosperous neighbors, kept a larger portion of their farms in woods than their northern counterparts. Fewer families pressed upon the land in the southern county.

The Reverend Abraham Essick, who had come from Franklin County but who lived in the Valley of Virginia, noted the difference the Mason-Dixon Line made. "During my visit to Pennsylvania I was deeply impressed by the contrast between the general appearance of the country and this," he wrote in his diary. "Naturally they are similar, both lying in the same valley, and presenting many of the same characteristics. But in Virginia the farms are large and the population sparse. The differences in cultivation, productiveness, and the general indications of thrift, are immensely in favor of Pennsylvania. It is usual to account for this on the grounds of Slavery."[39]

Northern travelers looked at the relative sparseness of people on the land in the South and viewed it as a lack of progress and energy. The Northerners saw scattered schoolhouses and churches, isolated villages and empty roads. White Southerners, however, thought they lived in places more beautiful and more humane than the crowded rural districts of the North. They argued that their farms, plantations, and towns were just as productive as those of the North, that white people in the South were actually better off than those in the North, that enslaved black people lived in the best possible arrangement for all concerned.

The farms of both Franklin and Augusta produced more grain than anything else, particularly corn and wheat. Those crops served as subtle indexes of the way farms worked in both counties. Franklin farmers preferred wheat, a crop more easily marketed than corn and one that was booming in the late 1850s, as towns and cities demanded flour they could not produce themselves. Augusta farmers preferred corn. The crop fed both the free population and the slave population as well as provided the raw material for the whiskey distilleries of the county. The richest farmers did use their deep supply of slave labor to produce more wheat than their neighbors, marketing it to the big mills down the railroad in Richmond.

Despite slavery, occupations for whites did not differ markedly between the two counties. In both places the largest single group of workers were unskilled: about three out of ten in Augusta, about four out of ten in Franklin. Most of them worked on farms. In both places professionals, merchants, clerks, and proprietors together accounted for one jobholder in ten. And about one woman in ten worked for wages in both places.

In both counties the poorest 40 percent of household heads owned nothing. The top 10 percent of the heads of households in Franklin and in Augusta controlled two-thirds of the real estate. The white class structure of the two counties diverged in only one important respect: the richest 10 percent in Franklin owned 57 percent of personal property, while thanks to the value of slaves, the richest 10 percent in Augusta owned 70 percent of all personal wealth.

Typifying much of the rural North, Franklin was hardly industrialized. Chambersburg claimed an advanced railroad shop and a paper mill, but much of the work of the county had barely changed for decades. Most of Franklin's manufacturing took place in small shops of a few men who produced leather goods, tinware, or wagons. People used the same techniques in their shops and on their farms as their fathers, even grandfathers. Workers at Thaddeus Stevens's ironworks still dug and processed the ore much as they had in earlier years. Farmers turned to mechanical reapers and other tools, but farming remained mainly sheer physical labor.

Augusta investors took advantage of slaveholding to create low-capital, high-labor industries. By using slaves in the months when they were not needed on the farm or plantation, industrial slaveholders had plenty of labor to cut trees and saw lumber, to shuck corn and maintain fires at distilleries, and to dig iron ore from the mountains. Such industries were not advanced, but they were profitable and fitted well into the overall economy of Augusta.

Augusta stood in the broad middle ground of the South in its slaveholding. In the South as a whole, about 25 percent of the white households owned at least one slave; in Augusta, about 22 percent did. African Americans accounted for one in five of the county's people, a percentage typical of hundreds of counties in the South, though of course lower than the districts of the Cotton South where the largest numbers of African Americans lived. Augusta was neither a black belt county nor a mountain county but something in between. It was, in other words, like hundreds of counties throughout the South.

Augusta and Franklin typified large parts of their states and regions. Dozens of counties in Virginia and Pennsylvania shared their number and proportion of free blacks, their population density, value of farms, and value of manufacturing, their voting patterns in recent elections. The farms in the Valley were richer than most in the rest of Virginia and Pennsylvania, the number of immigrants a bit lower; the proportion of manufacturing was about the same. But all in all, Franklin and Augusta embodied much of the nation's eastern border region.

From the economic perspective of white people, then, both Augusta and Franklin seemed prosperous and successful. Their farms were rich, and markets for their goods easy to find. While class distinctions were obvious to everyone, they did not create much overt comment or clear resentment in either place. Both counties, like their societies at large, looked out at the world with confidence.

3

SLOWLY THE BASE of John Brown's operations shifted south from Chambersburg to a farmhouse over the Mason-Dixon Line in Maryland, where Brown's young daughter and daughter-in-law fed the black and white men who gathered there in preparation for the attack. The men hid out in the attic during the day, planning, waiting, and sometimes arguing among themselves about Brown's intentions. Brown had hoped for many more men than the sixteen white and five black men who eventually joined him, but allies never came.

The attack began on October 16, a Sunday evening. Three of Brown's men remained at the Maryland farmhouse, ready to rally the slaves and the white men from southern Pennsylvania who, the raiders felt sure, would rise against slavery if presented with the opportunity. The other eighteen insurrectionists moved toward Harpers Ferry in the darkness. Brown told them that "if we lose our lives it will perhaps do more for the cause than our lives would be worth in any other way." It would be glorious to die as martyrs in God's cause of freedom. The wagon filled with pikes headed for the little town at the joining of the rivers in the Valley.

The band of men cut the telegraph lines. They silently captured night watchmen. They seized several people in the streets and brought them into an engine house as hostages. They sent raiders into the countryside to abduct Colonel Lewis Washington, a slaveholding planter and relative of George Washington.

But the plot began to go wrong almost immediately. A night watchman warned an approaching train that armed men were in town; the locomotive backed up to spread the word down the line. A free black man was shot as he tried to find out what had happened to a coworker; townspeople gathered with whatever weapons they could find; bells rang in alarm; riders raced through the countryside spreading news of the insurrection. Soon reports went out on the telegraph to Baltimore, Washington, and Richmond. Militia units surrounded the engine house, pinning Brown and his twelve allies inside. No slaves dared come to the abolitionists' defense.

Enraged and often drunken white men captured, shot, mutilated, and took target practice at the dead bodies of Brown's men, especially the black men. Shields Green, the former ally of Frederick Douglass's who had signed on with John Brown in Chambersburg, lay among those killed and desecrated. While federal troops set out from Washington, Brown's men fought back, wounding those who rushed the engine house. Brown tried negotiating, but to no effect. He was himself wounded, as were most of his men. When the troops arrived, the officer in charge, Robert E. Lee, sent another Virginia officer, J. E. B. Stuart, with a flag of truce and a note to the man inside.

Brown looked Stuart in the eye and refused to surrender. On a signal, soldiers rushed the building and began battering its doors. Despite gunfire from within, the soldiers quickly broke their way inside, overpowering Brown and his men. Brown himself received a sword wound. Militia rushed to the schoolhouse where Brown's allies had waited for the rebellious slaves, but all they found were pikes, rifles, and pistols. At the Maryland farm, soldiers discovered a large cache of papers that described in incriminating detail the plans of John Brown and his men to begin the end of American slavery.

ON THE VERY DAY of Brown's defeat a report of the raid arrived in Staunton. The article, rushed into print, combined fact and error in about equal proportions: "Rumors reached this place last night, about 8 o clock, by telegraph, of a negro insurrection at Harper's Ferry." The dispatch from Richmond breathlessly reported "that the negroes, under the lead of white men, had taken possession of the arsenal, and sent wagon loads of muskets and rifles to slaves in the surrounding country, and that large numbers had been killed.—They had cut and destroyed the telegraph wires."[40]

The Augusta newspaper immediately put its own spin on the report. There could be no doubt that *something* had happened at Harpers Ferry. "We think it probable, however, that a rebellion among the white oper-

John Brown on trial

atives at the Armory has been mistaken for slave insurrection; though it is probable that some negroes may have been induced to join them."[41]

Governor Henry A. Wise, fearing that Brown might yet serve as the rallying point for a rebellion by slaves or abolitionists or that Brown and his men would be murdered by the furious crowds, moved the captives eight miles away to Charlestown. A court was already in session there, so Brown and his raiders could be tried before violence erupted. The first hearing proceeded on October 25, a week after Brown's capture, with counsel assigned by the state. With an agitated mob outside the windows, the judge believed that he had to act quickly or risk a lynching.

The *Staunton Spectator* surveyed the vast expanse of newsprint devoted to Brown's raid, trying to find Northern voices that spoke with reason and forbearance. They had to look hard, but the "expressions of sympathy for the treasonable outbreak at Harper's Ferry," one paper did reassure Southerners, came only from "politicians and fanatical literateurs, who in no way express the sentiments of the mass of the Northern people."[42] To judge from the press, it was hard to tell what most white Northerners thought about John Brown. Even the ever-hopeful *Spectator*, however, could not deny that many people in the North seemed seized by irrational sympathy for Brown. The paper listed, without comment, the memorial services held for Brown in New York, Massachusetts, Rhode Island, Ohio, and New Hampshire.[43]

The moderates could not deny, either, that many people in the South—even in Virginia, even in Unionist Augusta County—succumbed to sectional fury rather than a measured response to what the *Spectator* considered a pathetic and quixotic act of a madman. Spontaneous meetings in Augusta issued harsh resolutions. John Brown's raid, one announced, "has been brought about by a mockish and sacrilegious sentiment, fostered and encouraged among a large number of the citizens of the non-slaveholding States of this Confederacy, under the false name of philanthropy." The Republicans had to accept the blame, the resolution argued, for creating the climate that produced John Brown. The people of Augusta declared themselves "prepared to say to the non-slaveholding States, with the determination of freemen, thus far you have gone, but you shall go no farther!" A meeting in Mount Solon raised the rhetorical stakes even higher: "The infamous treachery and ingratitude of the North has been fully revealed, and it is full time that the South should manifest its displeasure in some spirited and practical manner."[44]

One practical solution presented itself immediately: forming military companies to protect Augusta from any and all threats. A group in Staunton raised four hundred dollars to outfit a company and resolved that "the cultivation of a military spirit among our young men and the organization of volunteer military companies for the protection of our own firesides, the defense of the honor of our State and the resistance of invasion, come from what quarter it may, is demanded by the threatening aspect of affairs at the present time."[45]

John Imboden, one of the men who spoke at the rally, took leadership of the military efforts. He immediately traveled to Richmond and appealed to Governor Wise for two brass six-pounder cannon. Wise granted Imboden the valuable weapons on one condition: "All I ask in return is that whenever I call for these guns, and order you and your men to come with them, you will obey the call, whether I be in or out of office or the call be private or official." Imboden eagerly agreed to this remarkable request. He promised to "lacquer the guns, build them a shelter, drill his men, train his horses, and obey the call of the Governor, whenever made on him Governor or not Governor." Imboden returned home to Staunton to begin training his men.[46]

With such words and deeds flying throughout the South, the trial of

John Brown came quickly. The verdict from twelve Virginia jurors arrived after less than an hour's deliberation; to no one's surprise, it read "guilty." The judge sentenced Brown to hang on December 2, 1859. All his accomplices met the same verdict and sentence.

The *Staunton Spectator* wished Virginia would act more calmly and treat Brown with the trifling contempt he deserved. Hurrying Brown to the gallows, the paper warned, "looks too much as if the great State of Virginia was in great trepidation." Yet the trepidation seemed real enough. Reports of slave rebellion and abolitionist assault piled up on one other.[47]

Word of possible trouble in Charlestown, hours away even by railroad, prompted the forty-seven members of the West Augusta Guard to mobilize in defense of their county and their state. They caught a train to Harpers Ferry. Wild reports flew. "One day we would learn that there were 500 men a short distance off in the mountains," a member of the Guard told his readers back home in Augusta. "Another report was there were 1900 men marching against Charlestown, and would certainly make an attack upon us very soon, and a hundred and one reports of similar kind was every day circulated through camp." None of the reports proved true; nothing happened in the weeks while Virginia waited to hang John Brown. The soldiers soon became callous and began to talk in a parody of soldiers before battle. "Well John, Jim or Jake, as the case might be, I think we are bound to have a brush to-night. And so do I, was the invariable reply. Well, how many do you think we can whip? Oh, fully twice our number, of course."[48] They could see there would be no fighting, and they admitted that they felt a little foolish, rushing to put down an insurrection that never came. They waited, nevertheless, for John Brown's execution a few weeks later, just in case.

Several of John Brown's men escaped in the immediate aftermath of the raid and fled north across the Pennsylvania border into Franklin County. There allies from the Underground Railroad helped them for several days, secretly conveying them to safety. All but one escaped: John Cook, an important leader in the insurrection. Cook, a white man, had lived near Harpers Ferry for a year, even marrying a local woman, and had worked among local slaves. Hungry and desperate in the mountains of Franklin County, Cook appeared at the Hughes furnace, managed by "a Southern man," where Dan Logan happened to be visiting. Logan was, Alexander McClure reported, "a most accomplished natural detective, who had many times arrested fugitive slaves, and who was constantly advised of all rewards offered for slaves or fugitives from the South, as they very often took refuge in South Mountain, where Logan lived." Logan recognized Cook immediately. The fugitive "was under medium size, skin as soft as a woman's, and his deep blue eyes and wealth of blond hair made it easy to identify him."[49] Logan captured the surprised abolitionist.

Cook tried to talk his way out of the situation, invoking prominent relatives and suggesting bribes. Finally the fugitive persuaded Logan to take him to "someone in Chambersburg who might feel an interest in him." The slave catcher Logan had "actively supported" the Republican McClure in his political campaigning, remarkably enough, and so brought Cook to McClure's office. The bounty hunter begged McClure to help Cook escape, as he "did not want the responsibility of having a man hung" and because he "now regretted that he had arrested Cook."

McClure too wanted Cook to escape. "I talked with him for an hour on his wonderful exploits in Kansas, and found him a man of fine culture, rare intelligence, but keenly emotional." McClure told Cook that he expected him to escape, and if he did, "he must cease his reckless revolutionary methods against slavery." The young insurrectionist's "face at once flushed and he jumped up, declaring that as long as God gave him life he would battle to the death against the men who held the slaves in bonds." Despite their disagreement, McClure used his political connections to find the local man who had built the jail and ask "where a prisoner should be placed to best get out of jail." The builder gladly supplied the information, and McClure "started for home, confident that on the following night Cook would be free."

When McClure reached his house, he found two women waiting for him, including the "daughter of the Democratic Congressman of our town," McClure's political rival. Both women "were clad ready for the street with a considerable bundle on the floor beside them." Their plan, they told McClure, was to "use the contents of their bundle in dressing Cook in female apparel, when one of them would walk out of the jail with him and the other remain in the cell." The two women "were of unusual earnestness of purpose and heartily sympathized with the Free State people in the bloody Kansas struggle." McClure had "no doubt" they would carry out their plan if they could. He told them that they need not risk themselves, for Cook would be escaping the following night in any case. The women persisted, and McClure "had finally to be peremptory in forbidding their visit to the jail, and with tears in their eyes they said they would abandon it."

McClure was wrong about Cook's escape; an officer appeared from Virginia the next day and took Cook away to his trial and execution. The *Valley Spirit* told of Cook's departure: "He was in good spirits all the way except at one time when some allusion was made to his wife he was observed to shed tears. He talked very freely of the insurrection and related many incidents connected with it." The paper noted that "there seems to be a strong feeling springing up in this community in favor of Cook. He is looked upon as the dupe of that arch villain Brown whose fortunes he has been following until led to destruction."[50]

The Franklin papers wrestled over their county's role in the biggest news event of the decade. The Democrats' *Valley Spirit* was mortified. "Our community has by some means, of which we were entirely unaware, become mixed up with this insurrection. While we were harboring for months these desperadoes among us we do not believe that a single one of our white citizens was in any way connected with them, or even suspected their designs." Blacks were a different story, for "it is believed that a portion of them knew the object of these men, were associated with them, and would have joined them if successful."[51] The paper did not give the names of these black sympathizers, if it knew them. That was fortunate for Henry Watson, confidant of Brown and Douglass.

"The people of this valley can now appreciate the risk they run in giving countenance to declaimers against the South," the *Valley Spirit* warned. "Suppose BROWN and his associates had succeeded in inciting to insurrection several thousand slaves. The insurgents would have been driven North through this valley. They would have entered our houses, plundered us of our property, and perhaps murdered our wives and children." The moral was clear: "What has taken place at Harper's Ferry is but a trifle in comparison with what will some day occur, if conservative men of all political creeds do not unite with the Democracy to put down the sectional party that has disturbed the peace of the country."[52]

For its part, the *Transcript*, like Republican papers across the North, denounced and ridiculed John Brown even as it attacked the Slave Power. "There is not a man in the Republican ranks who is at all connected with, or has given any sympathy to this silly movement," Alexander McClure's paper insisted. Frederick Douglass was not a Republican; he and other abolitionists "have always been the bitterest opponents of the Republican party, because it was not ultra enough." The Republicans had no idea of "making war upon slavery in the States, either through the powers of the government or by force of arms; and the responsibility for this silly act must rest solely upon the heads of the few wild zealots who conceived it and have perished in trying to carry it into execution."[53]

The Democrats attacked John Brown and the Republicans; the Republicans attacked John Brown and the abolitionists. Neither said a word in behalf of his plan or of the enslaved people he tried to help. Brown's raid seemed to have done only what Frederick Douglass warned Brown it would do: "rivet the fetters more firmly than ever on the limbs of the enslaved."

4

WHILE JOHN BROWN'S TRIAL came and went, while the nation waited for his execution and talked incessantly about its meaning, elections stoked the fires of conflict and rhetoric in both the North and South.

The political system in the United States had undergone enormous, and disheartening, change in the 1850s. The decade had begun with two strong national parties mobilizing three-quarters of the nation's voters. The Democrats and the Whigs warred with each other across the country, offering sharply contrasting visions of America's future. The Democrats, North and South, championed freedom for white men untrammeled by government, reformers, Mexicans, blacks, or churches. The Whigs, North and South, championed education and moderate reform with the government helping steer the change in what they saw as a progressive direction, away from the influence of Irish, Catholics, and Germans. Though all believed in making money, men in counties that depended heavily on government-sponsored banks and railroads tended to be Whig; men in areas with less contact with outside markets tended to be Democrats.[54]

Men did not simply vote to reflect their economic or geographic interests, however, but made calculations less obvious, less rational, and more stubborn. Political identity was often rooted in religious background: Presbyterians and Congregationalists tended to vote Whig, while Baptists, Methodists, and Catholics tended to vote Democrat. Ethnic background proved crucial as well: men whose fathers, grandfathers, or even great-grandfathers had been English and Scots tended to vote Whig while those of Irish Catholic and German descent voted even more rigorously Democrat.

But these characteristics did not explain loyalties in any simple way. Where voters lived made a great deal of difference. Counties, thanks to the efforts and power of especially influential men, established political identities early in the history of the national party system. A leading man whose ethnic, religious, and economic characteristics would seem to have steered him to one party might have joined that party's opposition instead because he did not get along with someone there or because he saw room for faster advancement even in a currently losing cause. Moreover, when a leading man in a neighborhood proclaimed a loyalty to a party, his poorer neighbors often followed, whether out of respect, deference, or calculation of future advantage. Changes in leadership at the state or national level could throw local politics into disarray, as locally powerful men could find themselves suddenly shut out of patronage and influence. Whatever the particular geography, voters generally managed to divide themselves into two fairly evenly matched parties within every state in the Union. Counties too, even those that tended to give the majority to the same party year after year, contained plenty of men who worked hard for the opposition.

Once established, such loyalties proved hard to break. A man of goodwill and ability did not merely select a political party after rationally calculating which party better served his needs. Rather, he belonged to a party and counted political loyalty a manly virtue. Moreover, men counted on political networks for jobs, economic connections, and friendship. Whigs and Democrats imagined themselves embodying the virtues of their party and rejecting the vices of their opponents. Few men proclaimed themselves independent of party loyalty, for such a stance effectively removed them from influence and stature.[55]

The political system based on these complex and interlocking loyalties flourished throughout the 1830s and 1840s but began to break apart in the early 1850s. The Whigs went first. To many voters, the Whigs no longer seemed to offer a coherent platform, ideology, or winning strategy. That party had long tried to reconcile irreconcilable groups: the largest planters in the South and leading businessmen in the North, nativists and men of generous spirit, evangelical Christians eager to use the government to improve society and people who did not believe the Bible sanctioned such a role. The Whigs had long attempted to appeal both to conservatives who valued stability and to forward-looking men who valued the party's emphasis on progress and enlightenment. To avoid alienating any of these constituencies, the Whigs, even when they were strongest, repeatedly turned for their national ticket to innocuous candidates, men who stood for little except past military glory and good character.

Developments in the 1850s made such a strategy impossible to maintain. Before the railroad, telegraph, and newspapers tied the country together more tightly in those years, Whigs could get away with saying one thing in one place and its opposite in another. Once speeches and letters from one newspaper could *be quickly published elsewhere, the Democrats seized on the Whigs' inconsistencies. Nativist Whigs in a rural district might see their words used against urban Whigs who appealed to recent immigrants; antislavery Whigs in the North might see their words reprinted all over the South while proslavery Whigs could see their editorials reprinted and excoriated in New England.*

The Whigs, in trouble, proved eager to strike bargains with new parties that might bring new energy, direction, and voters. Alliances with the American Party, a nativist party that flourished nationwide in the mid-1850s before fading quickly, accelerated the Whigs' decline. These alliances offered only brief successes followed by a worsening factionalism in the wake of their failures. The opportunistic alliances just reinforced the sense of many voters that the Whigs stood for nothing in particular. The Whigs, who prided themselves on being among the most principled of men, were attacked for having no principles at all. Ironically, too, the great prosperity in the United States between 1848 and 1854, without the aid of Whig programs, persuaded some voters that they did not need the party and its proposed innovations.

This humiliating and rather sudden erosion occurred all over the country. It opened the way for the emergence in the North of the Republicans, who provided a congenial home for Whigs grown uncomfortable with their awkward national alliance with the largest slaveholders. It also opened the door in the South for secessionists, who faced less opposition every year from politically powerful advocates of Union.[56]

The dissolution of the Whigs hit Virginia hard, since many voters there had cast their loyalties firmly with that party. Some leading Virginia men went to the American party (dubbed by their opponents the Know-Nothings for their claims to know nothing about secret activities in their party) in the mid-1850s. Augusta, as a strong Whig county, had become a source of support for the American party when the Whigs faltered. The Staunton Spectator *briefly became a Know-Nothing paper. But the American Party did not flourish for long in Virginia, and Augusta supporters of the party found themselves left behind when the waters receded. The political turmoil of the North drove Whigs into the Republican party, but in the upper South former Whigs had nowhere to go.*

NEWSPAPER EDITORS SERVED as the eyes and ears of their communities. The editors knew everyone in town and wanted their patronage, but they also spoke for specific political, business, family, and even religious interests. They had to be neutral and partisan at the same time, cheerful boosters of the community at large and vigilant advocates of particular people within that community. The newspapers spoke with voices alternately personal and public, boasting and fearful, sarcastic and sincere.

The two newspapers of Augusta struggled, with uneven success, to contain these conflicting impulses. The *Staunton Spectator* had been founded back in 1823 and had long carried the banner of the Whig party. It claimed to have as wide a readership as any Virginia paper west of the Blue Ridge Mountains and spoke with the authority of a paper associated with the most prominent families of the Valley. Augusta had returned a large majority for the Whigs and that party's various permutations in every election except one since 1840. The Whig majority of Augusta had gradually declined to about 60 percent by 1859—when without a national party, they called themselves the Opposition—but it still dominated Augusta.

The emergence of the Democratic *Staunton Vindicator* in the early 1850s coincided with the emergence of new Democratic voters after a new constitution broadened the franchise. The Democrats envisioned themselves as the only truly national party. "Even-handed justice to all sections, and the perfect, unimpaired sovereignty of the States, is the motto of the democracy." The Southern Democrats charged that all Whigs, even the undeniably good men among them, were unwitting allies of the worst people in the United States, "the Black Republicans, the Abolitionists, and all the isms of the north, the Fanny Wright men, the anti-renters, the Mormons."[57]

While the two-party system dissolved all over the country, especially in the South, Virginia and Augusta voters refused to succumb to a one-party system. The Opposition did not attract many defectors from the Democrats, but neither could the Democrats, to their great frustration, attract defectors from this party with no national organization. Men in the Opposition continued to think of themselves as Whigs, to call themselves Whigs. Even though the name of their party had changed, it stood for the same things: stability, compromise, and progress.

The Whig men portrayed themselves as the only hope of the Union. The Whig leaders, with roots deep in Unionist attitudes and work, claimed that they were above faction and wanted only the protection of peace and property. It was the Democrats, they said, who agitated the slave issue and antagonized the North. That was true: the Democrats refused to let slavery sleep. They constantly goaded their opponents, charging that the old Whigs were soft on abolitionism because they valued Union above the Constitution.

Week in and week out, the newspapers of both parties filled their space with discussions of things political. An election for some position was always looming, raging, or being bemoaned or gloated over. Announcements, advertisements, notices, reminders, letters, jokes, diatribes, and exhortations appeared in elections ranging from local school commissioner to the governor to the president of the United States. If nothing was brewing nearby, political news from far-flung states would be imported. Somewhere something interesting and partisan was unfolding.

Augusta's newspapers listed more than a hundred men who participated in public political events during 1859 and 1860. Some joined committees, gave speeches, or donated money; others attended rallies, wrote letters, or ran for office. About three-quarters of these men worked for the Whigs, who apparently did a better job of both mobilizing and publicizing the work their partisans performed. Augusta's Whigs, like those everywhere in the United States, prided themselves on their dignity and respectability. About two-thirds of Whig activists owned slaves while only one-third of the Democrats did so. Moreover, Whig farms tended to be bigger and more valuable than those of Democrats.

But differences between Whig and Democratic activists in Augusta did not reflect sharp differences in wealth, status, or any other measurable attribute. Men wrapped up such a large part of themselves in their political parties that their partisan loyalty often overwhelmed other sources of identity. The best predictor of how a man would vote was simply how he had voted before. Men active enough in politics to appear in the newspapers were generally better off than the average man. The great majority, in both parties, were farmers. Activists of the two parties tended to be about the same age, in their early forties, older than most men.

Voter turnout in the county remained high throughout the 1850s, with about seven men out of ten going to the polls. "I feel the greatest loathing for these election scenes. The intoxication, profanity, rowdyism etc fill me with shame." Joseph Waddell, who had fought for the Whigs and now the Opposition in the *Spectator* throughout the 1850s, admitted his disgust to his diary. "Poor, miserable human nature! On such occasions a large class of people musters in town, that we never see other times. The ignorant and disgustingly besotted swagger about with all the self-importance of sovereigns, although many of them are led up to the polls like sheep to the shambles, with no more intelligence or free will."[58] The electorate contained men thoroughly conversant with the great issues of the day; it also contained men who knew little other than what the politicians buying drinks told them.

To men such as Waddell, the political system seemed out of kilter, broken. It still pulled men together, but only for displays of bravado and human weakness.

THE REPUBLICANS GREW stronger in the North and in Pennsylvania in the late 1850s. Conditions favored their growth. The Democrats bungled the economy and suffered an unmatched level of corruption in the Buchanan administration. The American Party quickly faded when immigration suddenly slowed and voters grew weary of the party's paranoia and secrecy. The South appeared ever more imperious in Congress and in the Supreme Court. The struggle in Kansas made the Democrats in Washington seem helpless in the face of the Slave Power. President James Buchanan and Senator Stephen Douglas openly fought over control of the party.

The Republicans seized on the opportunity to pull together a coalition of former Whigs, former Free-Soilers, former Know-Nothings, and former Democrats disgusted with the Buchanan administration and with the South. The Republicans indulged in nativism and anti-Catholicism but, after seeing the fury unleashed in the North by the prolonged battle over the fate of slavery in Kansas, made the expansion of slavery in the territories their main issue.[59]

The territories served as a screen on which both the North and the South projected their hopes and anxieties. To the Republicans, containing the Slave Power was the key. They were disgusted that the South, smaller in population than the North, had somehow managed to control the federal government throughout the history of the Republic. The nation should be run for the benefit of the white majority, the

Republicans argued, and that would not happen so long as Southerners and the Democratic party they dominated remained in control.

Since most Republicans had no intention of ending slavery where it existed, all their hopes for political power, for the expansion of the North's economy, and for the slow and peaceful end of slavery at some point generations ahead lay in closing the territories to slavery. If the Southern economy could not expand, Republicans believed, the inefficiencies of slavery would eventually catch up with the South and bring the haughty plantation economy to its knees. In Republican eyes, the South labored under a sick and static order unjust to its white majority as well as to its slaves. Republicans saw the vast and increasing production of Southern plantations merely as the result of fresh lands and slaves worked to their human limits, not as an indication that planters had harnessed forced labor to the banking, transportation, and manufacturing machinery of the modern world.[60]

The Democrats, sympathetic to and increasingly controlled by the South, had won in Franklin County throughout the early 1850s. In 1856 only a third of Franklin's voters, as in Pennsylvania as a whole, had cast ballots for John C. Frémont, the Republican candidate in the first election in which Republicans ran for the presidency.

In the late 1850s, though, the Republicans quickly gained a hearing in Franklin County. The crucial step occurred in 1852, when a venerable local paper, the *Repository and Transcript*, was bought by Alexander K. McClure. The *Transcript* had represented the Whig party for almost as long as that party had existed, from its early days as a loose coalition opposed to Andrew Jackson to its latter days as the party of property, evangelical faith, and progress. In 1859, while the national Republican party struggled to define itself and spread its message, the *Transcript* already spoke with confidence. It conveyed the core Republican message: contempt for the South and the Northern Democrats who did the South's bidding, especially the Northern Democrats who controlled Franklin County.

The Republican paper turned to ugly language to criticize the Democrats. "Nigger, nigger, nigger, is their only theme," the *Transcript* charged of its local opponents, "the interest of the nabobs of slavedom, the only rights worth battling for." The Republicans did not care about the detested South; they would not try to destroy slavery there. The Republicans cared about the white men of the North, of Pennsylvania, and of Franklin. "What have we of the North to do with the negro question? It gives us, of the Republican party, especially, no uneasiness. We had nothing to do with overrunning the country with the degraded, outcast race, nor are we particularly interested in getting rid of the burthen."[61]

The Republicans—local, state, or national—put forward no new ideas about ending slavery. They denounced immediate abolitionism, vaguely praised the colonization of gradually freed slaves to Africa, but offered no plan to erode slavery where it flourished. Emancipation was a Southern problem. "They who have reaped all the benefit arising from the unpaid labor of the poor wretches, who have grown rich, fat and lazy, upon the toil of these helpless, hapless creatures and their willing coadjutors of the North,—the nigger democracy—may devise ways and means to remove the curse of slavery where it exists; all we care about is that it shall not be extended."[62]

The Democrats' *Valley Spirit* was a relative newcomer to Chambersburg, only having moved down from Shippensburg, on Franklin's northern border, in 1852. The paper's message was simple: the Union must stand as the highest good, the greatest good. Black people did not matter and deserved no respect. The Republicans were hypocrites and fools, prattling on about the Slave Power when they themselves posed the greatest threat to the Union with their fanatical ranting that fed Southern paranoia. Fortunately, the Democrats noted with relief, the Republicans remained a minority in Franklin, in Pennsylvania, and in the North.

Despite the slurs they threw at each other, the Democrats and Republicans of Franklin did not differ very much in their wealth or the way they made their livings. Neither party's activists were richer than their counterparts, owned larger farms, or lived closer to town. Farmers and professionals were slightly more likely to vote Republican, while artisans and businessmen were more likely to vote Democratic. Those men depended on the South for their livelihoods and were not eager to provoke boycotts or movements for Southern self-sufficiency. In general, though, the men of the two parties appeared far more alike than not in any measurable way. That did not prevent them from hating each other; in fact, their similarity only fed the disgust.

In Franklin County a vibrant political culture hummed with activity. Not only did the two major newspapers of the county take their identity from the Republicans and Democrats, but so did many men there. Out of every hundred households, nine men cared enough about one party or the other to work in public on its behalf in 1859 and 1860. The *Transcript* and the *Valley Spirit* carried column after column of news about the doings of politicians, whether in Washington, in the capital at Harrisburg, in Kansas, or in states all across the nation. Each village and crossroads in Franklin sustained its own political leadership, dutifully reporting meetings, debates, speeches, and dinners to the party paper in Chambersburg.

Those politically active men represented a broad swath of Franklin's propertied male population. In both parties, farmers accounted for about a quarter of the activists, artisans another quarter, professionals another quarter, and businessmen the remainder. Poorer men appeared much less frequently, with only three laborers working for the Republicans and nine for the Democrats. On election day, though, about eight men of ten went to the polls in Franklin County. While they may not have cared enough to give their time or money to the parties, they did care enough to vote on election day. The families who bought the newspapers published in Chambersburg necessarily read about politics, for the papers published more political news than anything else. And that political news certainly bore enough drama for anyone after John Brown's raid.

AUGUSTA'S STATE SENATOR Alexander H. H. Stuart received the honor and the burden of writing the official response to Harpers Ferry for the Virginia legislature. The Democrats controlled both houses of that legislature as well as the governorship, but they turned to this well-known former Whig and Unionist to craft the commonwealth's official response. They knew that Northerners would respect Stuart. "We desire nothing but friendly relations with our sister States of the North," Stuart wrote. "We ask of them nothing to which they have not solemnly bound themselves by the compact of the Constitution. But we understand our rights, and we are resolutely determined to maintain them." Virginia cherished the constitutional bonds that held North and South together, "but when we are threatened with the knife of the assassin and torch of the incendiary, we cannot fold our arms in blind security."[63]

The report ended with resolutions that encouraged Virginians to take action. One resolution called for arming and equipping the militia "for active and efficient service." Another called for "encouraging the domestic manufactures of our own State, promoting direct trade with foreign countries, and establishing, as far as may be practicable, our commercial independence." Still another resolution invited the cooperation of "our sister States of the South" for establishing "more prompt and effectual punishment" of all "found guilty of conspiring against the peace of our community." Hard words, and hard words to write, from a Virginian who had devoted his life to binding the Union together.

Alexander Hugh Holmes Stuart came from Augusta's most prominent family. In his early fifties by the time of John Brown's raid, handsome, youthful for his years, and clean-shaven, Stuart owned one of the most impressive houses in Staunton, occupying a large lot near the center of town and displaying thick columns, broad porches, and elegant gardens. He and his wife owned ten slaves.

Stuart had acquired wide experience in public affairs. After attending William and Mary and the University of Virginia, he had returned home to Staunton in 1828 to practice law. He quickly became prominent in the Whig party and went to Richmond to represent Augusta for two terms in the General Assembly in the 1840s. President Millard Fillmore acknowledged Stuart's importance in 1850, when he named the Augusta man secretary of the interior, in which post he served for three years. As the Whigs disintegrated in the mid-1850s, Stuart associated himself with the American party, the Know-Nothings, and maintained the respect of his local constituents even when that party quickly collapsed. Augusta returned Stuart to the state senate in 1857.

Alexander H. H. Stuart

Despite his wealth and prominence, Stuart labored under the

burden of intense private loss even as he struggled with issues of great public importance. Briscoe Baldwin Stuart, the oldest son of the family, showed every sign of carrying on the Stuart tradition of leadership. He had attended the fine private schools of Staunton and then the University of Virginia, where he completed the law course and then returned home to practice law alongside his father. Baldwin became engaged to Elizabeth Luckett, a wealthy young woman from Louisiana who attended the Virginia Female Institute in Staunton. Their marriage, like many among the elite planter families who met one another at the spas and schools of Virginia, would nourish the ties between the border South and the deep South.

In the spring of 1859 Baldwin set out for the wedding in Louisiana. But traveling down the Mississippi River, his steamboat, the *St. Nicholas*, exploded. The first reports of the accident suggested that things might not be too bad, but soon the extent of Baldwin's injuries became clear. For two weeks young Stuart suffered agony from burns all over his body while wealthy families came to his aid. A Memphis paper noted that "he was not left as 'a stranger in a strange land,' but was nursed and waited on by the young men of our city as if he had been one of their own number." By the time his mother and father arrived in Memphis after a long and excruciating trip, hope had passed.[64]

Alexander Stuart and his wife brought their son's body back to Staunton. There "a large concourse of mourning friends and acquaintances" escorted him to Thornrose Cemetery, where other Stuarts lay. A gathering at the Staunton Lyceum, presided over by leading young men of the county, drafted a tribute of respect to Baldwin Stuart: "Whereas it has pleased Almighty God to call suddenly from our midst our beloved and treasured companion and friend," be it resolved "that while we deeply regret this fearful visitation, we bow in humble subordination to the will of that inscrutable Providence, who doeth all things for the best."[65] Soon after his loss, Alexander H. H. Stuart went back to work, burying his grief in service to Augusta, to Virginia, and the nation.

THE *Staunton Spectator* found a religious message in slavery as the nation talked of John Brown. "In one sense no one, white or black, is free in this world," the paper observed. God had a plan, and God had put slavery in America. Accordingly, there was only one Christian response to the burden that slavery put upon both slave and master: "When the man, whatever his complexion, recognizes the fact that his lot is ordained of God, and cheerfully acquiesces, he becomes a free man in the only true sense."[66] John Brown, refusing to acquiesce, had proved himself not merely a traitor but also a heretic, a blasphemer who dared speak for God.

The moral was clear. "We have never entertained a doubt that the condition of the Southern slaves is the best and most desirable for the negroes, as a class, that they have ever been found in or are capable of," the *Spectator* asserted. "There is abundant evidence to prove that the black man's lot as a slave, is vastly preferable to that of his free brethren at the North." The paper used the testimony of Henry Ward Beecher, a leading abolitionist and minister in Brooklyn, to indict white Northerners as hypocrites. According to the Reverend Beecher, free black people in the North " 'are almost without education, . . . cannot even ride in the cars of our city railroads, . . . are snuffed at in the house of God, or tolerated with ill-disguised disgust.' " The black man in the North, said Beecher, "is crowded down, down, down, through the most menial callings to the bottom of society. We heap upon them moral obloquy more atrocious than that which the master heaps upon the slave."[67] The South seemed better than the North in every way.

White Southerners, who had always seen abolitionists as sentimental, weepy, and irrational, felt their suspicions confirmed when the prominent abolitionist Lydia Maria Child wrote Virginia Governor Wise a public letter as John Brown lay wounded in jail. "I, and thousands of others, feel a natural impulse of sympathy for the brave and suffering man. . . . He needs mother or sister to dress his wounds, and speak soothingly to him. Will you allow me to perform that mission of humanity? If you will, may God bless you for the generous deed!"[68]

Though she and other abolitionists preached peace, even pacifism, Child admitted to Brown that "I admire your courage, moral and physical. I reverence you for the humanity which tempered your zeal. I sympathize with your cruel bereavements, your sufferings, and your wrongs. In brief, I love you and bless you." She spoke for many with such words, she claimed. "Thousands of hearts are throbbing with sympathy, as warm as mine. I think of you night and day, bleeding in prison, surrounded by hostile faces, sustained only by trust in God, and your own strong heart. I long to nurse you, to speak to you sisterly words of sympathy and consolation."

Governor Wise responded theatrically. Of course he would forward the dear lady's letter to Brown, through the proper channels. He would even welcome and protect her "among us, though it be to one who whetted knives of butchery for our mothers, sisters, daughters and babes." White Southerners thought they knew whom to blame for John Brown: the abolitionists and their hypocritical supporters among the Black Republicans. They had created John Brown.

THE WEST AUGUSTA GUARD stayed through John Brown's execution, to help and to watch. The county was proud of this militia unit. Unlike most militia around the country, which tended to neglect drilling in favor of drinking, the West Augusta Guard took its work seriously. "In the perfection of its equipments and efficiency of its drill, it was unsurpassed by any company in Virginia," boasted one observer. It appeared at every public occasion, it seemed, displaying its readiness to defend citizens from any challenge they might face.

Much of the Guard's polish and spirit came from its twenty-seven-year-old leader, William Smith Hanger Baylor. The only son of a prominent farmer and magistrate, "generous, ardent, and affectionate, with a most pleasing person and cordial address," one who knew him remembered, Baylor "was the idol of fond parents and the favorite of hosts of friends." Baylor had graduated from Washington College in Lexington and then proceeded to the University of Virginia, where he studied law. There Baylor had received the honor of delivering the final address to the graduates of 1853, selected by the prestigious Jefferson Literary and Debating Society. Returning to Staunton, Baylor immediately entered the bar and only four years later, 1857, was commonwealth's attorney, or district attorney. He became active among the Democrats of Augusta. Baylor married a young woman from eastern Virginia, Mary Hawes Johnson, in the fall of 1859. Already well-to-do, with six slaves of his own hired out to individuals and institutions in Augusta, he now came into the possession of twenty-eight more on a property in the Tidewater. Baylor was worth thirty thousand dollars.

William Smith Hanger Baylor

Baylor and his new wife were on their bridal tour at the time of John Brown's raid. Baylor had come down with typhoid fever on his journey and was resting in New York City when he heard of the attack at Harpers Ferry. "In the delirium of fever he imagined himself in command of his company, and not all the endearments of a devoted bride could divert his thoughts from the engrossing theme," a friend recalled. Baylor was therefore eager to perform his duty by taking the West Augusta Guard to Harpers Ferry in December.[69]

Virginia made the occasion of John Brown's execution as simple and somber as it could, demonstrating the state's adherence to the letter and spirit of the law. "The scaffold upon which the doomed man was executed was erected some half mile from the town in a large field containing some ten or fifteen acres," a report from Harpers Ferry related. "The field was laid off and staked—the stakes being about fifty feet apart, on each of which was hung a small white flag." The military companies formed two hollow squares around the scaffolding. Brown rode "in a small wagon containing his coffin, upon which he sat, as the wagon moved on toward the place of execution. Arrived at the place he ascended the scaffold with a firm step, merely remarking that the country before him was a beautiful one, but hoped those having him in charge would not detain him unnecessarily."[70]

The Virginians had to admit Brown's dignity as he came to the gallows. "No sign of fear was visible in his countenance; he looked calmly and resolutely at the crowd of soldiers surrounding him, but made no remark or allusion to his fate." Fifteen minutes later the executioner slashed the rope with an ax and John Brown fell through a trapdoor to dangle in the air. "Thus ended the existence of one, a great portion of whose life had been spent in warring against the laws and institutions of his country," the report concluded. "May his fate be a warning to all traitors in all future time."

The men of Augusta sighed in relief and in hope. They thought their state had acted honorably, that the Union might even be strengthened by the ordeal. "Happily for the peace of Virginia, for the reputation of our common country, and for all the high and holy bonds which bind us together in a great bond of Union and brotherhood, the mandate of the law has been strictly yet quietly enforced; justice has been meted out to the transgressors of the laws of God and man." Furthermore, Augusta had done more than its assigned part in the great drama. When the West Augusta Guard returned home, "they were met at the cars by a large number of admiring friends, desirous of welcoming the 'returned soldiers.' After parading Main street they proceeded to their armory room," where they found a "substantial banquet, to which they paid their compliments as only men who have been fed on crackers and middling for some time can." The time in the field had made Will Baylor's unit even better. "No one could have helped noticing the immense improvement in the drill of the Guards since they have been on duty." Although glad to get home, "they, to a man, express their entire readiness to perform any duty in defense of their State which its Executive may think necessary."[71]

The *Spectator*, always seeing itself as the model of Southern moderation, tried to explain to Northerners that contrary to reports and the panic in Charlestown, the whites of Virginia did not live in fear of insurrection. "It is a most egregious blunder to suppose that we who live in the enjoyment of all the benefits of the 'peculiar institution,' live also in constant dread of insurrection and rebellion, and go to our beds at night with the terrible apprehension that our throats may be cut before morning. Not a bit of it."[72]

Yet on a Wednesday night soon after John Brown's sentencing, Joseph Waddell, who may well have written the words of confidence and assurance in the *Spectator*, received a visit from James Wright. Wright, who had hired a slave, John, from Waddell, came to complain that "John had resisted him when he undertook to chastise him for some impudence, that he indulged in threats against him and the family, kept a pistol, went to bed with two hickory sticks etc etc. He said John must leave his place, that their lives were in danger." Waddell asked his brother Legh to check on things at the Wright house. Legh reported that Wright "had been too exacting, requiring too much work, and that the fears of the family had been unnecessarily aroused by the idle talk of the female servants about John's talk and conduct." Nevertheless, something had to be done.[73]

Waddell went to the Wrights' himself. There he found that "the family seemed rather nervous and John more alarmed, apparently, than anyone else!" The accusations proved ill founded, Waddell thought, based entirely upon the gossip of other slaves. "Wright had heard John make no threats, but the negroes had told him; he had seen no pistol and could find none, but the negroes had seen it." Wright did produce "a stout cudgel," which he had found in John's bed, "as proof positive of the boy's 'mischievous' intention." John, however, denied that he made any threat or ever had a pistol. "He acknowledges that he had cut the stick, he was going to a corn husking in the neighborhood, and having heard so much about bears, he wanted some means of defense. Some one else, he said, had put it in his bed." The newspapers of Augusta had indeed carried stories about bears, so the story was plausible.

Waddell took John away and apparently lost the money that came from his hire. But rather than be angry or alarmed at the threat John posed to white people, Waddell thought "the whole affair" was "extremely ludicrous." This had all happened because the "Harper's Ferry affair has certainly bewildered the Wright family." It bewildered many white people.

Stewing over John Brown and picking up on a resolution from Virginia's General Assembly, Staunton's *Vindicator* applauded a movement toward homespun cloth, divorcing the Southern market from the textile mills of detested New England. "We like it much. It has the sweet savor of the cargo of tea that was thrown overboard in other days." With self-discipline, "not one cent shall go from the South into the services of the Aid Societies, Underground Railroads, and Freedom Shriekers of the North, either through the merchant princes, manufacturers, institutions of learning, yankee book-sellers, yankee teachers, yankee pedlars, or any other channel."[74] Never mind that Augusta had produced exceedingly little homespun for years and that advertisements for all sorts of manufactured cloth filled the columns of the *Vindicator*.

The blending of patriotic purpose and main chance came home to Staunton when local capitalists raised twenty thousand dollars to incorporate a new Boot, Shoe and Leather Manufacturing Company. A local lawyer and farmer with seventeen slaves became president of the company, presiding over a board of directors constituted of some of the other large slaveholders in Augusta, including John Imboden. "We are glad to see this evidence of reviving enterprise," the *Vindicator* commented. "Instead hereafter of sending our hides to the North to be dressed, manufactured into Boots and Shoes, and then returned to us with a heavy profit to Northern enterprise, we will have a producing and consuming market of our own—facilitating home commerce and enriching our citizens."[75] An enterprise that, only a year earlier, would have been envisioned and perceived as a business venture, maybe a bit Yankee, had become charged with Southern independence.

5

JOHN BROWN HELD politics and politicians in contempt for their vacillation and compromise. But his death took much of its meaning from politics. Without political parties to channel the hard feelings unloosed in the winter of 1859–60, those feelings would have had little long-term consequence. Despite the harsh words, both the North and the South remained filled with people who wanted delay and forgetfulness. Abolitionists found themselves more distrusted and denounced in the North than before John Brown's raid. Both the Democrats and the Republicans distanced themselves from the violence, the racial mixing, and the religious fanaticism Brown seemed to embody.[76]

In other years the Unionism, caution, constitutionalism, and evasion that characterized most white Americans' response to the slavery issue would have dissipated into the ether of sectional distrust. But the American political system had broken apart in the late 1850s, and 1860 was an election year. In this fractured situation, people would declare loyalties, renounce enemies, and deny doubts. They would war with themselves, within their communities, as a substitute for war against more distant enemies, enemies they could not see and so imagined as they wished. Emotion and policy would build on one another, give meaning and force to one another.

Neither major party knew who would head its ticket in the November contests. President James Buchanan's administration held the power of patronage but little loyalty among the Democrats over whom he presided. He would not stand for reelection. Voters equated him with the Dred Scott *decision, in which the Supreme Court had taken an extreme proslavery position. Voters associated Buchanan with the political chaos of "Bleeding Kansas," which he did nothing to quell. When they thought of Buchanan, they thought of the Panic of 1857, of the humiliating corruption and factionalism within his own party.*[77]

The Republicans had grown stronger across the North in the elections of 1858 and 1859, and some believed they might even win the presidency if they could find the right candidate. Their party was new, untested, and unstable, however, made up of mismatched ingredients: nativism, antislavery, economic boosterism, reformism, religious intolerance, racism, free labor idealism, and regional chauvinism.

Many voters, North and South, believed in neither the Democrats nor the Republicans. They looked for a party that truly embodied Union and compromise; in their eyes, the Democrats talked of Union but favored the South while the Republicans talked of Union but only on Northern terms.

The American party system had evolved to hold things together, cementing the locality to the state and the state to the nation. Party identity and loyalty provided the cohesion. Normal politics had come to be based on fervent competition between two, and only two, national parties. It depended on the checks and balances of the various branches of government, on significant representation of the two parties in the House and the Senate, on the familiar ebb and flow of victors and losers in the various offices, on the ability of party leaders to enforce discipline and unity among their ranks, and on the willingness of men from the two parties to cooperate when they could. Though this system frequently stumbled, the balance and integration it offered remained the ideal.

The sharing of power in Washington depended on the replication of the two-party system throughout every other level of the political order. Officeholders in Congress or even the White House had to be able to lay claim to a constituency that supported them and their actions, or they could not expect to be in office long. Ideas, power, patronage, and money traveled up and down the political system, the high and the low giving legitimacy to one another.

This system held the divergent regions of the United States together through decades of expansion, economic boom and bust, nativism and abolitionism. It worked so well, in fact, that Americans relied on it alone to absorb the shock and strain of every kind of conflict. If the parties became sectional, if the parties abandoned any effort to reach across the border, there was little else to keep things from shattering. If normal politics died, the nation itself might perish as well. With everything riding on the election of 1860, the drama began with the Democrats, who held their convention in May in Charleston, South Carolina.

THE NEW EDITOR of the *Staunton Vindicator*, Samuel M. Yost, traveled all the way to South Carolina to watch history being made. The recent completion of the railroad to Augusta County made a two-day trip of what would have been, just a few years earlier, a long and dangerous journey by wagon and sea along the Outer Banks. Though Charleston was beautiful in May, Virginia was, predictably, even more beautiful. "The cool, refreshing breezes which invigorate and enliven the physical man in the Valley of Virginia, are sadly missed here. Those of us who had never experienced the heat of so Southern a latitude, were unprepared with wardrobe for the change of temperature, and consequently, are gradually losing, by profuse perspiration, our surplus flesh. The thermometer stands to-day about 93 degrees."[78] And it was still May.

Samuel Yost, only in his late twenties but well traveled, was not impressed with what he saw of the coastal South. The pinewoods of the South Atlantic coast struck Yost as empty and forbidding, though spring flowers and blossoms awakened "a lively remembrance of the months of June and July in Virginia." He was as amazed as any Yankee at the Spanish moss, "hanging in negligent grace from every bough and twig."[79]

Yost thought Charleston "handsome," with "brisk and large" businesses and "some of the most beautiful store-rooms I have ever seen." But "the negro population is far inferior to the same class in Virginia. One of our best negroes is worth a half-dozen of the dwarfish, disfigured, filthy creatures which swarm the streets of Charleston. Their dialect is different, and almost unintelligible, resembling more the chattering of a monkey or a parrot than the enunciation of a human being."[80]

Politics, however, not regional comparison, dominated Yost's reports back to Staunton. The editor, a Stephen A. Douglas man, was pleased to hear that most people thought the conciliatory Illinois senator had the "inside track," that the "North and Northwest are very candid in stating that their political existence depends upon his nomination." But things immediately spun out of control. The fire-eaters fought with the advocates of Douglas over the platform on which the Democratic candidate of 1860 would run. These deep South men demanded guarantees that slaveholders could take their slaves into the territories, ignoring all the struggles over that issue in the last decade. Delegates from Alabama, South Carolina, Arkansas, Louisiana, Texas, and Florida threatened to walk out of the convention if they did not rule the day.[81]

The men of Augusta, whether Democrats or Whigs, hated such displays. Instead they invoked the Virginia way, the border way, of dealing with slavery, the way they had inherited from Thomas Jefferson and all the state's leaders since: buy time with compromise and hope the wolf would leave the door. Yost assaulted the fire-eaters, who had stalked out of the convention when they could not control the nomination. "They went out. They are out, and we hope and trust will ever remain out. We look upon such men as no better than Northern fanatics. They care not for the Union. They would tear down the temple of liberty itself to accomplish the ends of selfish ambition, and erect upon the ruins of our common country, 'a Southern Confederacy!' It is for this they aim."[82]

The convention dissolved without naming anyone as its candidate, a humiliating failure for the most powerful party in the nation. The Democrats were to meet again two months later in Baltimore to try again. Yost returned home heartsick.

Meanwhile, with political conventions and debate stirring the air, Staunton held a celebration of its volunteer soldiers at the American Hotel. John Imboden's Staunton Artillery and Baylor's West Augusta Guard gathered "in full uniform and numbers, and truly the exhibition was handsome. Not in Virginia is there a military organization that surpasses in soldierly appearance, perfect discipline, and intrinsic and substantial worth," the *Vindicator* rhapsodized. Baylor received a "beautiful Damascus sword," its scabbard inscribed as "a token of affection and confidence from the West Augusta Guard to their Commander, Capt. Wm. S. H. Baylor, May, 1860," its blade inscribed with a Latin phrase and the motto "The Citizen Soldier." John Imboden received from the ladies of Staunton an "elegant Banner," also bearing Latin, and "on the top of the staff is a handsome bronzed eagle, with wings out-spread, indicating the onward tendency and destiny of the stars and stripes." After the banquet, the men, women, and children cheered and watched the militia march through the streets of Staunton. No one could be sure what the units might fight for, since the tension between local pride, state interest, and national identity was growing ever stronger, but the people of Augusta took comfort in knowing they had citizen soldiers ready to defend the county no matter what happened.[83]

THE DEMOCRATS IN FRANKLIN COUNTY watched the train wreck of the Charleston convention and knew what had been lost. "The division of the Democratic party by a geographical line upon the question of slavery, is the most ominous disaster that can happen to the country," the *Valley Spirit* warned. "When this bond is broken what remains to hold us together? What other national organization can take the place of the Democratic party, in case it is broken and scattered? This is a serious question, not only for Democrats, but for all men."[84]

The Republicans of Franklin, for their part, ridiculed the secessionists and made fun of the divisions among the Democrats. "After frightening a great many old women, and some timid men, at the North by their unsightly hobgoblin—dissolution of the Union, and a bloody civil war," the *Transcript* scoffed, the Democrats "have shown by their recent course that there is no danger to be apprehended from that source."[85] The Democrats had played with the fire of disunion talk and had burned only themselves.

Alexander McClure represented Pennsylvania as a delegate to the Republican National Convention in Chicago in June 1860. The Republicans made their nomination for the presidency after three intense ballots and much jockeying. Many observers had expected William Seward of New York, a longtime leader of the Republican party and a noted enemy of the South, to receive the nomination. He turned out to be, however, too strong an enemy of the South to win the support of several pivotal states along the border: Pennsylvania, Indiana, and Illinois, states necessary for Republican victory. Seward's main challenger going into the convention, Salmon P. Chase of Ohio, had been even more outspoken on slavery.

Abraham Lincoln of Illinois eventually emerged as the consensus candidate. Lincoln came from a key border state, had distinguished himself in his campaign against Stephen Douglas for the U.S. Senate in 1858, and had defined a position on slavery that combined principle with prudence. He acknowledged the constitutional right of slaveholders to keep slaves they already possessed but denied them any right to take slaves into the territories. Lincoln combined firmness on slavery with an appeal to moderate Northerners who would not have trusted Seward or Chase.

Lincoln consistently forswore any attempt to disturb slavery where it lay. He thought the South entitled to a Fugitive Slave Law (though he disliked it), would admit another slave state if the legislature of any new chose to allow slavery if slavery had not been introduced in the territorial stage (as he thought unlikely), would not abolish slavery in the District of Columbia (though he would very much like to see it disappear there), and would not disturb the domestic slave trade (though it disgusted him). Lincoln did not speak with the voice of an abolitionist or even as a Republican who took a particularly hard stand against slavery. That was why he had been nominated.[86] Lincoln was a man of the border.

McClure, chairman of his state's Central Committee, threw his support behind Abraham Lincoln early and watched his man rise to victory. McClure's *Transcript* embraced Lincoln with unchecked enthusiasm. The reasons have become part of American folklore: "He is the son of a poor man; he, by indomitable perseverance, raised himself from the depths of poverty and obscurity to be one of the first men of a great nation of Free men." Had Lincoln "been raised in the South—where he was born" he would not have had the chance to rise, but his family had migrated to "a young Free State," where he could flourish. In sum, "Elect Abraham Lincoln, the man of the people, the child of poverty, the youth of perseverance and application, the successful lawyer, the gifted statesman, the champion of Freedom, of Free homes for Free men, of keeping Slavery out of, so that poor white men may enter into the rich, teeming Territories of the great West."[87]

No wonder McClure grew enthusiastic over Abraham Lincoln. Not only had the young Franklin man attached his political future to Lincoln, but the party's platform sounded much like the editorials in the *Repository and Transcript* over the preceding months. The Republican platform went out of its way to silence those who saw their party as an abolitionist party. One plank announced that the Republicans "hold in abhorrence all schemes for disunion, come from whatever source they may"; the next plank held that "the rights of each State, to order and control its own domestic institutions according to its own judgment exclusively, is essential to that balance of power on which the perfection and endurance of her political faith depends." Slavery, in other words, could not be molested where it already existed. The same plank dismissed, without naming him, John Brown: "And we denounce the lawless invasion by armed force of any State or territory, no matter under what pretext, as among the gravest of crimes."

After such cautious hedging, and after more enthusiastic talk of the tariff, the Republican platform finally let fly when it got to the territorial issue. It asserted that "the normal conditions of all the Territory of the United States is that of freedom." Slavery could not be established in any territory by anyone. The platform also supported the Homestead Act, which would provide 160 acres to settlers in the West and called for a transcontinental railroad as well as harbor and river improvements. It excoriated those who would reopen the slave trade and distanced the party from the nativism with which many Republicans had been identified a few years earlier.

McClure put everything he had into the campaign of 1860. In fact, that year presented Pennsylvania with two campaigns, one for governor in October and another for president in November. That timing offered McClure a wonderful opportunity. If he could help elect Andrew G. Curtin, a strong ally of his and Lincoln's, to the governorship, he could lay the foundation for a Republican victory not only in Pennsylvania but throughout the North weeks later. He would also make himself a powerful man within the rapidly growing Republican party.

As soon as McClure got back to Chambersburg from Chicago in June, he began writing Lincoln, strengthening the ties with the new presidential candidate. Would Lincoln support sending two leading men from the party to take the stump in Pennsylvania? "I doubt not that we shall carry Pennsylvania," McClure told Lincoln, "but it is going to be a desperate contest." The Republicans were fortunate to have McClure, who, he bragged, had built "an organization that no combination can defeat." The Democrats promised to make things easier by breaking themselves apart at their convention in Baltimore, but the Republicans "shall continue to err on the safe side, by having every available vote within our reach on Election day." Lincoln wrote back with his recommendations and asked that McClure destroy the letter; the young operative obliged.[88]

Throughout July, August, and September, McClure sent one letter after another from Chambersburg to Lincoln, consulting on strategy and reporting on the mood of the voters. The second Democratic convention in Baltimore saw the Northern wing of the party nominate Stephen Douglas while the Southern wing, rapidly convening in another hall, nominated John C. Breckinridge of Kentucky, the current vice president under James Buchanan. The Democrats would have two men in the field in 1860, an unprecedented event. Douglas stood for compromise, Breckinridge for Southern rights and Democratic party orthodoxy.

Alexander McClure could hardly believe what the Democrats were doing. He wrote Lincoln that the Democrats had grown to hate each other so much that "both the Douglas men & the Breckenridge men here openly declare you to be preferable to the rival Democratic Candidate." Even more remarkable was the hatred some of the professed Douglas men held for Douglas. They just used Douglas, McClure thought, to get back at Buchanan for a "personal grudge," denying Breckinridge the victory in Buchanan's own state.[89]

The nomination of a fourth candidate for the presidency in 1860 offered an additional complication to an already complicated situation. The Constitutional Union Convention, disgusted with both the Democrats and the Republicans and fearing for the Union, sought to build on the foundations of the old Whig and American parties. It nominated a man from the border South, John Bell of Tennessee, and a man from the North as his running mate. Bell stood for what Southerners called Unionism, by which they meant a strict adherence to the Constitution. By *that*, they meant constitutional protection for slavery. Their Unionism was of a particular sort, self-interested and cautious. Yet their language was expansive and sentimental, talking of the whole Union, of the legacy of the fathers, of shared sacrifice.

Both the Republicans and the Democrats looked on the Constitutional Unionists with contempt. In the eyes of these partisans, a call to rise above partisanship was simply a retreat from the competition that lay at the heart of American politics. Hard decisions were made, the party men said, through contest and trial. In the language of rough-and-tumble politics, the Constitutional Unionists had nominated "Grandmother John Bell, a tough and toothless old politician."[90] Their strategy depended on a deadlock between the two major parties, throwing the election into the House of Representatives, where the party of compromise would triumph.

The conventions of 1860 neither created new ideas nor proposed new solutions. That was not their purpose. Instead they offered clarity by reducing indecision, by presenting clear-cut choices to voters. The candidates were now to talk as if their plans held out solutions to the conflict over slavery in the territories. This was not the time to introduce second thoughts or complexities, not the time to listen to opponents or those who claimed to mediate. This was the time to emphasize how deep and clear the differences ran.

McClure told Lincoln that "the Bell men are struggling fearfully to go anywhere but with us." The Bell men, the Constitutional Unionists, knew they could not risk association with the Republicans and have any hope of winning the votes of the upper South. Douglas, the more moderate Democrat, seemed most attractive to the Bell supporters, and McClure thought "a fusion between the Bell & Douglas men" was "altogether probable."[91] Meanwhile McClure worked to build a party organization of unprecedented strength throughout all Pennsylvania. "We have 'counted noses' in this State as nearly as it is possible to do, considering that such a thing never was attempted before in this State," the young Franklin man told Lincoln on the eve of the October gubernatorial election. The greatest danger was complacency, for though "the Democrats have been without organization," that party always fought "boldly."[92]

No need to worry: Pennsylvania went thoroughly against the Democrats in the October election, as did two other Northern states holding gubernatorial elections that month, Ohio and Indiana. "I congratulate you not so much upon your certain election to the Presidency," an elated McClure wrote Lincoln, "as upon the confidence with which the country hails your coming. You will have high expectations to meet, for the Nation greets your certain triumph with no ordinary hopes for the future happiness of the Republic."[93]

THE CONSTITUTIONAL UNIONISTS of Augusta thought they had an unassailable argument for the election in November. The Democrats could not vote for Lincoln, it went without saying, but neither could good Democrats vote for Douglas because, according to the party conventions that had nominated Breckinridge, such Southerners "would be traitors to the rights of the South, enemies of State equality and heedless violators of the Constitution." But neither could Augusta men vote for Breckinridge because, as many Democrats argued, "by doing so, they would be voting for a disunion ticket, which was nominated for the purpose of involving the North and the South in a sectional contest, which would lead directly and inevitably to disunion and civil war." Obviously, then, there remained "but one ticket for which they can vote, and by their votes remain true to the Union, the Constitution, the South and the equal rights of all the States, and that is the Constitutional, National, Union ticket—Bell and Everett."[94]

The disruption of 1860 might be just what Southern Unionists needed. With the Democrats committing suicide, perhaps the former Whigs of Virginia would finally have their chance, long overdue, within their own state. "For years and years seventy thousand gentlemen, comprising the pith and flower of the Virginia population, have been virtually disfranchised," the *Spectator* declaimed with undisguised resentment against the Democrats who had rushed to power in the 1850s. "Men of wealth, of learning, of influence, of the first order of ability in all things pertaining to public affairs, they have nevertheless had no more lot or part in the State government than if they had lived in China or Timbuctoo." But 1860 offered the chance of a lifetime. "A glorious hour is at hand for the Whigs of Virginia." Moreover, what was glorious for Virginia would be glorious for the Union. The great talents of Southern Union men, squandered for the last decade, would finally have a chance to save the entire country, steering it between the detested Republicans and the reviled Democrats. "A noble work, a great work, a task worthy, so unselfish, so unconquerable, so patriotic a band, is to be done."[95]

Fortunately for the Unionists, neither Douglas nor Breckinridge had won the hearts of the men who felt bound to support them; Democratic party officials sighed, and newspapers remained subdued. "The wires that once worked so smoothly and effectively are all crossed, tangled, intertwisted," the *Spectator* noted with satisfaction. The Democratic politicians, accustomed to moving people like marionettes, "were out-of-sorts, at logger-heads, undecided, stunned, paralyzed. The rank and file of the party are in like hapless condition. The fissure widens hourly—the breach yawns welcome to the Whigs. On, on gallant gentlemen, the citadel is yours!"[96]

Those who distrusted Douglas because he seemed to value the North over the South and slavery "should vote for Bell, who is as firm and true a friend of the 'peculiar institution' of the South as any man who was ever born upon its soil or breathed its atmosphere." Bell, from the patrician Whig point of view of Augusta, supported slavery for the right reasons:

He believed that slavery possessed "the sacred sanction of the Bible—that it is religiously, morally, socially, and politically right." He also understood that slavery "is the fountain from which springs the vast stream of our national wealth and prosperity—that it is the Midas which converts all it touches to gold." A Southern man did not have to sell out on slavery to support the Union.[97]

While the Constitutional Unionists spoke in quiet words of cooperation and optimism, the Democrats raged at one another. The *Vindicator* supported Stephen Douglas. He seemed to these moderate men of the border a way to have it all: remain a Democrat, defend Southern interests, and celebrate the Union as it was. If all Democrats would vote for Douglas, they argued, the Republicans would not have a chance at winning the presidency. Everything associated with Breckinridge, by contrast, spoke of division and self-defeating bravado. But the Breckinridge men enjoyed all the benefits of the patronage bestowed by President Buchanan. They did not support conciliation and compromise because their wing of the party, the dominant wing, did not support those things. Why throw away a chance at a government job in a state, county, or district that might go Democratic even if the Republicans won the presidency? The Breckinridge men treated Douglas like "fungi to be lopped off from the party organization."[98]

National politics became local politics when Stephen Douglas came to Augusta in early September. All along the Virginia Central Railroad as it crossed the Blue Ridge from the east, "groups of men, women and children were assembled at each Depot to catch a glimpse of the great statesman and patriot." In Staunton, an "immense concourse" of three thousand people, the "largest audience we have ever seen congregated" in the town, greeted Douglas at the train station. The Staunton Artillery escorted Douglas; the unit's captain, John Imboden, took the lead. Leading planter and businessman William G. Harman introduced Douglas, telling him, "To you, sir, all eyes are turned!" The people of the Valley, of Virginia, and of the nation were counting on Douglas to "roll back the swelling tide of sectionalism and fanaticism which threatens to engulf them," to preserve "this magnificent republican edifice reared by our fathers."[99]

Douglas, to repeated cheers, spoke modestly. He claimed that "he was not courting votes for the Presidency. If the people would put down the two sectional parties which are threatening the perpetuity of the Union—rebuke fanaticism both North and South—he did not care who they made President." Unlike the other men in the field, Douglas had seen all of America, North and South, and knew what people had in their hearts. He feared for the Union above all else. At the end of his speech, cheers echoing through Staunton, Senator Douglas went by carriage to the home of Michael G. Harman, where hundreds of people came to visit and where Turner's Cornet Band serenaded the visitor. After a day of rest Douglas headed down the Valley to Harrisonburg to spread his warning and plea once more.[100]

The Breckinridge Democrats fought back the best they could. Though John Breckinridge did not go on a personal speaking tour, he did send William Lowndes Yancey. A longtime fire-eater, a proponent of Southern defiance and independence, from Alabama, Yancey met a tepid reception in Augusta. Whereas Douglas had attracted three thousand listeners, Yancey pulled in only three hundred. The *Vindicator* made no show of graciousness to the guest from its own party. The paper declared that as a "specious reasoner, he has few superiors"; as a debater he was "totally and painfully deficient." The Augusta editor laughed at Yancey's debating style. Rather than respond to the logic of opponents who charged him of disunion, Yancey "indignantly exclaimed—'I scorn it—(stamp)—I trample it under my feet—(stamp)—I grind it beneath my heel'—(stamp). This kind of logic did not answer the demand of a reading, intelligent people, like the audience that listened to him."[101]

The paper resented Yancey's ignorance of the Valley. He could not understand that Augusta could remain unshaken both in its commitment to slavery and in its ties to the Union. "Mr. Yancey, when down in Alabama, remote from the 'slave depopulated' border State of old Virginia (all bosh—we have more slaves now than we had ten years ago) can write his disunion manifestoes." Yancey and the Breckinridge Democrats simply could not wrap their minds around the subtlety of the situation of the border. Like the Republicans, they thought only in opposites, not in the shifting shades of gray that enveloped the large part of the slaveholding South that called for Union. They could not understand that slavery and Union reinforced each other along the border, that a cool calculation of self-interest as well as sentimental attachment to other Americans led people on the border to see Union as their only salvation, as the best way to keep slavery strong in Virginia.[102]

The Unionists mobilized Augusta. The parties formed clubs in every hamlet, fourteen of them by early October, in Sherando, Churchville, Hamilton's School House, Middlebrook, and Mount Solon, with Greenville, Midway, Newport, and Craigsville joining in.[103] They put their tallest men on their highest horses to ride along the Valley Road. They rang bells at every opportunity. They advertised that seats would be provided for ladies at the speeches.[104] They brought in speakers from other states and counties. They enlisted any local man who could screw up the nerve to stand in front of his neighbors and speak. They printed the name of every man who came to their club meetings.

Though the fall rains had begun, and though the wind whistled down the hollows of the mountains, in October a giant rally in support of the Union swept through Augusta. "To see long processions coming into town simultaneously from every direction, . . . with their banners and bells, marching regularly and 'keeping step to the music of the Union,' was a spectacle worth witnessing, and one which animated and rejoiced every patriotic heart." The people of Augusta came to Staunton in "wagons, six-horse, four-horse and two-horse, they came in carriages, they came in buggies and on horse-back—they came by hundreds and fifties, they came till the town was filled with the mighty host." In Staunton hundreds lined the wet wooden sidewalks while watching "the waving of handkerchiefs from the windows of the houses by the fair hands of patriotic, Union-loving ladies." Observers could take away only one lesson from such an outpouring: "The great popular heart of Augusta throbs anxiously for the preservation of the Union, and is willing to spill the last drop of its blood in its defense."[105]

Even as the Unionists worked to get out the vote for Bell and Everett, they tried to soften the blow of what they increasingly feared would come: the election of Lincoln and the Republicans in the North. Be reasonable, they told their fellow Southerners. "Even though Lincoln should be elected, and should be disposed to commit some aggression upon the rights of the South, he could not do it. The Supreme Court is against the theories of his party. The Senate is against them and the Congress will be against them." All the secessionist warnings were nonsense and indeed posed a greater threat than Lincoln himself did. "To break up the Government under these circumstances, simply because Lincoln should be elected, would be adding madness to treason." In fact, "the danger is in the Cotton States, and not in the North. The spirit of prohibition as represented by Lincoln will be impotent for mischief, but the spirit of disunion, as represented by Yancey and other extremists of the South may be potential for indescribable evils."[106]

People worried privately as well as in public. "As to the election our prospects are gloomy enough," Lucas Thompson wrote John McCue on November 1. "Almost every person I see has despaired of defeating the Black Republican Lincoln." Thompson proclaimed himself more optimistic, though, for "I am Still hopeful of the election of Bell & Everitt or some one of the antirepublican tickets, and if the worst comes and Lincoln is elected their will be neither Secession or disunion." Secession, so often threatened, could not happen because "such a consequence would be of a piece with the Madness & folly of committing suicide for fear of dying." Wait for a truly threatening act, "which I verily believe will not be committed by Lincoln." Hold "to our glorious union as long as possible consistently with honor safety & liberty, for in disunion I can foresee woes innumerable, no remedy for our grievances but rather an aggravation of them all." Disunion would be "the greatest calamity that could befall not only the U S but the cause of free government throughout the world. We shall have a grand whig rally here tomorrow."[107]

Indeed, on November 2, four days before the election, the Union men of Augusta traveled through miserable mud and rain to the armory building in Staunton. "Though the weather was so unfavorable that we could not expect persons to leave their homes, yet they came by hundreds from all directions," exulted the *Spectator*. As before, they came in carriages, in wagons, and on horseback, "they came with banners and bells, and made the welkin ring with loud shouts for Bell and Everett. They came to testify their deep devotion to the Union." A long procession, accompanied by Turner's Cornet Band in a wagon drawn by six fine gray horses and bearing banners, "looked like an army of Union-loving men, and would have struck terror to the heart of the bravest disunionist." The banners, many of them bearing the names of their communities, read: "Constitution, Union, and Enforcement of the Laws!," "The Union Bell-Ringers!," and "In

Union There Is Strength!" One banner, bearing a female touch—"a beautiful wreath encircling the word 'UNION,' which was painted in the national colors—red, white and blue"—proclaimed that "The Belles Are for Union to a Man!" The parade marched "through the principal streets of the town, in all of which they were greeted with cheers from the men and the waving of handkerchiefs by the ladies."[108]

Alexander H. H. Stuart, longtime leader of the Whigs, Americans, and Unionists, spoke for an hour and thirty-five minutes. "He delivered an able, clear, and eloquent address, exhibiting a great deal of accurate information upon all the questions discussed. He gave a history of the rise and progress of the slavery agitation between the North and South so clearly and succinctly that no man could fail to understand it." Stuart offered a "withering rebuke of those unworthy sons" of Virginia who would allow it to be "dragged into a common destiny with the disunion States."[109]

Even the Democrats' *Vindicator* had to admit that the Union rally seemed a great success. "Bells and flags (expense being not a consideration) tossed and dingled, evidencing at least energy was not wanting in the contest."[110] The *Spectator*, glowing with pride, had no doubt that "those who traveled many miles through the mud and rain were more than compensated for all their toil and trouble." The moral seemed clear: "If the destiny of this country and the fate of the Union were in the control of Augusta, the watchman on the tower of Liberty might confidently exclaim: 'All is well—All is well—the country is safe!' "[111]

THE WIDE-AWAKES organized across the North for the 1860 election. A hundred young Franklin men joined the local unit and marched at every opportunity. Each Wide-Awake wore a black glazed cap and cape and carried "a neat, convenient torch—a swinging lamp, on a pole about six feet long."[112] The Chambersburg men "erected a nice pole, over an hundred feet high," in front of the *Transcript*'s office. "From the top of the pole floats a small streamer composed of red, white and blue ribbons. About twelve feet from the top there is a pretty blue Streamer with the names of our candidates—LINCOLN, HAMLIN, CURTIN,—thereon, in white letters. Some twelve feet lower down is suspended a handsome national flag."[113]

The Democrats made fun of the Wide-Awakes. "Many of them, if we may judge from appearance, will not be able to vote unless they begin at 19," the *Spirit* pointed out. "The Wide Awakes about here consist principally of capes, a small cap, a broom handle with a lamp tied to one, and a youthful aspirant to citizenship at the other. They spend their evenings in drilling, and learning to carry their torches perpendicular, when their bodies ought to be horizontal."[114]

As the appeal of the Wide-Awakes became clearer, the Democrats stepped up their attacks. The *Spirit* portrayed the Wide-Awakes as a secret society and charged them with disguised abolitionism. The paper imagined the order's initiation ceremony:

> Q. Do you believe in a supreme political being?
>
> A. I do; the almighty negro.
>
> Q. What are the chief objects of the Wide Awake Society?
>
> A. To disturb Democratic meetings, and to furnish conductors for the underground railroad.
>
> Q. What is your opinion of the great questions of the day?
>
> A. I believe that Abraham Lincoln was born; that he built a flatboat, and split three million rails.
>
> Q. If you are admitted a member of this society, do you promise to love the nigger, to cherish him as you would a brother, and cleave unto him through evil as well as good report, and hate the Democrats . . . ?
>
> A. This I solemnly promise to perform, so help me Abraham.
>
> The candidate is then invested with cap and cape, somebody gives him a slap on the side of the head, and tells him to be Wide Awake."[115]

Despite such contemptuous portrayals of their enemies, the Democrats were in trouble. Their meetings, which should have been festive affairs like those of the Republicans, were instead contentious fights over the most fundamental questions: Who is our candidate and what does he stand for? One meeting called for the support of Breckinridge; another, for Douglas. Both sides wasted more vitriol denouncing each other than attacking the Republicans. Without the glue of party unity every kind of self-interest, grudge, and division surfaced while their Republican opponents helped all they could by heckling from the sidelines. At the end of yet another meeting trying to establish peace among the Democrats, the Republican newspaper gleefully reported, "One of the orators of the occasion asked another of them to call for three cheers, and he asked the third speaker to call for them, but, as neither liked to venture upon so hazardous an undertaking, the meeting dispersed as quietly and solemnly as though they had just been attending a funeral."[116]

The Democratic party in Franklin—and throughout Pennsylvania and the North—fell apart in the months between the aborted conventions in June and the election in November 1860. Even the two editors of the *Valley Spirit* openly disagreed with each other. "The truth of the matter is simply this—the bone and sinew of the Democratic party are used by their leaders to vote but do not think and act for themselves; they use them as the nigger-drivers of the South use their Slaves—they must come when they are called and go when they are bidden. It is to this deep depth of degradation and humiliation that the great Democratic Party has at last fallen."[117] The Republicans could barely contain their excitement.

A "large majority" of the Democrats of Pennsylvania preferred the moderate Douglas over the pro-Southern Breckinridge, Alexander McClure observed, but "the entire patronage of the Buchanan administration was thrown into the breach against Douglas, and the factional conflict became extremely bitter and greatly chilled the hopes of Democratic victory."[118] The *Spirit*, torn between the competing loyalties of its two editors throughout the summer, finally did the unimaginable: it publicly changed its allegiance only a month before the election. It renounced Douglas as a maverick from party discipline and adopted Breckinridge as its candidate. Everything turned around party loyalty and solidarity, even if that meant abandoning the candidate the paper itself had championed for months in favor of a candidate for whom local Democrats had little affection or trust.

The *Spirit* fell into line and supported Breckinridge but offered scarcely a word about the candidate or what he stood for. The editors' hearts lay with any strategy that would avoid conflict between North and South. From their perspective, they were swallowing their pride and even their principles for a higher purpose. The Democratic paper told the story this way, blaming their fellow Northerners for the sectional crisis:

"For the last five years the air of the North has been surcharged with envenomed assaults upon the South. Every insulting epithet that malignant ingenuity could invent, has been applied to the Southern people." Everyone knew the insults, for they "are seen in every Republican newspaper and they are heard whenever a Republican orator opens his mouth. They can be uttered but for one object, and that object must be to exasperate the South to the point of withdrawing from the Union."[119]

The attacks on the South and slavery could only end in the breakup of the Union because the Republicans "know very well that they can never set one single bondman free by all their furious declamation against slavery. They know that fierce denunciation will never induce the people of the Southern States to abolish slavery. They know that Congress cannot abolish it. They know that the Constitution of the United States guarantees the Southern people the peaceable possession of their slaves, and they know that the South will never surrender her constitutional rights."[120]

The Republicans were not only disunionists but, unlike their Southern counterparts, dishonest disunionists. "They do not preach disunion openly, but they employ every means at their command to drive out the South and throw upon that section the odium of dissolving the Union. They want the damning work done, but they also want to escape the responsibility of doing it." While "the impartial historian" will agree that the secessionists lighted "the funeral pile of the Union," he will also record that it was the Republicans "that built it and placed the blazing torch in his hand."[121]

The Republicans did in fact call for Northerners to emulate Southern single-mindedness and unity. "We should practice a little more after the example of our Southern brethren," the *Transcript* counseled. "The people should study politics a little closer, and elect men to the Presidency and to seats in Congress who would die rather than wantonly trade off the cherished interests of their constituents." Some rudimentary mathematics showed that the North did not need to knuckle under to the South any longer. "The Free States are entitled to 183 votes in the Electoral College, while the Southern States have but 120. To elect a President by the people, 152 votes are necessary, so that the Free States can elect, and have 31 votes over."[122] The moral seemed obvious.

WITH DISCUSSIONS OF SLAVERY, justice, and American ideals filling its newspapers in the spring and summer of 1860, both the Democrats and the Republicans of Franklin County used black people for their own partisan purposes. Despite the high-flying rhetoric about justice, neither party displayed any sympathy toward their black neighbors.

Such callousness had a long pedigree among the Democrats. They had always exhibited Northern blacks as examples of what would happen if abolitionists, and now the Republicans, had their way. The Democrats went out of their way to make this point as the election loomed. "We believe it is the custom in Maryland, at Easter time, to allow the negroes the largest liberty," the *Valley Spirit* noted, as it described a group of black musicians who came into Chambersburg to play a concert. Although the musicians were almost certainly free people, the newspaper talked as if they were enslaved. Moreover, though they almost certainly came into Pennsylvania to earn money before a new audience and, as the paper admitted, enjoy themselves "among their 'free brethren,' on this side of the line," the paper talked as if they had come to aid the proslavery cause. "This Band had the audacity, on this occasion, to come into a free State as if for no other purpose than to show the sympathizers of John Brown, deceased, that their pikes and Sharpe's Rifles were not required to improve their condition, and that all the Republican philanthropy expended on the slave could be more appropriately used in bettering the condition of the free negro in the North." The *Spirit* felt free to put words in the mouths of these black musicians, who supposedly "returned home to 'bondage,' in the evening train, very well convinced, we have no doubt, that the worst form of Slavery that can possibly exist may be found among the negroes of Pennsylvania."[123]

The black people of Franklin had ideas about slavery and freedom different from those their white neighbors imagined. As the political heat rose in August 1860, black Franklin residents displayed their political allegiances in a quite public way. "It is a custom among the colored folks to celebrate the first of August in commemoration of the emancipation of the Slaves in the British West India Islands," the *Spirit* blandly noted of what was in fact a large public event. The free black people commemorated what they hoped would be the beginning of the end of slavery in the Western Hemisphere. Such a demonstration showed a political awareness among black people that Franklin whites never acknowledged, a global perspective on slavery and freedom that stretched far beyond the knowledge of most whites. The celebration brought together black people from towns across Franklin, staging "a grand pic-nic, military parade, and the other fixens of a jollification in such cases made and provided."[124]

The black celebration of abolition might have gone ignored by the Democratic paper, as it had in the past, if the *Spirit* had not seen an aid to its own political purpose in the gathering. The Democrats sought to associate the Republicans with the "bobolition selbration." They charged that the *Transcript* editors displayed their true loyalties "by hoisting a flag, or rather a rag, tied on a rail, from one of its port-holes, on which is the picture of a Crow with the name of Abe Lincoln underneath. It was a very fit occasion for the Transcript to show its colors and proclaim its abolition principles."[125]

Perhaps the *Transcript* had indeed put out some sort of flag for the black marchers. Across the North, African Americans supported the Republicans when and where they could vote. That did not include Pennsylvania, where the vote had been stripped away in the revised constitution of 1838. Before then, the *Transcript* charged, blacks had voted for the Democrats, though the Democrats now conveniently forgot that recent history. "The sap-heads are too dumb to know that a few years since negroes had the right to vote in Pennsylvania; that they exercised the right, and that they voted the Locofoco ticket. We remember having seen, upon more than one occasion, in this county, certain Locofoco township politicians leading up their 'culled brethren' to the polls and voting them for Jackson, for Van Buren and, generally having them to go 'the whole hog' for the D-e-m-o-c-r-a-c-y." In the eyes of the Republicans, black voters, like immigrant voters, were tools of the Democrats. The Republicans expressed no regret at black disfranchisement, although they would use black votes and influence when and where they could.[126]

In Franklin, as in Pennsylvania and much of the North, German voters were much coveted. The Republicans knew they could not count on the other major immigrant group, the Irish, who had long been an integral part of the Democratic alliance. In fact, the Republicans used anti-

Catholic appeals to cement the loyalty of their Protestant constituency, whispering about whether Stephen Douglas's Catholic wife had converted him to the Church of Rome and what influence she might exert over him.

But the Germans were different. Many German immigrants were Protestant, and many lived in the country. They seemed willing to listen to the Republicans, who devoted great energy to wooing German voters. Franklin Republicans put in the field local speakers who spoke German, and Republican Congressman Edward McPherson requested lists of German men he might write for their support.[127]

In their efforts to reach the Germans, the Republicans benefited enormously from the efforts of Carl Schurz, a famous writer and speaker. A refugee from the failed German Revolution of 1848, Schurz had come to the United States and the political freedom it offered; by the late 1850s he had become known throughout the nation for his eloquence and passion. Schurz wrote and spoke for the Republicans across the North, and in September 1860 he came to Franklin County. "This will be a rare treat," promised the Republican paper. "Only once in a life-time, to many of us, will this grand opportunity be presented. No person will fail to attend who can by any possibility be present." Schurz spoke in the afternoon in English, but that evening he was to "speak in german, his native language, to the citizens of Chambersburg who can understand him. The german portion of our population, who do not fully comprehend the objects of Republicanism, are particularly invited to listen to this great expounder of our political faith, himself a german by birth." The newspaper devoted pages to the texts of Schurz's speeches. Soon after his appearance a German Republican club formed in Franklin.[128]

ON ELECTION DAY, Tuesday, November 6, the *Staunton Spectator* published its last issue before the balloting. "This day, which has been looked to for some months with such deep anxiety by all patriots, has now arrived," the *Spectator* solemnly noted. "This day is pregnant with the fate of our country for weal or for woe."[129]

More than three-quarters of the eligible voters of Augusta County went to the polling places in their neighborhoods. The parties made sure that every man inclined to vote for their candidate did so, whether that meant giving him a ride in a buggy or stopping by his farm. The polling places, usually a store, church, or school, gathered a few election officials behind a book in which they recorded the votes made by the men who came before them. Curious neighbors stood about. Most men proudly voted a straight ticket. They had seen their party's ticket published in the newspaper every day for weeks; they had heard the speeches. Even if they had not been engaged in all the politicking going on around them, voters could have their memory refreshed by the party men who dispensed drinks and slaps on the back.

Men traveled to Augusta's twenty polling places over the course of the day. More than a thousand men, about a fourth of the voters in the county, voted in Staunton. The final tally surprised no one. The Unionist John Bell handily defeated the moderate Democrat Stephen Douglas, while John C. Breckinridge was only an afterthought. Bell received 2,553 votes, Douglas 1,094, and Breckinridge 218. More than 300 men who voted in the presidential election of 1860 had not voted in the gubernatorial election eighteen months earlier. The new voters, perhaps stirred by the momentous issues facing the country or perhaps pushed by energetic party men who would let no voter rest in November 1860, went disproportionately to the Unionists.

The convincing overall victory by Bell concealed many intricacies, and mysteries, within Augusta. Strong Breckinridge precincts hugged the broad middle plain of the county and the eastern border, for example, whereas strong Douglas precincts appeared in the northern flat region of the county above Staunton and high Bell precincts formed a ring along the westernmost boundary of the county, touching the Allegheny Mountains. No obvious reason is apparent for these patterns other than that men tended to vote like some of their neighbors. The precincts with the highest proportion of slaveholders and the richest farms voted in higher numbers for Breckinridge while Bell predominated in poorer districts, and Douglas voters appeared across the county and across the social spectrum. Perhaps the wealthy Breckinridge precincts thought themselves able to withstand the dangers of political unrest while the Bell precincts sought stability above all else. In general, however, few obvious connections appeared between economic standing and voting behavior.

After all the talk and effort, very few Augusta or Virginia voters changed parties in 1860. The strongest Whig districts of 1859 became the strongest

Constitutional Union districts; the strongest Democratic districts remained the strongest Democratic districts. The bitterest struggle was fought among Democrats, between those who went for Breckinridge and those who supported Douglas.

PENNSYLVANIA REPUBLICAN SENATOR SIMON CAMERON, supremely confident in the summer of 1860, had just one sweet anxiety as he wrote Abraham Lincoln of the prospects for the coming election. "I only regret that our opponents are not united," for Cameron wanted the satisfaction of defeating "their great man Douglas with all their forces concentrated." As it was, however, Douglas's "friends and those of Breckinridge are now more bitter against each other then they are against us and I fear that after the elections they will try to ascribe their defeat & our victory solely to their divisions." After all the years of watching the Democrats run the country and the state, Cameron longed for a total victory. The best way to keep their defeated foes from whining afterward was to make Lincoln's "majority a very large one." Cameron wanted to make the victory so overwhelming that it would be clear that he and his man could have defeated even the most unified Democracy.[130]

More than 8 of 10 eligible voters came to the polls distributed across the county. The fears of the *Valley Spirit* came to pass: about 150 Democrats abandoned the party. Furthermore, about 100 men who had not voted Republican in October decided to join in the triumph in November. Some may have fled from the Democrats, some may have come of age, or some may been especially moved by Abraham Lincoln to vote even though they had not voted before. All in all, 56 percent of Franklin men voted for the Republican presidential candidate. The turnout, the numbers, and the winner in Franklin typified the entire North.

Party strategists might have noticed some interesting patterns as they looked over the district-by-district voting returns. The Republicans did best in the southernmost districts of Franklin, where most of the black population lived. Though the black men themselves could not vote, proximity to African Americans seemed for some reason to encourage white men to vote for the party that would halt slavery's expansion. Perhaps black families had settled in areas where they knew whites were tolerant.

Republicans did well too in the towns and richer farming areas of Franklin, perhaps because their residents liked the emphasis of the party on economic development. It also appeared that the Germans, perhaps influenced by the visit of Carl Schurz, lined up behind the new party despite the nativism of some of its founders. Finally, the Wide-Awakes mobilized young men in a way the Democrats had not. In an election decided by hundreds of votes, even a marginal victory in each of these groups gave the Republicans a critical edge.

Although they had beaten a crippled opponent, Franklin Republicans and their stalwart paper, McClure's *Transcript*, gloried in the triumph. "The battle has been fought and the victory won! The spirit of the people rose with the fierceness of the contest!" The Republicans saw the conflict in epic terms: "No struggle, since the formation of our Government, was fraught with such important principles!" The Franklin Republicans saw only good things flowing from their victory. "The future, therefore, looks bright and cheerful. Lincoln's administration will prove the harbinger of better things to come."[131]

Across the North, as in Franklin County, more than eight out of ten men went to the polls on November 6. In every state many of those men voted for the Republicans for the first time. Three-fourths of these new Republicans were, like Lincoln himself, former Whigs. The rest were split about evenly between men who had been Democrats and those who had been Free-Soilers. Lincoln won in part because he made inroads into the border North, in southern Illinois, southern Indiana, and southern Ohio, where he pulled in 30 to 45 percent of the vote—not enough to win in those counties but enough to tip the balance in their states. Lincoln proved especially attractive to men under the age of twenty-five. Those young voters, eligible to cast a ballot for the first time in 1860, found the Republicans tailor-made for them: aggressive against the Slave Power and promising opportunity in a West filled with white men.[132]

Pennsylvania proved key to Lincoln's election. The fusion between Know-Nothings and Whigs, nativists and immigrants, old Free-Soilers and old Democrats, so delicate at the beginning, could hardly have worked better. More men from Pennsylvania switched to the Republicans than in any other state between 1856 and 1860: more than 120,000 of them, 24 percent of the electorate, voted for the party in 1860 though they had not in 1856. Only twelve Pennsylvania counties, thirty-five fewer than in 1856, went to the Democrats. Such abrupt swings had been almost unheard of in the United States during the fiercely bipartisan political wars over the preceding three decades. It was a product of Pennsylvania's unique mixture of Protestant Germans and nativists, of fervent antislavery men in the northern counties and conservative Union men in the southern counties, of squabbling Democrats and shrewd Republicans. The unlikely coalition fused in the heat of anger against the South.

The Republican victory was both impressive and deceptive. The party won half a million more votes than four years earlier; Lincoln carried every Northern state except New Jersey, which he split with Stephen Douglas, and he gathered 180 electoral votes, 27 more than necessary to take the election. Lincoln would have won in the electoral college even if all his opponents had combined their votes. The Republicans, though, knew the fragility of this stirring victory: if one-half of 1 percent of Northern voters in crucial places had voted differently, the election would have been thrown into the House of Representatives, where the Republicans were a minority. Abraham Lincoln, who won less than 40 percent of the popular vote in the country as a whole, would not have become president.[133]

Alexander McClure reflected in his memoirs on the meaning of this election. "A decided political revolution was generally expected in 1860, but none then dreamed that it would mean anything more than merely halting the extension of the slave power, and liberalizing the policy of the government in the support of free industries against the slave labor of the South," he wrote. "Had it been generally believed in 1860 that the election of Lincoln would bring the bloodiest civil war of modern times, and the sudden and complete overthrow of slavery at the point of the bayonet, it is doubtful whether the popular vote of the country would have invited such an appalling entertainment." Voters on both sides profoundly misunderstood and underestimated the other. "The North believed that the South was more bombastic than earnest in the threat of provoking civil war for the protection of slavery, and the South believed that the Northern people were mere money-getters, ready to yield anything rather than accept fratricidal conflict."[134]

Northerners and Southerners fought shadows. Southerners, even those close to the border, heard almost nothing accurate about the Republicans. When the Democratic press or speakers paused in their denunciations of one another long enough to talk about the Republicans at all, they painted them as the Black Republicans, a fantastical mixture of abolitionism, interracial love, and buffoonery. Northerners, for their part, heard of a white South filled with arrogant would-be aristocrats and sullen "poor whites," subject to the dictates of their white masters yet ready to throw off their shackles, given the opportunity, and join the Republicans.

Southerners did not understand the deep appeal the Republicans held for men who cared little about slavery as it stood. Northerners did not understand the democratic politics and broad prosperity of the white South. Both the North and the South were awash in political editorials and speeches, yet the information brought no real understanding of the nation as a whole.

6

TWO DAYS AFTER the election, its columns crammed with election news, the *Staunton Vindicator* carried a brief report from South Carolina, which noted: "There is the greatest enthusiasm for a Southern Confederacy here. Every hat has a cockade, and all minds are resolved to fight." The governor had sent a message to the South Carolina legislature asking it to stay in session to "take action to prepare the State for the crisis" in case Abraham Lincoln won the presidency. The governor thought secession the only honorable response and urged "that every man in the State between the ages of eighteen and forty-five, should be armed by the State with the most effectual weapons of modern warfare." Ten thousand volunteers should "be in readiness at the shortest notice." A similar report told of the "ardent disposition to act instead of talk" throughout Alabama, Mississippi, Georgia, Louisiana, and Florida.[135]

People in Augusta and most of Virginia thought otherwise. Even Staunton's Democratic paper, sympathetic to the states farther south, lamented that "Lincoln is elected President through the madness and the folly of the South herself." Augusta people certainly bore no part of the blame. "If wild infatuation shall rule the action of some of the extreme Southern States, and revolution is precipitated upon us, we can honestly lay our hand upon our heart and say we 'did it not,' " the Democratic paper assured itself and its readers. "We labored arduously, perseveringly and almost incessantly for what we frankly believed the best interests of our glorious old Commonwealth and our common Country, but it has been in vain."[136]

The Unionists, the former Whigs, considered themselves even more pure. "The ticket we supported bore aloft a *national* banner around which conservatives North and South should have rallied with the view of preventing the success of sectionalism North or South," the *Spectator* proclaimed. "Though we are mortified at the success of the Black Republicans in the Presidential election, yet we are rejoiced to know that the elections for Congressmen have resulted in giving us a very safe and decided majority against the Republicans in Congress." The Unionists felt sure that the Republicans' triumph would be "but a barren victory, and its fruits, like the apples of the Dead Sea, will turn to ashes upon their lips."[137]

The greatest danger in November 1860, the Unionists argued, lay not to the North but to the South, not in presidential tyranny but in rash secession. Before the election the secessionists appeared in Augusta as hardly more real than Abraham Lincoln. When William Lowndes Yancey came to Staunton, both papers ridiculed him. But now circumstances had abruptly changed, and the secessionists drove events. Forty-eight prominent Augusta men immediately called for a mass meeting to "consult as to what steps are necessary for the preservation of the Union in the present alarming condition of our Country." Those men lent their names to the cause, "irrespective of party." They included leading Democrats and leading Unionists, wealthy planters and enterprising entrepreneurs. They came together despite their differences to help prepare Augusta for the storms to come.[138]

Similar meetings took place all over the state, most of them roaring with the same message: Virginia must remain in the Union. East of the Blue Ridge, many of the public meetings denounced Lincoln and declared solidarity with the South, but virtually none called for the secession of Virginia. A Richmond newspaper, loud in its assertions of Southern rights, admitted that ninety-nine men out of every hundred opposed immediate secession.[139]

As the days passed, however, several Virginia newspapers began to call for the Old Dominion to secede from the Union. "That impulsive, mercurial sentiment that responds to sectional passion, regardless of consequences, seems to have taken possession of the leading Breckinridge papers of the State," the *Vindicator* warned through clenched teeth. "Hardly had the lightning flashed through the country the intelligence of the revolutionary movements of South Carolina" before the Breckinridge press began calling for a Southern convention.[140]

The spokesmen for secession had somehow gained a foothold in the birthplace of Washington and Jefferson. In a blistering editorial reprinted far beyond Augusta and Virginia, Samuel M. Yost of the *Vindicator* demanded to know "Where Are Our Statesmen?" "In these dark hours of our national existence, when political throes are shaking the fundamental law of the country . . . where is the statesman of Virginia to come forward and open up some way of deliverance? Echo answers, where?" In a biting attack on his own profession, Yost charged that weak-minded and undistinguished editors had "succeeded, by the aid of a few store-box and pot-house politicians, in raising a storm that utterly bewilders them, and which leaves them without compass or rudder to guide the vessel they have launched. The criminal ignorance or imbecility of the men who have brought about this fearful state of affairs can only properly be atoned for upon the gallows."[141] Rather than swinging from a rope, however, the advocates of secession seemed to be gaining influence.

Everyone in the nation waited to see what South Carolina and its neighbors would do. The Unionists of Augusta waited along with everyone else. "I am glad you are proceeding with deliberation," Alex Rives of Charlottesville wrote his friend Alexander H. H. Stuart. "Great unquiet and apprehension, pervades the Public here. A vague fear distresses us, lest our people should be maddened by occurrences at the South and dragged after the seceding states. I am clear for keeping the State out of that vortex."[142]

Men would say in private what they would not say in public. John Imboden wrote to his friend John McCue, a prominent and prosperous attorney from Augusta living in the next county to the east. Both men were in their late thirties, and both were substantial slaveholders. Imboden and McCue had been staunch Whigs but now spoke in distinctly non-Unionist language. "That the entire South will speedily have to leave the Confederacy under the present Constitution I entertain no doubt whatever," Imboden acknowledged, "but I dont think S.C. has put the issue upon a defensible ground—the mere election of a President under the Forms of law &c."[143]

Imboden let himself acknowledge what leading men in Augusta never said in public: slaveholders and nonslaveholders had different interests and different understandings of their interests. "You can't make the great mass of the people—especially the non slaveholders understand the political philosophy of our government, and the nice principles on which the Secessionists are now attempting to act," Imboden confided to his well-educated and well-to-do friend. "And there is great danger of creating a party with sympathies for the incoming administration, here in our midst." The Republicans, Imboden warned, might well establish a foothold in Augusta. Politics had already shifted beneath the feet of the South, and no one could say how it might shift again.[144]

If Virginia were to secede, its slaveholders would have to elevate the issue above slavery, take a higher political ground that united all white men in defense of their larger political rights. "The non slaveholder will fight for his section as long as the slaveholder if you can convince him that his political rights are really threatened, as a citizen. But he is not willing to leave his family & offer his life in a struggle which he believes is a mere contest between politicians in the spoils of office." As for Imboden himself, "I am for preparation now—defense when the equality of my State is actually denied."

Imboden fantasized about a conversation with Abraham Lincoln. "I would say to Lincoln 'You have been elected by the vote of only about one third of the people of the U. States. Your party is revolutionary in its organization, tendencies & aims. No man of your party ought to fill any national office if it can be prevented. We—the conservative 2/3rds of the American people still control the Senate & H. of Reps. of the U. States. We will use our power in those bodies to protect ourselves.' " Imboden thought the motives of Lincoln and the Republicans as clear as could be: "the subjugation of 15 States." Because that intent was obvious, "We therefore declare war upon you & your party as you have declared war upon us. You shall have no tools of yours in office to aid you in your unholy work." The unified opponents of Lincoln in Congress would refuse to approve any Republican appointments.

Knowing that this conversation would never take place, Imboden snapped out of his fantasy and suddenly descended into another kind of imagining. "I fear revolution is upon us. I expect Civil War before the 1st of June," he wrote McCue. "I am ready for it, if it comes but it will be awful in its consequences to the whole country. I shall be ruined by it." ...hought of his two sons and two daughters, all under twelve years old, ...vorried for them. "Instead of leaving my children as I had hoped well provided for they will be left, as I began life, poor, with the wide world before them." Even with this awful recognition, Imboden would not flinch from the implications of current events: "But while I cant help looking at such consequences, I would face them all, lose all, even life before I would submit to be less than the political equal of any man who treads American soil. I am afraid the die is cast and that no power on earth can avert the impending ruin of anarchy & bloodshed."

Imboden's letter embodied much of the thinking of the upper South in the first unreal months after Lincoln's election. From one paragraph to the next, Imboden jumped from one mood to another, from one kind of argument to its opposite. Others, without his education and political experience, proved even more volatile, eager to act even though they did not yet know how they would act.

ABRAHAM LINCOLN AND HIS PARTY held out the most exciting prospects the United States had ever seen, Franklin's *Transcript* rhapsodized. They "will begin with a clean sheet; no foul blots mar the pages of their record." Every American would benefit. The poor man would flourish under the tariff and the jobs it would create. "He who wants a home for himself and little ones, who has no means to procure one, is cheered with the expectation of the speedy passage of a Free Homestead bill." Most important, "all who desire the beautiful prairies of the far West preserved sacred from the polluting foot-prints of a slave" would see their vision fulfilled.[145]

The Republicans believed their party would soon spread into the South. Surely, they thought, the three-quarters of the Southern white population who owned no slaves only awaited the opportunity to strike against the haughty slaveowners who dominated their political, economic, and social lives. Surely, if given a chance, their party would appeal to the great majority of Southern whites who did not own slaves, especially in the border South. Once they saw Lincoln's true intentions, former Whigs, Americans, and Opposition voters would form the core of a Southern Republican party. The galling domination of slaveholders would be thrown off, a diversity of political opinion would again flourish in the South, and a new national party would prosper.

The Republicans painted the South as a vast wasteland. The Southern

THE "IRREPRESSIBLE CONFLICT."

AN AVALANCHE OF

VICTORY!

THE COUNTRY HAS SPOKEN!

There is a North!

FREEDOM NATIONAL!

SLAVERY SECTIONAL!

Franklin's Republican paper exults in the victory of 1860

states had controlled the federal government for sixty years, even though they were "comparatively weak in population, and with her elements of wealth undeveloped—in a great measure, destitute of internal improvements, those great arteries of trade and travel—almost without institutions of learning of any kind—in a state of semi barbarians, so far as regards the advancement of the manufactures and the mechanic arts." How could such a weak and corrupt society dominate the powerful and just North? It seemed simple: The few hundred thousand adult male slaveholders, "devoting their time and attention exclusively to politics, and possessing the principal part of the wealth of the South, are thus armed with an overpowering influence." The nonslaveholders were "kept in the back-ground or overshadowed by these lords-of-the-lash."[146] All the slaves and the nonslaveholders needed was the opportunity to break free of the slaveholders' dominion.

The Democrats of course saw different meanings in Lincoln's election. They saw only tragedy, a foolish excitement over partisan victory that would end in blood. "It is the first time in the history of the country that its national head has been elected by a purely sectional vote. What the result of this sectional triumph will be it is not difficult to conjecture. Fifteen States are without a President—they took no part in his election, and refuse their consent to come under an administration founded upon a sentiment hostile to their social system." The heedless insistence of the Republicans in electing a man adamantly opposed by almost half the states seemed likely to lead to fragmentation of the entire Union, with the Midwest and Atlantic states splintering from New England. "Let disintegration once begin, and no man can tell where it will stop."[147] The self-righteous and self-involved Republicans, caring nothing for Union, threatened the Union's very existence.

People voted for icons and symbols more than policies and issues in 1860. Voters did not calculate self-interest in terms of immediate economic benefit. If they had, neither side would have pushed the other as it did, for North and South relied on each other as key economic partners. Voters did not think about accomplishments of national scale and purpose. If they had, overtly sectional candidates would not have received so many votes. Voters did not worry over the welfare of black Americans, who were ignored when they were not ridiculed. Voters craved conflict and resolution.

The American political system after November 1860 sloughed off its decades-old form of politics, that of coalition, compromise, and efficacy. People had long called one another names and imagined terrible failings in their opponents during campaigns but then put those words aside when it came time to govern. That kind of politics, however, had been discredited by the events of the preceding ten years, given an air of impotence and corruption. Those who compromised with their sectional opponents came to be seen as weak at best. In the place of compromise had arisen a politics devoted to expressing anger and frustration. Neither side could tolerate trespass or negotiation. The politics of grievance devoted its energies to iden-

tifying enemies and drawing lines. It longed for some kind of culmination, some degree of satisfaction. This politics, to which some in both the North and the South had subscribed for decades, came to dominate the American political system in the winter of 1860–1861.

In the politics of grievance, leaders focused on two things. They dwelt, first, on what they portrayed as the fundamental differences in the character of the white people of the North and the South. Secessionists and Republicans increasingly emphasized the deficient morality of their opponents, their hypocrisy and corruption, their weakness and danger. Such enemies could not, must not be mollified or appeased. Second, both sides agreed that, as a result of these differences, all the boundaries between the North and the South had to be drawn more starkly. Since neither side could be trusted, only clearly marked lines between them would do.

Some Unionists of the border, for their own welfare, tried desperately to resist the politics of grievance. These men denied that the North and South lay in intrinsic conflict, blaming instead confusion, hard feelings, and corrupt leaders who had illegitimately grasped power and misled the good people. Such Unionists denied that boundaries between the North and South needed to be reinforced. They argued instead for the sort of mutual accommodation on which the nation had been built, an accommodation that accepted slavery as an inevitability. In their eyes, the politics of grievance was the politics of fools and madmen, people who could not tolerate the ambiguity of the world, the complexity of history, or the tangle of human motivation.

PART TWO

PATHS OF RIGHTEOUSNESS

WINTER 1860 TO SUMMER 1861

He restoreth my soul:
he leadeth me in the paths of righteousness
for his name's sake.

1

ALANSA ROUNDS was in her early twenties when she moved to Virginia from New York. Living and working at Loch Willow Academy in Churchville with her uncle Jedediah Hotchkiss, Alansa fell in love with Augusta County. She thrilled in the large and exciting social circle surrounding the academy. She loved to ramble in the countryside, to visit the elegant country houses of bishops and judges, to get to know the servants at these estates, and to meet young men and women her age.

In the fall of 1860 Alansa traveled to Augusta's Stribling Springs. Planters and their families came from throughout the South to Virginia's many springs every summer. Such visits helped knit the white South together, providing opportunities for social exchange and a vibrant scene of courtship. Alansa participated in a tournament staged in emulation of a fabled Middle Ages, a pageant in which white Southerners imagined themselves the heirs of a chivalric past. "Soul stirring band music echoed and re-echoed through forest and from rocky mountain side," she wrote excitedly. "The knights in gay and varied costume mounted on their restless steeds looked handsome and 'eager for the fray.' " The herald "sat his fine charger like a commanding general, as he announced the names of the riders, while one by one, each dashed forward and essayed to cast his spear through the coveted ring in the arch over his head. How hearty and contagious the cheering when the Herald announced the name of the successful knight who had won the honor of dancing with the 'Queen of Love and Beauty' at the coming Ball!"[1]

Alansa felt young and beautiful. "That night I wore my black and green silk; the fashionable flowing sleeves worn with embroidered lace undersleeves having several strips of pink ribbon run through the meshes lengthwise. At my neck and in my hair were bows of the same becoming color." When the dance started at nine, the procession began: "pretty young girls beautifully gowned, brilliant lights, and gay knights in costume; the Queen in crown and diamonds; the Maids of Honor none the less lovely." The herald, Franklin F. Sterrett, a friend of her uncle's, invited Alansa to stroll with him along the piazza decorated with Chinese lanterns. "I verily believe we were the happiest couple at that Tournament Ball!"

As the fall began to turn to winter in 1860, Alansa and her friends put on charades and tableaux at Loch Willow. The third tableau one evening was, unlikely as it seems, "Uncle Tom's Cabin." Uncle Tom "was personated by the Sterrett's oldest slave, grey headed Uncle Kit Matthews, and Nannie Gooch made the loveliest 'Eva.' " Nannie Gooch was the nine-year-old daughter of H. M. Gooch, who owned seventeen slaves. Alansa greatly enjoyed a cakewalk and a "darkey wedding" she saw in Augusta that winter. "Both were comical, mirthful and hilarious affairs to black and white alike. The refreshments proved 'tip top' and tony and lavishly prepared by these slaves and by them also dispensed to those 'down at the house' as well as all at the 'quarters.' " Alansa Rounds became engaged to Frank Sterrett that winter.

One of the deepest snows in memory fell on Augusta in January 1861. The snow lay lightly on the ground, glinting in the sunlight. "Bright and early the merry sleigh bells made music on our streets, and frolicksome men and boys amused themselves by tossing snow balls," an editor wistfully noted. "A real, genuine wintry snow rejuvenates age and makes us all feel like boys again."[2] The Valley of Virginia received only a few snows each year, and each was an event. The snow briefly immobilized trade and churchgoing, so people relaxed their usual routines.

Alansa shared "with other girls in the exciting, unexpected and ungraceful precipitate plunges into convenient snowdrifts!" She and Frank and their friends still held their steady round of tableaux, dinners, and musical evenings, but everyone knew that these days might not last. In January one state after another in the Cotton South left the Union. "Fun and social recreations were fast being relegated to the background and fiery political speeches took their places," Alansa noted. North and South "were daily growing more and more embittered and determined."[3]

The course of events seemed at once relentlessly logical and completely unreal. The *Vindicator* used the turning of the year as an opportunity to reflect on what had just happened. "It is no difficult task to trace the recent result of the Presidential election to the human agencies that brought it about," the paper admitted. Everyone knew about Douglas and Lincoln, Bell and Breckinridge. "But why it should have entered into the hearts of men to plot the destruction of the most perfect system of government the world has ever seen, is past finite comprehension, and is one of those unfathomable mysteries which the more confound us as we approach their investigation." Neither the Republicans nor the fire-eating Democrats could possibly be acting from "any rational motive" as they threw into jeopardy the Union, "the cause of human freedom, religious and political throughout the world."[4]

To hate the Republicans was not to love the fire-eaters. "We are far from justifying the erratic, senseless, ill-digested, childish, peevish, and miserably foolish action of the State of South Carolina," the *Vindicator* declared. "Of all the farces that have been enacted either in comedy or tragedy, since the Christian era, South Carolina has, in her recent movements, given us the most indisputable. There never has been witnessed such an entire absence of statesmanship, foresight and common sense in the politics of any people, as that she occupies before the world." At the beginning of January 1861 the new nation South Carolina was trying to create existed only in hastily constructed trappings. "Separate from a few palmetto leaves represented on canvas, a pitiful and foresaken asterix, and a large number of brass buttons, ornamented by blue ribbon, there is nothing to indicate her nationality."[5]

Yet the *Vindicator*, professing its devotion to the Union and holding South Carolina in contempt, slipped into an argument with profoundly different implications. The paper declared that the election of Lincoln had changed everything. The *Vindicator* had been a national Democratic paper, a Union paper. Now it would be a Virginia paper, a Southern paper, "whatever may betide, though civil war may rage and the country be drenched in blood, with Virginia and the South our destiny is cast."[6] The paper gave up, gave itself over to war and blood even though war and blood might yet be averted. Like a growing number of people on the border, the *Vindicator* declared a kind of passivity, a kind of fatalism, that itself became a political act full of consequence.

In January 1861 white Virginians thought and acted in non sequiturs.

They declared their love for the Union and threatened to leave it. They declared their faith in peace yet imagined the worst conceivable kind of war. Old beliefs and loyalties were forced into new combinations, twisted and torqued, distorted and deformed to fit unimaginable circumstances.

The Virginia legislature was to meet in extra session on January 7. The *Vindicator* wanted the legislature to call a state convention to decide if Virginia too would leave the Union.[7] The *Spectator*, on the other hand, wanted no convention—the meetings that were taking one Cotton South state after another out of the Union—if Virginia could avoid it.[8] Alexander H. H. Stuart reported the mood in Richmond to his daughter Fanny. "When I first arrived in Richmond I found the most alarming excitement prevailing, which threatened the most disastrous results," he recalled with a shiver. "All direct opposition was fruitless and we had for the time to give way." Unionists, of whom Stuart was a state leader, had taken the pulse of Virginia and decided that a convention might be the best way to keep the state in the Union after all.[9]

Delegates for a state convention to consider the future of Virginia in the Union would be elected in each county on February 4. "As for myself I have no desire to be a member," Stuart wrote his daughter, "and shall not seek the position. If the people desire it, of course I cannot refuse."[10] Voters would also decide if the document the convention produced would come before them for approval. Six of the seven Cotton South states, in a rush to secede, had simply declared the handiwork of their conventions the law of the land; the people had had no say. Virginia voters would decide if they would follow that path by voting for or against "reference," for submitting whatever decision the delegates reached to the voters before it became law. Opponents of reference argued that the delay might be fatal, that the Black Republicans might invade while Virginia vacillated. Supporters of reference argued that only the people could decide such a change in the history of Virginia.

While Virginia tried to find its way, leaders in Washington labored to find a compromise. Senator John J. Crittenden of Kentucky, chair of the "Committee of Thirteen," proposed an elaborate plan. The heart of the deal was a constitutional amendment to protect slavery forever and to legalize slavery in all federal territories south of that line in return for a prohibition of slavery north of the Missouri Compromise line. It was a lopsided compromise, giving the South virtually every protection of slavery it demanded. Alexander Stuart supported the Crittenden Compromise, as did most Virginia Unionists; a committee of the Virginia legislature reported that the state would accept the compromise. In the meantime they wanted to buy time for the compromise to be reached.

Stuart published a report to the people of Augusta about what was happening in the state capital. "Since the first day of the session, Richmond has been the scene of unexampled excitement. The disunionists from all parts of the State have been here full force, and have sought to bring every influence to bear to precipitate Virginia into secession and civil war."[11] The fire-eaters had long prepared for this day. The secessionists sought to pull together the Tidewater, the Piedmont, the Southside, the Southwest, and Richmond into an alliance that could take Virginia into the growing Southern confederacy.

Stuart invoked many arguments against secession, ranging from a discussion of taxes to demonstrations that secession was a Yankee idea, born at the Hartford Convention back during the War of 1812 with the British. But he argued above all that the North and the South needed each other. "In my opinion, there is no natural antagonism between the Northern and Southern States. On the contrary, each is necessary to the other. They are the complements of each other, and together constitute the most perfect social, industrial and political systems, that the world has ever seen." The differences between North and South were, if understood correctly, sources of strength. "The present condition of antagonism and alienation is unnatural. It is not the legitimate result of any conflict of the social and industrial systems of the two sections, but is the work of those 'DESIGNING MEN,' both North and South, against whom Washington so impressively warned us in his farewell address." Stuart picked up a favorite theme of Unionists: the Black Republicans and the fire-eaters caused all the problems. The people of the North and South loved and needed each other.

Stuart was by no means soft in his defense of slavery. Indeed, he sarcastically punctured arguments that would link secession to the protection of slavery. He could not see how slavery would be made safer "by surrendering the guarantees of the Constitution, and substantially bringing down the Canada frontier to the borders of Virginia." Such a step would "lead to emancipation and probably to emancipation in blood. Nor can I see how we would secure our rights in the territories by abandoning them." Yes, the Black Republicans were despicable and to blame for the crisis. But it simply did not make sense to leave the Union until every effort had been made to protect Virginia and its slavery with the Constitution that Virginia's own men had helped create.

Stuart painted horrific images of the war that would follow Virginia's departure from the Union. "Brother would be arrayed against brother, and the whole land would be drenched with blood. The border country would be ravaged and laid waste with fire and sword. Firesides and fields would be desolated by invading armies, and the wail of the widow and the orphan would be heard in all our valleys!" Stuart found much to fear even in matters of property values and tax rates. "Real estate would be depreciated more than 50 per cent; business in all its departments would be paralyzed; credit destroyed; personal property of all kinds impressed for public use; our slaves incited to insurrection; and ruin and desolation would overwhelm the whole country."

Soon after this statement Stuart told his daughter in a letter that he had "received no Staunton paper last night and therefore am quite in the dark as to what our people are doing in Augusta." But reading the papers would have shown him only that Augusta people thought anything and everything—and all of it strongly.[12] The same issue of the *Spectator* that carried Stuart's appeal for Union also carried a passionate article that discounted such appeals. "The North and the South are two different populations," wrote "A." "The Union cannot be saved." Pretty language aside, the issue was slavery. "The time for legislation or geographical compromise has passed. The North must agree, by a permanent compact, to recognize property in slaves, and to protect it wherever our common soil extends within the limits of the Constitution."[13] Such a declaration, ignoring everything that had happened in the politics of the nation for the last forty years, offered the South what it really wanted: complete freedom of conscience and complete freedom of action on slavery.

If "a drop of Southern blood should be shed by a Northern Administration in the effort to force back seceding States into the Union, then be it called secession, or revolution, let her people, as one man determine to make common cause with the oppressed." Demand complete

Northern capitulation, in other words, and wage war if the North sought to impose sovereignty. "In sixty days, according to all human foresight, every Southern man will be compelled by circumstances to take a decided stand for or against the South," this anonymous author felt certain. "The middle ground will then be untenable. We must abandon it then forever. It would be more graceful, more becoming, more manly to abandon it now." Such writers made certain to claim a peaceful purpose. "A solid front presented now will make bloodshed improbable, and our ruin impossible. Discord among the Southern States will inevitably plunge us into a gulf from which millions will never rise again." Such words revealed a longing for resolution at almost any cost, a thirst to have this maddening insult and indecision settled once and for all, with blood if necessary.[14]

Bellicose opinions were even more common in private correspondence. "I think it is time that they should arm the volunteer companies of the State. As in all probability they will be called out in the spring." Casper Branner, a student at Mossy Creek Academy in Augusta, wrote his father while the legislature debated. "Secession is on the increase here, I have heard men say in the last few days that they were strong secessionist, who before Christmas were quiet submissionist." There was a new word, "submissionist." Unionists were not the manly and principled characters they claimed to be but rather cowardly submissionists. "I think the time has come when submission can no longer be withstood, and we should claim our rights, if not in the Union we must out of it. The North will hear to no compromise, and the South will not submit to an unconstitutional party."[15]

Andrew Brooks, at Washington College in the county just south of his native Augusta, wrote his sister with stirring news: "From all I can hear, I think that the secessionists are rapidly gaining ground in Virginia." Young Brooks believed "that we are almost sure to have civil war." Judging from the "extensive military preparations going on in the north," the "threatening and insulting" language of the Republican papers, and the "overbearing and contemptuous actions of Congress in refusing compromises giving the South the barest justice," Brooks could only surmise that "it must be Lincoln's intention to compel the South to remain in the Union, if he can. And if he attempts that, the whole South will and ought to unite and oppose it." Already some young men of his college were proclaiming their readiness. "A week or two ago, a few of the boys secretly made and hoisted upon top of College a Disunion Flag, bearing a single red star and the word Disunion."[16]

J. H. Cochran, a young man of twenty-one from a prominent Augusta family, shouted his fury in bellicose letters to his mother while he was off in school in Richmond. He had read in the papers of a U.S. ship, the *Star of the West*, that was waiting in Brooklyn to "take the troops on board and attempt to foarce a passage to Sumpter. If she does I pray God that the Carolinians may be able to sink her with all on board."[17]

Americans of all sorts kept an eye on Charleston, South Carolina, and its federal port guarded by Fort Sumter. For months the fort had been a subject of angry debate. South Carolina officials demanded that Fort Sumter be turned over to them; President Buchanan and the federal government refused. Major Anderson, in command of the fort, did all he could to avoid conflict. But everyone knew his men were running out of food and that South Carolina would not tolerate this symbol of federal power at the very gates of the leading city of secession. The *Star of the West* did indeed steam down to Fort Sumter in January, and everyone who could read a newspaper knew it was coming, but it turned back after the South Carolinians hit the ship with a cannon shot. No supplies reached the fort. Buchanan decided to leave the resolution of the Charleston crisis to Abraham Lincoln, awaiting his inauguration in March.

Meanwhile every county in Virginia prepared to elect, on February 4, delegates to the state convention. Augusta, a large county, was entitled to three delegates, and the roster of candidates filled quickly. The candidates traveled as a group to twelve polling places scattered across the county. They spoke on every day except Sunday before the vote. The newspapers devoted long columns to the delegates' positions. Men took it upon themselves to write letters of support for one candidate or another. Both papers called for nonpartisan support for the "best" men and then unblushingly featured partisan delegates.[18]

The delegates bore familiar names. John Imboden was well known to the citizens of Augusta, serving not only as county court clerk but also as a captain in the militia. Imboden and his younger brother George, also an attorney, were prominent Whigs and Bell men, but of an unusually fiery sort. For John Imboden, who had dreamed of directing the disdain he felt at the Black Republican president, becoming a delegate to the state convention would be the next best thing.

John B. Baldwin

William G. Harman was even more prominent than Imboden, though he too was thirty-seven. He and his wife already had seven children. Harman owned the largest hotel in town and one of the largest plantations in the county; he was worth more than a quarter million dollars. His forty-four slaves represented one of the largest holdings in Augusta, and he hired out a number of those slaves to his neighbors. Augusta contained forty-six Harmans, and they counted among their number important planters, stock dealers, and attorneys. They were a family to be taken seriously. But they were also Douglas Democrats, and they had just lost Augusta the preceding fall.

Augusta people asked John B. Baldwin to come forward. A descendant of a leading Augusta family, Baldwin had excelled at the University of Virginia while still in his teens and become the law partner (and brother-in-law) of Alexander H. H. Stuart in Staunton. Forty years old and married, he and his wife had no children. Though Baldwin owned ten slaves, he possessed less wealth than his position might have suggested. Baldwin gave much of his energy to public service and the local militia, which he served as captain. He had been elected to the Virginia legislature as soon as he had reached the age of eligibility and had been known as an especially fine speaker throughout his adult life. When the moment of crisis descended on Augusta, people naturally listened to hear what he had to say. Because he was one of the strongest Whigs and Union men in Virginia, his opinions could easily be guessed.

People in Augusta knew too what George Baylor was likely to say.

Baylor, at fifty-five, was older than Imboden, Harman, and Baldwin and wealthier than any of them except Harman. Another attorney, Baylor had personal wealth of fifty-seven thousand dollars (equal to more than a million dollars today), including nine slaves. Augusta contained even more Baylors than Harmans. The Baylor family was a major slaveowning family. Seventy-five men, women, and children in the clan collectively owned eighty-one slaves. George Baylor and his kinsmen were Douglas Democrats. He had served in the Virginia Constitutional Convention of 1851, which had democratized the state's politics, and later as a captain in the militia. A prominent Lutheran, Baylor had given the land on which St. John's Church rested in Staunton.

The final man who agreed to run as a delegate to the convention, albeit belatedly after another candidate had dropped out, was Alexander H. H. Stuart. The *Vindicator* griped that Stuart should give up his seat in the state senate if he became a delegate, but Stuart's great popularity pushed such concerns aside.[19] Everyone knew Stuart, Augusta's most famous man: former cabinet official, former U.S. representative, scion of the most prominent family, possessor of a beautiful house and other property worth a hundred thousand dollars. Married to the former Frances Peyton and the father of seven beloved children, the fifty-three-year-old Stuart seemed to have everything. His law practice flourished, and he had long stood at the head of the strong Opposition party in Augusta. His ten slaves gave him a strong stake in protecting the institution and credibility when he called for preserving the Union, as he did at every opportunity.

The men who traveled throughout Augusta in the cold of late January 1861, putting themselves before the people and debating the future of the county, state, and maybe nation, fitted the profile of what the leading men of Augusta—and Virginia and the South—looked like: lawyers, slaveholders, members of prominent families, wealthy and well connected. Most had gone to the University of Virginia. They had property both in Staunton and in the county. They belonged to the most prominent churches (Stuart to Trinity Episcopal, Harman to First Presbyterian, and Baylor to St. John's Lutheran), and all invoked God in their cause. None of the candidates was a Breckinridge Democrat, but two, Harman and Baylor, were Douglas Democrats. Baldwin, Stuart, and Imboden had been staunch Whigs. All proclaimed their respect for their fellow candidates, their good friends. They all loved Augusta, they all loved Virginia, and they all loved the Union and the Founding Fathers who had created it. They all detested the Black Republicans and viewed South Carolina with disdain. They all desired peace, and they all feared war.

Despite the candidates' similarities, it soon became clear that voters trusted some of these men and not others. The *Vindicator* forswore any kind of party allegiance, but obviously preferred Imboden and Harman over the other four candidates. It made sense that the former Douglas paper would support Harman, a leading Douglas man—indeed, the Little Giant's host during his triumphant visit to Augusta back in the fall, when everything was so different. But why would the *Vindicator* support John Imboden, an Opposition man?[20]

Imboden's announcement to the people of Augusta revealed why. Of all the candidates, Imboden spoke most directly of slavery and race. Virginia, Imboden reminded his readers and listeners, had always lived up to its constitutional duties, sacrificing its own interests to those of the nation from the time of the Revolution on. What had this sacrifice gained for Virginia? "We this day see her and her institutions condemned and despised by an unprincipled Northern majority of wild political and religious fanatics, whose undisguised purpose it is to destroy all her future prosperity and greatness, by first subjugating her and the other slave States to the uncontrolled domination and power of the North, and finally, under the forms of the Constitution to effect the abolition of slavery and re-enact here the dark drama of St. Domingo." There it was, laid out cold: the Black Republicans were assaulting slavery and exalting black men.[21]

The Republican attack on slavery, Imboden raged, was driven by the highest kind of hypocrisy and would descend with immediate consequences. "They consider themselves commissioned by the Almighty to deliver the negro race from bondage and make them the equals of white men, though to accomplish this purpose it may be necessary to put arms in their hands and incite them to insurrection and the indiscriminate murder of our wives and children." John Brown's raid showed what the fruits of Republican leadership would be. Although Imboden thought the deep South states had "hastily" seceded and were wrong to do so,
that, however, it was their right to judge and act for themselves. T

have gone, and we are left now in the power and at the mercy of this party of the North, who are still with us in the Union." There was no choice. "The day for a time-serving, temporizing policy has passed. This sectional controversy must be settled, and now is the time. If it is not settled, or its settlement placed beyond a doubt before the 4th of March, in my humble judgment no settlement will then ever be possible. Lincoln will attempt the subjugation of the seceding States and then a terrific struggle will commence."[22]

Strong stuff, and listened to by large crowds, including "not a few ladies," wherever the delegates went.[23] The courthouse in Staunton was "crowded as closely as herrings in a barrel, and a great many were unable to get inside at all."[24] While the *Vindicator* applauded Imboden and cheered when Harman said almost exactly the same things, it expressed disgust when their opponents refused to face the central issue. They "confined themselves mostly to appeals in behalf of the preservation of the Union, without defining any particular policy, except to wait for future developments. They seemed to lose sight of the fact that the Union was already dissolved." The old Union men did not serve the county well by going on sentimentally. "It will not do to sing paeans to the Union and the stars and stripes when the waves of revolution and disunion are surging all around us."[25]

The Unionists of course thought Imboden and Harman much too eager to give themselves over to secession and blood. The *Spectator* thought the choice clear: "whether we will remain in the Union which has made us a great, free and happy people" or fall into secession and thus "into the bogs of anarchy and the bloody quagmire of civil war!" Everyone knew the election for the state convention on February 4 would be "the most important which has ever occurred in the whole history of our State," and so "every voter should be sure to be at the polls to record his vote for the candidate of his choice."[26] On the day of the election Frank Sterrett, the new husband of Alansa Rounds, made an entry in her diary: "Election day for State Convention, voted for Baldwin, Stuart and Baylor. Hope I gave judicious votes." Like his close friend Jedediah Hotchkiss, Sterrett was a Union man. (The newly married man playfully noted, in a reference to the love between himself and this young woman from New York, that "If Northern and Southern representatives were as friendly as two of their constituents, the prevailing difficulty could soon be settled!")[27]

The three most fervent Union candidates won in a landslide in Augusta. Stuart, Baldwin, and Baylor each took more than 3,000 votes; Imboden and Harman won only a few hundred each. Moreover, Augusta voted 3,394 to 263 to demand a chance to approve or reject whatever course the convention decided. The people wanted deliberation and process, not precipitous action. The election brought more than eight of ten eligible voters to the polls, nearly as many as in the momentous presidential election four months earlier.

The *Vindicator*, thoroughly disgusted with the results of the election, no longer evaded the key issue. "Harman and Imboden, the States Rights candidates, are as good Union men as Baldwin, Stuart and Baylor, but because they advocated the policy of prompt and decisive action on the part of Virginia, as the course best calculated to bring about a satisfactory adjustment of our National troubles, they were regarded as dangerous men to the peace of the country."[28] As John Imboden put it privately, "The idea got into the minds of the County that we were *immediate* secessionists, and it beat us to death."[29] Imboden and Harman, the *Vindicator* admitted, were voted against "by hundreds who believed their election would be equivalent to a declaration of war, and might cause pestilence and famine." The voters seemed to think "that those who could denounce the seceding States as the immediate authors of all our ills, and sing the praises of Northern patriotism the loudest, could preserve the peace of the country and save the Union. Well, we shall soon see who was right and who was wrong."[30]

Most of Virginia agreed with the Unionists of Augusta. Across the state fewer than a third of the delegates elected on February 4 favored immediate acts toward secession. All but a few counties west of the Blue Ridge voted for referring the convention's results back to the people for approval, in a kind of referendum on secession, and about half east of the Blue Ridge did so. The Unionists seized on the election as a complete vindication of their statesmanship, Virginia's sobriety, and the bright future of the Union. Observers in the seven states that had already seceded glumly interpreted the vote as a rebuke to the Cotton South.

The path of Augusta was the path of the border South. North Carolina and Tennessee voted against holding a convention at all. In all three states even nonslaveholders who had voted for the Breckinridge Democrats in 1860 turned against the bellicose secessionists. The nonslaveholding advocates of Union rebuffed the loudest advocates of the rights of slaveholders. The power that aggressive Democratic spokesmen for slaveholders had built throughout the 1850s seemed to collapse throughout the border South.[31]

The election for delegates in the upper South had suddenly reversed the nation's momentum. Everything since John Brown's raid and Lincoln's election had seemed to point toward regional conflict on an ever-growing scale. The secession of seven states, the ongoing crisis of Fort Sumter, and the growing heat of language on both sides seemed to make confrontation inevitable. But now voters in the largest states of the South, the most powerful slave states, had turned out in large numbers to stop the apparently unavoidable clash. The secessionists of the old plantation regions of the east had been handed a defeat they could barely stomach. Virginia prided itself on leading the entire border South into a position of national leadership. When the Unionist delegates met in Richmond, they dreamed of joining the pantheon of American heroes from the days of 1776.

Perhaps the nation had come just close enough to disaster to see the reality of the threat. Perhaps it would pull back from chaos and blood. The Staunton Spectator, *fervently Whig, and the* Chambersburg Valley Spirit, *fervently Democrat, printed the same poem in the early winter of 1861. "God Save Our Noble Union," pleaded an anonymous poet.*

'Twas left us by our fathers,
Those souls of priceless worth—
The noblest types of manhood
That ever walked the earth.
'Twas bought with fearful struggles,
By sacrifice sublime,
And stands a proud memento
For all the coming time—
God save the noble Union!

People on both sides of the Mason-Dixon Line knew what was at stake, knew what they were about to cast away.[32]

Abraham Lincoln, still in Illinois, listened to advice from fellow Republicans. Lincoln was himself a man of the border, born in Kentucky, raised in Indiana, elected by a state filled with Southern-born people. His wife's family were slaveholders. He thought he could reason with Southerners. Indeed, much of what Abraham Lincoln said and did for the next two years turned around his belief that reasonable men of the Southern border, both slaveholders and nonslaveholders, loved the Union and could be persuaded that their interests and loyalties lay within it. The letters he wrote in early 1861 often spoke to those Southerners in tones of hopefulness and patience.

Lincoln would not, he said, make patronage appointments depend on whether a man was a slaveholder or not; he would not disturb slavery in any way; he thought every state should control its own "domestic institutions according to its own judgment exclusively," for such autonomy was "essential to that balance of powers on which the perfection, and endurance of our political fabric depends."[33] *He professed not to worry too much about "fugitive slaves, District of Columbia, slave trade among the slave states," or anything else associated with slavery so long as "that what is done be comely, and not altogether outrageous." He did not care about slavery in New Mexico if slavery would expand no farther.*[34] *Slaveholders had not been hurt in any way by his election, and they would not be hurt by his administration. "What then is the matter with them? Why all this excitement? Why all these complaints?" This crisis, "as it is called," is "all artificial. It has no foundation in facts." Because there was nothing to it, "Let it alone and it will go down of itself."*[35]

Abraham Lincoln, and the Republican party in general, were willing to bargain on nearly everything regarding slavery. Only one thing was nonnegotiable: anything that permitted the expansion of slavery into the territories. That was the core of the Republican platform, the reason the party's men had been elected, the cause that had pulled together their large but fragile coalition. "Entertain no proposition for a compromise in regard to the extension of slavery," Lincoln wrote his allies in Washington. "The tug has to come, and better now than any time hereafter." He could not know that the "tug" would turn into an apocalyptic war, but Lincoln believed that to capitulate after the Republican victory of 1860 would be to give away the best chance the nation had to stop the spread of the slavery that had tortured the United States since its inception. If the Republicans backed down now, Lincoln felt certain, the advocates of "a slave empire" would not rest until they had taken Cuba and dragged the rest of the Union with them into the relentless expansion of slavery.[36]

The first day of February brought Texas, the seventh state, into the Confederacy. Three days later a convention gathered in Montgomery, Alabama, to form the new nation. Six days later that convention had drafted a temporary constitution and elected a provisional president, Jefferson Davis of Mississippi, a West Point graduate, an officer in the war with Mexico, a former United States senator and secretary of war. Over the next several weeks the Confederate lawmakers took their time polishing their founding documents and establishing their government. The Constitution of the Confederate States of American copied much of the United States Constitution, though it explicitly guaranteed the sovereignty of the individual states and named slavery explicitly rather than merely "persons held to service or labor." The new constitution outlawed the Confederacy's participation in the international slave trade and gave the new president, to be elected in a vote in November, a single six-year term.

Northerners and Southerners in Washington meanwhile labored to find some strategy to avoid war. They put together one compromise after another, trying to appease the various and competing strains of Republicans as well as the divided slave South. By the middle of February, with the recent election returns in Virginia and the other border South states holding out hope for reconciliation, the compromisers thought they were close to an agreement that would save the Union. The compromise would protect slavery everywhere it existed but give up what the Crittenden plan had insisted upon: protection of slavery in any territories the United States might ever obtain south of the Missouri Compromise line. If both sides would agree on that, the architects of compromise thought, everything else could be worked out. As their legislators worked, people on both sides of the Mason-Dixon Line waited to see what would happen when Abraham Lincoln arrived in Washington.

2

READING OF THE PREPONDERANCE of Unionists in Virginia's votes for convention delegates in February 1861, Thaddeus Stevens, congressman and Franklin County iron furnace owner, chuckled: "Well, well, well, old Virginia has tucked her tail between her legs and run, and thus ends the secession farce."[37] The Republicans thought they had stared down the Slave Power, breaking its will and revealing it for the sham it was. Without the enthusiastic support of the border states, the Cotton States' 10 percent of the nation's white population could not hope to hold out for long.

All across the North, Republicans watched the unfolding events with grim satisfaction, rising blood, and churning anxiety. It was good to watch the arrogant South twist and turn, caught in its own web of intrigue and bluster. It was good to hear the bitter words between the upper South and lower South. And as Thaddeus Stevens put it, it was good to watch the largest slave state ignominiously retreat from its most outrageous threats. But the satisfaction could run only so deep. The Union had already been divided and it might well divide more deeply. Pennsylvania, in particular, had conflicting loyalties. The state had been crucial to the Republican victory the preceding fall, its remarkably large swing to the Republicans doing much to cement Lincoln's win. Yet its conversion to the Republicans had been recent, and opposition to the party remained strong.

Despite the Republicans' triumph the previous fall, nearly half of Pennsylvania voters had not chosen Lincoln. The cascade of events in the South over the last few months had not made those Democrats lose their sympathy for their fellow white people across their border. Even the Republicans were divided. One voter wrote Senator Simon Cameron with his view of things: "All we want to save the Union, is to let the people of the north have a chance to say to the people of the south that they are ready to so amend the constitution as to give the south all the guarantees they ask. There are numerous men in this county who voted for Lincoln, that will vote for any amendment to the constitution (Crittenden, Douglass) or any thing else almost that has a reasonable face." Should there be war, the Democrats could not be counted on. "Will Mr. Curtin and M'Clure undertake to compel the democrats of this state to go south to fight their brethren. They will have a good time in doing it, I fancy."[38]

The Democrats did not accept the constitutional theories put forward by the Republicans or the strategies they pursued to keep the nation together. When the state legislature came into session, some people counseled that Pennsylvania raise a million dollars to supply the soldiers of the state. "What for?" asked the *Spirit*. "Pennsylvania is not threatened with an attack from any quarter." Moreover, "as a member of the Federal Union she has no right to assail any member of the Confederacy." The mere fact of preparation might bring on the conflict it supposedly sought to avoid. "The moment Pennsylvania commences making military preparations, that moment will the border States take the alarm, and proceed to arm their citizens for defence. Then the revolution will be upon us. Not cornered to the distant cotton States; but right at home, upon our borders."[39]

The Democrats scoffed at the Republicans' portrayal of the South as impoverished and weak. The Republicans "are ever swaggering and boasting of the superiority of the North over the South, and would fain make people believe that the South grows nothing but 'niggers,' that they consume more than they produce and have long ago eaten their masters out of house and lands, and that the South is only kept up by the alms bestowed upon it by the North." Though "there are many sap-heads in the community who really believe all this," many practical men did not.[40] Businessmen staged rallies across Pennsylvania and the border North to remind people how much they depended on the South.

The Democrats of Franklin held a public meeting in February to discuss "the present fearful crisis in our national affairs." The group resolved that "under the Constitution, all the States of the Union are equally sovereign and independent." The Democrats of Franklin stood united behind the Crittenden Compromise, happy to sanction the existence of slavery in perpetuity in exchange for the Union. J. McD. Sharpe, a twenty-nine-year-old attorney from Chambersburg who had already amassed twenty-two thousand dollars of property, delivered a long and potent address in which he calculated the costs of the Republicans' election. The speech occupied nearly an entire page of the *Spirit*. Sharpe could hardly believe what was happening before the eyes of the nation as a result of Lincoln's election. Three months ago " 'Hail Columbia' and 'Yankee Doodle,' thrilled with the deepest emotions of patriotism, the hearts of more than thirty millions of people, in thirty three sovereign states; now, these same national ballads are greeted with hisses, and in seven states of the old confederacy, have been banned and proscribed, and banished from their borders, as being the utterances of treason, against the new empire of 'the Confederate States of America.' "[41]

In those Southern states "the heavy tread of artillery, has usurped the swift step of the tradesmen and mechanic. The pomp and circumstance of glorious war, have banished from out their borders, all the arts of peace." The Northern states had been seized with the same "military frenzy. New companies are being formed and armed. The mechanic rushes from his shop, the merchant from his store and the professional man from his office to fill up the ranks. There is a growing thirst for military fame, and an impatience of restraint or delay." Such a portrait contained no exaggeration. "I have drawn no fancy sketch," Sharpe said, "I have deepened no hue, nor have I added a single sombre color, to the melancholy picture."

Sharpe set aside the usual language of political rivals, the manly language of sneer and bluff and sarcasm. Instead he begged. "I beseech the Republicans, in the name of humanity, in the name of justice, in the name of the fathers of the Republic, in the name of the children that have descended from their loins, in the name of an unborn posterity, in the name of all they hold dear on earth, or hope for in Heaven, to arise from this lethargy, and save the country." The border states, Sharpe argued, reached out for peace. "Virginia, 'the Mother of Statesmen and of Presidents,'—Virginia, containing within her borders the grave of Washington—that Mecca of America," needed only reassurance. With Jackson's Tennessee and Clay's Kentucky holding forth the olive branch as well, dare the North reject them? "If we do, fearful will be our responsibility, for the 'sic semper tyrannis' of Virginia will become the battle-cry of the United South."

Sharpe had no fear that the South would conquer the North. "But could we conquer the South, that is the question?" The American Revolution held out a sobering possibility that the North would not be victorious. "I would remind you, that three millions of raw, badly equipped and poorly armed militia men, in the days of the revolution, trusting in the justice of their cause, during the eight long years, resisted the flower of the British army, and at last, snatched from the lion of England, at the mouth of the cannon, the brightest jewels of the crown." And the South posed a far greater force than the American patriots of the Revolution. "The South is eight millions strong, rich in resources, skilled in the art of war, and fertile in military genius." Even if the North could muster the force necessary to conquer such a vast and well-fortified land, what then? "Commerce destroyed, cities burned to the ground, fields uncultivated, the people debauched, the arts of peace banished, and the fruits of industry relinquished for the more easily acquired spoils of robbery." Moreover, "what would we do with the South, after we had conquered her. Could we hold her in the Union by force? The idea is preposterous." The South simply would never submit. "The men of the South have loved liberty too long and too well, are too much like ourselves, not to prefer to die freemen, rather than to live slaves."

What course of action could Sharpe possibly recommend? The Republicans should prove they really meant what they said about preserving slavery where it was; they should accept the Crittenden Compromise. State treasuries in the North should repay slaveholders whose escaped slaves were not returned. But what of the territories, the crucial issue? The Republican argument is "that all the territory now owned by the Government must and shall be devoted to Northern settlement, and shall become the exclusive domicile and possession of the sons of the North to the total exclusion of Southern men, and their property and domestic institutions." As attractive as that prospect seemed to Northerners, it was not fair. "It will scarcely be denied, that the territories are the common property of the whole country," Sharpe argued, "purchased, as they are, with common treasure and common blood, how does the North acquire an exclusive ownership, an exclusive right to populate them?"

Sharpe thought the plan put forward by border Southerners the only honest means of dealing with the territories. Let them be divided between the North and the South "by a consentable line; let slavery be prohibited in all the territory north of it, and recognized as an existing institution, beyond Congressional or Legislative control, in all the territories south of it." This compromise "recognizes the equality of both sections in the Union, and will, without doing any real harm to the cause of freedom remove that nervous sensibility, which the south very naturally feels about her constitutional rights." Slaveowners would not go into New Mexico; they were free to go there now, and only twenty-four slaves lived in a territory the size of four Pennsylvanias. Self-interest, along with climate and land, would keep slavery out. Law was unnecessary, war even less so. "Dissolve the Union, for a mere abstraction, and the whole civilized world will cry shame on us and our children and our children's children to the latest generation will rise up and curse our memories."

Letters from Chambersburg to Republican Senator Simon Cameron revealed that some Republicans agreed with this sobering prediction and plea. "I can assure you Crittendon's course is the most proper and popular at this time," John Berryhill wrote, "and if you can't compromise, so as to retain Virginia, Maryland Tennessee, Kentucky, and Missouri in the Union, then let the Southern Fire eaters and rabid abolitionists and uncompromising shall I say, black Republicans, go their own way to distruction for that will be their distruction and I fear of the whole country." Pennsylvania should join "the Middle Portion of the Republic" to create "a separate, Independant, and free country." The "Middle Portion of the Republic" clearly embraced both the border North and the border South, a land of moderation and white freedom.[42]

IN THE PERIOD of enforced waiting in the late winter of 1861 between Lincoln's election and his inauguration, tempers began to boil in Augusta. The political language people used became far bloodier and more threatening than it had been just weeks earlier. "Before I'll bend my knee to Lincoln and Seward, and their Virginia cohorts, I will see this land run in rivers of blood," an anonymous writer, who earlier had supported Stephen Douglas and the Unionist cause, told the editor of the *Spectator*.[43]

Feelings ran even hotter in private. George Imboden was, like his older brother John, an attorney in Staunton. Though he was only twenty-three and could claim little money and no slaves, "I can in a few lines tell you where I stand. I am in favor of a united South, first last and all the time. Whether right or wrong, I go with the South. I am anti-disunion and anti coercion, but the union is dissolved and what's the use to shut our eyes to the fact." He acknowledged that slavery lay at the heart of the struggle. Virginia and the states of the Confederacy "have but one and the same destiny, one and the same interest, then what's the use to deny the true state of the case, and fool & cheat the people by singing hozanahs to the union when there is no union! I am called a fire eater disunionist &c &c. but I dont care what they call me. I am going to say what I think and believe and let consequences take care of themselves."[44]

John Cochran, writing from Richmond, was always ready to state his mind in his letters to his mother back home in Augusta. "You ask if things do not look more like peace. I think not—the air is redolant with the fumes of powder and I believe we will have war with the North in less than sixty days." Or at least he hoped. "If Virginia refuses to go out there will be a revolution in this state which will be the special wonder of the world and go down to posterity as the bloodiest picture in the book of time. I have said before and I say now that I will be free and will maintain my rights." Cochran, barely old enough to vote, declared: "I am a man who knows my rights." Secession was one of those rights, and "if the convention refuses to give us that there is another which I will maintain even at the foot of the gallows and that is rebelion. Rebelion has its horrors so has any other war. But like that gallant Henry who rose in rebellion aginst the mightiest empire on earth my words are 'give me liberty or give me death.' " Like George Imboden, John Cochran was ready to defy his elders and his neighbors, to "let consequences take care of themselves," to rise in revolution against would-be leaders.[45]

An even younger man, Casper Branner, wrote to his father from Augusta's Mossy Creek Academy. He dutifully reported on his studies (he had received a 90 in chemistry and a 98 in moral philosophy), but the point of the letter lay elsewhere. He noted with disgust that "Augusta has sent three Union Candidates" to the convention, as had neighboring Rockingham County. Branner was "fearful that the Convention will be made up of Union men, or we can hardly call them union men—submission would be the better name, for to wish to stay in this union as it now is would be downright submission." No use deceiving themselves, "the Black Republican party will hear no compromise, and will concede none of her privilidges whilst the dominant party and what good is that peace conference agoing to do?" Any compromises would be meaningless, Branner thought, for even "if the North made the proper promises, she would not keep them, because she has violated the constitution which she had sworn to obey and the consequence would be we will be hooked on to the north in a few years abolishionized and be trampled in the dust by the tyrannical heel of the North." Secession would not merely be a flight from wrong. It would be a blessing to Virginia. If the state seceded "with the south, it will be the great Commercial and Manufacturing state of the Southern Confederacy."[46]

On Washington's birthday, February 22, 1861, John Imboden led his battery of field guns along with a cornet band through the streets of Staunton. The unit fired a salute, "shaking the earth with the loud reports of their cannon." The editor of the *Spectator* proclaimed himself proud of these "excellent companies, composed as they are of as good material as ever marched to martial tread." But he could not help worrying that soon "they may be made food for powder."[47]

The secessionists had been calling for a separate Southern "nation" for years, and proslavery authors had crafted visions of a slave-based "civilization" ready to take its place alongside the other progressive Christian societies of the world. The border South had always contributed its share of energy to this effort. Virginia was the home of Thomas Dew, author of the first influential proslavery argument; Edmund Ruffin, fire-eater at large; and George Fitzhugh, author of books, such as Cannibals All!, *that carried the proslavery argument to the conclusion that slavery would be good for all working classes, regardless of their race. Some of Virginia's governors, especially Henry Wise, had been outspoken defenders of slavery. Some Richmond newspapers, such as the* Dispatch, *had long beat the drum of a separate Southern nation.*

With Lincoln's election and the secession of the Cotton States, more men began to listen to those who spoke of a distinctive Southern destiny. To judge from their letters, young men seemed especially open to the arguments of the secessionists. Males from their late teens through their twenties had always seen an American political life dominated by the sectional controversy. They could recall the North only when it hovered above them, denouncing and ridiculing them. They had heard of the "abolitionists" and "Black Republicans" at every turn, even if they had never met a representative of either. They had always known a politics built around apologizing for, wrestling with, or studiously avoiding slavery. They were tired of it, ready to take action, ready to take sides.

The Republicans of the North permitted themselves the gloating and boasting typical of the victorious side in American elections, the scoffing at their opponents, the fixation on the division of the spoils. Behind the scenes, however, they earnestly debated what they should do with the power they had so eagerly sought. Northern Democrats did not lessen their partisan attacks on the Republicans merely because some states had seceded. The Democrats did not seem concerned about closing ranks, about making common purpose with their fellow Northerners. Rather, they loudly blamed the Republicans for bringing on the crisis in the first place, for, as they saw it, goading the South into rebellion.

3

MANY PEOPLE FELT certain that the Virginia State Convention held out the best chance, the last chance, for the United States. The high turnout in the election of delegates in February and the great concentration of votes on behalf of the most cautious candidates across much of Virginia sent a clear signal both to secessionists and to the North. So long as the convention was in session, so long as it labored to find some kind of compromise, so long as it stood between the North and the Cotton South, the conflict could be contained. In time the border South and the border North might even be able to pull the seceded states back into the Union. After the close call of Lincoln's election, after this brush with disaster, a chastened United States could proceed to the God-ordained future everyone expected.

The convention would be difficult to keep on track. It had to permit full discussion, giving a chance for all 152 delegates to stand at the center stage of history. It had to entertain every permutation of constantly shifting opinion, and it had to do so with deliberation. The Unionists who dominated the convention thought time was on their side. The longer they could hold out, they believed, the greater the chance of some kind of compromise emerging from Washington, the greater the chance of one side or the other giving in enough to avert the war that Virginia so feared.

The conflict back home did not let up once John Baldwin, George Baylor, and Alexander Stuart of Augusta had taken their places at the convention in Richmond on February 13, only nine days after their election. Within two weeks the *Vindicator*, along with many other aggressive papers and citizens across the state, began complaining. "The sluggish progress of the State Convention," the paper charged, "is bringing down upon the devoted heads of the members of that body curses both loud and deep from a deceived and outraged constituency." Not only were the delegates spending up to two thousand dollars a day of the taxpayers' money, but "it was not expected that the Convention would sit longer than ten days at farthest, before it would either lay down an ultimatum and fix a time for compliance without, or adjourn at once without doing anything."[48]

The Democratic paper believed, correctly, that the convention was dominated by former Whigs and Opposition men. About eighty-five members had supported Bell, thirty-seven Douglas, and thirty Breckinridge. It contained men who had held, among other offices, president of the United States (John Tyler), positions in the cabinet (including Alexander Stuart), and governor. For most of the delegates, their glorious years lay behind them.[49] The convention was doomed from the outset, the *Vindicator* argued, by these "resurrected political hacks, whom the people have time and again consigned to the shades of private life." Unfamiliar with "such distinction and bewildered by the giddy height to which they have been elevated, they are totally at a loss."[50] The *Spectator* of course rose to the defense of the Augusta delegates. When George Baylor, a former Douglas Democrat, spoke before the convention, the former Whig paper applauded him. "It will be seen that he is 'all right,' and that he attacks the fiery dragon of secession in such gallant style as should entitle him to be canonized as 'St. George, the slayer of the fiery dragon.' "[51]

The convention talked interminably but came to no conclusion. All delegates, for different reasons, wanted delay: the Unionists to educate people about the costs of secession; the moderates to give mediation a chance; the secessionists to let the momentum of the Confederacy build. The convention invited representatives from the seceded states to make their case, to flatter Virginia with visions of becoming the New England of the Confederacy, the center of manufacturing and trade for a rich new nation the size of continental Europe. The Cotton South delegates denied any interest in reviving the international slave trade and assured Virginians that the state would benefit from a generous tariff policy to build up its industry.

The emissaries of the new Confederacy repeatedly emphasized the centrality of slavery, their great common bond, to the secessionist cause.

The Republican party, the commissioners warned, had been "founded upon the idea of unrelenting and eternal hostility to the institution of slavery." The Lincolnites wanted nothing less than "the ultimate extinction of slavery, and the degradation of the Southern people." The speeches swayed some members toward the secessionist cause, but most Unionists remained unmoved.[52]

The three Augusta delegates delivered speeches of their own over the course of the convention. Those speeches made clear just what it was that Augusta County's political leaders, elected by overwhelming majorities just weeks earlier, believed in. They all insisted that the day of political partisanship had passed, that it no longer mattered whether a man had been a Democrat or a Whig. Now all men were simply Virginians.

George Baylor went first of Augusta's three delegates, in late February, and spoke the language of unrepentant Unionism. Although he called himself an "obscure individual," he was proud to say that "I do not hail from an obscure place. I am from the town of Staunton, in the county of Augusta; and the county of Augusta is within an inch of the centre of the Commonwealth of Virginia." Baylor had listened to those who argued for Virginia to join the seceded states, but "the old Commonwealth of Virginia is not among the number that have gone out. No, sir; the stars and stripes are yet unfurled over her; and I, for one, say that I intend to hold on to the stars and stripes until the very last hope has fled." Baylor agreed with those who said that Virginia, and the rest of the South, had to protect their constitutional rights, but "did you ever hear of a man getting his rights by running away from them? I had thought that the best way, when you sought to secure your rights, was to look your adversary in the face and tell him what you wanted: to demand your rights and not run away from them."

Baylor had heard what people said about people like him, calling them submissionists. He accepted the name, for "if to contend for the honor of that flag for which Washington fought, and for which many of our soldiers gave up their lives in the revolutionary war, and again in the war of 1812—if that constitutes a Submissionist, I am one." Baylor admitted that submissionists "don't want to fight." It was true that "we don't want to go to war for the fun of the thing. We don't want to fight for military distinction and military honors. God forbid that I, or any of the people

I represent on this floor, should ever want to stain their hands in the blood of a brother for military glory." People talked of the beauty of the Southern Confederacy, "but I tell you that you will never have a better Government than the one which we have had—and which we yet have, I trust. I believe, sir, that the Constitution of the United States and the Government of the United States are the best Constitution and Government which ever God permitted a free people on this earth to enjoy." Virginia should exhaust every constitutional means it possessed before it abandoned that government. Baylor simply did not believe that Virginia had done all it could to protect its rights within the United States.

Patriotism and patience were not the only arguments George Baylor made. He also spoke in concrete terms of sheer self-interest. Virginia did not bow before King Cotton, for "we have more than one King in our own State." Virginia had "King Wheat, King Corn, King Potatoes [laughter], King Tobacco, King Flax and King Hemp." When those monarchs combined their power, Baylor argued, "they far over-ride King Cotton, with all the power that he may possess." Virginia, with its diverse economy, should not shackle itself to the desperation, and arrogance, of states that lived under a sole and imperious economic monarch.

All that said, Baylor made it clear that he would not back away from a fight if the North refused to acknowledge Virginia's rights under the Constitution. "When the honor and the dignity and the interest of the Commonwealth of Virginia require it, I tell you, sir, that I and the people I represent here, will want to be counted in the ring. Yes, sir, we will want to be there. It is not the men, Mr. President, who make the most noise about fighting, that are the first to go into it." In the meantime he had to be persuaded that every other avenue of redress had been exhausted. George Baylor would listen to the other speeches and watch to see how events played out.[53]

The speeches of the Virginia delegates, proceeding day after day, rehearsed and rehashed every issue that had divided the commonwealth for the last twenty years. Everything from taxation and internal improvements to the Constitution and the Bible came into play. Speeches appealed to logic and mystical bonds, to pocketbooks and principles. Speeches outlined the threats to slavery that came from leaving the Union and those that came from staying in the Union. Some speeches insisted upon the fundamental differences between Northern and Southern "civilizations" while others insisted on the fundamental similarity of the people across the border. All of them bought time for something to happen, somewhere.

Most Unionists and moderates put their faith in the bipartisan peace commission in Washington, which was trying to end the sectional conflict by constitutionally guaranteeing the safety of slavery forever and the right to expand slavery in the territories below the Missouri Compromise line. The commission finally came to an agreement, but its members had little faith that their work would be approved by Congress, then adjourning, in time to make any difference. One of the Virginia commissioners, Jonathan Brockenbrough of Lexington, passed through Staunton on his way back home from Washington. His brief interview could not have been more direct or less heartening. "He expressed it as his opinion that there was very little hope of an adjustment of our national difficulties," the *Vindicator* reported. "The Judge seemed to feel exceedingly despondent for the country, and loth to contemplate the sad disasters which loom up in the future for the only truly free government in the world."[54]

Everyone waited to see what Abraham Lincoln would say in his inaugural speech. Lincoln had been quiet since his election, working behind the scenes to build his cabinet, to cement alliances within his diverse and contentious party, and to determine the best way to resolve the crisis engulfing the nation. He had consulted with trusted advisers on his inaugural; he moderated parts of it on the advice of William Seward, who had been laboring with Southern Unionists to avert the spread of secession and the outbreak of war.

Lincoln's speech of March 4 struck the familiar notes of this man of the border. He addressed those Southerners "who really love the Union," trying to talk past the passions of elemental politics. Before destroying the "national fabric, with all its benefits, its memories, and its hopes, would it not be wise to ascertain precisely why we do it? Will you hazard so desperate a step, while there is any possibility that any portion of the ills you fly from, have no real existence?" Whatever the debate over the Constitution, some facts were clear. "Physically speaking, we cannot separate. We cannot remove our respective sections from each other, nor build an impassable wall between them." The different parts of the country "cannot but remain face to face." Would aliens and enemies be better neighbors than friends? Lincoln was willing to amend the Constitution so that slavery would be guaranteed forever, something he thought the document already granted. He thought that calling a national convention to resolve all the issues that bedeviled the nation would be the best way to approach the problem, the best way to set aside emotion.[55]

Lincoln's carefully modulated speech sparked all kinds of responses, largely dictated by what people wanted the speech to say. Staunton's Spectator *reprinted it in full on its first page and knew that "it will be read with great interest by all of our readers." The address was "understood by some to indicate a purpose to enforce the laws at all hazards, and by others that the laws will be enforced only so far as it can be done peacefully. It cannot be known certainly which is the proper construction, till the policy of the administration shall be more clearly indicated by its acts." Lincoln announced that he would "hold, occupy and possess the property and places belonging to the Government," by which people knew he meant, most pressingly, Fort Sumter. But he also announced that "there will be no invasion, no using of force against or among the people anywhere." What did those words mean in practice? No one knew. The maddening wait would continue until something happened.*[56]

THE CONFEDERACY STRENGTHENED itself. Southern-born officers in the United States Army and Navy resigned in great numbers to stand by their states, and the Confederacy persuaded men of stature to assume office. "With the flower of the American Army in command of 50,000 well drilled troops; the most gifted and experienced statesmen of the age in charge of its civil departments; a treasury well supplied with funds; and sustained by the hearts and hands of a united people," the *Staunton Vindicator* enthused, "the new Confederacy bids fair to become one of the most successful and prosperous governments on the globe." The Augusta paper clearly dreamed of becoming a part of an edifice whose "foundations are being carefully and firmly laid; its columns erected to meet all the shocks and throes incident to new enterprises, and its arches formed to bear the weight of an empire baptised in blood, if needs be."[57]

In the meantime the Virginia State Convention did nothing but talk. "Lincoln threatens coercion, yet our Convention hesitates to secede," the *Vindicator* moaned. "The Peace Conference patch-work is repudiated by Congress, yet the Convention hesitates to secede." The Confederacy "opens wide its gates and beseeches Virginia to take her stand under the folds of that banner which bears upon it the blessed motto of Constitutional freedom and State equality, yet the Convention hesitates to secede."[58] One of the Confederate commissioners decided, correctly, that Virginia would "not take sides until she is absolutely forced."[59]

John B. Baldwin addressed the convention on March 21. Like George Baylor before him weeks earlier, Baldwin boasted of Augusta County and claimed that as " a representative county of this Commonwealth" it stood for all Virginia. "Situated at the centre of the State, connected with both East and West by the great lines of travel and improvement, and with the great Valley, midway of which she stands, she is connected with each and all by every tie, social and industrial, that can bind communities together." Augusta was "identified with every interest and every institution that is recognized as of value in Virginia." By this statement Baldwin made it clear he meant slavery.

Baldwin went right to the heart of the matter. When all was said and done, "there is but one single subject of complaint which Virginia has to make against the government under which we live; a complaint made by the whole South, and that is on the subject of African slavery." The problem could hardly be any more general, for Virginians and other Southerners had controlled and shaped the federal government since its beginning. Every speech the delegates had heard in all their time of deliberation, before and after Lincoln's inauguration, returned to slavery. Baldwin could not have been any more direct in his own ideas about slavery: "I have always entertained the opinion that African slavery, as it exists in Virginia, is a right and a good thing—on every ground, moral, social, religious, political and economical—a blessing alike to the master and the slave—a blessing to the nonslaveholder and the slaveholder." He did not see any sign that slavery would become extinct. To the contrary, "if it can be done by fair, legitimate and honest expansion and extension, I have no objection that this mild, beneficent and patriarchal institution may cover the whole earth as the waters cover the great deep." Baldwin foresaw the expansion of slavery within western Virginia and continued development of slavery in the rest of the state. Let the black population grow as it would, he argued, for the South could never have too many slaves.

No secessionist from South Carolina or Mississippi could have given a more wholehearted endorsement of slavery. But Baldwin's unalloyed faith in slavery did not lead to secession. He warned of the "kinship of extremes," of the similarity of the Black Republicans and of the new "Cotton Confederacy" when it came to slavery in Virginia and the rest of the upper South. The Republicans promised to kill slavery by cutting it off, by building "a wall of fire all around the institution of slavery, and letting it die out within that circle." The Cotton Confederacy would do the same thing by different means, for it had declared it to be its policy "that the slaves of the border States shall be pent up within their present limits, and forever prevented from going into the Cotton States." Baldwin spoke for the white people of the border "as a Southern man, as a slave-holder in Virginia." As such, "I never can consent that this great interest, this great institution of the South shall be placed under the ban of government." Slavery could never be treated "as an inferior property to be subjected to any sort of restriction or limitation."

Like so many Unionists, Baldwin based all his thinking, all his strategizing on a sophisticated geopolitics of slavery. He opposed joining the Cotton Confederacy in March 1861 precisely because he recognized the centrality of slavery to Virginia. Virginia slavery had flourished within the Union right up to the present day; slavery's productivity and slave prices had never been higher. Slavery had grown and developed and adapted in a continually changing United States. Abandoning the Union, a great good in its own right, made no sense. The Cotton Confederacy offered a threat to Virginia's slavery by isolating it, hedging in the potential for growth that all property needed to maintain its value. Virginia should stay in the United States unless the Republicans turned the government against what it was made to protect: the property, equality, and freedom of all the white people who lived under it. In the meantime John Baldwin, along with George Baylor and Alexander H. H. Stuart, would remain a staunch defender of both slavery and the Union.[60]

Back home, however, some men began to change their minds. Augusta men who had talked so fervently of Union in the presidential election four months earlier now spoke publicly of seceding regardless of what the state convention might eventually decree. "Honor, freedom, justice, good faith, all are to be crushed under the Juggernaut of abolition villainy," the Democratic paper shouted. "We put it to the farmer, the mechanic, the professional man, to men of every grade of wealth and every occupation, if this deed shall be perpetrated by the Convention with impunity?" The *Vindicator* claimed to answer for Augusta: "They are not now, and never will be, willing to pass from a state of freedom to a condition of vassalage—to bend their necks to the yoke of abolition servitude. The Convention cannot consign us to Northern despotism." It did not matter what the old men, the decrepit Whigs, of the convention might do. "The Convention may delay—the Convention may jeopardize our safety—the Convention may put to useless sacrifice many valuable lives, but the people of Virginia, in the strength of that integrity and power and patriotism, high above all Conventions, will force their representatives to strike the blow in behalf of that civil, religious and political liberty which constitutes the chief glory and pride of our beloved Commonwealth."[61]

By late March Virginians had become exhausted from endless constitutional debates, economic theorizing, and lessons from ancient history, exhausted with apparently clear-cut choices that suddenly branched into yet other clear-cut choices. People tried to give new names to their opponents and themselves, defining their predilections so that they appeared in the best possible light.

The secessionists of the Confederacy, of Virginia, and of Augusta expertly narrowed the range of choices. "The question is *not* 'Union,'" the *Vindicator* argued. "That is irretrievably, hopelessly broken up. No compromise of right—no palliation of wrong, or denunciation of its resistance, can restore its fallen columns." Only one question mattered: "Where shall we go? With the North or the South?"[62]

Once the secessionists had drawn the boundaries in that way, slavery, the fundamental issue sometimes buried in the layer upon layer of constitutional debate, immediately reasserted itself. With boundaries being redrawn, people no longer debated a matter of hypothetical slaves in hypothetical territories, but real slaves in Augusta County and Virginia. If the state goes with the North, "what are we to do with our Negroes?" the *Vindicator* asked rhetorically. "Converted into pests and vampyres as they soon must be in such connexion, they will suck out the very lifeblood of the Commonwealth. And there will be no help for us. The North would gloat over our distresses, while the South, in self-defense, would be compelled to close her doors against us. The 'irrepressible conflict' will then be upon us with all its horrors." The next step in the logic was clear: "Who will not say, give us war, give us anything, extermination itself, rather than such a consuming life of degradation and ruin?" The paper did not speak with the bold confidence of John Baldwin of the future of slavery in a Virginia isolated from most of the other slave states.[63]

Though the institution of slavery remained sturdy, it depended on a complex and extensive political and economic web. Those who read the papers of Augusta carefully might notice signs of what would happen if slavery became suspect as a long-term investment. Joseph Mitchell was selling a prime property, a 418-acre farm, lying 3 miles west of Staunton, bisected by the Virginia Central Railroad. He was also selling "Nine Young and Likely Negroes: "a Woman 33 years of age, who is a good Cook, Ironer and Washer, with a pleasant disposition; a Man 21 years of age, who is a No. one hand; the remainder are from 3 to 14 years old, all stout and well grown. The Negroes are healthy, robust and likely." Such slaves certainly did not sound like "vampyres," but what if their value plummeted overnight? What if they had to be fed and housed but were worth less each year? Would slavery prosper? Would it long endure?[64]

Driven by such calculations and such fears, white men would soon fight white men if Virginia stayed in the Union, John Imboden warned his friend John McCue. In a letter filled with bitter charges of slander, lying, and cowardice against Alexander H. H. Stuart, Imboden predicted that "we are going to have fearful times here in Virginia. I am afraid we shall have a war amongst ourselves." For his own part, this well-to-do lawyer and county court clerk had "made up my mind that if Va submits to the dishonor of standing by and seeing war made in the Seceded states, I will leave Va." Despite Imboden's best efforts and despite the escalating rhetoric of race war, the people of Augusta seemed determined to stay in the Union. "I am persuaded that a majority of our people here are ready for that. I am not and never will be. We must have immediately the constitutional guarantees of the Crittenden plan at least or go with the South. If these are refused, and Va submit, I never will. I shall go to Florida or Louisiana, take my family & cast my lot there for life."[65]

John Cochran watched the convention with disgust, fearing some deal with the North. If Virginia accepted any such plan, "woe to Virginia this proud old mother of states. For close upon the heals of such a cowardly submission" would follow "a general exodous of the owners of slaves with their slaves, and with the money for their lands in their pockets. Then will come dishonor disgrace and repudiation. Then will this fair land be polluted with the presence of hoards of yankees and other such like vermin." Cochran saw Augusta's Alexander Stuart as one of the worst traitors to Virginia, who would join his compatriots after the ruin of the Old Dominion to "lift their heads and glory in the consciousness of having acquired high offices among their colaborers the abolitionists by selling and disgracing their native state." Cochran perceived only one way "to avert such dire calamities to the old commonwealth and that is by revolution. Some will say that the remedy is worse than the disease—but sooner would I see this fair land drenched in the blood of contending brothers than to see such a fate as the submissionist are preparing for her accomplished." Cochran was "trusting in 'God and keeping my powder dry.' I intend to make the best fight I can. And I think there are enough of my way of thinking to inaugurate a revolution which will be triumphant." Cochran, like Imboden, saw revolution and civil war within Virginia. While Imboden would move to the Confederacy, Cochran vowed to stay and fight.[66]

Virginia had to act with the Confederacy or be abandoned by the Confederacy. Some white leaders were certain that if they did not go along with the other slave states, slavery in Virginia would die from either race war or the exodus of slaveowners.

The Confederate states urged Virginia on. A "patriotic letter" from a South Carolina woman asked her cousin in Virginia "O, could we, my Cousin, for one moment crouch to Yankee tyranny? No, never! never! I for one, woman as I am, would willingly spend my last breath, if need be, in behalf of the Southern Confederacy." She was willing to "bid farewell" to her three sons and "cheer them on to the field of battle." Though "I know my heart would fill to overflowing—still I should commit them to Him alone who rules our destinies, and trust to the final result." But why was Virginia slow to join the struggle for Southern freedom? "What is my own native Virginia about? Why has she acted so tardily and shown such a lack of independence?" Nearly all of this woman's family lived in Virginia, and she wondered if there could even "be one of them who intends to submit to Black Republican rule? I cannot, will not believe it, until I hear it direct from some one of you, for in my veins still runs that blood which has always been opposed to imposition and insult." The Yankees had been dealing out both imposition and insult for thirty-five years now, she believed, and she could barely understand how "Virginia should be so slow to act when she has been most injured and insulted."[67]

As the weeks passed and the range of debate steadily narrowed, the matter increasingly boiled down to whether Lincoln would use "coercion" to resupply Fort Sumter. The president received conflicting advice from everyone, from his most trusted advisers to the newspapers of the North. The *Vindicator* eagerly reprinted parts of an article in the *New York Times* encouraging Lincoln to give up the fort for reasons both military and diplomatic. According to the Staunton paper, the *Times* judged Lincoln too inactive, too indecisive, especially in comparison with the new Confederacy of the Cotton States.[68]

Little did the Augusta paper know that John B. Baldwin had just talked with Lincoln about these issues at the heart of the national struggle. William Seward, Lincoln's former rival for the Republican nomination and now his secretary of state, was hoping to dissuade Lincoln from sending a ship to Fort Sumter, which he was sure would trigger armed conflict. Seward thought that if the President could talk to a Virginia Unionist face-to-face, the crisis might be averted. Unionists remained in control of the Virginia Convention, after all, and had struggled tenaciously for months to keep Virginia from seceding. Seward sent an emissary to Richmond to get George Summers, a trusted Unionist from Charlestown in the western part of the state. An important vote was coming up in the convention, however, and Summers, the floor leader of the Unionists, thought he would better serve the cause by staying in Richmond. He suggested that leading Unionists choose another of their number to go. They selected Augusta's John Baldwin, defender of slavery within the Union. He left with Seward's emissary that evening, April 3, and arrived in Washington at breakfast the next day.[69]

Taken to the president's house, Baldwin waited. Lincoln met the emissary cordially and looked for a quiet room in which the two of them could talk privately. Baldwin recalled the meeting in detail. "Why do you not all adjourn the Virginia Convention?" the president asked. Lincoln saw the convention as a threat to the Union, the sort of body that had rushed seven other states out of the Union. With the convention in session for weeks now, Virginia had its finger on a hair trigger. The slightest jolt could cause it to fire, and secessionists from the Confederacy were shaking the convention as hard as they could. Baldwin protested that the convention was in fact dominated by men such as himself, men who shared Lincoln's goal of keeping Virginia in the Union, and that it thus stood as a bulwark against secession. If the convention adjourned, "leaving these questions unsettled in the midst of all the trouble that is on us, it would place the Union men of Virginia in the attitude of confessing an inability to meet the occasion." Virginia would simply call another convention, one dominated by secessionists. All the convention wanted, Baldwin assured Lincoln, was a constitutional guarantee of the South's "peculiar rights" associated with the protection of slavery. If the convention had that guarantee, "it will give us a stand-point from which we can bring back the seceded States."

Baldwin, a forthright man, boldly told President Lincoln that "if I had the control of your thumb and forefinger five minutes I could settle the whole question." Lincoln asked him to elaborate. "I would issue a proclamation to the American people, somewhat after this style: I would state the fact that you had become President of the United States as the result of a partisan struggle partaking of more bitterness than had usually marked such struggles; that, in the process of that struggle, there had naturally arisen a great deal of misunderstanding and misrepresentation of the motives and intentions of both sides." Baldwin struck the note that Unionists on both sides had struck all along: the crisis was the result of misunderstanding, false information, and underestimation. Lincoln merely needed to set the record straight, and peace would follow.

After clearly expressing his benevolent intentions, Baldwin continued, President Lincoln should "appeal to the American people to settle the question in the spirit in which the Constitution was made—American fashion—by consultation and votes instead of appeal to arms. And I would call a national convention of the people of the United States and urge upon them to come together and settle this thing." In the meantime, as a gesture of goodwill, Lincoln should withdraw federal forces from Fort Sumter and Fort Pickens in Florida, declaring that he was "determined, if the seceded States chose to make a collision, that they should come clear out of their way and do it." If Lincoln would follow that path, Baldwin believed, "there is national feeling enough in the seceded States themselves and all over the country to rally to your support, and you would gather more friends than any man in the country has ever had."

Gathering friends was not "what I am thinking about," Lincoln responded "rather impatiently," Baldwin reported. "If I could be satisfied that I am right, and that I do what is right, I do not care whether people stand by me or not." Baldwin apologized for having talked to Lincoln as if he were a "politician" rather than a "gentleman." Lincoln "laughed a little at that." Baldwin and the president talked about the military and financial considerations of giving up Fort Sumter but ran into the nub of the matter. Lincoln did not think he could withdraw without violating his oath of office and alienating his own party. Baldwin replied: "Sir, if there is a gun fired at Sumter, as sure as there is a God in heaven the thing is gone. Virginia herself, strong as the Union majority in the Convention is now, will be out in forty-eight hours." Lincoln said that such an event was "impossible." Baldwin pleaded: "Mr. President, I did not come here to argue with you; I am here as a witness. I know the sentiments of the people of Virginia, and you do not." Baldwin told Lincoln that he had two weeks in which to save the country; the Unionists could not hold out much longer. With that, Baldwin left. He had nothing in writing and no assurances from President Lincoln.

Lincoln left no record of his meeting with Baldwin. Another leading Virginia Unionist, John M. Botts, later challenged Baldwin's version. Botts argued that Baldwin had helped bring on Virginia's secession by refusing Lincoln's offer to evacuate Fort Sumter if the Virginia Convention would adjourn. Lincoln supposedly told Botts that Baldwin "would not listen to it for a moment; he hardly treated me with civility." Baldwin insisted that Lincoln made no such offer, saying instead as soon as Baldwin arrived that he had come "too late." In any case, the result was the same: both Lincoln and Baldwin left the meeting convinced that fighting of some sort could not be averted. That was April 4. Later that day Lincoln made the final arrangements for the mission to Fort Sumter.[70]

Later that day too Baldwin gave a speech, previously scheduled, in

Alexandria, just outside Washington. A Unionist paper from that town deemed it "one of the most powerful and convincing speeches ever delivered in Alexandria—a speech full of sound reasoning, moving pathos and true eloquence." The *Spectator* eagerly reprinted word of this Augusta man's success, for Baldwin attracted "one of the largest, if not *the* largest, audience" ever assembled in Alexandria's Liberty Hall. Baldwin "did not believe for a moment that the *people* wanted to overturn and break up" the Union. He called for "a Convention of the Border States" to put forward "a Constitution and invite all the States, North and South, willing to adopt it, to come in and thus reconstruct the Union." The speech, the local reporter judged, was "thoroughly Union, and evidently struck a responsive chord in the breast of the people of Alexandria."[71]

Baldwin returned to Richmond and privately told his Unionist friends of his discouraging meeting with Lincoln. Unwilling either to adjourn the convention or to precipitate secession, and unaware of the ships sailing toward Fort Sumter, the Virginia Convention voted on April 8 to send a delegation of three men to visit Lincoln and ask of his plans. Alexander H. H. Stuart was one of the men selected. They set out on April 9, but a terrible storm washed out much of the railroad from Richmond, and they did not arrive in Washington until April 12. They came to the president at one o'clock, and he said he would be delighted to see them the next morning at nine. When they arrived, Lincoln had already read of their mission in the newspapers and simply referred them to his inaugural address, in which he announced his duty, and his intention, to "hold, occupy, and possess" all property of the United States and to collect all duties. The delegation received the response glumly and returned home.

The growing number of secessionists in Virginia discounted such efforts even before their results were known. The commissioners "will no doubt call upon 'King Abram,' " the *Vindicator* predicted, "who will amuse them prodigiously with 'flat boat yarns,' and again assure them that 'nothing hurts anybody'—'nobody is going wrong.' " The paper believed that "nothing but war will satisfy the intense hatred that is borne at the North to the institutions of the South—nothing can satisfy their hatred but the shedding of 'their brother's blood.' It is too late now to talk of 'Compromise,' 'Conference,' or 'Commission.' The golden hour, when all this train of horrors could have been avoided has been lost, by the miserable submission policy that rules in the Convention at Richmond." If only Virginia had stood up to Lincoln at the beginning, the *Vindicator* maintained, "there never would have sailed the first man from New York against the South."[72] The Unionists of Virginia shared the blame for the war with the Republicans.

Slavery in Virginia seemed threatened no matter what course the state followed. The *Vindicator* admitted that it was possible that "a dissolution of the Union on the slave line" would destroy the institution in Virginia. "We do not think so. But admit it did. In that case, the slaves would be gradually removed South, and the change would not so seriously affect the private fortunes of individuals, or the general prosperity of the State." But what would happen if Virginia should stay in the Union, or, as the newly secessionist *Vindicator* called it, the "Northern Confederacy"? Abolitionism would not relent until slavery had been destroyed. Then, "with six hundred thousand Negroes amongst us, denied all outlet, and rendered worthless and uncontrollable, a nuisance and a pest, not only their whole value as property would be annihilated, but Virginia herself, ere long, would cease to be a house for the decent, industrious white man." Worse, "a degraded race of negroes and mixed bloods would huddle into the deserted homes of her people, and a desolation and ruin spread out around them, like that which, under British emancipation, has blasted the most fruitless isles of the Indies." The secessionist who defined the issue in this way deprived opponents of defensible ground. "What son of Virginia can hesitate as to his duty, when such a choice is presented to him? Nay, is it not an insult to our manhood to speak of it as a choice? War is an evil, but not the worst. Life itself has limits to its value. And he must be a dastard indeed who will not defend his friends and his home."[73]

The more slavery was endangered, the more fervently the Virginia secessionists embraced the institution. In the easy and prosperous days of the 1850s the white people of Augusta had rarely bothered to offer a defense of the institution. When the crisis descended, though, the secessionists of the county rushed to celebrate slavery, devoting long columns to proslavery diatribes from the hotly secessionist *Richmond Dispatch*. "Nothing could be more preposterous, nothing more stupid, than the dogma that slavery is a curse to the country," one article sputtered. "On the contrary, the heaviest calamity that could befall any slave State on this continent, the greatest curse that an angry Providence could inflict upon the South, would be the destruction of its slave institution."[74]

The *Vindicator* printed these words on April 12. By April 14 the Confederates in Charleston had fired on Fort Sumter and the hungry and weary men inside had surrendered. On that day John Cochran sent his mother the latest news, available in Richmond before it reached Augusta. "News of the surrender of Fort Sumpter was received here yesterday after a bombardment of nearly thirty hours (not counting the time that both parties ceased firing during the night.)" Young Cochran, unlike the Unionists of the convention, felt no dismay at the news. Indeed, he and his many secessionist compatriots used the opportunity to taunt those men of caution. "We fired a salute of one hundred guns in honor of the victory on the square under the very noses of the Traitors to the state who hold their daily 'pow wow' in the capitol," he bragged. The crowd in the street "hoisted the flag of the Confederated States upon the capitol where it remained until removed in the darkness of night." Bonfires set by the crowd "blased in main streat until 12 Oclock at night and the city looked like an immense hive."[75]

The following day, the fifteenth, Lincoln issued a call for seventy-five thousand volunteers to put down the rebellion in South Carolina. On the sixteenth, the *Spectator*, one of the staunchest Union papers in Virginia and the South, announced the news from Charleston with bitterness and disbelief: "War has actually commenced. After all his declarations in favor of peace, President Lincoln has taken a course calculated inevitably to provoke a collision, and to unite the whole South in armed resistance. It seems that he attempted to throw supplies into Fort Sumter and thus the war began." George Baylor, one of Augusta's delegates in Richmond, sent a dispatch to his fellow citizens telling them that Lincoln had called out thousands of militia. The paper had to insert the news at the last minute but could not refrain from a brief but potent editorial about Lincoln's call for troops: "Where from? For what? The Colonel wishes to know what the people here think. There is but one sentiment—every man is ready to take up arms."[76]

Some men did not wait. John Imboden, always in the forefront of activity and frustrated by being relegated to the margins in the vote for convention delegates, late in the day on April 15 received a telegram summoning him to Richmond. He caught a train in Staunton and headed east. He arrived early in the morning. Before he had even reached his hotel, Imboden ran into former Governor Henry Wise, who looked exhausted and who spoke of "his impatience at the delay of the Convention and of the dark prospect of events."[77]

Wise asked Imboden if he recalled "what passed between you and me when I was governor, at the moment you thanked me for the order permitting you to have two brass field pieces for your company of artillery in Staunton?" Imboden did recall; he had promised to obey any request Wise made of him whether Wise was governor or not. Wise said he had been joking before, but not now. "I want those guns with which to aid in the immediate capture of the United States arsenal at Harper's Ferry; can they be had with all the men you can raise?" Imboden declared that he was ready to move.[78]

When Governor John Letcher refused to authorize the assault, Wise, Imboden, and others of a small group, including the superintendent of the arsenal at Harpers Ferry, resolved to act on their own responsibility. Even while they planned, Wise received a telegram telling him that federal troops were on their way to the arsenal. Imboden wired to Staunton to tell his men to be ready. He loaded a railroad car with ammunition from the Virginia Armory and headed west over the Blue Ridge to Augusta. When he arrived early on April 17, he found the Staunton Artillery and West Augusta Guard, a hundred men, ready at the platform along with a large crowd of supporters. Imboden also found a telegram waiting for him from Governor Letcher, telling him that Virginia had seceded and ordering the Staunton Artillery to Harpers Ferry. Several of the officers gave speeches, and several ministers gave prayers. The *Spectator* proclaimed it the most exciting scene in Staunton's history. "There was a general feeling that the crisis was a solemn one, united with a firm and universal determination to resist the scheme set on foot by President Lincoln to subjugate the South." The train pulled out, heading north.

Meanwhile Alexander H. H. Stuart of Augusta labored in Richmond to head off any conflict. He gave a speech that told of his interview with President Lincoln three days earlier. In that speech Stuart revealed that Lincoln had talked with the delegates more fully than they had originally suggested. Stuart had offered the president elaborate advice on ways to avoid a conflict over the forts, calculating lost revenues and laying out technicalities. Lincoln, though he disagreed with Stuart's argument, had replied with characteristic charm. The president hardly seemed bellicose or rash. The delegates had left the meeting without hope for an immediate solution but continued to believe that their dreams of maintaining the Union in some way might yet come to pass. When Lincoln's proclamation calling for troops arrived, Stuart telegraphed Secretary of State William Seward in disbelief, asking if the call could possibly be authentic. Seward replied that it had indeed come from Lincoln's hand.[79]

Stuart, like many constituents back in Augusta, gave up hope of keeping Virginia in the Union after he read that proclamation. He spoke in anguish to his fellow delegates: "If there be any man upon this floor who has cherished a more ardent, a more decided, a more, I must say, religious and sincere love for this Union than any other, I claim to be that man." Stuart revealed how deeply the feelings ran. Seventy-nine years before, "the people of Augusta deputed my father to this city as a member of the Convention to ratify and adopt the Constitution which formed this Union." To renounce the Union was to renounce that personal legacy. Yet Stuart thought that he, and Virginia, must make that renunciation.[80]

Three options lay before the convention on April 16, he argued. The first was to remain in the Union and "lend our forces and our arms to the subjugation of our Southern sisters." Stuart believed "there is no man upon this floor who is prepared to stand here in that attitude." The second alternative was to secede immediately. Immediate secession, he warned, would make Virginia the battleground, "the Flanders" of the war to come. That would be a great help to the Republicans, giving them a much cheaper and healthier place to fight than in South Carolina or Florida. By seceding on its own, the convention would transfer the war to Virginia, "to a country that furnishes every supply that is necessary for the support of troops; to a climate that is entirely salubrious to the Northern troops." Immediate secession would leave Virginia surrounded on every side by states still in the Union—and with an ocean to bring navies to invade its coast.

The third possibility, Stuart's preference, was to cooperate with other slave states that had not yet seceded. Better to coordinate with North Carolina, Tennessee, and Kentucky (and Maryland, if possible), Stuart argued, to make sure they all went out together and in accord. Faced with a bloc of powerful and unified border slave states, Lincoln would be much less eager to resort to arms. Virginia would not become a battleground.

Stuart had not given up hope for the Northern people. He wanted Virginia to appeal across the border as well, approaching Illinois, Indiana, Ohio, Pennsylvania, New York, and New Jersey. He would "invite them to disconnect themselves from the extreme North and Northwest." Stuart maintained his faith in "business relations, private interests, social ties, the ties of brotherhood, the ties of intermarriage and of communication, in every form and shape in which they can take place." He felt certain that these bonds would "counterbalance this odious fanaticism." A border empire, uniting the reasonable people across the boundary of slavery, might yet save the legacy of their fathers.

But Virginia would not wait—or listen to Stuart any longer. On April 17 Henry Wise arrived at the convention. He "rose in his seat and drawing a large Virginia horse-pistol from his bosom, laid it before him and proceeded to harangue the body in the most violent and denunciatory manner." He told the body of a secret meeting the day before and of his plan to seize Harpers Ferry before the United States could. The people of Virginia, Wise announced, had "waited on the convention too long in vain," so he had acted on his own accord. John Baldwin of Augusta, furious, demanded to know who his allies were. Wise told him that the "patriotic volunteer revolutionists" were Baldwin's "friends and neighbors of Staunton . . . marching under my order to take their own arms for their own defense." Baldwin, "aghast," sat down in silence.[81]

As if to embody the irrational and yet powerful emotions unleashed by these events, George Baylor, fellow delegate from Augusta and hitherto a strong proponent of Union, rushed toward Wise "with tears streaming down his cheeks and exclaiming 'Let me grasp your hand; I don't agree with you; I don't approve of your acts, but I love you, I love you.' "[82]

That day, April 17, the convention voted to secede, 88 to 55. After the balloting, some delegates changed their votes to lend greater weight to the majority, making it 103 to 46. Augusta's representatives refused to change their votes; the county stood alone in the central Valley in its apparent unanimity against immediate secession. The counties immediately above and below Augusta split their votes, but the rest of the Valley, from near the Maryland border all the way down to the border with Tennessee, threw themselves behind the Confederacy without a dissenting ballot.

On April 17, the day Virginia left the Union, the officers of Augusta's volunteer companies had met at John Imboden's office. The units, "comprising an aggregate of 422 men, rank and file, uniformed and armed, do hereby agree to the formation of a Regiment of Volunteers to be numbered the 5th." They elected William Smith Hanger Baylor, the colonel of the West Augusta Guard militia, colonel of the new regiment. He had long been captain of Augusta's militia and volunteer units, leading the West Augusta Guard to Harpers Ferry in the wake of John Brown's raid back in the autumn of 1859. Everyone admired Will Baylor and was glad to have him in the lead of their regiment.[83]

By the next day the train carrying John Imboden and the Staunton Artillery finally had reached Harpers Ferry after an arduous trip; Imboden put a gun to the head of the engineer along one stretch of track for going too slowly. Having dragged the guns and horses from one train to the next and then up the heights overlooking the town, the troops prepared to attack at dawn any Federal troops they might encounter. As they arrived, however, they noticed the lights of fires burning the armory, fires set by the Union troops that had beaten them to the crucial spot. The Confed-

The destruction of Harpers Ferry

eracy lost twenty thousand pistols and rifles in the fire, but they saved the workshops and machinery along with five thousand muskets and the parts for three thousand more. Exhausted, they set up their guns to protect Harpers Ferry.[84]

Fort Sumter and Lincoln's call for troops pushed Virginia over the line its leaders had themselves drawn, the line that defined the boundary between the legitimate power of the nation and of the state, the boundary of sovereignty that allowed Virginia to stay in the Union even though it opposed its current president. Lincoln's refusal to remove the Federal soldiers from the fort declared that the United States still considered the fort its property despite South Carolina's secession. It meant that Lincoln would not accept the legitimacy of secession. The president considered the men currently in control of South Carolina mere "combinations," illegitimate pretenders to power, unreflective of popular will.

Many white Virginians had long agreed with the deep South that states could leave the Union if they so chose. They based their arguments on the Virginia and Kentucky Resolutions of 1798, which declared that the Constitution was a compact of states and that those states had the right "to interpose, for arresting the progress of the evil, and for maintaining within their respective limits, the authorities, rights and liberties appertaining to them." Such Virginians, holding tight to the notion that the Union was a confederation of states, *not people, the product of state conventions that acted in the name of the people who elected them, had invoked and developed this doctrine at periods of crisis throughout the first half of the nineteenth century. Many of their Unionist neighbors had dismissed such ideas and instead appealed to a notion of the Union, also the product of Virginians, as the highest good. Fort Sumter forced people to decide which view they held, which notion of sovereignty would predominate. A constitutional question that had long endured without immediacy or consequence suddenly seemed critical, for it provided a rationale for those who could no longer abide the Yankees. The call of states' rights suddenly echoed through Virginia.*[85]

Even Fort Sumter might have passed, however, had Lincoln not called for the arming of volunteers. The one thing that almost all Virginia Unionists agreed upon was that the Republicans could not "coerce" a state. Resupplying Fort Sumter was seen as coercion by many Southerners, but border South Unionists could, and did, argue that it was not. The proclamation calling for militia, however, was another matter. Lincoln called all "loyal citizens to favor, facilitate and aid this effort to maintain the honor, the integrity, and the existence of our National Union, and the perpetuity of popular government." That call included Virginia and all the other slaveholding states still in the Union. They had to decide whether to contribute men to put down secession. They had to choose one way or another, or so they thought. They told themselves that principles, or their forefathers, or their God forbade anything but armed resistance.[86]

The Southern Unionists had worked frantically to avoid any kind of clear-cut declaration of allegiances. Inaction, they argued, gave time for the Confederacy to wilt, time for the dominant Unionism of the upper South to grow stronger. With the call for militia, however, all the ideological and emotional elements that that been held in suspension for so long immediately combined and combusted. Had pro-Confederate sympathizers attempted to stage a coup against the Virginia Convention, as some dreamed and advocated, the upper boundary of the Confederacy might have been drawn to the south of Virginia or even North Carolina. Ideals and emotions might have gone to the Unionist side, as they did in Kentucky and Maryland when pro-Confederates pushed too hard.

But Lincoln believed that he had no choice but to fortify the United States against the rebellion in South Carolina. He saw the leaders of the Confederacy as outlaws, treasonous and treacherous. Their acts could not be tolerated if the federal government were to maintain its integrity, if he were to sustain his oath. Surely, Lincoln thought, the good men of the South, the majority of the South, forced to choose between anarchy and the nation they had helped create, would choose the Union. In any case he could not call for militia from only the nonslaveholding states. Convinced that he acted both from right and from prudence, he called for all the states of the Union to help put down the rebels in South Carolina.

With Lincoln's proclamation came Virginia's decision. It came with stunning rapidity, given all the months, all the years of talk and vacillation that had come before. The decision came from what seemed to many white Virginians the unavoidable logic of the situation: Virginia was a slave state; the Republicans had announced their intention of limiting slavery; slavery was protected by the sovereignty of the state; an attack on that sovereignty by military force was an assault on the freedom of property and political representation that sovereignty embodied. When the federal government protected the freedom and future of slavery by recognizing the sovereignty of the states, Virginia's Unionists could tolerate the insult the Republicans represented; when the federal government rejected that sovereignty, the threat could no longer be denied even by those who loved the Union.

Abraham Lincoln, working from a different understanding of nation, could not understand or acknowledge a reading of the Constitution that placed the rights of the states over the integrity of the Union. His own logic made perfect sense given his belief that nation superseded state, that the states had given sovereignty to the Union when they signed the Constitution. He therefore saw illegal rebels where white Southerners saw principled revolutionaries. Lincoln's view came to dominate after the Civil War, but in 1861 the ambiguity of the Constitution on the issue of sovereignty and its quiet on the issues surrounding slavery made it possible for men who loved the Union to leave the Union.[87]

The call for militia fused forces that had been in contention and balance in Virginia. Before that call the defenders of Union claimed the high ground of the Revolution, of the Constitution, of law and order. After the call advocates of secession could lay claim to those same ideals. Emotion and rationality suddenly aligned in the moment of secession; economic self-interest and high-minded constitutionalism coincided. Slavery had come to embody all the rights of white men, to stand for all that was worth fighting and dying for under the American Constitution.

After Virginia's decision everything shifted within the upper South. North Carolina and Tennessee left the Union after Virginia despite their even stronger Unionism. The geopolitics of slavery and of warfare demanded as much. Now the white people of the upper South suddenly professed to know where they belonged, what they must do. Earlier words of Union and peace had to be disavowed, denied, forgotten.

4

FRANKLIN COUNTY, with the rest of the North, had watched the events of early April with avid interest and unceasing commentary. The Democrats kept up a steady round of criticism and warnings about Lincoln's every action; the Republicans kept up a steady round of defense and encouragement. Right up to the very day of Fort Sumter, secession had divided the North even as it divided the South.[88]

An issue of the *Spirit* should have appeared on April 17. But no paper came out because the young men who worked there, like their counterparts in counties all over the country, had left the office, rushing to fill the ranks of volunteers called out in response to Lincoln's proclamation. Two days later a new Republican Franklin County paper appeared, published twice every week, the *Semi-Weekly Dispatch*. It announced its first issue on April 19 with a compelling rationale: "Weekly newspapers are too slow for the times."[89]

The new paper launched its first issue with good partisan insults against the Democrats. "The capture of Fort Sumter is the first bitter fruit of the vacillating and effeminate Administration of JAS. BUCHANAN," the bachelor president. Under that Democrat, "Treason stalked abroad in open day in our National Capital; plunder seemed to have become a ruling passion among our officers." By contrast, since Lincoln assumed office, "in the short space of six weeks, order has been brought out of political confusion, the public offices have been filled with good and true men, a scattered army and a dispersed navy have been gathered together, the public defenses have been duly cared for, and in every movement, our new President has thus far shown himself the man." If war came, so be it. "The consequences of all this firmness and manliness of President LINCOLN may be a war with the so-called Southern Confederacy; but it will merely be an earlier commencement that the end may be the sooner, and will, doubtless, under the Divine blessing, avert from our beloved land, those terrible evils of anarchy, toward which we were so rapidly and fatally drifting. There are worse evils than war."[90]

The citizens of Chambersburg immediately demonstrated their Union feeling by raising in the Diamond a Union pole "bearing aloft 'The Star-Spangled Banner of the Free.' It is 128 feet high, surmounted by a golden ball, with a Streamer floating to the breeze. When the Pole assumed an upright position, one long, loud and tremendous cheer from the crowd (numbering from 1800 to 2000) rent the air." A group of "ladies on the veranda of the Franklin House sung 'The Star Spangled Banner' in a style worthy of their patriotism." Seven speakers, including Alexander K. McClure, addressed the crowd "in a style so thrilling and animating as stirred the very souls of their auditors, and so great was the feeling exhibited that the faces of many stern men were seen bathed in tears. Our citizens are 'not wild with excitement,' but stern determination is visible in every countenance." American flags of all sizes appeared throughout the stores, streets, and houses of Chambersburg.[91]

On the evening of the eighteenth, Chambersburg came together in a town meeting at the courthouse. George Chambers, after whose ancestor the town had been named, presided. The meeting, with the "greatest enthusiasm," blasted out a series of resolutions with the most insulting language the assemblage could say in public. The story line was simple. "A band of traitorous spirits" had for years "been plotting the dismemberment of our glorious Confederacy, the hope of struggling Freedom throughout the World and the asylum of the oppressed and down trodden of all Nations." The "hellish efforts" of these traitors had now led the people of the seven Cotton States "to establish a rebel Government" that has "stolen the treasure, seized the Fortresses, and taken possession of the National Vessels, Arms and Munitions of War, belonging to the Union." The "Arch Traitor of them all—the Benedict Arnold of the South—Jefferson Davis—the President of the so called 'Confederate States' has boldly and openly threatened to march upon the Capitol of our Country at the head of 25,000 men, and drive out the Constituted Authorities of the land, and seat himself in the mansion and Chair of State." In the face of these depredations, President Lincoln had rightly called "upon the soldiery of the nation, who are faithful to their Country, without respect to party feelings or predilections, to the number of 75,000 to rally in defence of the Constitution and the Laws."[92]

Chambersburg could not wait to do its part. "The time has come for all men to sink the Partizan in the Patriot, to forego political principles and party animosities, until the danger that threatens our national existence is past, and to rally as one man, with one heart, one mind, and one purpose at the call of the constituted authorities of the land, for the maintenance of the Constitution and the Laws." The people of Chambersburg proclaimed happiness "that the gallant soldiery of our noble State and the Country generally, have so speedily and so cheerfully responded to the call of their Country, in numbers far over the aggregate desired." The Chambers Artillery and other volunteers would leave town the next morning to serve Pennsylvania and the Union.[93]

The people who remained behind offered the departing men "most sincere and heart-felt wishes for their individual preservation from death or grievous injury during their absence, and our ardent prayers that they may each and all be speedily restored to the arms of those who so patriotically part with them at the call of duty." The meeting sought to put the volunteers' minds to rest, for those at the meeting "pledge to each one of these our friends, our sacred honors, that we will see that their wives and children, and whoever elsewhere is dependant upon them, shall not, during their absence, lack for any thing temporal that money and willing hearts can provide." The people of Chambersburg spread a "sumptuous banquet" before the volunteers, presented a "very handsome sword" to their lieutenant, and offered "a fervent prayer in behalf of our noble soldiers and the cause they are about to defend."[94]

The supervisor of Thaddeus Stevens's Caledonia furnace wrote his employer down in Washington to give him good news and bad. The news from the Republican and Union point of view was excellent, W. E. Camp reported. "The wildest state of excitement reigns here. Our best men have tendered their services and everybody left back is anxious to go." Stevens the businessman might have been less pleased with the report on that front: "Business in this place is entirely suspended—stores all shut up. $6000 was raised yesterday to support the families of the soldiers during their absence. If it would be policy to stop operations at Caledonia, our force to a man will go. & I will go with them." In the spirit of patriotism, Stevens could hardly resist.[95]

The *Valley Spirit*, which had berated the Republicans and Abraham Lincoln at every opportunity, which had defended the South for years and the Confederacy since its inception, exploded in headlines proclaiming its change of heart:

WAR-FEELING IN CHAMBERSBURG

GREAT UNANIMITY AND ENTHUSIASM.

Men and Money Freely Offered.

THE TOWN DECORATED WITH FLAGS.

PUBLIC MEETING OF CITIZENS.

ELOQUENT AND PATRIOTIC SPEECHES.

All Parties Uniting on a Common
Platform to Maintain the Constitution and the Laws.

The Democratic paper noted that three Democrats addressed the crowd along with many Republicans. "The utmost harmony and good feeling prevailed at the meeting." Some leading citizens volunteered to head a committee on contributions; others volunteered to supply pocket Bibles to the soldiers. Fifty men volunteered to serve in the Home Guard.[96]

The 150 men of the Chambers Artillery mustered into service for three months and headed for Washington, D.C. "The fathers, mothers, brothers, sisters, wives and children of the volunteers, together with the entire population of the place, were collected at the Depot to bid farewell to the gallant band and witness their departure." The young men of the unit "seemed much less affected at parting than their friends. While almost every eye in the vast throng was bathed in tears the soldiers seemed in the most joyous spirits and cheered their friends with words of consolation and hope."[97]

The *Spirit* paused long enough in its thrilling account of unity to acknowledge that it had abruptly changed its entire tone and outlook. "A formidable band of traitors have broken up the Union and made war against the government," it explained. "While we considered them friends we battled for their rights in the Union, but when they determine to break up the Union and array themselves as enemies against us, we are their enemies. They are no longer of our household but enemies up in arms against us." While the formation of the Confederacy had not led the paper to renounce the Southerners as traitors, the assault on Fort Sumter and the massing of troops had changed everything. "Let us then be up and doing and crush the monster before it crushes us," the suddenly belligerent paper cried. "Let us be watchful on every side and allow no man to slumber at his post while the flag of his country is in danger. Let the watch-word of all be—'READY, AIM, FIRE.' "[98]

The "war spirit" that seized the people on both sides of the Mason-Dixon Line amazed the Reverend Abraham Essick. "No one could have imagined that the sober-minded Pennsylvanians could be so aroused. Yet it seems that she is taking the lead in furnishing men and means and all the essentials of war. Such unanimity I never heard of. Conservative men, who did all in their power to avert the collision before our flag was dishonored, are now burning with indignation. I have not heard a dissenting voice." Through "all classes of the community," even among the ministers, "the sentiment is universal, that the government must be sustained, rebellion suppressed and the honor of the nation vindicated. May God defend the right!"[99]

The Civil War did not approach the border like a slowly building storm. It came like an earthquake, with uneven and unpredictable periods of quiet between abrupt seismic shifts that shook the entire landscape. It came by sudden realignments, its tremors giving no indication of the scale of the violence that would soon follow. People changed their minds overnight, reversing what they had said and done for years.

The crisis came in a strange way. It was rehearsed through elaborate debate and deliberation, through what Abraham Lincoln called "airy" and "theoretical" concerns. People on the border, dedicated to peace and moderation, imagined all the permutations and outcomes, calculating carefully what would be won and lost by each strategy. Border Unionists gained momentum after the first secession, pulling Virginia and its neighbors toward compromise and reconciliation. Partisans in the border North fought with one another over every petty issue until the day the Confederate troops fired on Fort Sumter. Abraham Lincoln bent over backward to appease the border South, giving in on everything except slavery in the territories and the fort at Charleston.

Then everything changed because Lincoln sought to resupply that fort. Actually overnight, the Virginia Convention, so cautious and plodding, threw itself to the Confederacy with the support of the great majority of the voters east of the Allegheny Mountains, including the Valley. By doing so, they gave themselves to a war that they had every reason to dread. Over the border in Franklin and Pennsylvania, the Democrats abandoned arguments that war with the South would be wrong, unconstitutional, stupid, and unmanly. They gave themselves over entirely to the new cause.

Each side had a simple explanation for the other's sudden change: the people on the other side were hypocrites, claiming to fight for one thing while really fighting for another. The South felt certain the North fought for dominion and an abolition born of sheer spite, envy, and a puritanical self-righteousness. The North felt certain the South fought to extend slavery like a disease throughout North America, infecting white people in the established states with its black slaves. Both knew the other side used the language of the Constitution as a mere shield and excuse.

Indeed, the inconsistencies were striking. The North went to war to keep people in a Union based on the consent of the governed, to maintain connection with a slaveholding society it despised. Northern leaders expressed barely a word of concern for the millions of people currently enslaved. The South, for its part, went to war under the flag of freedom to maintain a massive and growing human slavery. The South risked war and the disintegration of a nation it had dominated to maintain rights that remained unchallenged in any concrete way.

But both sides had reasons that seemed deep and compelling to themselves. The North clearly believed in the global importance of Union, the anarchy that would follow in the North if the South were permitted to leave and other parts of the Union broke away, and the illegality of secession. Northerners believed that the Confederacy did not speak or act for most white Southerners, that a white Southern Unionist majority only awaited help and a signal to step forward. The South clearly believed that the safety and integrity of its entire society were challenged by the Republicans, a party that had arisen for the express reason of dominating the South. The South believed too that the Constitution gave states the right to leave if they so wished and that the election of Abraham Lincoln had been nothing other than an attempt to drive the South away through electoral means. The South now wanted to leave, whether the Republicans offered an immediate threat, a long-term threat, or no real threat at all.

People defended their actions through the words of the Constitution. Like a prism, the Constitution focused and intensified the sectional struggle. Rather than fight for slavery, the South said, it fought for the right of slavery, a right won and decreed by their ancestors who helped create the United States, and the right to remove itself from a union it had voluntarily joined. Rather than fight against slavery, the North said, it fought to preserve the government the Constitution created, to stop outlaws and traitors from usurping it.

Slavery lay at the root of the South's actions, and white Southerners were not squeamish about saying so. Since all civil society in the South, everything touched by the public realm of law and government, rested on slavery, that civil society necessarily defended slavery as a crucial part of itself. White Southerners did not isolate slavery as the "real" reason they were fighting because slavery could not be separated from the rest; it was so tightly bound up with their sense of who they were that it could not be isolated. They spoke easily, as they had for decades, of God's plan to use the South to Christianize Africans. They spoke of enslaved people's love for their masters and mistresses, of the bonds that tied them together. They spoke of the waste and bloodshed that would accompany emancipation, of the desolation of the South, of the slow death of the former slaves.

Along with the constitutional language and the language of slavery emerged another language, a language of elemental loyalties, a language of loyalty to family and locale, of native soil and the sacrifices of the fathers. It was a language everyone knew how to speak. It was a language older than the Constitution. It drew on cultural memories even older than the Bible, memories of Greeks and Romans. It spoke from instincts embedded in the human mind and body. It was a language made for wartime, and people on both sides of the border spoke it fluently.

Both the North and the South claimed the sanction of God. They read their Bibles selectively, turning to the language of retribution and vengeance in the Old Testament rather than to the language of forgiveness and brotherly love in the New. They defined righteousness as they wanted to define it, as they needed to define it, not for His name's sake but for the sake of worldly ends.

Law and right, duty and honor, fate and history, so tangled only weeks before, suddenly aligned for both the North and the South. The paths of righteousness suddenly appeared straight and smooth.

5

THE CREATION OF the Confederacy and the consolidation of the North into a newly configured nation recast people's conception of themselves. They saw their families and communities as well as their government in unfamiliar ways. Their nationalism, a feeling of oneness with unseen others, shifted to a smaller, more homogeneous, more comfortable group.[100]

The demonization of the enemy burned with new intensity. Each side imagined the worst in the other's character and motives. Each portrayed its own purpose as an essential step in the world's moral improvement. The Confederacy told itself that it fought for the ideals of Christian stewardship, constitutional government, and white freedom. The Union declared that it fought on behalf of all republican government everywhere and for all time.[101]

Men made a great display of burying political animosity with their immediate neighbors, of standing shoulder to shoulder against the invading enemy from the North or the outlaws from the South. Rich and poor alike would sacrifice for the common good. The language of manliness, always evident in public talk, flourished.

Women suddenly appeared in prominent roles on the center stage of public life. They took it upon themselves, with warm public thanks, to prepare their men for war. They took it upon themselves to proffer symbolic gifts of wreaths and flowers, flags and uniforms. Men bathed women in adulation, and women reciprocated. The charged air led to fervent courtship as well as to the rapid enlistment of single men.

Before the war, people North and South had gloried in, defined themselves by their differences of political parties. But now they could not afford such arguments. In a time filled with opportunities for personal pride and ambition they had to appear to swallow pride and ambition. In a time filled with chances for glory and distinction they had to subordinate themselves to the cause if glory and distinction were to become theirs.

Everyone knew the stories of the American Revolution, of privation, trial, and triumph. Everyone knew too the stories of the Bible, of testing and deliverance.

Many people knew the stories of the ancient world, of the Spartan soldiers and their women. People knew how they were supposed to act in times of war and crisis. People followed the scripts and took great pleasure in speaking the lines they already knew.

AUGUSTA WAS SWEPT UP in delicious unity. The *Spectator* claimed that Augusta's devotion to secession ran deeper because of the county's earlier passion for Union. "As soon as the last ray of hope had been extinguished, as soon as they had seen the President's proclamation, the herald of civil war, and heard the call to arms, they sprang to their feet, donned their military dress, shouldered their guns, bade their fathers and mothers, brothers and sisters a hurried and affectionate farewell, and marched with speed to the place of rendevous." The Unionists of Augusta were "still for Union—a Union of brave and patriotic men for the defence of our State." Union proved an ideal whose form could change, whose boundaries could be redrawn without changing the ideas to which that Union devoted itself. Two young men left the *Spectator*'s office that day to take up arms for the new cause.[102]

The people of Augusta raged at their former friends in the North. A banker from New York wrote John M. McCue the day after Fort Sumter. It was the sort of letter that had often crossed the border in the decades before April 1861, a letter calling on men of goodwill and good sense to cool the conflict in a spirit of cooperation. It alluded lightly and obliquely to slavery as "the cause which created this contention," but only to warn that slavery might be destroyed if the border South joined the Confederacy. The letter from New York contained nothing incendiary or insulting. Indeed, it gave itself over to a kind of language that men usually shunned. "When I heard that South Carolina fired coolly and deliberately and wantonly upon our flag," the New Yorker admitted, "I cried like a child, that our brothers should fire into us." The banker asked McCue what he thought and what Virginia would do.[103]

McCue published the New Yorker's letter, using it as a target for acrid sarcasm—and impressive vocabulary and alliteration: "Could you, and the myrmidons of abolition, of agrarianism and all that is abominable in a free government, see, as I have had the opportunity within the past few days, the spirit of our people, your craven hearts would collapse within your cowardly carcasses." McCue, a businessman and lawyer of wide associations, knew the power New York could deploy. But "when our brave and gallant sons are exterminated, if such could be, you will find our wives and daughters more than a match for all the Beechers, and Cheevers and Stowes and that damnable set that you have so long paid Court to, and encouraged, until you have brought this affliction upon the country." It was not the "institutions" of the South that caused the war, not slavery, McCue argued, but "the misguided frenzy and folly and madness of your people, that has been the cause; and that people that has fattened and flourished upon the labor of this institution, and in your pharasaical and puritanical self-righteousness, after hoarding this wealth, would say to us, 'stand aside, we are holier than thou,' and cannot live under the same government with you." The North's "damnable hypocrisy makes my blood boil."[104]

The South imagined the North as craven and cheap, the land of the bigoted Puritan and the tightfisted Yankee, the last refuge of the drunken and worthless vagabond from Ireland or Germany. The South, by contrast, prided itself on fighting a purely defensive war: "We are repelling aggression. We are defending our firesides and homes."[105] The war meant that the "flower of Southern honor and chivalry will cross swords with rowdies, cut-throats and burglars from the corrupt cesspools of Northern cities." The calculus was cruel, for "whenever the South shall lose a soldier, it will lose a valuable citizen, whose loss will be sensibly felt, whereas the North would be benefitted if a large portion of its soldiers would never return from the battlefield." Yet who could deny that the South would triumph over such Yankee scum?[106]

John Imboden and the Staunton Artillery remained at Harpers Ferry after their desperate attempt to save it from the Federal forces, alongside Will Baylor and the West Augusta Guard he commanded. On April 22 Baylor wrote a public letter back home. The Augusta men, he told their relatives and neighbors, were "now encamped on the most romantic and commanding spots about Harper's Ferry." Their position was "the post of danger, and therefore the post of honour, and we will maintain it against every enemy." Baylor apologized for boasting, but "the pride which I have for the gallant fellows under me, may make me exceed propriety. Their conduct reminds me of the glorious deeds of our forefathers, and their name and memory shall never be disgraced by their sons." Baylor, Imboden, and their men imagined themselves the heirs to the American Revolution, minutemen rushing to the defense of their homes. "The men work willingly, eat heartily, and sleep as soundly on the ground, as a prince in a palace.—They are ready for a fight, and I believe are eager to show their courage in driving back any invading foe."[107]

Colonel Thomas J. Jackson arrived to take charge a couple of weeks later and quickly brought military order to the rather ragtag occupation. He gave the troops the option of enlisting for one year or the entire war. "For the war! For the war!" they all shouted. Imboden delivered the muster roll of his men to Jackson, saying, "There, colonel, is the roll of your first company mustered in for the war." Jackson thanked Imboden and Baylor warmly.[108] Augusta men, notwithstanding their Unionist heritage, had given themselves to the Civil War from its very first moments and pledged to remain until its very end.

Augusta men quickly attained important posts under the command of Jackson. The Confederacy removed the former heads of militia units from command, and Jackson had to be careful that he not lose the service of excellent men in the process of transition. John Harman, a veteran of the Mexican War and a man impressive for his size, strength, and profanity, became Jackson's first, and only, quartermaster, responsible for equipping and sustaining the entire command. Kenton Harper, sixty years old and another veteran of the war with Mexico, had arrived at Harpers Ferry as a general of a militia unit but accepted a position as colonel in the 5th Virginia. Will Baylor attained the respect of Jackson by staying with his former militia unit instead of going off to Richmond to lobby for a more elevated post. Baylor could have played upon his popularity, but instead he subordinated his personal ambition. Jackson soon made him a captain.[109]

The final popular vote on secession in Virginia arrived on May 23, weeks after the state had seceded in deed. The tortured and hopeful language of compromise had been replaced by simplistic and superheated rhetoric. "Is it not the threatened policy of the North to invade our State and take from us by brute force, our lands, our houses, and all that we possess, and divide it among themselves?" asked a former Augusta Unionist. "Their cry is 'booty and beauty,' which means, in plain English, as I understand it, to steal our lands from us, and ravish our females. Any one that doubts can get the newspapers and read for themselves." Northern newspapers said nothing like this, but Virginians felt certain they did.[110]

By May 1861 no one in Augusta could talk of loyalty to the old Union, no matter his or her true feelings. "We look upon such conduct as treason, and deserving the halter," the *Vindicator* screamed. "There can be no other interpretation given to action of that character." The threats lay right on the surface. "Mark the prediction: the man who casts his suffrage against the Ordinance of Separation, will regret it as long as he lives, and posterity will curse his children." A well-known dentist who regularly visited Augusta made the mistake of airing "very obnoxious sentiments, declaring that Lincoln was right and his Administration was Washington-like." Agitated citizens threatened the offending dentist with "summary punishment," but several gentlemen stepped in to argue that he should merely be escorted from the county.[111] Staunton bridled when a New York paper charged that several Northern shoemakers working in a local factory had been driven from town. They merely "preferred to leave." And they did.[112]

Alexander H. H. Stuart, leader of the Unionists, was "asked" by twenty-five of his "friends and fellow citizens" to announce his position on the current state of affairs. Everyone knew that Stuart had fought for Union throughout the entire crisis and a New York paper had even reported that he had been "compelled to leave from Virginia."[113] That was untrue, but Stuart did not capitulate easily. He still thought his plans for a border state convention would have saved the Union and the South. But he had lost, and now, he wrote, "it is the duty of all good citizens to stand by the action of the State. It is no time for crimination or recrimination. We cannot stop now to enquire who brought the troubles upon us, or why. It is enough to know that they are upon us, and we must meet them like men. We must stand shoulder to shoulder. Our State is threatened with invasion, and we must repel them as best we can." At the same time that Stuart made this bleak plea, this admission of personal defeat and what he feared would be the defeat of the South, he announced that he would not seek reelection to Virginia's senate. He would become a private man and allow others to preside over the destruction of Augusta and Virginia.[114]

The clergy tried to preach Christianity and righteous war at the same time. They found it hard to locate the right language. When a statement from several ministers appeared in the *Spectator*, whose editor emphasized the ministers' former Unionism, a correspondent rushed to set the record straight in the *Vindicator*. The ministers, "Fair Play" argued, "are peace-loving and God-fearing men; but at the same time patriots." The correspondent insisted that everyone read this key sentence from their statement: "If the Southern States of the Union are persistently refused their just rights in the Confederacy and its common territories, and the peculiar property, *then, in our opinion, the Southern people must conclude that these causes do exist, and that the catastrophe, however lamentable, must be met, sorrowfully indeed, and yet with the resolution of Freemen.*" The clergy acknowledged the role of slavery, using the familiar circumlocution "peculiar property." They also acknowledged that war, catastrophe, must descend on the nation. As their defender insisted, the Christian leaders of Virginia were not "tame submissionists."[115]

Most Augusta people claimed to have no reservations at all. "This is election day," sixteen-year-old Mary Smiley wrote her brother, who had just joined the Augusta volunteers. "It has been beautiful so far even the morning appears to favor the election for ratifying what the convention has done." Mary was sure that "a great majority of the people will go for secession, revolution or what ever it is called. The greatest number of the papers urge the people to ratify the acts of the Convention to present a bold and united front to the North against its tyranny. Even to the Spectator which you know was as strong a union paper as could be found. I don't hear of many union people about here now."[116]

Indeed, only 10 men in Augusta, scattered one by one around the county, voted against secession. Given that the election was not in doubt, the turnout was remarkable, for 3,130 men voted. They did so to send a message to Abraham Lincoln: do not count on the South's dividing, on former Unionists' betraying the Confederacy. You will have to defeat us; we shall not buckle. Up and down the Valley the vote was the same, with massive turnout and virtually no public dissent tolerated. Some people who had been reluctant to secede proved eager to fight.[117]

Anger at the North came accompanied by a warm sense of unity at home. Alansa Sterrett, the young New Yorker recently wedded to Frank

Sterrett of the West Augusta Guard, described the excitement in her diary: "Frank took me to attend a Band Concert at the Armory. Band looked superb in their new uniforms and with silver instruments glistening in an artificial light. 'Dixie' created a furor of delight! Orchestra of stringed instruments very sweet."[118] A week later, with Frank gone to Richmond to get weapons for his unit, Alansa spent the day working for the new cause: "8:30 to 3 P.M. ladies sewing on knapsacks for the cavalrymen. Everybody excited and stirring." It was not only sewing that kept the ladies busy, for "Kate Seig practiced with Mr. Cook's revolver." That evening the household gathered in the library to "hear Uncle Jed read the news."

As the days passed, the signs of Frank's military future multiplied. Alansa "was giving Nannie music lesson when a package arrived for me, a lovely portfolio with Frank's picture inside, a sweet note, and gold pen and pencil!" That afternoon the young bride "watched Cavalry drill, admirably done. Swords flashed in sunlight and bugle played at intervals. Their noble Captain looked very handsome and rode superbly. I was justly proud of 'My own brave Cavalier.' " That evening Alansa's cavalier came to her "to honor my 24th birthday! Lovely moonlight night, windows open to the breeze." A few days later she received a "letter from Pa and Ma. Both very anxious about my safety and begging me to try and get home while I could." Her uncle Jed Hotchkiss, himself a New Yorker, read the letters and "said I could not and should not go home. Was safe here. Unsafe to travel now." Truth be told, Alansa showed no desire to leave.

WITHIN WEEKS OF FORT SUMTER and the secession of the upper South, Franklin saw itself transformed by mobilization for war. Not many men rushed to volunteer in Franklin in the spring of 1861. A few dozen joined one regiment or another of the light infantry or cavalry, but no concerted effort at enlistment had yet begun in the county.

The war came to Franklin in a more abrupt way: the county became the home of Camp Slifer, located on the Baltimore Road to the southeast of Chambersburg. "This usually quiet town now presents a very animated and soldier like appearance, as the sound of the drum, the running to and fro of soldiers, and all the pomp and circumstance of glorious war, are the distinguishing features of our streets." Two regiments, about a thousand men in each, had gathered in Chambersburg before the opening of the camp, "stationed at the Fair grounds and hotels, but in one day the sheds in the new camp were erected." With an efficient general in command, "order has taken the place of disorder, and well drilled soldiers are now seen on parade instead of raw recruits."[119]

If the soldiers were impressive, this visitor to Chambersburg thought, the citizens were inspiring, "generous in their contributions, and profuse in their kindness to the soldiers and officers." As in all such reports, the ladies came in for special praise, for they, "God bless them, smile upon us so sweetly as almost to captivate us all." Martial imagery playfully described the romantic maneuvering. "Some of the fair damsels have 'laid siege' to the hearts of the gallant beaux in our company."[120]

Military excitement filled the air. Alex Cressler, a twenty-one-year-old teacher from northern Franklin who had recently moved down to Chambersburg, wrote his friend Henry Bitner, a nineteen-year-old farm hand and teacher back in their old neighborhood. "I have been somewhat disappointed in not seeing you up here to see the men playing sol-

Chambersburg mobilizes for war

dier," Cressler wrote enthusiastically in May—on new stationery bearing the American flag in full color. Governor Curtin was coming to Camp Slifer to review the troops. Four thousand men, five regiments, had already gathered there. "My but they do look pretty, Just come and see," Cressler wrote somewhat wistfully. "Three Regiments were in yesterday afternoon and make a long line of people, who with their glittering bayonets under the rays of the shining sun, accompanied by their Bands, or marshal music, and the heavy and steady tramp of three thousand men, make all who stand and look on, feel, that they are not soldiers."[121]

Cressler permitted himself to imagine the battles soon to come, both in their glory and in their cost. As impressive as the marching in Chambersburg was, "all this can but give a very faint idea of the appearance of one hundred and fifty thousand human beings marched into the field of battle by the warming and thrilling sound of almost countless drums." No one could adequately imagine, the young man thought, "the feeling of that immense congregation of human souls when the sound of the booming cannon first disturbs the quiet of that breast and paints death and destruction all around." Cressler admitted to his old school friend that they could never "realize the horrors of such a sight until we ourselves behold it, and such humanity forbids us from wishing." Yet desire and dread refused to stay distinct.

Word was already coming of Rebels mobilizing in Maryland, and the young teacher felt certain that "we will have a bloody time here" on the border. Cressler had come to believe that war would be necessary, and "what could be more cheering to the hearts of freeman such as we are, than to see that the whole north will move to the work, as one mighty machine none of the parts being wanting, but all complete." Divine motive power drove the great machine of the North, fueled not "by steam, but the hearts blood of millions, and the smiles of Heaven." Through the machine of the Union, secession would "be crushed out of existence, and like a mighty cloud, it will rain Union sentiments on every farm and plantation south of Mason's and Dixon's Line."

The people of the North were convinced that God watched over the Union cause. "The mighty uprisings of the people, and tremendous outburst of patriotism throughout the entire North," the *Dispatch* proclaimed, "can only be explained upon the hypothesis, that agencies more

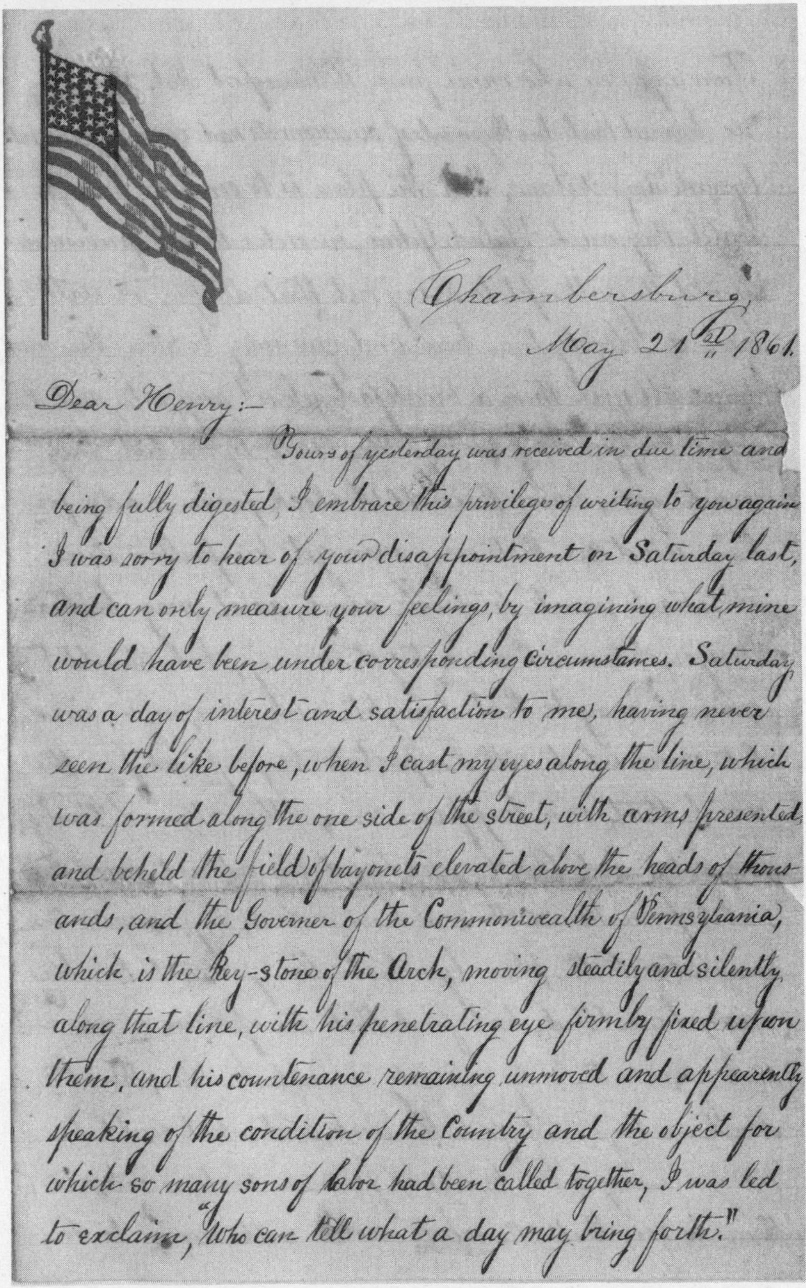

Chambersburg
May 21st 1861.

Dear Henry:-

Yours of yesterday was received in due time and being fully digested, I embrace this privilege of writing to you again. I was sorry to hear of your disappointment on Saturday last, and can only measure your feelings, by imagining what mine would have been under corresponding circumstances. Saturday was a day of interest and satisfaction to me, having never seen the like before, when I cast my eyes along the line, which was formed along the one side of the street, with arms presented, and beheld the field of bayonets elevated above the heads of thousands, and the Governer of the Commonwealth of Pennsylvania, which is the Key-stone of the Arch, moving steadily and silently along that line, with his penetrating eye firmly fixed upon them, and his countenance remaining unmoved and apparently speaking of the condition of the Country and the object for which so many sons of labor had been called together, I was led to exclaim, "Who can tell what a day may bring forth."

Alex Cressler describes thrilling preparations for war

than human are at work amongst us." The course of history had changed too quickly for any secular explanation. "Love of country has burst so suddenly and sublimely upon us, that the most sanguine have been surprised and amazed." The war brought wonderful change. "When you see the miser unlocking his coffers and giving his hoards to his country, flags flying from churches of every creed, and whole populations giving up work and rushing into the army, may we not feel that we are in the hands of God, and that He has become our Protector and our President?" Sacred and worldly had become one.[122]

The scenes repeated across the North. In the six weeks since Fort Sumter people were moved not by "patriotism merely" but by "religious phrenzy," a reporter joyously noted. "The Star Spangled Banner has become quite a chant and a chorus everywhere. It is hymned in churches, shouted in taverns, sounded in the streets, and made familiar to the lips of beauty and the lisp of childhood." The religious fervor ran even in the veins of fiercely partisan political warriors. "As to party feeling, he who shows it is shunned like a plague. We have forgotten all of the past save that which teaches us to love our country, and look only upon the future to save and fight for her." There could be only one lesson to draw from such displays: "Our cause must prevail, and the designs of Providence in thus visiting us, must be those of ultimate and substantial good." To judge from His signs, God had already determined that the Union would triumph and that justice and glory would triumph alongside it.[123]

6

AUGUSTA'S FIRST PASS at enlistment in April had mainly taken in men who had been active in the militia units. Many other young men in the county declared themselves eager to serve. In May a recruiting poster from "Head Quarters, Virginia Forces," in Staunton called out: "MEN OF VIRGINIA, TO THE RESCUE!" The plea defined the enemy in reference to slavery: "Your soil has been invaded by your Abolition foes, and we call upon you to rally at once, and drive them back." The Confederate army wanted volunteers to march immediately. "Come one! Come ALL! and render the service due to your State and Country. Fly to arms and succour your brave brothers who are now in the field." After the blazing words about the abolitionists and brotherhood came the more historical plea: "The sentiment of Virginia's inspired orator, 'Give me Liberty or give me Death' " should "animate every loyal son of the Old Dominion! Let us drive back the invading foot of a brutal and desperate foe, or leave to posterity that we died bravely defending our homes and firesides,—the honor of our wives and daughters and the sacred graves of our ancestors!" This one recruiting handbill covered most of the ideological bases that drove the Confederacy, ranging from the defense of slavery to the defense of the hearth, from aid to living brothers to honor for forefathers. Every potential recruit could find something to justify the sacrifice.[124]

From this round of recruiting came the formation of yet another set of eight companies in Augusta, these for the 52d Virginia Infantry. The new companies included the Augusta Fencibles, Waynesboro Guards, Letcher Guard (named after Virginia's governor), Harper Guard (named after Kenton Harper, a local veteran of the Mexican War), Cline's Company (named after their captain, Joseph E. Cline), Veteran Guards, and the Staunton Pioneers. This wave of recruitment brought in even

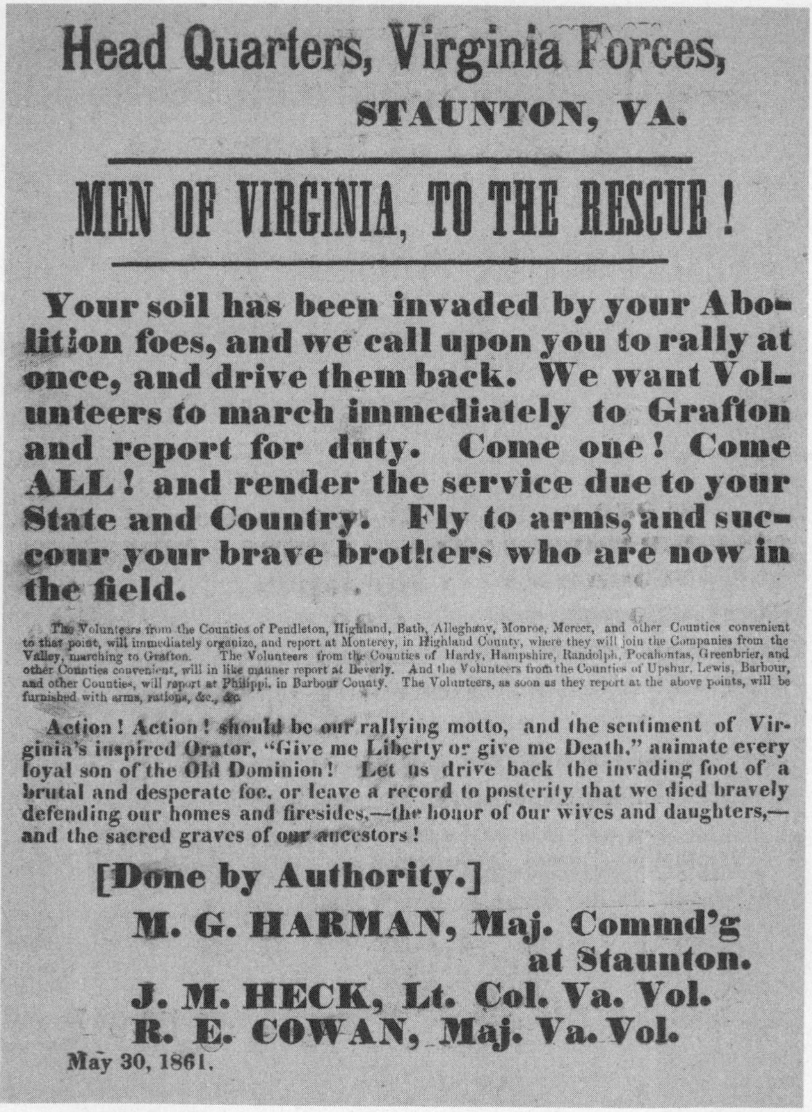

Head Quarters, Virginia Forces,

STAUNTON, VA.

MEN OF VIRGINIA, TO THE RESCUE!

Your soil has been invaded by your Abolition foes, and we call upon you to rally at once, and drive them back. We want Volunteers to march immediately to Grafton and report for duty. Come one! Come ALL! and render the service due to your State and Country. Fly to arms, and succour your brave brothers who are now in the field.

The Volunteers from the Counties of Pendleton, Highland, Bath, Alleghany, Monroe, Mercer, and other Counties convenient to that point, will immediately organize, and report at Monterey, in Highland County, where they will join the Companies from the Valley, marching to Grafton. The Volunteers from the Counties of Hardy, Hampshire, Randolph, Pocahontas, Greenbrier, and other Counties convenient, will in like manner report at Beverly. And the Volunteers from the Counties of Upshur, Lewis, Barbour, and other Counties, will report at Philippi, in Barbour County. The Volunteers, as soon as they report at the above points, will be furnished with arms, rations, &c., &c.

Action! Action! should be our rallying motto, and the sentiment of Virginia's inspired Orator, "Give me Liberty or give me Death," animate every loyal son of the Old Dominion! Let us drive back the invading foot of a brutal and desperate foe, or leave a record to posterity that we died bravely defending our homes and firesides,—the honor of our wives and daughters,—and the sacred graves of our ancestors!

[Done by Authority.]

M. G. HARMAN, Maj. Commd'g at Staunton.

J. M. HECK, Lt. Col. Va. Vol.

R. E. COWAN, Maj. Va. Vol.

May 30, 1861.

Augusta men called to fight "abolition foes"

more men than the first. By the end of August another nine hundred men had joined from Augusta, bringing the total to more than fifteen hundred since April.

These volunteers, like those that were to follow them, represented in many ways a cross section of the younger white men of the county. More than half were farmers or laborers, just as in Augusta as a whole. Artisans, about a third of the workingmen in the county, made up about a third of those who were to fight for the Confederacy. Professional men, accounting for about eight men in a hundred in the county, accounted for exactly the same proportion in the new regiments being formed in Augusta. Most of the men had just become men; the largest single proportion was either twenty-one or twenty-two years old. With eighteen as the minimum age for enlistment, dozens of youngsters in their teens signed up, as did men up into their thirties. The average age of those who fought from Augusta rose over the next few years as men with families stepped into service.

Those who enlisted for the Confederacy in Augusta, though, differed from their neighbors in important ways. While young men from middle-class and wealthy families signed up in numbers roughly proportional to their share of Augusta society, the poorest families produced twice as many soldiers relative to their numbers in the county. Only 20 percent of the households in Augusta owned less than a thousand dollars' worth of property, but over 40 percent of the soldiers came from households that poor, their poverty masked by the census taker's calling them "farmer" even though they owned no land. Heads of households were less likely to join up, since they had family responsibilities to take care of, but such men still accounted for about a third of all those who enlisted in 1861. About a fifth of those who signed up were eldest sons, meaning that about half the new soldiers from Augusta County were second, third, or fourth sons or men who lived as boarders in the houses of families to which they did not belong by blood. All in all, Augusta's soldiers in 1861 came from among the most expendable young men, the least integrated, or the least fettered, in the county.

Augusta County men dominated the leadership ranks as well as the enlisted ranks of the 5th and 52d. Neighboring Rockbridge County, the home of the Virginia Military Institute, chafed at the exalted position of Augusta men. Rockbridge supplied three of the twelve companies in the 52d yet saw coveted officer positions elude them. A disgruntled Rockbridge soldier wrote a facetious letter to his county's newspaper evaluating the Augusta officers appointed by Governor Letcher, a letter reprinted by the *Spectator*: "General Baldwin is the Colonel. This is regarded as a good appointment, for Col. Baldwin has the intellect to carry him through any position that may be assigned him." In fact, John B. Baldwin, former Unionist and delegate to the convention, had also been appointed inspector general of the Confederacy. "But it don't stop here," the Rockbridge soldier sarcastically noted. "Augusta must be treble loaded with rank and titles."[125]

Michael G. Harman had been appointed Baldwin's lieutenant colonel. Harman, a self-made entrepreneur, hotel owner, planter, large-scale slaveowner, and prominent Douglas Democrat, had already been made quartermaster general for western Virginia. It was over his name that recruiting posters went out all over the Valley. "By his flaming proclamations," the Rockbridge man caustically observed, Harman had already "made himself familiar as household words to all the people of West Augusta and a thousand other Western places besides, under his stirring appeals and over his flaming signature of 'Quartermaster and Major Commanding.' " Now Harman had been given another plum position, "so that Mike can rise in his stirrups, mount a new shoulder strap and equestrianize through the thoroughfares of Staunton with Ostrich feather streaming out behind and a longer title floating out before." Why not go the whole way, the critic asked, and make Mike Harman "revered as Lord of Augusta and Duke of Staunton?" Such complaints mattered. Virginia leaders could not afford to ignore local leaders and local feelings. Soon John D. Ross of Rockbridge was named major of the 52d Virginia.[126]

Augusta had acquitted itself well in the first test of loyalty to the Confederacy. Despite all the votes for Unionists at every stage of the conflict, the commencement of war changed the calculus. The border had shifted. Virginia had become capital of the new nation, the center of attention, the likely battlefield. "Abolition foes" threatened Virginia soil, and people had to stand together, just as their ancestors had. Augusta's white men joined the Confederacy in large numbers and with a burning desire to fight. Loyalties could change to fit the times.

DESPITE ALL THE FINE WORDS, conflict appeared in every facet of mobilization for war in Franklin County. Were the men in Franklin's

Camp Slifer well fed by J. Allison Eyster, who seemed "indefatigable in his exertions to procure the best produce our market affords suitable for soldiers fare"? Or perhaps people should believe the visitor who reported that "a great deal of the bread is of very poor quality, and in many cases, the men have not enough, even of that."[127] Were the men above petty concerns for their own comfort and welfare or were they in fact already warning that if the food did not get better, "they should return to their homes whenever their three months of enlistment are up"?[128]

Were the soldiers respectful to residents or should accounts of soldiers bullying old men lead citizens to question "the morals or bravery of some of the troops stationed here"?[129] Could it be true that a soldier had threatened to break down the door of a good citizen's house if he were not let in?[130] Had the men of the Federal army, unified by "integrity, intelligence, and patriotism," cast away the old bonds of party, or did Democratic newspapers across the North in fact still make "invidious slurs upon the Republican party," holding it "responsible for the war now forced upon us"?[131]

The Democrats railed at the attempts by the Republicans to use the war to suppress free speech. "Talk gently of the slaveholding South, whisper softly of despotic Russia," the Democrats hissed, "for here exists in the so-called free North today a petty tyranny of opinion and expression, which outrivals in its malignant hatred of free institutions and popular government, the worst despotism of ancient or modern times." The Democrats sarcastically observed that in the United States of 1861 "to discuss the action of the government renders our citizens 'traitors,' to seek to bring back our rulers to their constitutional duty and to make them respect their solemn oath, is to 'give aid and comfort to the rebels.' "[132]

Many Northern Democrats still talked of peace even though war seemed an inevitability by late June, when thousands of troops poured through Chambersburg, "We owe it not only to the South, but to ourselves, to see to it before we proceed further, that we have not fallen short of our constitutional obligations," the *Valley Spirit* dared suggest. The Democrats found it "clear that the great mass of the Southern people believe that they are warring for their just rights," for "it is impossible that such unanimity could be the result of anything but a deep conviction of the justice of their cause." The *Spirit* wanted to show "these honest but misguided people that we intend no infringement of their rights." Despite secession and military mobilization, the Democrats still supported a congressional compromise to work out things peacefully. Surely, they argued, "the glory of preserving the Union would be all the greater if we could preserve it without bloodshed." They, like their Republican neighbors, thought the Union would triumph, but the Democrats were not so sure that "the conquest of the South" would be "a mere frolic for our soldiers."[133]

The nature of the enemy seemed uncertain, even to the Republicans. Had the majority of Southern whites been dragged, against their goodwill, good judgment, and true wishes, into the war by scheming demagogues so that "many loyal hearts still beat beneath Southern bosoms"? If so, that meant that the "warfare upon the Rebellion in their midst" should be "characterized by humanity and magnanimity as our cause is by justice and fidelity."[134] Or was the Confederacy in fact unified by its villainy top to bottom, worthy only of contempt, "their own masses—rude, ignorant, coarse, and in many cases, desperate and semi-barbarous," the willing prey of lying secessionists? If so, war would have to be unrelenting. The Union had to prepare simultaneously to dispense mercy and exact vengeance.[135]

TENSIONS BETWEEN BLACKS and whites in Franklin flared almost immediately in response to the coming war. "A pair of drunken negroes" entered a confectionery store in Chambersburg, the Republican paper reported, "and after purchasing a few nick-nacks, proceeded to make themselves quite familiar in their remarks, when the woman requested them to leave the store." The incident was not crime as usual, the paper thought, but had a political meaning. The black men retorted "that in these times every one expressed their opinions, and they would express theirs. They became so outrageous as to draw a pistol and threaten her life." The white woman eventually called on a neighbor, and "the rascals were driven off, making threats against her, and swearing that they had a right to cut whosoever's throat they pleased."[136]

Relations between local black people and white soldiers grew desperate. One Saturday in May 1861, weeks after Fort Sumter and the confrontation in the confectionery store, a group of soldiers, apparently in search of whiskey, went to the home of Frank Jones, a mulatto man who lived outside Chambersburg. Jones was working in his garden when his wife answered the door. The soldiers demanded entry, and when Mrs. Jones resisted, they sought to push their way in and fired a gun through the window. Jones, running into his house, grabbed his shotgun and fired at one of the men as the band burst through the door. Soldiers hit Mrs. Jones in the face and "knocked the children about." In the struggle Jones shot a second soldier in the leg. A crowd swarmed around the house. Soldiers, infuriated at the sight of their wounded compatriots, rushed Jones, shouting, "Kill the nigger." Jones ran three-quarters of a mile to the home of Franklin's prosecuting attorney, George Eyster, where he hid in a chimney.[137]

The soldiers caught up with Jones and told Mrs. Eyster they wanted to take him to jail. A lieutenant who had pursued Jones from his home, however, ordered the soldiers to step aside. He then shot Jones point-blank in the chest. The black man tried to escape, but the lieutenant shot him four more times in the back while another soldier beat him over the head with a heavy club and others bayoneted him. Jones "was a long time dying." He cried "piteously," but the lieutenant and soldiers refused "any one to afford him any relief." A "large and excited crowd" gathered and threatened "to burn the body, quarter it, &c. Several shots, one of which accidentally struck a soldier in the right groin, inflicting a severe wound, were fired, at the dead body." After others mutilated the body, the prosecuting attorney persuaded a superior officer to dispatch men to take the body to the jail to protect it. Jones's twenty wounds included one from a sword, "passing through the arm, entering the chest, breaking a rib, and then deeply penetrating the lung."[138]

What had Frank Jones done to unleash such fury among the men of the U.S. Army? A neighbor had been selling whiskey. Jones, "fearing disturbance from it, entered complaint against him for selling liquor without license." The customers for that whiskey, the *Dispatch* dryly related, "finding their supply cut off, swore vengeance against Jones." Neither of Chambersburg's papers offered editorial comment on the murder.[139]

These accounts of the murder of Frank Jones appeared alongside articles that told of fugitive slaves flooding across the border into the North. Hundreds were already coming through Philadelphia. The former slaves understood the opportunity the chaos of war offered; they escaped at the first evidence of overt conflict between the North and the South. The runaways "exhibit a consummate knowledge of the questions at issue," the *Dispatch* reported, and "are ready to make use of any exigency that may arrive." Yet the enslaved people who fled into Franklin County hardly found an antislavery haven. A runaway slave woman had already been captured in Chambersburg by a constable and thrown into jail.[140]

Slaves seized the first opportunity for freedom below the border, when the Union took Fort Monroe on the Virginia coast. "As our readers are aware, numbers of slaves have been escaping from their masters, and taken refuge with Major General Butler, since his occupation of Fortress Monroe," the *Dispatch* reported. "In many cases their reputed owners have asked their delivery under the Fugitive Slave Law." Butler promptly returned slaves to owners who took the oath of allegiance to the government of the United States but kept slaves from owners who refused to adopt the oath. Butler put the fugitive slaves—"contrabands," he called them, property seized in war—to work in his camp. Simon Cameron, former Republican senator from Pennsylvania and now Lincoln's secretary of war, approved of Butler's plan. The ultimate fate of the escaped slaves would be "reserved for future determination."[141]

Slaves who were freed, Republican papers argued, should be colonized if they so chose. "The expense wouldn't be formidable" during wartime. "From military 'lines' established near Charleston, Savannah, Mobile, New Orleans, &c., into which the contraband negroes would flock, they might be 'sluiced off' to St. Domingo or Central America, with great rapidity and economy." Such a plan would have two crucial advantages for the North: it "would quiet any sensitiveness in relation to a too sudden and great increase of our free negro population," and "no question of constitutionality can be raised, as the war power covers the case."[142] The opportunity for which whites had longed, to purge their nation of black people, suddenly presented itself. President Lincoln found the idea of colonization appealing.

Despite such plans, the role of slavery in the war remained unclear. Were the people of Franklin to listen to the *New York Tribune*, which argued that "even those who are moved by no higher motive than a desire to be relieved from an agitation which, for a whole generation, has absorbed so much of the time, talents, and temper of the country, eagerly hail the present exigency as the Heaven-ordained opportunity for striking an exterminating blow at the root of the evil"?[143] Or should they listen to their own *Dispatch*? It argued that slavery "is not a question for the North but for the South. Let it be our business to preserve our own liberties, by sustaining our Constitutional Government, and let the adjustment of the Slavery Question be an after consideration, or find its own adjustment."[144] Northerners spoke of the "future determination" and "adjustment" of slavery because Northern attitudes toward slavery remained profoundly unsettled.

Although only a few minor battles had been fought by the early summer of 1861, and none in a place where slavery was strong, the North was already hearing of the determined desire of the enslaved to be free. "The ebony 'contrabands' are everywhere to be seen," a letter from a soldier at Fortress Monroe reported back to Franklin in early July. "The one to whose skill my boots owe their extravagant polish says his master left him, and he had no alternative but to come to the fortress," the Union soldier joked. The apparently requisite stereotypical humor out of the way, the white man from Franklin reported that the escaped slave "thinks the cause of the North eminently just, and agrees with one of his dark companions in expressing an earnest desire that Jeff. Davis may be roasted alive." Despite the slaves' thoroughly political act of escape and these thoroughly political words, the Northern soldier imagined that the enslaved people did not really understand what was going on. "The contraband women and children occupy an old house near the fortress and laugh and sing away the long warm days in blissful ignorance of the magnitude of the contest of which their race is the innocent cause."[145] Maybe something other than ignorance lifted their hearts.

THE EDITORS OF Augusta's newspapers now talked of slavery only metaphorically. They spoke of Northern newspapers muzzled by the Republicans, by "the tyrants who would enslave them" and of Northern citizens afraid to speak their mind who thus "must become slaves, in order to enjoy exemption from molestation." They quoted a New York Democratic paper raging against the Republicans, who, "getting into power under the pretence or regard for the negro, had riveted the chains of slavery upon millions of white men." The Augusta editors argued that the Northern armies "have invaded to subjugate and destroy an innocent people. Our enslavement is their object." The white people of Augusta and the South remained resolutely silent about the real slavery over which they presided, a slavery whose centrality in the Confederacy and secession they had freely acknowledged over the preceding two years.[146]

For their part, some enslaved Virginians seized, and created, every kind of opportunity for a measure of freedom, even at great cost to themselves. The *Vindicator* coolly told the story of an enslaved woman in Augusta County, a "fine looking negro woman aged about 28 years, belonging to Mr. Joseph Cline, living about four miles from Staunton." Cline, for whom a company had been named in the 52d Virginia, owned seven slaves, three male and four female; six of them were mulatto, including, presumably, this "fine looking" woman. "Becoming unruly, he determined to bring her to town and sell her. While she was going to get her clothes, she picked up an axe which she had concealed, and deliberately cut off three of her fingers, taking two licks at them. She was brought to town, placed in jail, and her hand was dressed by Dr. Baldwin. She did the act for the double purpose of preventing her sale and taking revenge upon her master."[147]

Such business was distasteful and thus not dwelt upon. Both the *Spectator* and the *Vindicator* preferred articles attesting to the gratitude with which the enslaved people of Virginia viewed slavery. A tribute to a beloved elderly slave showed how it was done. "Old Uncle Frederick Hill, for a number of years a servant at the Hospital at this place, died one day last week," the *Vindicator* intoned. "Uncle Frederick was as regular in his visits to the Vindicator office, every Saturday, as clock work, until the past month, during which time he was too feeble. His funeral was largely attended by colored and white persons and as much respect paid his memory as if he had been one of our most respected citizens. Frederick was truly a pious man, and one of the most faithful servants we have ever known."[148]

Despite such reassuring episodes, the black people of Augusta weighed on the minds of white citizens caught up in the political turmoil of 1861. "There are a number of free negroes about town, who are not registered, and consequently have no business here," the *Vindicator* complained. "It is duty of the proper authorities to forthwith commence the correction of the serious evil by notifying them to leave, or suffer the penalty imposed by law of remaining."[149] The paper may have had in mind the eighteen former slaves who had been freed by Elizabeth Via's will four years earlier. The court had refused them permission to stay in Virginia, yet they remained. Two weeks later the county court clerk listed them in the registry but noted that they were "without leave to remain in this State." The clerk, John Imboden, acknowledged no last names for the free black people, nine males and nine females, whose ages were sixty-five, thirty, twenty-eight, twenty-six, twenty-four, twenty-two, twelve, eleven, ten, eight, six, four, three, two, twenty months, and eighteen months.[150] Perhaps these free black people, who had ignored the law for four years, managed to evade it once more in the confusion of the spring of 1861, when Imboden ran for delegate to the secession convention and then became swept up in military planning. They were not mentioned again in the registry.

The article that complained of unregistered free blacks complained about slaves and lax masters as well. "Another source of great annoyance to our town is the policy of permitting slaves to hire their own time, or get persons to stand as their masters. The habit induces idleness among slaves, and is the cause of all kinds of trafficing among them, which is more or less connected with petty thefts. These evils should be radically corrected without delay. The quicker the better."[151] The *Spectator* posted a notice from the Augusta County jailer reporting that the Staunton jail held three runaways from Richmond. The paper noted that the "owners of said Negroes are requested to come forward, prove property, pay charges, and take away, else they will be dealt with as the law directs." The law directed that the men would be sold, notwithstanding their claims of being free.[152] While the political crisis swept up Augusta, slavery ground on.

7

AUGUSTA VOLUNTEERS FORMED eight new companies for the 5th Virginia with names devoted to their neighborhood and their weapons: the Mountain Guard, Southern Guard, Augusta Greys, West View Infantry, Staunton Rifles, Augusta Rifles, Ready Rifles, and West Augusta Guard. Other men went into the Staunton Artillery, the "Valley Rangers" (Company E of the 1st Virginia Cavalry), or the Churchville Cavalry and Valley Cavalry of the 14th Virginia Cavalry. Most came into Staunton to join, but others went to the smaller towns nearby, especially Waynesboro and Fishersville in eastern Augusta. Men enlisted in groups, in dozens at a time or two and three together. Within two weeks of secession, nearly eight hundred Augusta men had joined the Confederate army for three months. About one hundred served in the artillery, three hundred in the cavalry, and four hundred in the infantry.

The trip to Harpers Ferry proved exciting and memorable for the soldiers. Michael Reid Hanger, a twenty-year-old carpenter from Staunton, working in Lexington when the war began, enlisted as soon as possible. He and his comrades were "put up at the Va House got breakfast and Asbury McCluerer & my self went to see some ladies came back at 10 oclock AM." That evening "we started out was Escorted out of town with the band of musick & we all got aboard of stages hacks and prseeded to Mt Sidney got there at dark." The new soldiers "had quite a nice time of it" the next day as well. "Our lady Acquaintences they were so verry Agreeable that I hated verry much to part with them though we bid them Adieu." Hanger and his comrades took "the cars" most of the way north but marched eighteen miles near Winchester, finally arriving at Harpers Ferry.[153]

William Francis Brand—Willie, he was called by those who knew him—joined Company E of the 5th Virginia on April 18. Relatively tall at five feet ten inches, with blue eyes and dark hair, the twenty-year-old miller struck a handsome pose in his new uniform. The second of four brothers of a middling nonslaveholding farmer from Greenville in Augusta, Willie Brand wrote to Amanda Catherine ("Kate") Armentrout back home in the first weeks after his departure with his new unit. The 5th had enjoyed a glorious journey up to Harpers Ferry. "The Ladies all along the road seemed so pleasant that it cheered us onward thare hankerchiefs ware continually waveing & we generally gave them three loud cheers."

When time for the official vote for secession arrived on May 23, Willie Brand told Kate, "all of the Augusta grays voted for secession but two & they did not vote. fifteen or twenty of us was not old enough but our Capt told us to vote if we could & every one of us voted. one of our low life men talked like he wold oppose our votes and the gentle man was about to get him self in to business he got so bad scared that he went and voted for secession." Brand had grown to despise the Yankees. "It will not be long I hope until we shall soundly whip the deamons of the North for the blood thirsy villions has invaded our soil at different points & taken property & searched houses for money." He fretted over how hard it was to keep the Sabbath, with all the cardplaying and other temptations, but reading the Bible with a mess mate "seemed to revive my low spirits. I shall ever put my trust in the lord who is able to do what so ever he will."[154]

Soldiers kept their promise to write, and so did their families. Thomas Smiley, a nineteen-year-old who had signed up in Company D on the first day of recruitment, came from a typical Augusta family. Like three-fourths of white families in the county, the Smileys owned no slaves, but they did own a farm whose 150 improved acres produced corn, wheat, oats, and rye as well as twelve cattle, ten sheep, seven horses, and seven pigs. The farm was worth about fifty-five hundred dollars. Thomas had two younger sisters, Mary and Latitia; the family of five was about average for Augusta.

When Thomas's mother wrote him a few days after his departure, she had only one thing on her mind, her son's salvation. "It is with a trembling hand and a sad heart that I take this pencil in my hand to drop you a line but fearing that I may never have another opportunity I will exort

Thomas and Mary Smiley

you once more to put your trust in the mighty god of Jacob take Jesus Christ for your Saviour and then if you ever fall in the battle field you will still be safe." In case these words did not comfort her young son, Mrs. Smiley added that "there has been much fervent prayer offered for you and the dear friends who has gone from amongst us. O will you not pray for yourself. Nothing more." His aunt Ellen joined in the crusade to make sure Thomas knew Christ. "It is seldom that I employ the sacred hours of the Sabbath in writing letters. But as this may be the only opportunity I shall have of writing to you I feel as if I cannot let it pass," his aunt began. "Meet God you must, whether prepared or unprepared and how soon you know not. Death may summon you to his presence." If that chilling image proved inadequate to push Thomas into action, perhaps guilt would: "I am not the only one that feels deep solicitude for you. Your dear Mother told me the night you left home If I only had good evidence of Thomas being a true Christian it would make parting much easier." Thomas wrote back politely but did not mention religion.[155]

Mary, his sixteen-year-old sister, wrote different kinds of letters. It was not that she did not care about religion. She reported that "Providence congregation looked sadder last Sabbath than it has done for many a long day," and she bragged that she did especially well in her Sunday school lessons. Mary acknowledged too that Thomas might not return. "Farewell dear brother. do your duty as a soldier and as a man and if I never see you again may we meet above." But she seemed more interested in other things going on in the community.[156]

Mary Smiley, unlike the adults who talked in hushed tones about anything to do with slavery or the black people in their midst, was direct. "There has been a Home Guard formed around here and I suppose it is needed for some of the negroes are not to be trusted even around here and then they are backed by some of the mean white folks," Mary wrote. The Home Guard was a sort of military police force created to keep order. Already whites worried about their slaves and distrusted their neighbors; quick and rough justice would keep both in line.[157] Mary passed on a letter from their young cousin Maggie, who saw the purpose of the war with a stark racial clarity. She declared: "If I was a man I would take none of the *negro lovers* prisoners I would do my best to kill the last one of them."[158]

Young women participated vicariously in the war. "Thomas have you received your secession badge yet Hannah was telling us that she had made one for you," Mary wrote of the contribution from another cousin. Mary apparently admired the patch, but "Ma told her she ought not to have done it as it would be a mark for the enemy to shoot at."[159] Mary had no such fear, and she laughed at Lincoln's message to Congress. He "says that a majority of the people in all the Seceded States are in favor of the Union. What a fool and I hope to his sorrow he may find it out."[160]

Mary sternly patrolled the boundaries of loyalty in the community. She shed no tears when their pastor was driven away. "Dr. Junkin preached at Providence Sunday his last sermon there I expect. I believe he said he was coming to preach to the *rebels* so I have heard. He had to resign at the college on account of his union sentiments and he has started for Philadelphia this morning."[161] Mary reported with disgust that some of their neighbors, especially the Hutchens family, a household of ten with children the same age as Mary and Thomas, still held to the Union. "Hutchens are all unionists I belive even to the women. Some of us got to arguing with Eliza yesterday but we might as well have tried to make her believe that the sun shines in the night as to make a secessionist of her, and this is the way with all the unionists." Even some of Thomas's best friends in the army had close relatives of dubious loyalty. "Tell John Beard he must try to make a secessionist of his father and

Sam," Mary admonished her brother.[162] Mary had heard of a company in which the Confederate oath of allegiance was accepted by all but two members, one of whom was a captain who "says he is too religious to fight—he won't fight against his relatives who are nearly all in the North. That if he went he wouldn't fire a ball at the Yankees and that he didn't know whether he would take his company North or South. Don't you think he ought to have the words Traitor to his country, branded on his fore head, as heretick was branded on in ancient times?"[163]

These young women resented local boys and men who shirked their duty, whatever the cause. Mary's aunts "have been telling us that John Berry has got home. I do think it is a shame that he has got off on the plea of bad health. it makes the balance of us dissatisfied. I hope his father will get a good scolding. I think it is very dishonorable for him to get off that way when others in that company are as weakly as John and others are going away that *are* in bad health."[164] Thomas's cousin Hannah was even less charitable. "I suppose you have heard that Bill Anderson started away with the troop and went as far as Staunton and was taken sick. I expect he wanted some excuse to get back home anyhow. I tell you I don't believe in cowardice (in time of war no way) and we have too much of this great evil about here. If I were a man I would have gone long before this and would now be serving my country." Brave young men like Thomas, on the other hand, could take heart from the reception they would get from patriotic young women. "If you all ever return I have no doubt but you will be considered great and learned men. I guess every girl would fight for a soldier and me with the rest."[165] Women, long the symbols and advocates of Union, seemed to convert their loyalties to the Confederacy even faster than men. Young women may have been the most ardent Rebels of all in 1861. John Imboden proudly described his young wife, Mary, as "a red hot Southern Confederacy woman."[166]

News from the front made it home in a matter of days and then circulated quickly. "Ma says that if you have any thing rather private to write home to write it on a slip of paper and put it in as your letters are read or heard by a great many," Mary warned Thomas. "Every one is anxious to hear the news from the camp."[167] News went the other way as well. Thomas's mother sent him copies of the *Spectator*: "I will send you two Staunton papers you will find a piece in each marked which I want you to read."[168] When Thomas got the measles and did not tell his family, they found out anyway. "We hear that you are sick, in the hospital with the measles," his sister upbraided him. "We heard that you were sick from letters that were written to people out of the neighborhood. You I suppose meant it for the best not to let us know that you were sick, but I say never do that way again, truth is always better than uncertainty."[169]

The correspondents of John McGuffin, a twenty-three-year-old clerk in the 5th Virginia, were women in his family, a cousin from neighboring Albemarle County and his mother. Those women mixed political messages with messages of personal concern. "John be careful of your moustache, goatee imperial & whiskers if you do go. I could not bear for you to write me that one of old Abe's men had deprived you of a part of them," his cousin, a schoolteacher, kidded him. "Putting all jesting aside, I fear you will have to go. How much I dread it." Unlike some women, this female correspondent was hardly bellicose. "I entertain the hope that we will only have a brush & all will be restored to peace & harmony again. What a state of affairs! Our quiet Union the envy of the old countries broken in pieces." What made the division so painful was the way it had come, "First one corner & then another, scale by scale. Not by one unanimous & universal crack, as if done by men blindfolded, but inch by inch here a little & there a little with their eyes open to its awful effect." Despite the penetrating comment, this young woman quickly dismissed her insight and replaced it with feeling. "I am not a great hand on 'politics' but my 'war' calls forth my every sentiment & exercises my every nerve."[170]

John McGuffin's mother felt the war deeply as well. "Every person old & Young Man Woman and children being anxious to hear the news from the army of Harpers Ferry and other points. We are full of excitement and prayers are daily & hourly offered for the preservation of our brave soldiers." His mother's letter was filled with news of the few men in the Valley who dared vote against secession on May 23, for "to find a Union man would be a wonder." She told of a supposed spy jailed in Staunton.[171]

The boundary between the war and home blurred in these early days. No one had any idea of what to expect from a civil war. "Every person is putting his house in order about here so that when called by our Governor they will be prepared to take up arms in our Common defense," McGuffin's mother told him. "Our Crops are looking finely better than for some years so that Mr. Lincoln will find it about as hard to starve us out as it will be to whip us into terms." She, like everyone else, hung on every report and dreaded the worst. "I am the more anxious at present for the reason that we have just heard the report of another battle at Shepperdstown where you are, and that your Co. was engaged in it, hence my writing before I again heard from you." She apologized for writing twice before he had a chance to reply, but she could not help herself.[172] When John responded, she was "truly grateful" and swore not to believe everything she heard, for "it is no use believing any reports now."[173]

While they waited, the women of Augusta threw themselves into the cause. Young ladies who had cheered for Bell and waved handkerchiefs for the Union a few months earlier now sewed uniforms for the volunteers, "scarcely permitting twenty-four hours to pass after the order had been placed in their hands, ere the full uniform, neatly made, was presented to the young soldier." The young girls "entwined their brows with glorywreaths of evergreen, which beautifully reflect the fresh and buoyant courage of their hearts." Looking upon these acts of devotion from the young, the *Vindicator* quietly intoned, "God bless the sweet girls, and God speed and protect the brave boys."[174]

Thomas Smiley's aunt told him that the ladies of her rural neighborhood "have been sewing for more than a week fitting out Mr. Curry's company. I think they ought to be well fitted out as they have had 4 and sometimes 5 sewing machines employed besides a number sewing by hand."[175] Some of the sewing projects sounded less than promising. "Some of the Ladyes are making soldiers cloakes out of their Piano covers," Smiley's mother wrote. "I have none but I will send you one of my oil cloth table covers; which I want you to spread down when you have to make your bed on the ground. It will keep the dampness from you. I want you also to wear it around you when you stand guard when it is raining."[176]

Alansa Sterrett sewed so much that she became ill and had to set her diary aside. But she did record one event because it was so humiliating. Her new husband, Frank Sterrett, wrote with embarrassment from the mountains to admit that the enemy had "surprised the 'Rebs' so suddenly that his Cavalry Co. had to make precipitate flight, leaving behind horses, tents and baggage." The Northern press exulted in what it called the Philippi Races because the Confederates ran so fast from that place. Alansa blushed to read that "among the 'spoils' was Frank's valise, and the following day one of *my letters* was published in the 'Wheeling Intelligencer' headed 'A model love-letter'! A very aggravating and mortifying fact to Frank and me!" As a result, Frank "asked me to burn every letter of his and all he should write me thereafter! That was a heart breaking request, but he declared he should destroy all of mine." Alansa decided to meet the spirit, if not the fact, of his request while saving "my precious war-treasures. Put them in a close wooden box and secreted the box under one of the floor-planks of the attic at Loch Willow." When Frank wrote again, however, and asked if she had burned his letters, "I had to confess what I had done and Frank said it would not be safe to leave them there." Alansa complied with his wishes.[177]

THROUGHOUT JULY TROOPS from Augusta marched, maneuvered, waited, rushed, camped, and broke camp along the northern border of Virginia. They faced U.S. troops under the command of General George McClellan, a cocky and inspiring young veteran of the Mexican War, a military observer in the Crimean War, and the president of the Ohio and Mississippi Railroad. McClellan's Army of Occupation put three brigades against Confederate forces that sought to bottle up the Yankees in northwestern Virginia, sealing off turnpikes, passes, and the Baltimore and Ohio Railroad. The Confederates feared that the Federals would rush down into the Valley.

Michael Reid Hanger, the twenty-one-year-old carpenter from Augusta, recorded each movement in his diary. There was some fighting early on, with a few of his friends wounded and a number of Union prisoners taken, but he spent most of his time in preparation for battles that did not come. One day "we remained in line of battle for an hour or two, and finding that the Yankes were not coming, we retired from the field, and went to cooking supper." The next day, he wrote laconically, "we are now drawn up and I think we are going to Winchester, though it is hard to tell." Usually not one to complain, Hanger admitted that "we are all very tired and very much fatigued. We left behind us beautiful fields of wheat, already cut and shocked which I suppose will all be destroyed by the enemy." The waste was painful to behold.[178]

Virtually every day saw Hanger and his fellows moved from one place to another in a restless anticipation of the enemy. Both sides wanted to control the crucial rivers, bridges, roads, and railroads between the northern end of the Valley and Washington, D.C. The Confederates had retreated from Harpers Ferry south into the Valley near Winchester. The Union hoped to drive them deeper into the Valley so that another Union force could separate them from a Confederate force east of the mountains at Manassas. The Union wanted to protect Washington and take Richmond, recently made the capital of the Confederacy, before the Confederate Congress could meet on July 20. The Confederates, for their part, wanted to keep pressure on Washington and be ready to help defend their own capital. Spies, male and female, worked throughout the contested area, carrying word of movements. Neither army was really ready to fight, but the political pressures mounted. Maybe a convincing battle would cause the other side to give in.

John Lightner watched the mounting war fever with mixed feelings and unusual honesty. Back at Washington College in May the nineteen-year-old Lightner had written Kate Armentrout in Augusta that "I hardly know what to write about, for you hear nothing but war, war, all the time. People are entirely too much taken up with the excitement." Lightner came from a prosperous slaveholding family in Augusta and showed promising signs as a student. Despite his religious reservations about war and the emotions it unleashed, he enlisted in the Confederacy in June. A week later, now a private in the 4th Virginia Infantry posted near the Potomac River, "I met with a great many of my old acquaintances, in the different regiments stationed here, which makes it more pleasant than it otherwise would be," he wrote Kate. "They all seem very cheerful and lively, and most too anxious to come into deadly conflict with their enemy. I know I don't want to fight. I'm a great lover of peace, and would give a million, if I had it, to be in Lincoln's position one day, peace would come if I could bring it. I abhor the idea of war, and believed once that it was morally wrong on all occasions." Recent events had changed his mind, however, for "this war is certainly a holy and great one, on our side; the other is none else than unconstitutional, brought on by wicked usurpation of power." He was to fight with a clear conscience until he died that February of typhoid fever.[179]

Measles and typhoid fever raced through the ranks of men who had not had the illnesses as children and thus held no immunity. Of one Augusta County company of fewer than one hundred men, twenty-one lay in Winchester hospitals in the summer of 1861. Three were to die in July, five more in August, seven more in September. Some made it home before they died of fever or pneumonia; others died in camp.

The *Spectator* hungrily printed reports of the gallantry of Augusta men on the scattered battlefields of the early war. With only skirmishes occurring, people could dwell on each act of gallantry and every loss. After a conflict at Falling Waters, an anonymous Augusta man wrote to tell the people back home of the deeds he had seen. Captain O. Grinnan, formerly a twenty-five-year-old professor at Jed Hotchkiss's Loch Willow school, "fought like a Trojan, and his zeal was emulated by the youngest member of the Company, and it was with great difficulty the Company could be induced to retreat at all. All will concur with me that Old Augusta has had no cause to blush for any of her sons on this field."

One man had died in that battle: George Rupe, "a most worthy, industrious and excellent young man, who displayed a noble and unselfish spirit in his last moments, when he urged his four comrades who were carrying him out of the field, 'to let him alone and make their escape, twas better to leave a dying man to his fate, than four should be killed to save him.' " Rupe was thirty-one, a bachelor carpenter who had lived with another young carpenter and his small family. "His comrades will keep green his memory."[180] This was what people had imagined war might be like: selfless charges, brave leadership, and ennobling death, duly recorded and mourned.

The northwestern area of Virginia bore great military, political, and symbolic importance. Much of the Baltimore and Ohio Railroad ran through the region, which also contained the largest concentration of Southern Unionists accessible to Northern aid and support. The valleys and passes of the mountains offered potential paths for armies into the rich Shenandoah Valley and from there into Richmond itself. Everyone expected some of the war's first and most important fighting to take place in western Virginia.

Unionists rebelled in the far northwestern part of the state, on the border with Pennsylvania and Ohio. "Since the action of the convention, handing the state of Virginia over to the confederate states, without the knowledge or consent of the people, like a lot of herds or slaves," a friend from Morgantown wrote Alexander Stuart, "the excitement in N.W. Virginia, is becoming most intense, and, indeed, in some quarters, terrible." So furious were the Unionists that "the clamor here for a division of the state is becoming loud and universal. I fear it will become uncontrollable."[181] Conflict between eastern and western Virginia, fueled for generations by struggles over taxation, representation in the legislature, support for railroads and canals, and perceived arrogance in the east, broke into the open when secession forced people to declare their loyalties. Some people in the northwestern part of the state saw an opportunity to take control of their own political destiny by rejecting secession.

Unionist sentiment did not dominate all of the west, however. In fact, in the secession vote of May 23 all but four thousand of the thirty-four thousand votes against secession in the western part of the state came from the extreme northwest. Southern papers claimed, with reason, that the presence of U.S. forces along the Ohio River encouraged men in that section to support the Union and reject the Confederacy. Secessionists did much better, often triumphing, where no Union army lay and where self-interest and loyalty were far less obvious in the large area that bordered the Shenandoah Valley.[182]

Given the presence of secessionist feeling in western Virginia, the task of the Union soldiers there, General McClellan announced to his men, was to "restore peace and confidence, to protect the majesty of the law, and to rescue our brethren from the grasp of armed traitors."[183] By July the Union general had twenty thousand men with him, some guarding the B&O Railroad, some protecting Charleston, but most pressing in on Confederate forces. The Southerners had only forty-five thousand men to resist McClellan.

Jed Hotchkiss chose this threatening time to offer his services to the Confederate army. Hotchkiss, a thirty-one year-old man born in New York, had been keeping his school in northern Augusta County going for the first few months of the war. But in June, after many of his students and fellow teachers had left, Hotchkiss set out for the mountains of western Virginia, where the 52d Virginia Infantry and the 14th Virginia Cavalry encamped not far from Augusta. A man of great energy and skill in surveying and drawing, he was hoping to work as an engineer or topographer. His first letters described the landscape with the close attention of the amateur botanist. "The sides of the mountains are finely variegated with the flowers of the laurel, snow white, and the deep yellow evening primrose," he wrote his wife. The tall mountains to the west of Augusta "milk the clouds, for the dew covers everything like a rain, it looks beautiful on the leaves."[184]

Despite his Northern origins, relatives, and friends, Hotchkiss believed in the Southern cause. "All we ask of the North is to be left alone in the enjoyment of inherited rights," he told his wife in one of his first letters home. "We shall surely conquer but Oh how many precious lives must be lost, & how many homes made desolate before the end shall come." He had faith "in the God of justice to vindicate our cause."[185]

No sooner had Hotchkiss arrived at camp in the mountains than a Union force attacked at Rich Mountain, driving most of the Confederates from their positions. On July 10, McClellan turned Brigadier General William Rosecrans, one of his favorites, against the Southerners at Rich Mountain. The Federals, coming around the side of the mountain through the brush, brambles, rocks, and ravines without the sound of an ax, surprised the Virginia men and drove them from the summit. The next day Rosecrans pursued the Confederates through the Cheat River valley in a driving rain that mired down the Southerners' supply train in thick mud. The Rebels lost their general, Robert S. Garnett, when a bullet struck him in the back; he was the first officer on either side to die in the Civil War. The Federals captured 555 men.[186]

Augusta men were caught in the defeat at Rich Mountain. The United States captured sixteen men, three more suffered wounds, and one, James Wilson, died. Wilson, a twenty-six year-old farmhand, a private in the 14th Virginia Cavalry, was the eldest of several brothers of a "most respectable" family with ten thousand dollars of real property and one slave. Soon after Wilson's death, his father appeared at the quartermaster's office in Staunton to ask if a gun could be supplied for a son joining the Churchville Cavalry. "Some one present asked if another son belonging to the same company had not been killed by the enemy at Rich

Mountain. 'Yes,' said the gentleman with emotion, 'and his brother goes to take his place.' "[187]

Thoughtful people might worry about the safety of Staunton itself. Michael G. Harman, a prominent Staunton Democrat businessman before the war and now a prominent quartermaster and recruiter, wrote General Robert E. Lee an alarming letter in the wake of Rich Mountain. Harman urged Lee to fortify the western border of the Valley as soon as possible. Not only did the Federal troops present a military threat there, but "I would urge upon you the great importance of keeping the enemy from ever touching this country, for Union men, in great numbers, would be found here in this county, and other counties in the valley, if the Federal troops were here in force to protect them." Despite the nearly unanimous vote for the secession ordinance, Unionism still ran deep in Augusta, Harman warned. "It is necessary, to keep all our people loyal, to keep the enemy from having an opportunity to tamper with many of them. Of course, I would not express this opinion where it would be spoken of, as it would have a bad effect; but I assure you it is nevertheless true."[188]

One of the staunchest Unionists, however, threw himself into support for the Confederacy and thought that Michael Harman damaged the cause with his frantic and rough recruiting. Alexander H. H. Stuart wrote the Confederate secretary of war to urge him to put "a military officer of intelligence and character in command of the post. Everything is now in the hands of the quartermaster, M. G. Harman, who is a civilian unacquainted with military law or usages, and who has rendered himself exceedingly obnoxious to officers and soldiers." If the secretary would send an agent to look into matters in Staunton, he "would learn things that would surprise you. The officer in command here should be a calm, dignified man, who would possess the confidence of the public. The expenditures at this point are enormous and the public interests would not suffer from being vigilantly looked after." Harman was pushing too hard too fast. "You can scarcely imagine the depth of the feeling occasioned by the call for the militia en masse," Stuart warned. "Men go to the battle-field with very little alacrity when they feel that they leave their wives and children exposed to horrors to which their own perils are as nothing."[189] Staunton and Augusta occupied critical positions for the Confederacy; they would have to be treated with care.

THE NORTH PRESENTED a confusing scene in the summer of 1861. The U.S. army had grown rapidly and with great enthusiasm. A Franklin man in the 2d Regiment Pennsylvania Volunteers wrote home from the unit's posting near Hagerstown to reassure folks back home that "all the boys are in good spirits, and are getting along a great deal better than they expected." Things were looking up, for "now that we have received new pantaloons, of light blue, our appearance is greatly improved." Morale grew strong. "Few men of course feel disposed to rush recklessly into the very jaws of death, but 'conquer or die' is the universal motto among us." His letter ended with bluster: "We wish to spend the Fourth in Virginia, and I hope this wish will be gratified. Instead of firing blank cartridge, we are eager to throw in the solid lead!"[190]

The Union had a great hero in General McClellan, the Young Napoleon. Battles in western Virginia in June and early July at Rich Mountain had shown how fortunate the nation was to claim him as a leader. "Within less than one week he has met and vanquished, a rebel force of at least 10,000 men," boasted Chambersburg's *Dispatch*. "His triumphant message to head quarters is, 'Our success is complete, and Secession is killed in this part of the country.' "[191] Indeed, the North began to think it had perhaps misjudged its enemy. The Southerners seemed cowardly. They had "run" at several battles in western Virginia, and "it really looks as if they were all cowards and not fit to fight with brave men," commented Franklin's Republican paper. "It has been suggested here that the mystic letters of the Virginians, F. F. V., really mean Fast Flying Virginians." The First Families of Virginia, for all their pride, proved weak when tested.[192]

With the armies in the field and the sacrifices already telling at home, the pressures began to build for some kind of decisive action. "On to Richmond!" Northern papers urged. If decisive battles were not won soon, the three-month volunteers from the spring and early summer would be passing out of the army before they had had a chance to fight. If the war were not decided soon, the economic depression that lay across the country North and South would deepen as the fall and winter descended. Abraham Lincoln had to put down the rebellion to keep other border states in the Union, to show that the Confederacy could claim no legitimacy.

At Chambersburg on June 3 Union troops heard an address from their commanding generals as they prepared to head south into Virginia. The soldiers would soon "meet the insurgents" and vanquish "those who have raised their parricidal hands against our country." The U.S. soldiers should have no doubts: "You are not the aggressors." Instead "a turbulent faction, misled by ambitious rulers in a time of profound peace and national prosperity, have occupied your forts and turned the guns against you . . . and now seek to perpetuate a reign of terror over loyal citizens." The troops would be fighting against illegitimate renegades, outlaws. "You are going on American soil, to sustain the civil power, to relieve the oppressed, and to retake that which is unlawfully held." In case anyone thought otherwise, this was not a war against slavery. "You must bear in mind you are going for the good of the whole country, and that while it is your duty to punish sedition, you must protect the loyal, and, should occasion offer, at once suppress servile insurrection." Should the soldiers remember these things, "success will crown your efforts; a grateful country and a happy people will reward you."[193]

Alexander K. McClure entertained Union generals as they headed to Virginia to crush the rebellion. Major General Robert Patterson, a sixty-nine-year-old veteran of the War of 1812, camped on McClure's farm. The young attorney invited the general and his staff to dinner, and they sat on his porch on that "pleasant May evening," smoking cigars and looking out over the lush fields around Chambersburg. Several of the generals and colonels "freely discussed" the "whole question of the war." They eagerly "agreed that it might be necessary to fight one general battle, but beyond that the war could not possibly be extended." The North had the numbers; a victory in that one battle would "inevitably" bring compromise and peace.[194]

Only two men on McClure's porch did not join in the optimism. One, Colonel George H. Thomas, was a Virginian. He warned "how terribly the South was in earnest," McClure observed, "and how desperately its people would fight for their homes." His fellow officers only occasionally asked Colonel Thomas a direct question, "to which he always answered very courteously and without expressing any decided opinion." The other dissenter in the group was General Abner Doubleday (later to be erroneously credited with the invention of baseball), who had been "in immediate intercourse with the Southern people. He declared with great earnestness that if one general battle was fought between the North and the South, it would precipitate the bloodiest war of the century." When Doubleday was called away to his command that evening and left the rest of the party sitting on the porch with their cigars, General Patterson remarked that it was a shame that Doubleday was "gone in the head."[195] Everyone knew the war would be over soon, the Federal army victorious and the Union restored.

The people of Augusta and Franklin did not start the Civil War; Virginia and Pennsylvania did not start the Civil War. Left to themselves, the white people of the border would never have descended into such conflict. But when the war came, they gave themselves to it with a startling passion.

Virginia's decision to secede was simultaneously calculating and high-minded, ideological and emotional. Everyone from the governor down to the average person watched as events slowly unfolded. All had plenty of time to weigh consequences and to listen to the arguments for and against leaving the Union. Despite their proclamations of confidence, however, their language betrayed a people visceral in their fear of invasion, infiltration, and insurrection. Despite their claims of nationalism, they defined their rights in constitutional terms so brittle that Abraham Lincoln seemed destined to offend them unless he capitulated completely to their demands. Despite their calls for peace, they seemed to welcome the catharsis that came with war.

Heckling from the side, the North watched and waited as the Confederacy formed and then grew. It did not take the Southern talk seriously. In their hearts, Northerners too seemed to welcome the culmination of so much talk, the chance to repay so much bragging and threatening. Despite their words, they proved eager to fight the South, eager to put the Slave Power in its place, eager to show what their free society could do. The secret of the Civil War was that many Americans wanted it to come, wanted to prove their patriotism and demonstrate that they held God's favor.

PART THREE

THE SHADOW OF DEATH

SUMMER 1861 TO SUMMER 1862

Yea, though I walk through the valley of the shadow of death,
I will fear no evil: for thou art with me;
thy rod and thy staff they comfort me.

1

War came to Augusta and Franklin like a force of nature, uncontrollable and unpredictable. People in the way were often devastated, swept up, and cast aside, the work of decades destroyed overnight. A place could be safe one day, overwhelmed the next. Attacks could come from any direction. A battle hundreds of miles away could flood a town with men wounded, dying, and dead. No one, including generals and presidents, could tell where the war would be raging a month later. Whether on the home front or on the battlefield, war proved to be nothing like what people had imagined.

In July 1861 armies of thirty-five thousand Union men and twenty thousand Confederates converged around Manassas, Virginia, an important rail junction. The Army of Northeastern Virginia, under Brigadier General Irvin McDowell, planned on taking Richmond, the Confederate capital, and bringing the ignominious conflict to the quick end the Northerners thought it deserved. The Southerners sought to block the Northern effort, with General P. G. T. Beauregard's Army of the Potomac occupying Manassas and General Joseph Johnston's Army of the Shenandoah ready to move from the west.

On July 18 Beauregard arrayed his seven brigades along four miles of the stream called Bull Run; the troops stretched from a bridge on the Warrenton Turnpike to the north to the Orange and Alexandria Railroad to the south. After a day of fighting on July 18 along the steep and slippery banks of Bull Run, Johnston rushed in from the Valley to reinforce Beauregard. Union General Robert Patterson, who had predicted easy victory from Alexander K. McClure's porch two weeks earlier, became confused by the movements of cavalry under Colonel J. E. B. Stuart and sat in the Valley, away from the growing conflict at Manassas. The men of Augusta's 5th Virginia Infantry came with Johnston, under the command of Thomas J. Jackson. On July 20, both sides prepared for the first major battle of the American Civil War. It was to start before dawn the following day.[1]

John Imboden

JOHN IMBODEN AND HIS MEN had been in the field for months, longer than any other Virginia troops, ever since their rush to Harpers Ferry. Partly with Imboden's own money ("good tents purchased and paid for by the Captain out of his private means costing $298"), partly with the support of the people of Augusta ("a suit around consisting of a grey cap, and flannel shirt, grey woolen pants, and woolen socks"), and partly with what they could take from the citizens around them ("26 impressed horses to be substituted by state horses as soon as possible"), the Staunton Artillery had helped capture fifty-six locomotives and three hundred railroad cars. Their four bronze guns constituted their most valuable possessions as they protected the Confederate troops gathering in northern Virginia.[2]

Having arrived at the Manassas Gap Railroad after marching all night and having slept in the rain after they arrived, the Staunton Artillery was not ready to fight on July 21. "You will have plenty of time to cook and eat, to the music of a battle in which we will probably take little or no part," General Barnard Bee reassured Imboden. As they moved to their positions, however, the Staunton men found themselves in a key position to fire on massing Union troops. "We were almost under cover by reason of a slight swell in the ground immediately in our front," Imboden wrote. "Our shot passed not six inches above the surface of the ground." The enemy could see only the heads of the men as they loaded and fired. The Staunton men fired low and ricocheted the "shot and shrapnel on the hard, smooth, open field" that sloped away from them. "The effect was very destructive to the enemy."

The Staunton Artillery fought alone in the position for two hours, Federal shells bursting among the men and horses. No other Confederates were in sight, for orders to retreat had been lost with the courier killed on the way with the message. Men fell on the ground, exhausted from the heat and the backbreaking work. They had used almost all their ammunition, having fired 460 rounds, before they finally began to retreat. As they did so, Imboden met General Thomas Jackson, a thirty-seven-year-old West Point graduate, Mexican War veteran, and, for the last decade, somewhat eccentric professor of mathematics at Virginia Military Institute in the Valley town of Lexington. Jackson commanded the 1st Brigade. Imboden, angry at General Bee for leaving the Staunton Artillery behind, used profanity as he explained his situation to Jackson; he immediately saw the cursing was "displeasing." Jackson ordered Imboden's men to move with him and then "withdraw your battery, as it has been so torn to pieces, and let your men rest."

Imboden asked permission to fire the last three rounds of shrapnel as they prepared to retire. In his eagerness, he sheepishly admitted, "I forgot to step back far enough from the muzzle, and, as I wanted to see the shell strike, I squatted to be under the smoke, and gave the word 'Fire.' " The blast threw Imboden twenty feet. He thought the gun had burst, but in fact, pent-up gas had shot sideways as the shell left the muzzle. Blood ran from his ear, but he recovered "in time to see the shell explode in the enemy's ranks," taking down six Union men.

Michael Hanger, the young carpenter from Augusta in the 5th Virginia Infantry, described the situation he and his comrades faced. "5 O'clock A.M. we can hear the cannon firing from the hills in front, and a little below us. The Yankees are endeavoring to draw us in that direction. The Junction is strongly fortifiyed, with breastworks and entrenchments around in every possible direction." Put into position, Hanger and his comrades lay there for three and a half hours. "Then we was ordered to rais and fire and charge bayonetts. There was an Awfull fire kept up The yankees had flanked round on our left had planted six peaces of Artilery & had A cross fire on us when we charged the yankees fell back and we captured their artilery The ground was covered with dead & wounded."[3]

Things got worse the next day. "It is now raining very hard, and has been all night. the wounded on the battle field must have suffered greatly last night. It is a very muddy and disagreeable day. A great many more forces came to the Junction today I went to the battle feild to help bury the dead the Awfulls scene I evir witnessed In my life hundreds of dead

& wounded on the feild yet the yankees sent in a flag of truce and got some of thier wounded." Hanger gave no fuller evaluation of the battle. He did not say who had won and lost. He only listed the names of the men of his company who had been wounded.[4] He did not give the name the battle was to bear. The Confederates called it Manassas, after the nearby town; the Union called it Bull Run, naming it after the nearby river, as became its custom.

The telegraph brought word of the battle to Staunton the very day of its outbreak. At first the telegraph reported only that a "great battle" had transpired, former editor of the *Staunton Spectator* and now Confederate clerk Joseph Waddell anxiously wrote in his journal. "The victory is attributed to our side. The enemy were said to be retreating, pursued by our cavalry. Total loss (on both sides, it is presumed), ten thousand to twelve thousand." With such vast losses rumored and with many Augusta men on the field, it was hardly a surprise, as Waddell put it with understatement, that "the utmost desire, not without apprehension, is felt to obtain full particulars." That night another telegram arrived. One member of the Staunton Artillery had been killed, as had two infantrymen. Fourteen men had been wounded.[5]

Three days later Waddell received a letter from his cousin Lyttleton, a quartermaster sergeant in the Staunton Artillery. Lyttleton had begun his letter the morning of the battle at Manassas, Joseph wrote, and "in the midst of a sentence he breaks off to say that he heard the report of cannon and must go to his post." Lyttleton returned at five and took up the letter again, "but at the close of the letter could not say definitely what was the result. On a separate piece of paper he states that General Johnston had come along and announced a victory!" Over the next few days Waddell gathered details about the battle. "The booty captured after the battle near Manassas is said to be immense," he happily recorded. "The Federalists seem to have anticipated an easy march to Richmond, and were provided with all sorts of conveniences and luxuries. Many females and children accompanied their army, and female apparel and even children's toys were found scattered over the ground."[6]

An Augusta man who had fought at Manassas sent a full report of the battle to the *Spectator*. It painted an elaborate set piece in the hyperbolic language of instant history: "The noble and brave Billy Woodward exclaimed, 'I will never retreat. "Give me liberty or give me death.'" His lips had scarcely given utterance to these heroic words, when a ball pierced his brave heart." When the artillery opened fire, it appeared to the correspondent "as if Heaven and earth were being rent asunder, so terrible was the crash and roar of the monster instruments of death."[7]

The newspaper painted its picture on the broadest canvas and in the brightest colors. "In the direction of Manassas Junction a large column of men approaching, and filing past them with the swiftness of the wind, was a splendid body of cavalry, numbering probably a thousand." The cavalry "came rushing on like a mighty torrent, with drawn sabres glittering in the evening's bright sunbeams, mounted on steeds which seemed to be maddened by the contest that was being waged by man against his fellow man." Numbered in this 1st Virginia Cavalry were dozens of men from Augusta, "commanded by the gallant Col. Stuart," J. E. B. Stuart, a cousin of Alexander H. H. Stuart's. At this crucial point General P. G. T. Beauregard appeared and addressed the Augusta men: "Fight on, brave Virginia boys; the day is ours everywhere else, and it must be here also." Following their general, "with a loud cheer, we rushed forward, determined to do as commanded or die."[8]

When Confederate reinforcements arrived via railroad, with "the most terrible volley of musketry" and "a shout that rent the air" (later to be known as the Rebel yell), the battle quickly turned. "The enemy, terror stricken, broke ranks and fled in the wildest confusion over the hill." The Confederate cavalry charged the broken Union ranks, "sending terror and dismay" among them. "The guns of the captured batteries were turned against them"; the guns, posted on high ground and along roads, "raked and crushed their disordered columns dreadfully, and shout after shout rent the air from victorious Southern troops."[9]

General Jackson offered his official report of the battle, the battle in which he earned the nickname that followed him through the rest of his life, Stonewall. (General Bee, killed soon thereafter, rallied his men by shouting, "Look! There is Jackson standing like a stone wall! Rally behind the Virginians.") General Jackson's report was neither the clipped account of the foot soldier who saw only a fraction of the battle nor the dramatic rendering of the young man writing to his hometown newspaper with phrases already clichéd. Rather, Stonewall Jackson offered an evaluation of men, of leaders, and of the brigade as a whole. Like all the other reports of the Battle of Manassas, it offered a highly stylized, even formulaic presentation.

Jackson mainly distributed accolades. Captain John Imboden of Augusta, recently a court clerk keeping tabs on free blacks, was "dauntless." Others under Jackson's command were "heroic," acted "nobly," and "deserved great praise." Some made "gallant" charges and performed in a "highly meritorious" way. Colonel J. E. B. Stuart played a central role with his cavalry (as Stuart's own report noted with poorly disguised pride). No one was singled out for failing in any way. Jackson ended his report with a somber accounting of the losses from his brigade: eleven officers, fourteen noncommissioned officers, and eighty-six privates were killed; nearly four hundred more were wounded or missing. Given the number of soldiers involved, the numbers were not high, certainly nowhere near the twelve thousand reported in the early telegraph messages. But they were high enough, shocking to a people who had never known war.[10]

The 5th Virginia lost four killed in the first major battle of the war, three months after their enlistments. Three were privates: Asbury McClure, a twenty-one-year-old carpenter; Joab Seely, a twenty-four-year-old cigar maker from Staunton; and Thomas Killeen, born in Ireland but a clerk in Staunton at the time of Fort Sumter.[11] The 5th also lost a first sergeant, Benjamin Franklin Shuey. The oldest son of propertyless farmers, he was buried in his church cemetery with the epitaph "One of the Best Young Men of Whom Augusta County Could Boast."[12]

Sixteen Augusta men were wounded. Nelson Andrew, nineteen years old, would never again be fit for duty. William Peyton Johnson, a twenty-six-year-old cabinetmaker, had his face shattered by a ball, the bone beneath his right eye fractured and his optic nerve damaged. Most of the others healed enough to go back to their units and fight in the next battle.

The victory at Manassas brought immediate glory to Augusta's men. They had experienced what they all had dreamed of: engagement in a major battle with a stunning victory over a larger force without great losses. Their own leaders had been singled out for the highest praise. They became known as the Stonewall Brigade. Few of their friends and comrades had been killed. Some Southerners dared hope that the battle would break the Union will, that the decisive battle everyone expected to determine the war had already occurred.

John Imboden got a good story out of the fight. A friend of Imboden's, after it had become clear the Confederates would win the day, came upon Jefferson Davis, himself a veteran of the hard war with Mexico in the 1840s, on hand to witness the victory. The friend "rushed up to the President, seized his hand, and huzzahed at the top of his voice. I could see that Mr. Davis was greatly amused, and I was convulsed with laughter." The friend pointed toward Imboden and "exclaimed, to the great amusement of all who heard him: 'Mr. President, there's my captain, and I want to introduce *you* to *him*.' " Davis eyed Imboden "for a moment, as if he thought I was an odd-looking captain. I had on a battered slouch hat, a red flannel shirt with only one sleeve, corduroy trousers, and heavy cavalry boots. I was begrimed with burnt powder, dust, and blood from my ear and arm, and must have been about as hard-looking a specimen of a captain as was ever seen. Nevertheless, the President grasped my hand with a cordial salutation, and after a few words passed on."[13] Imboden was deaf in his left ear from the blast for the rest of his life.

A battle proved to be an enormously complicated thing, marked by ever-changing patterns of structure and chance, of intention and accident, of personality and anonymity. It required years and mountains of reports, maps, papers, memoirs, and analyses to understand the battle as a whole. Even then essential elements of understanding were left out, for no human could know or relate all the flood of thought, emotion, and experience that enveloped those who fought.

A full account of the battle at Manassas, written in retrospect and after the evidence from both sides had been sifted and measured, might stress the use the Confederates made of the telegraph and railroads to concentrate their forces and rush in reinforcements. It might emphasize the quickness with which infantry, equipped with muskets, could move, dispensing with careful and unbroken lines. It might emphasize the advantages the Confederates enjoyed in defending ground rather than trying to seize it. It might note that similar numbers of Confederate and Union men were lost as a result of the battle: 387 killed and 1,582 wounded for the South; 460 killed and 1,124 wounded for the North. But the North and the South knew only one important thing in July 1861: the Confederates had beaten the Federal army.

THE NORTH HAD EXPECTED its army of proud volunteers to triumph in one climactic battle. When that battle turned into a rout, with Union soldiers fleeing the field in a panic, Northerners were stunned. Franklin responded to the defeat at Bull Run with a rush of mixed emotions. Local families held no intimate stake in the humiliating loss because no men who fought there had come from Franklin, but people believed that the battle reflected on the entire Union cause. The character of its men, the quality of its leadership, and the unity of its purpose all seemed in doubt.

Alexander K. McClure wrote an ally in disgust: "What a sad chapter in our National History is that of Sunday last. If not speedily redeemed, our nationality will tremble in the scale with a more than doubtful issue." The state's soldiers had been among those who ran, and the state "seems to be crippled at every step. Her troops were badly officered & leave a record, which however justifiable when closely scrutinized, will ever be a blot upon our fame."[14]

Some responded with defiance. The defeat has "not conquered us," the *Valley Spirit* proclaimed following Bull Run. "The shrieks of the wounded and the groans of the dying—the wail of the widow and the tears of the orphan will arouse the entire united North, who will 'strike until the last armed foe expires.' " With the loss of this battle, "the lion of the Nation has been aroused, and he will soon enter the arena in his might." The paper expected vast numbers of Pennsylvanians to pour into the army to vindicate the loss.[15]

Rumors spread that Southerners had acted brutally toward the fallen Union soldiers. Robert Taggart wrote his brother John, a captain in the 9th Pennsylvania Reserve Infantry, to thank him for sending a revolver. Though a handgun would not be of much use in regular battle, Taggart had been "informed by a number of the N.Y. Zouaves, and others, who were engaged in the recent Bull's run affair, that they proved the means of saving quite a number of the wounded from being murdered. They say the secessionists have no mercy on the wounded, but when ever they pass on the field or elsewhere, one who cannot take himself away, they instantly bayonet him." This "game," Taggart admitted, "is now being played as a general thing on both sides." After one major battle, inhumanity seemed already to have broken loose.[16]

Alex Cressler, a young schoolteacher in Chambersburg, bristled to a friend that "the cruel manner in which our wounded heroes were treated will forever remain on the pages of history as a living testimony against the humanity of the slave drivers of the South." Perhaps, Cressler thought, Bull Run was penance for slavery, maybe a warning of what awaited the white North if it were defeated. "We permitted the south to inflict upon a poor and helpless race of Gods creatures the most unjust tortures that was heaped upon any race of human beings," Cressler wrote Henry Bitner. A defeated North would have "to bow down on our knees, that a like burthen may be placed upon our shoulders." But could that ever happen? "Will we sacrifice ourselves and our children to the everlasting curse of slavedom? No, but we will cheerfully sacrifice our all upon the alter of our Country and stand by the Constitution and the laws until the last drop of our heart's blood shall have oozed from [our] bosoms."[17]

Blasting the inhumanity of the foe and proclaiming a willingness for collective sacrifice went only so far. If more defeats were not to follow, the North would have to cast a cold eye on its failure. What had gone wrong? The generals were the logical place to start, and Robert Patterson, in command of Union forces in the Shenandoah Valley, who had been so confident on Alexander McClure's porch, seemed most to blame. The Union had unforgivably permitted the two parts of the secessionist army to communicate with each other via telegraph and to join together via railroad. "Had a written agreement, drawn up by Jeff. Davis himself, between Gen. Patterson and Gen. Johnson, been regularly signed, sealed and delivered, containing full stipulations respecting the method to be pursued by both," the Republican *Dispatch* charged, "such an instrument could not have been drawn by Mr. J. Davis more to his own liking than the farce enacted by this forced-to-show-his-colors General." Robert Patterson had to go.[18]

Across the North the Democrats launched an attack on all the men in charge of the Union cause. "It is becoming more and more evident every day that the present Administration is not competent to conduct this war," the *Valley Spirit* railed in the week after Bull Run. "So far, with the exception of McCLELLAN'S brilliant successes, it has been a series of blunders and mishaps."[19] It was not merely that Lincoln and his subordinates were incompetent, as Democrats deemed them to be, but that the Republican leaders "boldly avowed day after day that the Constitution must be invaded, overstepped, or in other words, trampled upon, in order to carry on and carry out this war. This is corruption of the rankest sort."[20] The Republicans, with their supposed disregard of habeas corpus and freedom of the press, threatened to destroy the liberty they claimed to fight to preserve.

"All abolitionists ought to have a halter slipped around their necks the moment they open their mouths on the subject of abolishing slavery anywhere at this critical moment," the Democrats declaimed.[21] Democrats warned that the Union had to be careful. If the North made it appear that the war endangered slavery, "the effect will be to unite the most of the South as one man against the cause of Union." Just as bad, a move against slavery in any form would "engender throughout the North wide spread and embarrassing opposition," dividing an already divided people.[22]

Northerners believed there might be deeper reasons for their defeat than incompetence or unjust policies. Was it possible that the Union attack on a Sunday had contributed to their failure? It was certainly the case, the *Dispatch* noted, "that our forces attacked the rebels on Sunday at Bull's Run." The editor of the paper was "not inclined to be superstitious, but we firmly believe in the overruling hand of a Divine Providence, who will not suffer iniquity to go unpunished." There could be no doubt that "our cause is just and righteous, and must finally prevail; but we shall be scourged for past national sins, and it behooves us to guard well, that the continued commission of others does not protract the scourge." President Lincoln and his generals must hereafter keep the dictates of Divine Providence in mind.[23]

As the weeks passed, the North came to realize that Bull Run had not hurt its cause very much. The signs of its strength remained clear: "Washington more impregnable than ever; Northern troops hurrying in at a rate that far more than makes up for the expiration of the three month enlistments; and an unconquerable General opposed to them." Faced with these facts, the Union thought the Confederates had begun "to ask themselves how many such fields must be fought and won before they establish their Secession." The North saw deep flaws in the Southern cause: "With ports blockaded, business stagnant, negroes preparing for insurrection, and paper trash circulating in place of specie, the prospect for them is indeed very dismal, and they begin to feel it so."[24]

Despite much talk of sacrifice, up to the end of the summer of 1861 the war had touched Franklin County lightly. With more than 40,000 residents, Franklin had sent only 250 men to the nation's service. The two companies of the Chambers Artillery, formed in the first days of the conflict, returned home at the end of July, their three months of duty expired. The unit's experiences had not been stirring, for it had not seen "actual battle," as the *Dispatch* delicately put it.[25] The other Chambersburg paper observed that the men even "improved in personal appearance" as a result of their service.[26]

Just as the Franklin County soldiers were returning in late July, prominent men in the county decided to raise a regiment from Franklin. They had better reason than most. "We occupy a border county," a paper reminded its readers, and "we might yet be compelled to meet the enemy on our own soil, and witness not only the destruction of our fields and dwellings, but the ruthless murder of wives and little ones." Faced with dire threats, how could Franklin hesitate to mobilize? If each township in the county formed one company—about one hundred men, with three of them officers, five sergeants, and eight corporals—Franklin could gather a regiment of its own, a thousand men in ten to twelve companies.[27]

A few days later a mass meeting gathered at the courthouse on the Diamond in Chambersburg. The local brass band played "some soul-stirring music." Many people gathered. But when the time came to sign up, to the mortification of Franklin County, only thirteen men stepped forward. "The result was anything else than creditable to the military spirit of the town," the *Dispatch* admitted with considerable understatement, "especially in view of our close proximity to the enemy."[28] Franklin County had put on a good show of patriotism and talked a good fight. But it failed to respond when real sacrifices had to be made.

The recruiters tried again in the fall of 1861, when Franklin men were invited to fight for the 77th Pennsylvania Regiment. This time they had better luck, 164 men filling two companies of the new regiment. Between November and January another 100 men joined the 107th Pennsylvania Regiment. Despite the willingness of these young men to serve, the fact remained that by January 1862, eight months after secession and six months after the defeat at Manassas, fewer than 400 Franklin men had joined the Union army and the first ones to enlist had already fulfilled their three months of service.

2

THE PEOPLE OF AUGUSTA, close to the mountains of western Virginia, knew that the victory at Manassas had not put the balance sheet so clearly in favor of the South as others imagined. Even as sixteen-year-old Mary Smiley exulted over the victory, she noted that "we have got back enough of provisions and men now to pay for what was taken from us in Western Va." There, the battles had not gone nearly as well.[29]

The Confederacy, determined to regain control of western Virginia, put General Robert E. Lee in command. Lee possessed a prominent Virginia background, a degree from West Point, and a sterling reputation as a man and a soldier. Only months earlier he had turned down command of the Union army and resigned his commission in the U.S. Army. He had been put in charge of coordinating all Virginia forces, working out of Richmond. There his skills as a field commander had been wasted, and Southern leaders looked with hope upon Lee's new command in the mountains of his native state.

Jed Hotchkiss, the New York schoolmaster from Augusta County, was impressed with the new leader and thought him and his fellow officers "perfect gentlemen." When the general came for a day to the camp where Hotchkiss stayed, "all were pleased with him." Lee visited troops elsewhere and "praised our men especially & complimented the Augusta *Lee* Rifles."[30]

It had taken Hotchkiss a while to find his place in the army. The elite Engineer Corps was not eager to employ a self-taught civilian topographer when West Point had produced many trained military men, but when Will Baylor introduced Hotchkiss to Stonewall Jackson, the general was impressed with Hotchkiss's Christian morality and self-discipline as well as his remarkable ability to make comprehensible the complex landscape of the Valley Hotchkiss knew so well. In March 1862 Jackson gave

The Valley becomes the scene of war

Hotchkiss the task that changed his life and that of the general and army he was serving: "I want you to make me a map of the Valley, from Harpers Ferry to Lexington, showing all the points of offence and defence in those places." The young "professor," as men called him, was to be given two horses, a wagon and driver, and a tent; he already owned the drafting tools he needed. He set to work immediately on the map of the Valley, a map that grew large and ever more detailed to guide Stonewall Jackson's decisions. Jackson and Robert E. Lee soon came to trust Hotchkiss completely and rely on his maps, knowledge, energy, and advice.[31]

Though Hotchkiss often had to work on the Sabbath, he found time to keep his eyes on the higher purposes. He heard preaching "just behind our tents, in the nice grassy yard of Esq. Stephenson & the whole Regt. was marched out & seated on the grass." A presiding elder from a nearby Methodist church preached from 2nd Timothy 4-6—"a very good sermon, adapted to the times & place—the men all listened attentively." The next week Augusta's Reverend Luther Emerson, a prominent and prosperous Presbyterian, "preached for us today from Ps. 118-6—a very good brief sermon—the parson is about as good looking as ever—is very sound on the question of State rights &c."[32]

General Lee had appointed Hotchkiss to work "making maps of the country & putting down the information in reference to the enemy's position, that we obtain from scouts prisoners &c. I get 100 dollars a month." He wanted to come home, but "I cannot afford to lose my place in such hard times as these, when a few month's service will enable me to get money enough to keep us comfortable for some time, and I shall certainly spend the winter at home teaching a short 3 months or so session—leaving the army as soon as it goes into winter quarters." In the meantime serving among officers had its advantages. "I have also sent you 4 lbs. of sugar, 3 lbs of rice & 1 pound of coffee—and am sorry that I cannot send you more—but I can only get these things by certifying that they are for 'my own use'—and as such I send them to you." An upright man, Hotchkiss felt some guilt about his misdirection of government property. "You can use them and say nothing about it to any one," he told Sara, "not even telling the children where they came from." He did offer one metaphorical rationalization: so great was his love for his family that he offered the supplies "as part & parcel of myself."[33]

Hotchkiss was appalled at the conditions in occupied and war-torn western Virginia. "I have been trying today to get some washing done," he wrote Sara, "but the pollution of the place is such that the waters are not in a condition to wash with, unless brought from some ways." In fact, the Confederate camp "is the worst place in the state for men to be that are not well—there are few houses & they are full of all sorts & conditions & the sick have a hard time, some of them die daily." Hotchkiss came to share a tent with Dr. John Opie. Opie was "a good fine fellow," and "the only drawback is the frequent calls on the Dr & the numerous cases that he has to treat." Hotchkiss found the complaints of the soldiers from the mountains "quite amusing." The young teacher was "surprised at the seeming want of any power of endurance in these mountain men—they wear down very soon and seem unable to endure any fatigue & more of them are sick than any other class of soldiers here."[34] Hotchkiss was seeing the effects of crowding upon men who had lived on relatively isolated farms. Diseases such as mumps and measles that soldiers from towns and cities had passed through in childhood hit vulnerable country men hard.

A few weeks later, having moved on to another mountain camp,

Hotchkiss told of finding twenty sick men at one house, where an "old lady was seeing to them all." She and one other woman were the only two women he had seen willing to work as "an angel of mercy." In fact, Hotchkiss thought, "more of the men have died for the want of nurses & proper diet than any other cause—the women here flee away from the army instead of coming to its aid & cheering up the men by their presence—there are enough of them here but they seem to think it indelicate or beneath them—or something—I do not know what—to take care of the sick soldiers." Hotchkiss could not escape from the sick men. "I can hear them groan here where I am from the upper story of the tavern which is converted into a hospital."[35]

Not surprisingly, Hotchkiss himself fell sick. He had started a journal of his experiences in the Confederate army but had neither the time nor the energy to make many entries for September 1861. The month began with a short note: "am quite ill." After three days of this "typhoid attack," Hotchkiss went back to work, making a reconnaissance, and on September 9 even marched "to attack enemy." The effort proved too much, and he collapsed. He wrote his brother Nelson and explained what had happened. "We went to their very presence but the result was a failure and the exposure used up a good many, myself among the rest." For two days Hotchkiss had lain ill, and "all alone as I was yesterday, twenty times did I cry like a child at the thoughts of home and the thousand attentions I should have." He asked Nelson to bring their wagon to come get him, a two-day drive. "How I long to see every one on the place, white and black." A week later Hotchkiss scratched in his last entry for 1861: "Very ill and attempting to start homeward." He finally made it back to Loch Willow, where he stayed with Sara and the girls throughout the winter.[36]

Enlisted men did not enjoy the same freedom of movement or range of amenities as Jed Hotchkiss. A. W. Kersh, a thirty-three-year-old cabinetmaker, also served in the mountains in the summer and fall of 1861, but his experience was quite different from Hotchkiss's. Kersh had lived and worked with his brother George back in Augusta until he joined the 52d. His regiment had experienced no glorious battles such as Manassas, only skirmishes and periods of waiting for the well-fortified Union troops to show themselves. "Our men cant fight them where they are to any advantage it is their intention now I believe to surround them and cut off their supplies if they can their provisions must be scarce now," Kersh wrote his brother. Most of the news turned around health. "Since I written first Some of us have been taken sick Junius R Craun has the yellow Jaundice he is getting well again William Cupp has been right poorly getting better Joseph Goin William vanfossen also went to the Hospital the three some of the boys has got the Measles some the Mumps none but James Craun in our mess sick as to myself I am well as common the boys are all in good spirits and seem anxious for a brush with the Yankees."[37]

Henry Dedrick had joined the 52d in Waynesboro in July. A twenty-four-year-old farmer, short, with dark hair and blue eyes, he had joined with a group of neighbors he called the creek boys. Writing to his young wife, Dedrick tried to be cheerful.[38] His first letter reported: "I am getting as fat! as a pig. Dear Lissa you wanted to know what we had to eat. We have plenty of good beef and some bacon and flour, sugar and coffee and rice. We have plenty to eat we get some butter at times as we can get it."[39] Soon, however, the letters took a darker turn. Many of their friends in his company had grown sick. "Bridge is not well, he has not been well for two weeks, and Ephriam Sillings has not been well for about three weeks. They both had the yellow jaundice."[40]

Like all the soldiers, Dedrick worried about providing for his family. "Dear Wife I have no money to send to you and I don't know when I will get any." He told Lissa that if she needed money, she "must try to sell some rye if you can spare it, and if you can't spare it you must try and sell one of the calves and get what you can." Henry had only words to offer, and those seemed empty enough. "You must try and do the best you can while I am absent from you, but I hope and trust that I will return again safe and sound."[41] Much to Dedrick's relief, he was paid a couple of weeks later. "Lissa we drawed our money yesterday and I will send you fifteen dollars in this letter." Henry included twelve dollars more and told his wife that "if you need any you must take as much of it as you want." As he put the letter in the envelope, he added a firm admonition: "Lissa, I don't want you to lend out one cent of it to nobody on occasion at all."[42]

Henry finally received a letter from Lissa, and it apparently struck the same notes as so many other letters from home. "Dear and Dearest wife," the soldier responded, "you wanted to know if I was trying to get religion or not. I have been tryhing and I intend to try all that I can, but I tell you it is a hard place here in camp. I will tell you more about it the next time."[43] Despite the danger in which he lived and his desire for faith, he depended on Lissa to intercede with God for protection. "If I should not return no more I hope that we will meet in heaven and there to meet to part no more for ever and ever. I want you all to pray for me that I may get there and I will do all I can to meet you all there."[44]

Some of the other men had received boxes of food or clothes, and Henry hinted that getting a parcel would be nice. "If you have anything to send me if you have a chance you may send it and if you don't have any chance it don't make any difference."[45] When a box did arrive, in freezing January, it apparently made a difference after all. Henry was clearly thrilled to receive the "ten apples and twenty cakes and the sausage and the hickory nuts that you put in my pants pocket. Tell mother and Amanda and Carry that I am much obliged to them for their kindness and I got the bottle of whiskey. James McDaniel give it to me but did not tell me who sent it to me, but I think you sent it to me."[46]

As the weeks passed and the winter descended, Henry Dedrick's thoughts became more bitter, sliding quickly from warm thoughts of home to suspicion. "I hope when these few lines comes to hand they may find you and the baby well and all the rest of my inquiring friends if there be any. I find that there is but few in these days, every man that is now at home is for his self and they take every advantage of them who is now in the army serving their country. I do hope that it will be our time next." Dedrick did not say what "advantages" the men back home were taking, but rumors of high prices had grown common. Henry urged Lissa to take care of their rye and corn. "If you have any you must keep it for grain is a going to be scarce after while."[47]

The months dragged by with no action, no progress. The passing time was marked only by things Dedrick could not see. His father had written to say that he had visited with Lissa and their little boy, Willie. "He said when he started from there that little Willie cried and hollered after him." The young boy yearned for his father, gone now for eight months. "He said that he left with a sad heart to think that the little boy would cry after him and to think that I was out here and did not know whether we would ever meet on earth any more or not." Henry's father admitted "that he had to shed tears when he was writing to think about it." Henry could barely stand it. "Dear Lissa you don't know how it hurt my feelings to read it." The envelope from his father had contained something else, "the pattern of our sweet little boys hand. I was glad to see it. It has growed very much since I seen it."[48]

The Confederate troops in the mountains could not overcome the larger and better supported Union forces. Robert E. Lee, unable to push the Federal army out of the mountains, found himself ridiculed in the Southern press as "Granny Lee" and "Evacuating Lee." The transformation of western Virginia into an area under Union control heightened the danger in the Valley, making it the vulnerable western border of the Confederacy.

3

BUSINESS OF ALMOST all kinds has been paralyzed, and the majority of persons will suffer heavy losses," the *Staunton Spectator* admitted in June. Only months after soldiers had gone into the field, Staunton newspapers were urging their readers to economize. "The Revolution in which we are now engaged will demand heavy sacrifices, and we should prepare ourselves as well as possible to bear them. No money should now be expended for luxuries or mere display." Well-to-do people, especially women, had a special responsibility. "We hope that those whose means would enable them to dress extravagantly will set the example of appearing in a dress which will combine neatness, cheapness and durability," the Augusta paper admonished its readers. "We hope to see unpretending calico dresses, which have been banished from the towns, again introduced. Who will set the example? What lady will lead in this laudable enterprise?"[49]

A Georgia soldier passed through Augusta in July 1861 and painted a flattering portrait of the Valley county for his paper back home. "The citizens of Staunton treated us very kindly. More enthusiasm I have not seen anywhere." Indeed, "scarcely an hour in the day passed without something being sent to the camp for our comfort. The same spirit that animated the hearts of our mothers in the days of '76 is still to be found in Old Virginia." In Waynesboro "we found tables spread with an abundance of provisions for every man on board. We all partook freely of the good things set before us, and gave three hearty cheers for Waynesboro—but especially the ladies—bade them farewell, and went on our way rejoicing." The Georgia man was struck by the bounty of the Valley, "emphatically a land of milk and butter, and the milk has flown freely to the weary soldier wherever it was to be had."[50]

With a large army in the field, the people on the home front heard continual pleas for support. Let the spirit of selflessness "not only animate our heroic soldiers—as it did on the glorious fields of Bull Run," urged the *Spectator*, "let it not only cause our planters and property holders to empty their barns, and to hold their wagons and their laborers at the call of our generals—as did the patriotic populations around Manassas." The spirit of selflessness, the paper urged, should also take a more prosaic and perhaps painful form. "Let there be no murmuring when the government asks for money! Let there be no repining when the tax gatherer comes." Cheerful contributions would not be sacrifice at all, but investment and insurance. If a selfish populace starved their army, "then will land, slaves, mules, horses, cattle bonds and stocks become worthless, except to the rapacious Yankee invaders."[51]

Should anyone in Augusta forget the sacrifices of others, he had only to visit Staunton, which had become overnight the "great Hospital for the Western Army." Disease and defeat had stricken many men in the mountains. "We have had a horrid view of war," Joseph Waddell noted in his diary when wagonloads of wounded men began coming in from the mountains in July 1861, in the wake of the battle at Rich Mountain. With no places prepared for the wounded, Staunton residents scrambled to find locations for them. They covered the floors of the sheriff's office and the courthouse. "The sight was a sickening one—one man gasping with asthma, another burning with fever, and another shaking with chills." Four days later the streets of Staunton were "full of soldiers, many of whom are lying against the houses and on store boxes. A free negro woman," Waddell noted, "took three of them home with her to get something to eat and a place to lie down."[52]

Five hundred sick soldiers, stricken with "pneumonia, measles, mumps, typhoid fever and dysentery," quickly filled the buildings. The women of Staunton, the *Richmond Whig* reported, "minister tenderly to their wants as far as possible. With lavish liberality, they have emptied their larders, their store rooms and their purses, to add to their comfort. But their supplies are well nigh exhausted." Staunton issued a plea to "their sisters of the South" to help in the overwhelming work of tending for so many suffering men.[53]

Joseph Waddell gave a less enthusiastic view of the women's efforts. "The ladies are bent upon nursing at the hospital," he derisively noted in his journal. He heard some "ludicrous stories of their performances. Mrs.———was very anxious to 'do something' " and persuaded one of the doctors to give her two prescriptions to administer. In her excitement and inexperience, however, she confused them. "It is said that these ladies rub the fever patients and dose the rheumatics. One man had his face washed by one lady after another till he was perfectly clean or very tired of it." Waddell, despite his skepticism, admitted that most of the women learned quickly and soon performed admirably.[54] They had plenty of practice, for by October the Deaf, Dumb, and Blind Institute had become a hospital and Staunton contained 750 ill and wounded men. It expected 500 more from the mountains.

The entire county was being worked to the bone. Augusta had sent more than twenty-five hundred men to the Confederate army, the *Whig* reported, and many had already fought bravely at Manassas. The county had only half "of her white agricultural labour" and "almost every farmer has been required to surrender one or more wagons and teams" to help carry soldiers and supplies into the mountains to the west. Some feared, in fact, "that the withdrawal of so much labor, both human and animal, may seriously affect the next year's crop." Despite these deep and real fears, "all are in good spirits and unalterably fixed in the determination to resist to the last Yankee aggression."[55]

Over the course of the fall the Confederate armies in northwestern Virginia depended "almost entirely upon supplies collected in Staunton" and shipped by wagon from there. One day in September, Joseph Waddell watched as thirty-two wagons went out, followed by thirty-six the next day; a few weeks later, eighty-one wagons left from Staunton for the troops in the mountains. "Teams going and coming all the time, and a constant rush of team-owners, wagon-masters, teamsters, etc," he recorded in December. "Old or broken down horses are coming in from the army in droves nearly every day, and better ones are sent out as fast as they can be procured."[56]

John B. Baldwin, who had in April pleaded for the Union and even met with Abraham Lincoln, had been elected colonel of the 52d Virginia Infantry Regiment. In October he pleaded with Judah P. Benjamin, Confederate secretary of war, for supplies for his men high in the Allegheny Mountains. "You are no doubt aware that the army on this line cannot depend upon the surrounding country for supplies of any kind. The country at the best is sparsely populated, and produces no surplus of any kind of provision except live stock, and the troubles of the times have brought upon the people an unusual scarcity of all kinds of supplies." They had to rely on Staunton for food and forage, but Staunton lay sixty miles away. The road to Staunton, good in the summer, had become impassable with the rain and snow of winter. One major storm would mean that all their horses would starve within two weeks. The soldiers had inadequate housing and no tools to build huts for themselves, despite being surrounded by timber. "Already the weather has been such as to freeze the tents of my regiment solid after a soaking rain and to coat the water in vessels with thick ice." Baldwin begged the Confederate government for supplies.[57]

EVERYONE IN STAUNTON could see that people should economize in every way possible, forswearing expensive clothes and display. Yet "the indifference of some, the thoughtlessness of others, and the selfish rapacity of not a few, constantly remind us that all are not patriots who profess to be Southern in feeling," the *Spectator* warned. "All are not to be trusted who are loudest in their expressions of devotion to a cause which they appreciate only to the extent that it can be made to fill their pockets."[58] The apparent unanimity of the Confederacy hid traitors who cared for themselves more than for the cause.

A blistering letter to the editor of the *Spectator*, written from the military camp of Monterey in the dead of winter, took the people of Augusta to task for their hypocrisy and selfishness. "When the call was made for volunteers to drive from our soil the invader," "Monterey" reminded his fellow citizens, thousands of the best men of Augusta "left their homes and all that was dear to them and marched to the scene of action, where they have been exposed to privation and dangers of almost every kind." The soldiers did not complain. They felt sure that those who remained behind in Augusta would help take care of their wives and children. "But, to the astonishment of the soldiers, many who were left at home, in whom they had the utmost confidence, have to a great extent, proved to them that they intend to make a fortune at the soldiers' expense." Selfish men were bleeding the Confederacy dry. Prices had risen 300 percent and more because speculators drove up prices. These profits were "robbed from the families of the poor soldiers."[59]

"Now, I am a soldier, and have but little of this world's goods," Monterey admitted, "but I have left in good old Augusta a wife and four lovely little children which have, so far, been well taken care of." His family was depending on him for support, and "if things continue as they are during the war, they must suffer." This Augusta man and his fellow soldiers were heartbroken that their male neighbors, sitting snugly in their homes safe in the Valley and having "managed to dodge the active service of their country," would extort obscene profits from the wives and children of men protecting them from the invading North. This soldier in the field did not direct his charge at only a few men back home. It seemed to him that "a large number of those who are not in the army feel as though they have no part nor lot in the defence of their own homes and rights; they do not seem to be willing to make any sacrifice of time and money."[60] Any military victory along the border seemed meaningless if everything the Confederacy claimed to fight for was being betrayed at home.

WITH LITTLE HARD NEWS coming from the war in the fall of 1861, the Chambersburg newspapers were fortunate that politics still flourished to fill their columns with stirring conflict. The partisan language was, if anything, even nastier than in the days before Fort Sumter. The Democrats accused the Republicans of using the war for selfish ends and unconstitutional purposes. The Republicans charged the Democrats with treason. As summer turned to fall, Franklin County, like the North in general, found itself divided and quarreling. People knew their communities held vast potential for making war, but that power could not be conjured up as easily as many had imagined.

Some of the controversy grew over freedom of the press. The Republican papers of Franklin attacked local Democrats for reading antiwar papers. The Democrats laughed. Listening to the Republicans, argued the *Spirit*, one would think that Orrstown—a longtime Democratic stronghold in northern Franklin—"is a perfect hot-bed of treason, and the inhabitants, in and around it, a set of 'rebels,' 'traitors,' 'secessionists' and everything else that is vile!" The *Spirit* pretended to be aghast. To offer an accusation against one's neighbors would, "once upon a time, have been looked upon as very unChristian-like conduct, to say nothing of punishing the slanderers as the law provides, but in this LINCOLN era the largest liberty may be taken with men's characters, persons and property, and there is no redress, nor dare you raise a finger or utter a word against it."[61]

The Republicans gave as good as they got when the local elections heated up. The key votes were for delegates to the state legislature, which was to elect Pennsylvania's U.S. senator. To show the dubious loyalty of the Democrats, the Republican *Dispatch* offered alleged quotations from and about Democratic candidates from various times in the past:

> "I have no part in this war—have no sympathies with it—and will give nothing towards its support." (Associate Judge)
>
> "When it comes to fighting, I will be with the South." (proprietor of the Valley Spirit "just before the outbreak of the rebellion")
>
> "If there was any shooting to be done, he would go to the other side of the Line and would shoot North." (man in running for Associate Judge nomination before withdrawing)
>
> "All the patriotism, all the statesmanship, and all the religion was with the South." (an unspecified officer in the Court House)[62]

The Valley Spirit, its competitors charged, embodied Democratic treason. "It is filled with attacks, both open and covert, on the war and on the Administration. Extracts from disloyal papers like itself, teem in its columns. It reiterates the Secession argument that the present Administration has brought all the present trouble upon the Country." Riots had broken out in other Pennsylvania towns against outspoken Democratic papers, the Republicans warned, and the Spirit was lucky it had not met with the same fate.[63]

Resentment built against the Lincoln administration and its party as military progress and business stagnated while taxes increased. For the Republicans to win in the October elections, they needed to forge an alliance with Union Democrats or War Democrats, men who placed the war effort over partisan loyalty and belief. To the Republicans, the choice was clear: "All who are unconditionally for the Union will vote for the Union candidates for the Legislature, and all who are for compromising with the rebels will vote for the Democratic candidates."[64]

The *Spirit* refused to accept the Republican argument that to be loyal, one had to support the Republican administration. As election day approached, the Democrats urged their men to the polls. "The issue is forced upon you, to decide in favor of Democracy or of Sectional Black Republicanism and Abolitionism." The Democrats seemed unembarrassed to tar their foes with the same words the secessionists and Confederates used; they seemed undaunted by charges of treason. They considered the Republicans sheer hypocrites, hiding political ambition behind the war and cries for nonpartisanship. The Republicans were "at this very time more intensely and uncompromisingly partizan than they have ever been in the past."[65]

Come election day, the Union party of the Republicans and the War Democrats won in Franklin County. In the key contest for the state legislature their candidates won 56 percent of the vote, the same percentage as had voted for Lincoln a year earlier. Turnout was high for an off-year election: about sixty-four hundred men voted, only nine hundred fewer than in the preceding year, when the momentous election for the presidency electrified the country and before men departed the county for military service.[66]

Although the Union party won every office, the Republicans were dismayed that such a large portion of Franklin's men refused to stand behind Abraham Lincoln and his administration in this time of crisis. "We should have shown the enemy a solid front," the *Dispatch* lamented. A strong vote in favor of the Republicans would have "gone farther to dispirit the rebels than a defeat on the battle-field."[67] The Democrats, though they had lost, professed themselves to be heartened. "This vote shows that the Democratic party is not to be trifled with, and those who imagined they could merge it into a 'no party' have received a serious backset."[68]

The only good news, Republican leader Alexander McClure sighed, was that "there were no State officers to be elected in Pennsylvania," for "the Republicans would have lost."[69] The Civil War simply was not popular in Pennsylvania in 1861, "with the Democrats next to solid against coercing the South by war, most of the Know Nothings cherishing the same convictions, and a very large proportion of the Republicans unwilling to accept fratricidal war unless it should be absolutely unavoidable." Illinois and Indiana too would been have lost in 1861, McClure judged, had there been offices for the taking, though Ohio and New York were more solidly Republican. Had the War Democrats not sided with the Republicans in Pennsylvania, that state might well have gone to the party opposed to Lincoln and the war he oversaw.[70]

Slavery increasingly lay at the heart of the conflict between the Democrats and the Republicans. The Democrats brought up the issue far more than the Republicans, for the Democrats still sought to label the Republicans an abolitionist party. The Democrats charged that the Republicans would in time issue a proclamation of emancipation that "would bring sure and irretrievable defeat from the day on which it was promulgated." At that time, Democrats warned, "Two-thirds of the army would refuse to march another step or serve another day in such a crusade." The only men who would enlist in it would be abolitionists, "and we should immediately have a powerful revolutionary party at the North as well as at the South. It would plunge the country into general anarchy, and destroy the hopes of the Union forever."[71]

To make matters worse, Democrats scoffed, such a proclamation would free no slaves. "Who is to carry copies of the proclamation to the plantation and distribute them there? If the agents of distribution go, singly or in small squads, they will swing from the next tree." Some Republicans argued that making the abolition of slavery the point of the war would lead the Union to victory. But, argued the Democrats, if the proclamation were "carried by armies, it cannot reach the slaves until the opposing armies have first been conquered. But how can it be the means of victory if it can take place only after victory has been achieved?"[72] Democrats attacked the notion too that slaves could be freed as property of war, "contrabands." The abolitionists had always "contended that slaves were not property, but persons. Now they assert that these same negro slaves are as much property, and is as liable to confiscation as horses, oxen and munitions of war." The hypocrisy seemed clear: "If the slaves are property in one sense, why not in all?"[73]

Enslaved people rush to the hope of freedom in 1861

The *Spirit* argued that the best way to "turn the world topsy turvey" would be to permit the abolitionists to "go on in their plan of turning loose 4,000,000 indolent negroes." White workers would starve when "the negroes would spread over the North to fill the alms-houses and be supported by white labor, or underwork it." The effects of immediate emancipation would not be restricted to the economic realm. "Civilization would be put back a hundred years, Republican institutions destroyed, and our country follow in the footsteps of Mexico and Central America, where a hideous and disgusting mongrelism has made the fairest country in the world 'a hell upon earth.' " Of all the times to end slavery wartime was the worst. Any hint of emancipation would unleash unpredictable and uncontrollable force, taking on a life of its own. "The South was never as secure against the danger of slave insurrections as it is at this time, when the white population is in arms," the *Spirit* pointed out. "If the slaves were ever so much disposed to rise they could make no headway so long as every rifle, and sword, and shot gun, and every ounce of ammunition in the South, is in the possession of their masters."[74]

Abolitionists were indeed pressing the Lincoln administration to make emancipation a top priority of the Union war effort. Frederick Douglass and others argued that enslaved men, if guaranteed their freedom, would help overthrow the Confederacy. The Republicans, including Lincoln, vacillated. Some party leaders wanted to free the slaves but could not see how to unify the country behind the cause; others wanted only to restore the Union and leave slavery alone.

The Republicans in Franklin took a bold step in December 1861, one that put them far ahead of many Republicans on the leading question: they supported making the war a war against slavery. Before the war Franklin Republicans had warned against disturbing slavery where it existed, granting that it was protected by local law and the Constitution. But now that the slaveholders had "madly rushed into revolution, and convulsed our country with civil war and bloodshed, we are for striking the monster down!" They took that position as a way of defeating the Slave Power, the conspiracy of slaveholders they believed had unfairly dominated the government of the United States since its inception. The Constitution and Union had to be preserved intact, "cost what it may, and if Slavery be in the way of their preservation, let this hateful source of all our trouble be destroyed." They felt sure that if they destroyed slavery, "the world would resound with one universal acclaim of Amen and Amen!"[75]

The Democrats vehemently disagreed, arguing that abolitionism would shatter the Union cause and prolong the war. Generals Scott and McClellan had promised that the war would be over as soon as the vast Union army building strength in Virginia could be readied and marched to Richmond. With such fair prospects for an end to the war and the reunification of the nation so soon at hand, the *Spirit* asked, "is that abomination of all abominations—abolitionism—to be permitted to frustrate the designs of our Generals, upset their predictions, and kindle a new rebellion in the country before the existing one is quelled?" The paper, as was its style, put things crudely: "Will the administration let us know in plain words what we are fighting for—is it Sambo or the Union?"[76]

Even Republicans who proclaimed emancipation a war aim had no vision of ending slavery and leaving the slaves in the United States. They could not imagine a country in which four million former slaves claimed [illegible]m. Those former slaves were invariably pictured in the abstract, as [illegible]iscriminate mass without purpose or home. Like Abraham Lincoln himself, most white Republicans dreamed of colonization in 1861, of ridding the United States of black people. In this regard, their vision remained constant: Republicans had never put the interests, desires, and loyalties of black people at the center of their vision. That did not change with secession.

Republicans who wanted to end slavery were continually planning for ways to dispense with the freed slaves, ways to "avoid the expense of supporting crowds of slaves in idleness." They spoke of moving freed slaves to the lands earlier set aside for American Indians in Louisiana and Arkansas, apprenticing them to white Northern settlers there, and "leaving the question of their final disposition to be settled by Congress at the close of the war. All contrabands, as fast as they come into camp, to be promptly forwarded thither."[77] If not the Indian lands, Haiti, which "is naturally attracting the attention of the intelligent colored men of this country," would do. Its "genial clime" seemed perfectly suited to black Americans. The paper printed an invitation from Haiti's president "to the colored people of the world": "Listen, then, all ye negroes and mulattoes who, in the vast continent of America, suffer from the prejudices of caste. The Republic calls you; she invites you to bring to her your arms and your minds." The *Dispatch* claimed to have heard of "six or eight enterprising colored persons of this place who have it in contemplation to emigrate to Hayti."[78]

Lincoln listened to the abolitionists who said that the North faced an opportunity of a century to bring slavery to an end. "To fight against slaveholders, without fighting against slavery, is but a half-hearted business, and paralyzes the hands engaged in it," Frederick Douglass argued.[79] But the president also listened to those many Northerners loyal to the Union cause who argued that freeing the slaves would be suicide. While he listened, he waited.

WITH NO BATTLES on which to focus, people waged a war of words on the enemy. The months of war had deepened the contempt Southerners felt for Northerners. The *Staunton Spectator*, which had for years championed the bonds of kinship, sympathy, and interest across the border, and which had argued in the face of withering personal criticism for compromise and concession to maintain Union, gave itself over entirely to the Confederacy. "We would not now consent at any time, or under any circumstances, to be again brought into Governmental association with the people of the North," the paper snarled. "We are opposed to reconstruction on any terms whatever. The silver chord has been severed, the golden bowl has been broken, the Union lies in ruins and we hope it will never, never, NEVER be reconstructed."[80]

The Yankees suppressed free speech, the editorials charged, waging "a reign of terror." The papers claimed that "journals are suppressed for denouncing the actions of the Government. Editors are lynched and their printing offices destroyed by the mob. Forced loans are demanded of the banks." Indeed, charged the Southerners, "no Neapolitan despotism or Spanish Inquisition ever exceeded in the measure of its cruelty, the present Dictatorship at Washington." While people in the North tore at one another, the Confederate States, by contrast, "are calm and impregnable." In the midst of war, "no man in the South complains that his individual rights are trespassed upon. No State feels that she is in danger of losing her liberties. Our independence is a fact. Our prosperity is beyond a contingency."[81]

Even bad news could be used to good effect. "The Northern papers seem to be surprised because our papers speak of the sickness prevailing in some regiments of the Confederate armies," the *Spectator* observed. There was a powerful reason for reporting it: "The Southern papers, and Southern letter writers, and Southern officials, tell the whole truth about the condition of their army and their country, whether good or bad, favorable or unfavorable, and thus the people of the South are at all times informed of the real condition of affairs." Truthful Northern papers, by contrast, "are gutted and destroyed by Northern mobs, or suppressed by Northern officials, and their editors arrested or imprisoned without the privilege of a hearing or the hope of redress."[82]

The North could not afford honesty because people there had worked themselves into a desperate situation. "Never did a people swagger more in the outset, or thunder more in the preparation, of hostilities than did they," Southerners gloated. "Amid insolence and bombast and bravado, such as the world never saw, they raised, equipped and organized the 'Grand Army' that was to quarter in the Capital of the Rebels by the 4th of July, at farthest." As a result of the North's bragging, every setback and delay seemed a disaster. "The Confederate States, on the other hand, promised nothing, threatened nothing but simply asked to be 'let alone.'" They could bide their time, secure in their borders.[83]

The South's own determination to purge itself of dissidents, by contrast, was entirely benign. Jefferson Davis proclaimed that anyone who did not accept the legitimacy and sovereignty of the Confederacy had forty days to leave the new nation. "The distance to abolitiondom is short and the coast clear, and the man who is not loyal to the Southern Confederacy has no business in it," the *Spectator* announced. "Ours should be a harmonious and homogeneous people."[84]

The appearance of harmony was much heightened by the sudden disappearance of most Southern newspapers. In counties around Augusta, twenty-three papers had been published before the war began; a year later only seven remained, and only three of them came out each week. Those three, moreover, were only half as long as before: a single page printed on both sides. The politically engaged and poorly paid young men on which newspapers normally relied had gone off to war. Paper became scarce and expensive even while subscribers had less money. The papers that remained could hardly afford to alienate readers and legislators with dissidence.[85]

The insistence on harmony meant that good Southerners should refrain from criticizing their generals. Manassas had shown what happened when political and military leaders permitted themselves to be hounded by an impatient and ill-informed public. Thanks to relentless cries of "On to Richmond!" a Union army unready to fight had been thrown into battle too early. Those blowhards in the South who yelled, "On to Washington!" were fools, judged the *Spectator*. "What do they know about the condition of our readiness to advance?" asked the paper. "When and where did they receive a military education?"[86]

Some disagreed. The North would not relent until crushed, an anonymous correspondent to the *Spectator* argued. The South's borders and coastlines were too vast to guard. Better to concentrate all Confederate troops and drive to Baltimore and to Harrisburg, the capital of Pennsylvania, with armies of one hundred thousand each while holding another hundred thousand to threaten Washington. With control of the border and the Potomac in the hands of the Confederates, the North would crumble from within. Class warfare would erupt throughout

Yankeedom. "Starvation will raise up allies for us there. The war between capital and labour will break out when 'bread or blood' is emblazoned, as it will be, on the banners of the street mobs there." The approach of the Confederate army would "accelerate the disintegration of society in all the doomed cities of the North, and their streets will flow with blood, and their dark places be lighted up with conflagrations before our cannon are placed in battery on their suburbs."[87] Southerners believed that the North roiled with discontent, with furies only waiting opportunity to escape.

Virtually all commentators emphasized the strength and resources of the South. "There is no country as rich in resources as the South," boasted the *Spectator*. "It is God's favored region, on which his hand has lavished boundless wealth." A single glance at the map demonstrated that the South had been "furnished and destined by the Creator of all things to be the seat of a mighty and flourishing nation." The Southern population perfectly suited its bountiful landscape. "In her slave population of four and a half million, she has a body of laborers, hardy, industrious, reliable, and adapted to her industrial pursuits." Those slaves were worth "double the number of white inhabitants at the North, in productive capacity, and the value of their labor." The white population, for its part, was "animated by an intense love of freedom, an unbending pride, an indomitable personal courage, and a lofty chivalry of character, they can neither be awed by fear nor subdued by force."[88] How could such a nation, black and white, lose?

Patriotic language and bloody emotion were not reserved for public display. Mary Ann Sibert, a twenty-two-year-old woman working as a nurse at Mossy Creek, received a steady stream of letters from Clinton Hatcher, a beau stationed in northern Virginia. Mary Ann's father, Lorenzo, had won a burst of local fame the previous year as the inventor of a repeating rifle, the "Virginia Gun" or the "Pacificator." Now Clinton, obviously in love with Mary Ann, longed for battle.

Across the summer and fall Clinton Hatcher's anger against the Yankees grew ever more heated. In May he boasted to Mary Ann that "I had the pleasure of casting the first vote of my life last Thursday and was happy to give it in so good a cause as that of ratifying the ordinance of Secession." In July, with Manassas under his belt, Clinton announced: "I would give all that I possess for the pleasure of marching into Washington at the point of a bayonette. I have just heard of one of my classmates, a Virginian by birth who is now in Lincoln's army. If I see him once a ball from my musket or revolver will settle it if I am not killed first. Nothing would do me so much good as to take the life of such a traitor to his state." In September, Clinton dreamed of getting wounded "if I could only be taken to the Mossy Creek hospital. I am sure I should never think of pain if I could have your kind and tender attentions. I envy those soldiers who will be near you and hear your sweet voice speak words of comfort."

The next letter Mary Ann Sibert received was not from Clinton Hatcher but from his cousin Thaddeus, on the day before Christmas, giving the details of Clinton's death. "He fought like a hero all day with his company and in the evening in making a charge on the enemy he rushed on and became separated from his company." He fired alongside that unit until they had pushed the Federals back. "The fight was just closing and Clinton going on to the river bank, when within thirty yards of the bluffs the enemy discharged one more and the last volley when Clinton fell with a ball shot through his heart." The young Clinton's "last words were come on Boys let's give them one more charge." Thaddeus admired his cousin, but "poor fellow, I fear he was too rash. I sometimes think if he had have had less courage he would not have been killed. He thought it his duty to defend to the uttermost his native country and in so doing sacrificed his life." Thaddeus assured Mary Ann that he would "plant the rose as you requested."[89]

As THE FALL of 1861 began to settle over the country and bring the fighting to a pause, the people of Chambersburg took stock of the Union war effort. The months since the firing on Fort Sumter had not seen the Northern victory everyone expected, but they did show other remarkable accomplishments: "An army of over three hundred thousand men has been raised, organized, equipped, transported, and drilled ready for action." The navy had been transformed. "A fleet that was spread over the waters of the entire globe, has been called home, repaired and is in active service. Dozens of craft of all sorts had been manned, armed, and equipped. In the meantime "two forts, seven hundred prisoners, two hundred and three prizes have been captured by the fleet." These things had been "done whilst our army was in a state of disorganization, and our government affairs in chaotic confusion. What can be done in the next three months with perfect order, great power, great leaders, and a great cause?"[90]

The war marked a new era in the history of the world and its warfare, the *Valley Spirit* argued. While all around Washington vast armies pitched their camps, "west of the mountains the Union forces are pressing downward into Virginia, clearing Kentucky of the enemy, driving the hordes of General Price southward into Arkansas, and preparing for the great advance down the Mississippi." All along the border, "from Kansas to the ocean every State, almost every county, is occupied by one or the other of the two forces now striving for the supremacy or overthrow of the Union." This line of war extended "more than a thousand miles, and the men that are on it, or thronging toward it, arms in hand, will soon be nearly a million."[91]

The paper watched with awe: "This stupendous display of force may well be compared with the greatest wars which history has recorded." The stakes of the war bore the same grandeur. "It is no diplomatic quarrel, no dispute over the prices of goods, nor even the succession on a throne of a line of kings. But the question is whether a nation shall continue to exist, first among the nations of the earth, or shall be henceforth two, or ten, or thirty petty provinces."[92] Slavery received no mention in the Democrats' understanding of the vast war gathering strength all around them.

The war bred demoralization far from the battlefields as men abandoned responsibilities at home. The newspapers of Franklin County reported the results with a mixture of shock, sadness, and titillation. One story told of a girl who "gave birth to a child and deposited the body in the vault of a Privy at the residence where she was hired." The child "though fully matured had never breathed." Another told of a man, a merchant, father of several children, and church elder in another community, who arrived in Chambersburg with "a young lady whom he represented as his wife." The girl, "whose ruin he has accomplished, was from a rural district, and became acquainted with Klink by dealing at his store."[93]

Some stories were about poverty and desperation rather than sex. "A woman from the country, while in Eyster & Bro's Store a few days ago, was observed taking a piece of Calico, secreting it under her shawl and leaving the Store. She was followed and the goods taken from her." The *Dispatch* expressed only sympathy. "The woman, doubtless, was prompted to the act more from her needy circumstances than from inate dishonesty." The paper used her shoplifting as an opportunity to admonish the community: "Those who are in affluent circumstances, without a single wish or want ungratified, know not of the sufferings of the poor, whose children, from sheer necessity, are illy clad and poorly fed, and who, in the chilly hours of night occupy but squalid and cheerless beds."[94]

The *Valley Spirit*, harsher in its judgments, noted the rash of crime and wondered, "Where Are We Drifting?" All the crimes seemed crimes of desperation. "One of our Merchants was swindled out of about $75 worth of silks by a young girl. A 'contraband' relieved another Merchant of a couple of hams in a sharp way. An attempt at 'shoplifting' a piece of calico, by a woman, was made in one of our stores the other day. An overcoat was stolen from one of our Hotels last week. A young man was robbed on our public streets a few nights ago." The clear moral: "We seem to be 'advancing backwards' in honesty and morality." After only a few months of distant war the effects had been felt in deprivation and sexual exploitation.[95]

Faced with defeat and disappointment, President Lincoln declared a day of "public humiliation, prayer and fasting" in the fall of 1861. The *Dispatch* hoped that "the day will be observed in a proper and becoming manner, and not, as many do on such solemn occasions, in feasting, drunkenness and revelry." The paper welcomed the opportunity to appeal to "the Supreme Ruler of the Universe, who can raise up as well as cast down nations." Because the United States was "passing under His afflicting rod, it becomes us to humble ourselves in the dust and to cry mightily unto Him, to spare us from His just indignation and from His righteous wrath, which our multitude of National transgressions have so justly merited." The ministers of Franklin County asked that people go to their own churches on the morning of fast day and then gather for a meeting of everyone in the early afternoon. "It is sincerely hoped, that all our citizens will join in a general and devout religious observance of the day, so befitting a Christian People, especially at such a time as this."[96]

The day of humiliation and prayer had been declared, the Reverend Abraham Essick wrote in his diary, "in view of the deplorable state of the country." He offered to his Lutheran congregation "a sermon on our national sins from 2 Chron. 7.14." That verse read: "If my people, which are called by my name, shall humble themselves, and pray, and seek my face, and turn from their wicked ways; then will I hear from heaven, and will forgive their sin, and will heal their land." The church "was filled to its utmost capacity, and the audience unusually devout and attentive." Essick told his church members that "truly we have great reason to humble ourselves. Pride, avarice, intemperance, lack of charity, profanity, sabbath-breaking and various other sins, are rife. To purge out these God is, doubtless, scourging the nation. From all such good Lord deliver us!"[97] Perhaps the war, in some way that men could not now see, would be God's means of leading the Union to a spiritual rebirth.

On the last day of 1861 the Reverend Mr. Essick paused to look back over the preceding year. "It has been a year of sad and stirring events in this land. From a quiet and peacable people, who scarcely knew or thought anything about war, the military feeling has been aroused through out the entire land." Essick had lived and preached across the border in Virginia for several years, but his loyalties clearly lay with Pennsylvania and the North. "Upwards of six hundred thousand soldiers are in the field from the loyal states, for the purpose of putting down the great rebellion, which threatens to destroy our beneficent government." Unlike many of his neighbors, Essick did not underestimate the enemy's power. "How many are in arms against us, we cannot tell; but the number is very great—perhaps not much less than our own army."[98]

Essick, a man of profound optimism born of faith, could not understand how such a calamity could descend upon the United States. "I deplore the existence of this unnatural war with all my heart. There was no justifiable ground for it. Nobody was suffering from bad government. The country (especially the southern states) was never more prosperous than when the war commenced." To make matters even worse, the war on the border where Essick had lived his entire life "is a war between brethren. Families are literally divided, brother against brother, and father against son, in numerous cases one member of a family being in the northern army while another is in the southern." This man of God could imagine only one explanation: "For our sins, the Lord is chastising the nation. What the issue will be no mortal can predict. Our trust is in the Lord. But for this I would despair. The Lord reigneth, let the earth rejoice."

Ironically, "the country was never more blessed with a full harvest. The whole country has been healthy, there being no prevailing epidemics, on this account the country was never in a better condition to sustain a war." Moreover, "our government is greatly annoyed by the sympathy manifested on the other side of the ocean, especially in England and France, with this deplorable rebellion." There could be only one reason for the Europeans' vacillation: "the jealousy with which the great powers have been viewing our nation. The United States have been growing immensely in all the elements of greatness. The experiment of free institutions has shown here a degree of prosperity unequalled in the whole world." The American example threatened the "aristocratic nations" and "hence the desire to have it dismembered and weakened. They are disposed to favor the south the more also because it is there where they find the nearest approach to an aristocracy, among the slaveholders." Despite these disheartening obstacles, "the people of the North are firm in their sense of right, and, I think are determined to sustain the government and preserve the union at all sacrifices."

His accounting of public events done, Essick permitted himself to look over his own life. His ministry had flourished. "I have worked hard—rather beyond my strength—and have been cheered with many token of success." His young wife and newborn child had died exactly two years before, "a sore affliction to us all," but his surviving "children are a great comfort to me. Though young they are becoming almost necessary companions. They are all ardently attached to me, and show a commendable degree of respect and obedience." As he sat in his "snug and comfortable studio," while "the sky is clear and many bright stars are twinkling" and his "dear little pets are all snugly in bed and sound asleep," the young minister's mind was "thronged with many thoughts of the past, and my heart stirred with recollections both fond and sad. May the gracious Father of us all forgive the delinquencies of the past, and prepare for the emergencies of the future."

VIRGINIA HAD NOT STARTED the war, but neither would it be trampled upon. A tongue-in-cheek epic written by the editor of the *Staunton Spectator* in his New Year's Day issue of 1862 told the story of Virginia and the Confederacy:

I told you last spring of old Abe's "Proclamation,"
That insulted the South, and united our nation:
Virginia declared, tho' opposed to secession,
She'd never submit to a tyrant's oppression.
Since war is declared, no longer she waits,
But hastens to join the Confederate States.
Her sons were in armor, and ready to come,
At the sound of her bugle, the tap of her drum—
The preacher and lawyer, the stout mountaineer,
Men of all callings and trades volunteer,
To meet, with cold steel on Virginia's dear soil,
The legions who come to insult her and spoil.
The Boy bids adieu to his father and mother,
The maid, with a smile and a tear, to her lover—
'Tis glory to go, 'twere shame to remain—
Virginia ne'er called on her brave sons in vain!

The history seemed promising enough, though its culmination proved far distant.[99]

For months the 52d Virginia Infantry had sat on top of Allegheny Mountain only thirty miles to the west of Augusta, freezing in windy cabins, awaiting a Federal attack. "We had snow here on the 24th about 4 inches deep," George Kersh wrote his brother in January. "It stormed and blowed like the Dickens here it blowed the snow through our old clapboard roofs and sifted it over us."[100] Augusta men in the other major regiment drawn from the county, the 5th Virginia Infantry, protected the northern part of the Valley with Stonewall Jackson. While January conditions there were not as harsh as in the mountains to the west, they were harsh enough. "We marched on a solid sheet of ice," Thomas Smiley wrote to his sister Mary. "The wagons running on the road packed down the snow and it got so icy a person could hardly stand on his feet the horses falling down wagons sliding off the road and breaking to pieces there was several men slipped down and broke their legs and arms there was a great many horses killed and crippled."[101]

In the absence of action, the Confederacy occupied itself with imagining how discouraged the North must feel. "With an empty treasury, a ruined credit, an enormous public debt, and heavy taxation, it is impossible for her to maintain hostilities of such gigantic proportions as those which the war has now assumed," Virginia papers felt certain. "The Northern volunteers are not fighting from patriotism or for defence, but for pay, and when they cease to get that, they will cease to be soldiers." When the Yankee treasury had grown empty, "the grand army will melt away like morning mist, and disorganization and mutiny be the order of the day."[102] The South was sure the North would soon be torn by class warfare. "It is an ugly fix. The time is approaching when the Lincolnite dynasty will be at a loss to know which most to fear—the armies of the South, or the armies of the North. It will be easier to run from the one than to get rid of the other."[103]

The "Lincolnite dynasty" would have to claim at least one victory, however, before it could call off the war. "It must have something to show for the blood it has spilt and the money it has squandered. Therefore, we look for more bloody work, and more 'grand' movements upon the Southern rebels, ere the contest flags and closes."[104] The Confederacy would have to expect at least one more struggle such as Manassas before the war would come to an end, one more stanza in its epic.

"IT IS UNDENIABLE," proclaimed the *Valley Spirit* in early January, "that every move our army has made has been a blunder, our naval expeditions proved failures, and our battles resulted in defeats." The paper felt compelled to tell the truth, and the truth hurt. "Can any man say that this wicked rebellion is any nearer being crushed out today than nine months ago, although millions upon millions of dollars have been expended and thousands of valuable lives lost in the unnatural conflict?"[105]

Even the Republican paper of Franklin was distraught over the course of the war. The most frustrating event—or lack of an event—was the failure of General George McClellan, now in control of the Federal forces in the east, to advance toward Richmond. He had built a vast army in

Virginia. Why would he refuse to move? "If our army is not now ready to strike the enemy, when will it be?" asked the *Dispatch*. "It has been undergoing organization and discipline for the last six months, and nothing has been withheld, in the shape of munitions and equipments, to render it invincible, that an extravagant expenditure of money could procure."[106]

While tens of thousands of men flowed into the army, the Lincoln administration tried to hold the issue of slavery at bay. One Republican faction, the radicals, wanted to use the war to destroy slavery by confiscating the property of the Rebels. The Senate invited leading abolitionists to address the body. Antislavery bills proliferated, coming before committees run by New Englanders eager to promote abolitionism as a purpose of the war. Another faction, the conservatives, wanted to follow a much more cautious course, allowing slavery to die slowly by the actions of the slave states themselves, accompanied with colonization of the freed slaves to Africa or Latin America. They were in no hurry. Lincoln tried to steer a course between the radicals and the conservatives but met fierce crosscurrents.

Franklin's Democratic paper sputtered with fury that "the everlasting nigger" was being "dished up to us morning, noon and night, in such form and shape as our tormentors think best adapted to their malignant purposes." Though President Lincoln seemed to be reasonable on slavery, the abolitionists "are holding caucuses, offering resolutions in Congress, making speeches and cutting up various other antics characteristic of the race." The *Spirit*, along with other Northern Democratic papers, argued that "it is full time that something was done with these incendiaries, for they are really doing more injury to the country than the Secessionists." The abolitionists "have been instrumental in plunging the country into war, and now they are doing everything in their power to prolong it, and to add to its horrors." Rather than fight, the abolitionists busy themselves "concocting schemes that must result in making the strife more sanguinary than the most blood-thirsty could desire."[107]

The *Spirit* certainly did its own part to divide public sentiment. The paper repeatedly equated the secessionists and the abolitionists, blaming the latter for causing the war. "It is these atrocious sentiments, and others like them, that have provoked the present war, and to prolong it to the 'bitter end' the nigger is dragged into the contest by his wooly-head at every turn until it has resolved itself into a war for the special benefit of Sambo, and his abolition admirers." The abolitionists had no desire "to fight for the maintenance of the Union or the defence of our Constitution and Government." No wonder "that the Southern people felt alarmed at their position in the Union, with four hundred millions of property in slaves endangered by the advent of such a fiendish party to power."[108]

Abolitionism was no distant threat. It had broken out in Franklin County. "We have men—ah, Christian men—in our own county who are as rabid Abolitionists at heart as Lloyd Garrison or Wendell Phillips," charged the *Spirit*. Though these Franklin men "pretend to be followers of the 'meek and lowly Jesus,' " they would rather let every foot of the country "be drenched in fraternal blood than concede one iota of their miserable idiosyncrasies. These are the men of the same stamp of the New England Puritans, who killed the Indians, hung the Quakers, drove out the Baptists, drowned women for witches, and all in the name of Religion! Have we the evidence that this species of fanaticism is rampant among us? We think we have."[109]

For evidence the *Spirit* held up a petition circulating in Franklin. The petition proclaimed that the Christian denominations should testify "on behalf of human right, Law, and liberty together with an unequivocal condemnation of Southern Treason, and Slavery." Toward that end the signers of the petition resolved that "we will unite in sustaining the men in the Cabinet and in Congress who will advocate the cause of universal emancipation of the slave population and their colonization in a southern territory to be under the protection, care and government of these United States." The petition was signed by 111 residents of Franklin.[110]

The Democrats could not believe it. "We confess we were mistaken in regard to the extent of the anti-slavery feeling among us. We could not suppose that patriotism was at such a low ebb." The result of abolition would be vast suffering and a lost war for Union. Even with the colonization called for by the petition, "to free four millions of ignorant negroes would be one of the most inhuman acts that could be inflicted on the people—white and black, north and south."[111] The Democrats warned that "if the North is flooded with Abolition petitions, and the emancipation of the negroes made the object of the war in the eyes of the Southern people we wipe out the last vestige of Union sentiment in the South."[112]

The Republican papers of Franklin had always denied the charge of abolitionism, but by January 1862 some Republicans had begun to embrace the cause more openly. "What is there so hideous, so odious or so terrible in the term Abolitionist, when applied to an individual or a party, to distinguish it from another party, that induces the new editor of the Spirit to howl so terribly about it?" asked the *Dispatch*. To judge from the Democrats' depictions, an abolitionist "cannot be anything less than a monstrous, hideous hobgoblin, the sight of which would not only frighten children into spasms, but would make ignorant men—such as the Spirit only can influence—tremble with mortal fear."[113]

The Republicans went on the offensive. "As a general thing, ninety-nine out of every hundred men, who profess to be Abolitionists, are the most upright, moral, pious men of the community in which they dwell, and they have naturally become Abolitionists in their endeavors to carry out Christ's injunction: 'Whatsoever ye would that men should do to you, do ye even so to them.' " Despite its defense of abolitionism in the abstract, however, the *Dispatch* pulled away. "We are not now, nor were we ever an Abolitionist; not because we believe there is anything intrinsically wrong in the doctrine, but from prudential motives." They followed the Republican line, the Lincoln position: "We are for the preservation of our Constitution and Union, at all hazards, and if Slavery stands in the way of their preservation, then we are for striking down Slavery—or, in other words, we then become an Abolitionist."[114]

The first months of the Civil War saw remarkable contrasts and surprises. As in all wars, people thrown into conflict with one another learned to hate. Southern Unionists and Northern Democrats, who had long counted each other as allies and friends, suddenly vilified each other. People of common religious, ethnic, political, and even family backgrounds quickly came to imagine people like themselves as alien, bloodthirsty, corrupt.[115]

For all the rousing speeches, for all the eloquence and bombast against their enemies, internal solidarity shattered almost immediately in both the North and the South. People sacrificed for the cause but thought that many others did not sacrifice enough. Men of few means stepped forward to fight but sometimes regretted their sacrifice when they heard of the deprivations their families faced back home. On both sides people quarreled and chastised one another. On both sides people criticized their military and political leaders. On both sides people worried that their communities, states, and nations lacked the character to sustain a prolonged war.

Many Northerners had felt certain that nonslaveholders would vote against secession, would resist serving in the army, and would love the Union more than the Confederacy. At every step the North had been wrong. Many white Southerners had felt certain that Northern workingmen and immigrants would rebel against the capitalists and abolitionists the Southerners blamed for starting the war. That too had been wrong. Both the North and South summoned the will to put vast armies in the field in a remarkably short time. They rallied behind those armies even as they watched for signs that the cracks in their social order might break wide open.

Michael Hege, a Mennonite in Franklin County, summarized the events of 1861. He told of the firing on Fort Sumter, Lincoln's call for men, and the creation of the Union camp in the county. He ended with two somber sentences: "On the 20'th of July, there was the great butchering of Bull Run. Then there was a very great unrest in the whole land." People waited for battles to give shape to the chaos.[116]

4

THE WAR HAD not touched Franklin County very heavily by early 1862. Camp Slifer still brought men into Franklin, but complaints about the soldiers subsided, and townsfolk became used to their presence. No men from the county had been caught up in a serious battle, and the enemy did not threaten the border.

The United States had built an army of more than 575,000 by January 1, 1862. The officers in charge of these men changed as politics, illness, bickering, failures, and successes shuffled leaders as well as soldiers. Tension grew between President Lincoln and George McClellan, who was removed as general in chief. Battles broke out early in the year in East Tennessee and along the coast of the Carolinas.

The most important struggle, though, took place farther west in the cold winter of early 1862. The Confederates were trying to protect a distended front from Missouri across southern Kentucky and northern Tennessee, keeping the Federals out of the middle of the Confederacy. General Ulysses S. Grant, then only one of a number of relatively anonymous Union leaders, led gunboats and infantry against Fort Henry and Fort Donelson in Tennessee. In freezing battles in February the United States seized Nashville. The Union suddenly controlled a large part of the central Confederacy. In addition to encircling much of Middle Tennessee, the Tennessee River swept down into northern Alabama.

The 77th Pennsylvania Regiment, with 164 men from Franklin County filling Company A, occupied Nashville. The Tennessee capital seemed a long way from Chambersburg. A corporal wrote back to the *Spirit* with a rather forlorn letter, ending with a plea: "Mr. EDITOR if our friends at home would only write us letters oftener and give us all the home news they would often raise our drooping spirits."[117]

The Franklin men of the 77th had their own news to share. Henry

Erisman, a twenty-six-year-old shoemaker from Franklin, wrote back home with his impressions of the Tennessee capital, now the proudest acquisition of the Union army: "Nashville is a Purty Place and it has the appearance of being a buisness Place at one time but Buisness is suspended there now. all the stores and Buisness shops are Closed and the City is diserted of nearly all its inhabitants except the Ladys." Despite all the talk in the North about the vast reservoirs of latent Unionism in the upper South, Private Erisman saw no evidence of sympathy for his cause. The ladies "are all secesh and wear a secesh flag for Aprons and have a belt around their waists with an Ivory handled Colt Revolving Pistol of the best quality sticking in it. Nashville and all the surround Country is secesh and they dont try to hide it nether."[118] The Union army would not find the conquered South a congenial place. Nevertheless, in a matter of a few weeks in early February 1862 the border had shifted radically, entirely to the benefit of the Union.

News from the Western theater died down for a while but then returned with horrifying abruptness in early April. Franklin men had been caught up in a battle along the border of Tennessee and Mississippi at a place called Pittsburg Landing, what the Rebels called Shiloh. Ulysses Grant and William T. Sherman were surprised on April 6 by the arrival of forty-five thousand Confederates, desperate to stop the incursion of the Federal forces into the middle of the Cotton South. The Confederates attacked from the southwest, determined to push the Yankees into the Tennessee River. Confusion filled both sides as they fought on for two days. It appeared that the Rebels would win until twenty-five thousand Northern reinforcements arrived by steamboat and ferry.

"The slaughter on both sides has been immense,"[119] read a Franklin paper, and "hundreds of bodies and the carcasses of horses innumerable lay festering in the sun, while the air seemed black with buzzards, attracted thither by the stench which filled the atmosphere for miles around."[120] The Confederates lost seventeen hundred killed and eight thousand wounded; the Federals lost almost exactly the same numbers and the same proportions. "We had the bodies of the dead piled up in places like cord wood. It was the most terrific battle ever fought in this country," Colonel F. S. Stumbaugh of Franklin wrote home.[121]

The county held its breath at news of such a horrifying battle. "We await with mingled feelings of pride and anxiety to hear from this regiment—of pride, hoping that it has covered itself with glory in defence of the honor of their country and her flag, and of anxiety for some who may have fallen to rise no more," the *Dispatch* quietly observed. Though the 77th had played a key role in the battle, it had, miraculously, lost three killed and ten wounded, a low casualty rate for that struggle, in which twenty thousand men fell, about equally divided between Union and Confederate. "The only wonder is that we were not all killed. God and right must be on our side," Lieutenant Colonel Peter Housum gratefully observed.[122] The relative lack of dead and wounded, officers later agreed, resulted from the position of the 77th: lying flat on the ground and firing into the Rebel ranks as the enemy charged in.[123]

Within days the chaplain of the 77th, the Reverend J. M. Thomas, arrived in Chambersburg "to impart information, to those having friends in that portion of the army, concerning their condition, and to take on his return any message they might have to send. During his short stay here he visited most of the families of those of the 77th regiment who reside in the place." While the chaplain had some hard visits to make to parent and wives who had lost loved ones, his general report was reassuring. "He speaks in terms of praise of the moral and physical condition of the men, few are ever observed intoxicated or heard using profane language. Many hold regular prayer meetings, and other religious exercises, in their tents. The general health, and physical condition of the regiment in every respect, the Chaplain pronounces excellent."[124] The battle at Corinth, which came on the heels of Shiloh and gave the Union control of the railroad into Memphis from the south, took no toll on the 77th. So far Franklin had been lucky.

THE NORTH CONTINUED to struggle with slavery even as its armies triumphed. On March 6 President Lincoln addressed Congress, asking for money to compensate any state "for the inconveniences, public and private" demanded by the end of slavery. His expressed goal was to keep the three border slave states—Kentucky, Maryland, and Missouri—in the Union and perhaps entice back in some states that had left, allowing them to avoid the catastrophic costs of uncompensated emancipation. Lincoln wanted the end of slavery to come slowly, for "in my judgment, gradual and not sudden emancipation is better for all." Anyone who looked at the figures the government was spending on the war, he observed, could see that compensated emancipation would be much less costly than fighting until slavery had been destroyed.[125]

The Democratic paper in Franklin liked the president's message, for "we certainly like his plan of buying the negroes much better than that of killing the white race to free the black." Lincoln needed to remember of course that black and white could not possibly live together in a spirit of equality after emancipation, for "it is a law of nature" that "two antagonistic races cannot exist side by side without one holding the other in subjection."[126] Colonization would be essential. On March 13, Congress passed an article of war that forbade Union army officers from giving sanctuary to slaves who escaped to the Union army. The factions of Republicans wrestled with one another in Congress, some working for abolition, others undoing that work whenever they could.

The Republicans ended slavery in the District of Columbia as they wished to end it everywhere, compensating owners and providing for colonization. "The Bill appropriates One Million of Dollars to compensate owners of this species of property for the loss they may sustain, and One Hundred Thousand more to defray the expenses of those who may wish to emigrate to the land of their fathers," the *Dispatch* reported. The moral seemed clear: "This is an evidence that the world does move. It is an act worthy of our Country and the Age, and, with all our boasted love of liberty, is the first public tribute to Freedom adopted by our Government since the Declaration of Independence."[127]

Such idealistic and inspiring language came packaged with disavowals and reservations. The Republicans had no intention of unleashing emancipation, their Franklin paper argued, if emancipation meant "the immediate and general disruption of the servile relations existing between the white and black races in the Southern States, and a radical change in the social system of the Southern part of the Confederacy."[128] When word came that the Republican secretary of war had decided to uniform and arm former slaves freed on the South Atlantic coast, the Franklin newspaper expressed only grudging support. "We have no idea that these blacks would ever make good soldiers in the field. But for garrison duty, with a proper proportion of well-trained white officers, they may be very serviceable." Black soldiers could stand Southern heat that white soldiers could not. "Doubtless, with the taste for finery that characterizes the Africans, they will be very proud of their uniforms, and the pleasure of wearing them will excite their ambition to make good soldiers."[129]

The change of governmental policy did not alter the hearts and minds of Franklin soldiers in the field. John Miller served in a unit, containing a number of Franklin men, that took Port Royal, South Carolina, one of the first places with a large black population occupied by the Union. Miller wrote his brother George to report that "they are raising a nigger regiment there to do the guarding as it is getting too hot a white man cant stand it." Miller was dubious and blunt: "I don't think it will do any good as they will throw down their arms sooner than fight alongside niggers."[130] When Bob Taggart wrote his brother back home in Franklin about his impressions of Tidewater Virginia, the description included black people merely as part of the depressing landscape: "Whitehouse station is a miserable looking place. The only thing to be seen are 'Government Hospitals' '*Undertaker's'* shops, *Embalmers* of the dead, Suiters, & niggers."[131]

The Democrats complained relentlessly of the Republicans' attention to the slaves, no matter how hedged and patronizing such attention might be. "Congress has no time to act upon anything but the nigger," the *Spirit* railed. "The dark-skinned individual occupies the attention of Congress to the exclusion of everything for the benefit of the white man and the honor and peace of the country."[132] The Republican fixation on black people, the Democratic papers warned, threatened the North in a more direct way. "The Niggers are coming—Fine Prospects Ahead," a headline sarcastically warned as it quoted a Philadelphia paper about the arrival of ninety-seven former slaves. "An immense crowd followed the contrabands, shrieking, mimicking and tormenting them. At the saloon they were plentifully fed at the tables where a hundred thousand soldiers have been refreshed." Local black people came to meet the new arrivals and welcome them into their homes. "The negroes who have arrived are dressed in the coarsest garb of hemp, and those that stray around the city are singled out for universal criticism and laughter," the Philadelphia paper reported. "They have brought their grandmothers and children away, and we saw among the arrivals one woman upwards of a hundred years old, who stated that she had more than twenty children." All in all,

Philadelphia's white citizens proclaimed themselves "incensed at the appearance of these people, and the laboring people are particularly chagrined."[133]

Former slaves began to appear in Franklin almost daily. They "are becoming quite saucy since they consider themselves free," the *Valley Spirit* complained. "They talk about the 'poor white trash' here with as much disdain as if they really belonged to the F.F.V.'s. Their abolition friends will have to teach them better manners or they will meet with a serious backset one of these days." The paper, bitterly opposed to abolition, thought that a visit to the black part of Chambersburg would "cure" President Lincoln "of his 'emancipation policy' or he is more of a 'woolly-head' than we take him to be."[134]

The *Valley Spirit* devoted considerable space to Nip Scott, "an individual of the kullered persuasion," who "returned from the wars last week covered all over with glory." Scott had served as "private commissary" to the colonel of the 77th Pennsylvania at Pittsburg Landing. "Nip is quite a lion among the wolves of Wolfstown while fighting his battles o'er again and recounting his hair-breadth escapes on field and flood," the paper said, referring to the black neighborhood of Chambersburg. "Nip called to see us and gave a 'gleamy' account of our boys in Tennessee. He considers the 77th the crack regiment of the army—that it did all the fighting, took all the prisoners and killed all the rebels at Pittsburg Landing he is quite sure." The paper gave its account of the interview:

> We inquired of Nip if he was in the battle?
>
> "No sa I warn't."
>
> "How near were you to the fight?"
>
> "Well you see de Colonel, in de afternoon you see, sent for me you see, to bring him somthin to eat you see. I slung de habbersack ober my back and started for de field on de double quick you see, and got up whar de balls war wizzen and den—"
>
> "Well, what then Nip?"
>
> "I'd radder you wouldn't ax me anything more 'bout dat."
>
> "You did'nt retreat I hope?"
>
> "No S-ar. Dat is not de word we use out dar—I retired, sa in good order."

"Did the Colonel get nothing to eat all day?"
"No sa, muffin by dis individual nigger."
"Were you afraid of being shot?"
"No, sa, but I didn't want to be."

The editor, far from the battlefield, smugly ridiculed Scott's accounts of his experiences at the site of the largest and bloodiest battle yet seen in North America.[135]

Finally, the North felt it could afford to laugh—if only at blacks. Despite the turmoil over the future of slavery, the Union looked upon the victories throughout the South with relief and satisfaction in the spring of 1862. Much had been accomplished, from Tennessee, Mississippi, and Arkansas to Port Royal, Norfolk, and New Orleans. With General McClellan assembling a vast army on the Peninsula in Virginia, it seemed only a matter of months before the nightmare of the war could end. One more battle might do it.

5

THE CONFEDERACY PUT the best face on the losses of the winter and early spring of 1862. "We are not disposed to take a gloomy view of the seemingly sad reverses with which our arms have recently met. We do not feel discouraged by them; on the contrary, we believe that they will eventually result in good to the cause of the South," proclaimed the *Spectator*. "These reverses are but the thunder-claps which were necessary to arouse the giant of Southern energy from its false repose." Just as Manassas had stirred the North, now defeats in the West would stir the South. "The news of these reverses falls upon the ears of the brave and patriotic like the sound of the trumpet calling to arms."[136]

The most important effect of the setbacks, Confederate patriots hoped, would be to spur enlistment and reenlistment. After all, the year-long terms of the first volunteers would soon expire. The patriots of the secession spring would have fulfilled their obligation and could look forward to others taking their place on the battlefields. The Confederate Congress decided that it had no choice but to institute the first draft law in American history. In April 1862 that body decreed that all healthy white men between eighteen and thirty-five years of age were liable for three years' service. Those who had volunteered a year before for a one-year term would be required to serve two more years. The Confederate government did not want to draft men; it hoped the law would encourage men to enlist on their own rather than suffer the ignominy of being drafted.

Some wondered if enough Southern men would eagerly sacrifice themselves. The *Spectator* put on a brave face, expressing certainty that nine-tenths of the Virginia volunteers would reenlist come spring. Just as important, "we believe that thousands will now cheerfully volunteer, who have not done so heretofore, for the reason that they did not feel that their services were needed." The Confederacy was talking of conscription, a draft law to fill its ranks, but "this county has too fair a name and her sons are too proud of it to allow the stigma of a forced draft to be put upon it."[137]

The paper's confidence in Augusta proved justified: despite its dangers and despite the hardships enlistment would cause for those left behind, Augusta men continued to enlist in 1862. Nearly six hundred men who had not signed up in 1861 did so in 1862. They continued to pour into the units where their brothers and friends served (or had served): the 5th Virginia Infantry, the 52d Virginia Infantry, the Staunton Artillery, the 1st Virginia Cavalry. The Confederacy as a whole increased by about two hundred thousand men in 1862, fewer than half of them conscripts.

With one significant difference, the Augusta men who enlisted in 1862 differed little in most measurable ways from those who had signed up the year before. Heads of households were still more likely to remain at home, and men with less than a thousand dollars of property still signed up in numbers twice as large as their numbers in the county as a whole; indeed, they were a bit more likely to do so. But the percentage of men between the ages of twenty-six and thirty-five increased appreciably, and the number of firstborn sons rose as well. Those who might have stayed on the farm or in the shop now realized that the war would not end soon and that a draft might force them into service. They would have to go.

Not every man from Augusta proved eager to fight. The mere talk of conscription frightened some men enough to drive them away. Harvey Bear, a hardworking farmer from Churchville who had little to say about politics in his terse farm diary, took the time to complain about those who would not do their duty. "Some men from our neighborhood disgraced themselves and families by running to the mountain, to avoid being drafted," he observed. The pressure to bend to the needs of the Confederacy mounted when the Union army posed an immediate threat. A man's former politics did not matter.[138]

The *Spectator* reprinted a letter from a sixteen-year-old Staunton boy "in reply to a letter from his father requesting him not to re-enlist." The father thought that he himself might be drafted, and he wanted his son to stay at home to help his mother. "You and Ma are opposed to my re-enlisting in the army," the son replied. "If every parent gave such counsel, what would become of our country? I cannot consent to leave the army and quit the service when my country is bleeding and my countrymen are struggling for independence, and to leave my comrades to battle with the foe in their efforts to drive them from our land." It was true that there seemed to be some who "would rather stay at home, enjoying the luxuries of life and speculating off the poor soldiers who are in the service, guarding their homes." But merely because some men acted that way was no "reason why I should do the same. No, NEVER." This young man declared that "I for one would rather suffer banishment and exile—I would rather fill a soldier's honorable grave and sleep peacefully beneath the green sod of the Valley."[139]

Other men who had served in the Confederate army spoke in more uncertain terms. "I have not reenlisted yet and don't know when I will," James McCutchan of the 5th Virginia wrote his cousin Kate from the front in late February. "9 of our company have reenlisted. we have to the 10th of March to deside. I rather expect most of us will reenlist by that time some will stand the draft. I sometimes think that I will just float along let come what will." McCutchan resented the men back home who were content to serve in the militia and stay in Augusta. "I would not hesitate a moment to reenlist if I thought my going would not stop some malitiamen from coming. What are they all thinking about it[?] I guess some of them would like if we would reenlist, if I were in there place I would too."[140] Doubt, envy, and resentment piled up on top of one another.

Three weeks later, with the thirty-day grace period for reenlistment before a man was considered a draftee coming to its end, McCutchan still vacillated. "Most all of our company have reenlisted I haven't & I don't intend to do it, but I mean to stay & fight for my country & her rights." He proclaimed himself too proud to reenlist and accept the bonus that went with that decision. He would show "to my friends and to this World that my service can't be bought for fifty dollars." That did not mean that he would leave the service, however, for "this is the darkest hour the Confederacy has ever seen. Now is the time for every one & patriot's spirit to rally 'round the Bonnie Blue Flag & fight & never cease to fight while there is an enemy South of Mason's & Dixon's line." Despite his mixed feelings, McCutchan, like the great majority of the other men in his company, did in fact reenlist—this time for three years.[141]

Adam W. Kersh of the 52d had his doubts as well. "You were speaking of reenlisting," he wrote his brother in March. "I have not reenlisted yet nor none of our company have yet. it is a heap talk in the regiment about reenlisting. I have come to the conclusion to wait awhile and see how I get along with my first twelve months before I reenlist." Like almost all his comrades, Kersh did decide to sign up again.[142] It was hard not to. The Confederacy promised volunteers that they could serve in the unit of their choice, but draftees had to go wherever they were sent and bear the stigma of "conscript" on top of that.

Word from home eroded morale. The winter had been hard not only for soldiers in the mountains but also for their families. Though no invading armies had descended on Augusta, cold weather, food shortages, and high prices had. Mary Dedrick, a young wife with a small child at home in Fishersville, wrote her husband, Henry, a private with the 52d: "Times is hard here and if this war continues I don't know what poor people is to do." Things that they had taken for granted before—a horse for transportation and even firewood—had become hard to get. If "I want a horse I have to pay 25 cts for it and if I want a little wagon I have to pay 50 cts. for it and everything is so high. You don't know what hard times I have here about wood. Your Father did haul me a little and Aunt Becky got some hauled and when that is done I don't know what I will do." Mary offered what comfort she could. "I am glad that you are not give up trying to get to heaven. In this world we have tribulation. But in Christ we have consolation. I hope we will meet around the throne one day or other. Dear Henry strive for heaven." And he should see their son, for "nine days from today your baby will be a year old."[143]

Henry longed for home, a longing made all the worse for being so close. "I was up on the top of a ridge yesterday and I could see the Blue Ridge. I could see the laurel and Spring Hollow and I said to my self now if I was up in that hollow how soon I could get home." But he could not, and he had to end the letter because he was "so cold I can't write. I was glad to get some of your hair. It is very pretty. May god bless you all. Nothing more but remain your affectionate husband until death."[144] As bad as things were at home, Mary Dedrick worried about her husband. "Dear Henry my thoughts were fixed on you all them cold snowy days last week. I don't know how you poor fellows can stand it. I know you all have a hard time out there in them cold cotton hats." When she read about Henry looking down on Augusta from Allegheny Mountain, "Tears came twinkling from my eyes when I came to where you said that you came out on a hill and seen the Laurel Spring hollow and saying to yourself how soon could I get home if I was there." She could only pray that "you will be nearer home than that hollow before long. Dear Henry no one knows how bad I want to see you. No one knows how bad it is to be from each other, only those that have tried it." If the pain and loneliness in her words were not clear enough, Mary spelled them out: "one thing I do sincerely hope that you may never volunteer again for no one knows how bad I want you to be in peace at home again."[145]

Joseph Waddell, thirty-nine years old, well educated and public-spirited but with a wife, three adopted children, a sister, his mother-in-law, and her sister living with him, struggled with enlistment as he sat in Staunton. "The military bills pending in the Legislature cause much anxiety," he noted in his journal in February, "as they contemplate a draughting, to raise a force of 65,800 men." A couple of weeks later he observed that "a good many persons have hired substitutes for the war, in anticipation of the draught. Great anxiety felt by many who, from one cause or another, do not wish to enter the army." Waddell counted himself among the anxious many and spoke with his wife about the matter. "I have had a talk with Virginia as to my going into the army. She, very naturally, does not wish me to go, and thinks I ought not, but I am doubtful as to my duty. It is very unpleasant to me to reflect that others are encountering dangers and hardships, while I am safe at home. I earnestly pray that God will guide me and dispose of me for his glory." Finally, Waddell sought and received a medical discharge for extreme nearsightedness.[146]

People made fun of those men who tried to get out of serving. The Confederacy exempted men with disabilities, and the *Spectator* worried, in mock alarm, that the draft law had created more disabilities than any disaster that had ever descended on Virginia. On the day the draft took effect, "a countless host of disabled men were evoked from the bosom of this State, and it was made manifest that our good old mother had a vast number of weak, enfeebled, diseased, crippled, deformed, and sickly children—many shaky in the knees, weak in the back, and faint-hearted. If our weakness be our strength, and our host of disabled men our shield of defence, our State is indeed invincible." The paper suggested that if the governor would publish the number of Virginia men exempted by disability the Federal troops would surely flee such a land "as from a city with the plague."[147]

The spring of 1862 witnessed the highest rates of desertion Augusta County units would ever know. No more than a few men had deserted from the 5th or 52d in any month since the war began, but in March 1862, with battles assuredly waiting, with crops to get in the ground, with squabbles over enlistment and reenlistment filling the air, with the long and hard winter finally breaking, dozens of Augusta men left their units without permission. Twelve deserted in March, 24 in April, 12 in May, 9 in June. That pace remained unbroken in July and August before gradually fading away in the winter. All told, 108 Augusta men deserted in 1862, about 3 percent of all the men from the county in the Confederate army at the time.

Most of the men, fighting so close to home, did not find it hard to walk away from camp. Some became sick, went home to mend, and chose not to return. Others fled to West Virginia or Maryland. A few went to the Union, but most seem to have avoided fighting altogether. The case of William Harrison Rosen revealed what could drive a man to the dangerous and humiliating step of desertion. In Rosen's file, someone told of "tragedies at home" in 1862, "as in the deaths from illness of his wife, three children, his father and mother, and his brother." Rosen returned from desertion to fight throughout 1863 and into 1864. Others too reappeared on the rolls after deserting.

The struggles with reenlistment and desertion wore at morale. "Croakers"—"the long faced men of faint hearts and weak nerves, who go up and down the country, seeking to impart their own despondency and cowardice to all with whom they come in contact"—cast a pall. "We would suggest to have petticoats put upon these miserable creatures, and curls hung about their craven foreheads, but for the insult we should thereby offer to our brave women."[148]

About 1,220 men applied for exemptions in Augusta in the spring of 1862. Of those, 270 were refused while another 211 bought substitutes. Another 470 applicants were exempted for illness or disability, and 290 for their essential work. Those workers included physicians and druggists, government officials and deputy sheriffs, millers and blacksmiths, bank officers and stage drivers. The largest group was those who worked on railroads, in mines, and in manufacturing, 160 men. Overseers of slaves accounted for 15 of the exemptions.[149]

With workingmen in such demand, the role of slaves increased even more. The *Spectator*, down to one sheet, made space for one of its few advertisements in the spring of 1862. "Two Runaways!" the announcement began. "Ran away from the subscriber, at Mossy Creek Iron Works, on Sunday night, the 23rd of March, two NEGRO MEN, hired for the present year, named THORNTON and DAVID." Both men had been hired from distant counties to help fill the labor shortage at the ironworks.[150] With labor so scarce that dozens of able-bodied white men had been exempted from Confederate service, the loss of two hired slaves dealt a blow not only to the owner of the ironworks but to the Confederate cause. In the growing turmoil of war, however, runaways would find it easier and easier to escape. The vigilance once directed toward them was now directed at the Yankees.

While the armies watched one another in the Valley, people worried about another threat to the Confederacy: whiskey. "It is supposed that, in this county, FIFTY THOUSAND bushels of grain are consumed monthly by the fifty or sixty distilleries which are now in active operation," the *Spectator* observed. "As liquor will command any price, the distilleries can afford to pay an enormous price for grain, and the consequence will be that corn will become so high in price that the poor will have to suffer, as they will not be able to buy." A petition circulated throughout the county asking the state legislature to shut down the distilleries.[151]

Liquor plagued the army. "Since I have been in the service I have seen youths as it were fresh from the endearing circles of home, and warm from their mother's bosom, staggering and reeling and swearing," a letter from the camp of the 52d at Camp Allegheny reported.[152] A warning went out to the friends of the men in the regiment that "if they wish to bring or send boxes of provisions, clothing &c. to their friends in camp, they must know that there is no whiskey in the wagon, conveying the articles into camp, for Gen. Johnson has determined that, in case whiskey is found in a wagon conveying such articles he will confiscate the whole load. He has the boxes opened and examined and though whiskey may be found in but few of them, he confiscates the whole load."[153] This warning did not prevent a sly request from A. W. Kersh to his brother back home: "If you come you may bring those two shirts and a bottle of Professor Woods hair restorative that I have on the shop loft in that old walnut chest I think I left it in there when I left home if it is not there it is locked up in my desk."[154]

6

JOHN IMBODEN, hero of Manassas, grew frustrated with the prospects for promotion in the artillery. He saw a chance with the new draft law of 1862 to recruit other men like himself, eager to fight. Eternally ambitious, Imboden longed to play a larger role in the history unfolding around him. As he surveyed the possibilities, he thought the greatest scope for his talents as a recruiter, leader, and fighter lay with a new kind of unit, partisan rangers. With the Confederates spread thinly throughout northern Virginia and the mountains on the western slope of the Valley, loosely organized bands of guerrilla fighters kept the Federal troops off-balance. They called themselves independents or irregulars; the North called them bushwhackers and outlaws.

As soon as he heard that the Confederate government would authorize the formation of ten such units for service in Virginia, Imboden wrote President Jefferson Davis "about raising a legion for guerrilla service in the Mountains." Not only would such service provide Imboden with a chance to lead his own unit, but the partisans offered something the regular army did not: in addition to their standard pay, the guerrillas would be paid the going rate for any arms and munitions they captured. Fighting could be a money-making proposition. Imboden won a place as colonel in such a unit under the command of Stonewall Jackson in the spring of 1862. He immediately set to work raising companies to fight in the no-man's-land west of the Blue Ridge Mountains.[155]

Always good at public relations, the new leader quickly distributed broadsides to stores, courthouses, and crossroads calling for men to join Imboden's Partisan Rangers. "My purpose is to wage the most active warfare against our brutal invaders and their domestic allies, to hang about their camps and shoot down every sentinel, picket, courier, and wagon driver we can find," the broadside brazenly announced. They would attack "convoys and forage trains and thus render the country so unsafe that they will not dare to move except in large bodies." Only certain kinds of soldiers need apply: "It is only *men* I want, men who will pull the trigger on a Yankee with as much alacrity as they would on a mad dog; men whose consciences won't be disturbed by the sight of a vandal carcass."

Such fighting provided what men such as Imboden himself wanted and what he knew many others did as well, a place where, he advertised in a Richmond newspaper, "individual prowess is not swallowed up in the mere mechanism of the great masses of men." Their fighting would "rely on great celerity of movement, sleepless vigilance, good marksmanship and plenty of old-fashioned rough fighting and bushwhacking." The paper enthusiastically supported Imboden, arguing that partisan fighting was, "beyond a doubt, the most attractive branch of service (and would attract the attention) of all young men of daring and adventurous natures." Sure enough, in less than two months Imboden raised four complete companies and had four more nearly at full strength. He chose Staunton for his headquarters.

In May, Imboden wrote the secretary of war to request additional supplies. The people of Staunton had contributed twenty-five hundred dollars, but he needed more. He wanted to cross the Alleghenies in July to recruit yet more men. He had heard that "hundreds of men will join me as soon as I can penetrate their country." The "bogus" federally supported government there did not command their loyalty, Imboden felt sure, and half the men in the mountain counties "are represented as ready to join me as soon as I can appear amongst them with arms to put in their hands." Already Imboden had "agents at work in the heart of the Northwest sending out to me small parties of two or three unarmed men at a time." The partisan ranger felt sure that "we can do more for our cause in that region through the instrumentality of the true men there (and there are thousands of them), if properly managed, than has been accomplished by more regular military operations. But to begin I must have money and arms." He asked for five hundred of the fine Belgian or Austrian rifles that General Jackson had captured, either of which were "admirably adapted to our purposes." Imboden sought nothing less than the recovery of the Northwest for Virginia and the Confederacy.[156]

When Jacob Hildebrand of Augusta visited his son Benjamin in camp, the pious Mennonite noted with some satisfaction that he "got into Camp Shanandoah about 11th o'clock The Provost Marshall searched my wagon for whiskey but found none as I had none."[157] From the outbreak of the conflict the Mennonites and German Baptists of the Valley had struggled with their consciences. (Outsiders often used "Dunker" or "Tunker" to refer to all people they associated with the Mennonite Church despite doctrinal differences, the most obvious being the Dunkers' belief in immersion during baptism.) About four hundred families of the two faiths lived in Augusta and neighboring Rockingham, the center of their community in the Valley. The Dunkers opposed participation in slavery, and a few voted against secession, but most remained quiet in their opposition. The newspapers of Augusta never singled out the Dunkers before secession, and church members seem to have blended into the county's life without difficulty. The Dunkers' confession of faith required them to subordinate themselves to worldly government. Even if persecuted, they were not to "calumniate, slander, or defame, or with weapons of war to oppose or resist; but by faith look to God, to whom vengeance belongeth."[158]

The Dunkers had paid a small fine rather than serve in the militia before the Civil War, but once war broke out that option no longer lay open to them. Two Confederate officers came to a Valley Dunker church in the spring of 1861 to announce that all men between the ages of eighteen and forty-five must report for duty in the militia. The whole congregation was in tears, as their minister addressed them in choking and trembling voice. The Dunker men proclaimed that they would not kill anyone despite the weapons thrust into their hands. A number of men from the church hired substitutes to fight in their place, and several more purchased mail routes and postmasterships to keep them from service.

Stonewall Jackson, himself a deeply religious man, grappled with these matters of conscience as the pressure of the Union in the Valley drove the Confederacy to bring every man into the cause. Jackson wrote Virginia's governor to describe the men and their beliefs. "They can be made to fire but can very easily take bad aim," he pointed out. He proposed making the men teamsters, organized into their own companies. They would continue to drill, in case necessity forced them into action, but otherwise would remain free from obligation to fight. The governor approved the plan.

Before Jackson's leniency had become known, however, more than seventy men from the churches tried to flee the Valley rather than serve. During the preceding year of war the church had decided that opposition to military service was appropriate, and when the draft arrived in the spring of 1862, the Mennonites and Dunkers resisted. They looked to the new state of West Virginia emerging on the western border of Augusta, where they might find the Union army and refuge from the Confederate conscription. Along the way sympathetic families hid the fleeing men, sometimes under trapdoors, and showed them mountain passes where they might escape. These homes were called depots, and their guides pilots.

In early March 1862, the Confederate draft looming, a large group of Mennonites and Dunkers crossed over the mountains to the west. Many citizens watched them pass and did nothing, but two Confederate scouts intercepted them. The dissenters, searched and arrested, were marched to Richmond to prison. They passed east through Staunton on the way. "These were persons who, to avoid the general levy as well as the draft, were attempting to 'work their way' into the lines of the enemy when they were captured and brought here," the *Spectator* noted. "As most of them were members of the Tunker denomination and non-combatants by profession and practice, we suppose their conduct be attributable to a desire to avoid being participants in the war either on one side or the other." The editor felt confident of the loyalty of his Dunker and Mennonite neighbors. "Unless we be mistaken, if they sympathize with the enemy, they are not true exponents of the great mass of the members of that church. They are good and harmless citizens in times of peace, and we cannot believe them to be traitors in times of war."[159]

The seventy men were sent to Castle Thunder in Richmond, where they were met with considerable sympathy by their captors as well as by Union prisoners. Of those men, twenty-seven agreed to "volunteer" and asked to be placed in Stonewall Jackson's brigade, the brigade from their counties. The remainder were freed after a month in prison and returned home to farm. They were represented in court by Colonel John B. Baldwin of Staunton, former Unionist delegate to the Virginia Convention and now an officer in the 52d Virginia Infantry and member of the Confederate Congress.[160]

Not all the Mennonites and Dunkers joined in the resistance. Even some of the most prominent members of the church enthusiastically supported the Confederacy. Few families in the church were more prominent than the Hildebrands, who owned rich farms in eastern Augusta County and donated land on which an important church was built in 1826. Jacob Hildebrand, forty years old, worked a small but prosperous farm near Fishersville with his wife, Catherine, and their four children, Benjamin, Gideon, Michael, and Mary Susan. They owned no slaves.

Jacob Hildebrand had paid attention to politics in the 1860 election and even had dinner with Michael G. Harman, the leading Douglas Democrat in Augusta and a general in the militia. Hildebrand's son Benjamin, eighteen years old in 1861, joined the 52d Virginia Infantry early, in July 1861, well before the draft law had even been considered. The journal that Jacob Hildebrand kept in 1862 showed no anguish over his son's service or doubt about the cause for which he fought.[161]

In March 1862, with Confederate conscription threatening, Hildebrand noted: "I have to report in Staunton and from there to Winchester, as the enemy are said to be there in large numbers." He did not complain, merely observing that "God only knows whether I shall ever return again. Yet one thing I know that I have commited all things into his hands knowing that he careth for us and that he is able to keep that which I have commited to him." Hildcbrand "understood that the Yankees Draft the malitia as fast as they get posession of Va. and that they are to fight in the front Ranks against the south."[162]

Though he claimed not to put any faith in dreams, Hildebrand reported that his wife dreamed that "some barn had caught on fire, which caused great alarm, and that it burned many of the shingles off it when the fire was put out, and left some shingles on and all the Rafters stood upright not being damaged." He did not "pretend to be a Daniel to interpert dreams but will call the barn the Southern confederacy, the Rafters the States composing the confederacy, the shingles the People of the States." In other words, the Confederacy might be under fire, but the states and the people would emerge unharmed. The next day, while in Staunton, Hildebrand heard of the seventy Mennonites and Dunkers captured by the Confederacy. He merely noted that the men "had 32 horses and & $12000 in gold and silver. They were sent to Richmond today They are from the lower end of this county and Rockingham." Apparently he did not know them.[163]

Hildebrand himself had to go before the Board of Exemption at Staunton early the next week. "The crowd was too large could get no admitance." Returning the next day, he was declared "exempt on the eveidenc of Doctors A. J. Hamilton and Thomas B. Fuqua. Disease of the Heart." Hildebrand seemed neither concerned about his medical condition nor elated by the news of his exemption. He wrote to his son Benjamin, up on Allegheny Mountain, and heard that the young man was "well when he wrote." On April 6, Hildebrand learned at church that his son's regiment, the 52d, had left Allegheny Mountain and had moved into the Valley. The season for fighting had returned to Virginia.[164]

STONEWALL JACKSON AND his thirty-six hundred men had long been based in Winchester in the northern Valley. The Confederates knew that the Union army under McClellan was gathering a massive force on the Virginia coast with which to attack Richmond. In order to keep the Federals from uniting all their forces, taking the capital, and bringing the war to the early close that the North expected and demanded, Jackson and his men were ordered to remain active in the Valley, preventing the Union from concentrating its forces in Virginia. Tens of thousands of Federal troops that could have been marching on Richmond instead tried to make sure that Jackson stayed in the Valley and did not march on Washington.

The Valley was well worth protecting for its own sake, for the South could not afford to lose the rich farms and productive mills concentrated there. Alexander H. H. Stuart wrote to the secretary of war in April 1862 to warn that so much food had been stockpiled in the Valley that it offered a threat to the Confederacy. "The counties of Augusta, Rockingham, and Rockbridge now abound with supplies of wheat, flour, corn, pork, bacon, cattle and sheep. Last year's crop of corn and wheat were the largest ever raised in those counties, and the growing crops are remarkably promising. The invasion of the western counties compelled the inhabitants to drive their stock to the Valley, and thus we have on hand a double supply of cattle, hogs and sheep." This "vast surplus" would grow even greater "when the growing crop matures, sixty days hence." The bounty held military significance, for the Union army could live on this food for a year should it fall into their hands; if the Confederacy kept the Valley, they would benefit immeasurably.[165]

The Valley also offered protection for the rest of the state, serving as a barrier against the long-threatened invasion from the west. "I have only to say that if this valley is lost Virginia is lost," Stonewall Jackson wrote that spring.[166] In fact, one member of Jackson's command wrote back home, "It would be hard to convince him that the axis of the world does not stick somewhere between Winchester and Lexington."[167] Augusta lay right on that axis.

The 52d Regiment had waited for six months on the top of Allegheny Mountain to defend against Union forces that might try to rush through the gaps of the mountains to take Staunton. But in late March they came down from their perch to aid Jackson. Meanwhile the 5th Virginia, like the rest of Jackson's troops, had been moving up and down the Valley in the lingering winterlike weather of March 1862. They had left cozy Winchester when a much larger Federal force threatened them. Jackson hated to abandon the hospitable town and would not rest until he retook it. On March 23, a Sunday, Jackson attacked what he thought were four regiments, or about 4,000 men, in Kernstown, just south of Winchester. It turned out that the Union in fact had 12,000 men. The failed attack cost the Confederates 80 dead, 375 severely wounded, and 263 captured. The Augusta men of the 5th found themselves alone on a small hill, defending Jackson's entire brigade while it regrouped and then retreated. "The Fifth Virginia stood the shock of battle and stopped the advance of the foe," Jed Hotchkiss, recovered from illness and back with Jackson, wrote his wife the day after the battle.[168]

Kernstown was a defeat for the Confederacy and for Stonewall Jackson, but it brought them an unanticipated benefit. Their Federal opponents mistook the Rebels' rather heedless attack and fierce fighting as evidence of much larger numbers than the Southerners actually possessed. The Union army, exaggerating the threat that Jackson and his Valley men presented, decided that it could not risk moving any of the Federal troops from the Valley to aid McClellan. In fact, two brigades, eight thousand men, that had already crossed the Blue Ridge on their way to McClellan stopped and turned back to the Valley. A bruising defeat had somehow turned into a strategic victory for Jackson and the Confederacy.

With armies on the move in the Valley, the war threatened to descend directly on Staunton at any time. Joseph Waddell kept his finger on the pulse of the town. Each evening he recorded the rumors, reports, and conversations he had heard that day. From his position in Staunton's quartermaster's office, Waddell was well placed to hear the latest news from passengers on the train, from the telegraph office, from couriers passing through town, and from the quartermaster general himself. What he heard in March 1862 was disheartening.

"The first news I heard this morning was that the Federalists were in force at Woodstock! I did not believe it, but still the report was repeated." The little town of Woodstock was only a few dozen miles to the northeast of Staunton. People had known that Stonewall Jackson was somewhere in the northern Valley and they knew that the Union had sent Nathaniel Banks with three divisions from the east to destroy Jackson. But they had no idea of where the two armies might fall into battle. Waddell, and the rest of the town, came to believe "that a battle would certainly come off." He went home to meet with his wife, Virginia, and his niece Kate. "Va. decided at once that she would stay at home. Kate was at a loss to know what to do." Signs of an impending battle appeared. "Some 8 or 10 stage loads of sick soldiers arrived this evening. A large number of wagons with supplies from the army also arrived today. The wagon on which a large cannon was drawn, broke down opposite the Valley Hotel, and the piece was lying there at 3 o'clock this afternoon. A train of wagons went down the Valley this morning, to aid in bringing up the stores, and a large party of volunteers from Roanoke went along. The ten stages take down others in the morning. For the last week or more, two or three stages full of recruits have left here every day."[169]

All this nervous apprehension was perhaps warranted. Staunton offered no natural means of defense—no bluffs on which to post cannon and no rivers behind which to take a stand—so armies were unlikely to occupy or lay siege to it. But as the anchor of the Virginia Central Railroad in the Valley, Staunton found itself swept up in every Confederate maneuver in the Valley. As an essential link in the supply chain the town received warnings when railroad cars suddenly appeared or wagons suddenly left. As the main hospital for a large part of the state the town felt the aftershocks of conflicts when dying and wounded men poured into Staunton. As a temporary haven for refugees the town shared in other people's distress.

The war appeared in Staunton like a parade. Waddell offered snapshots of what he saw. "The volunteers were dressed in every imaginable style," he observed when new recruits came through on their way to Jackson's army. "Some wore slouch hats, some caps of their own manufacture, and others the old-fashioned high-crowned kind; the only thing *uniform* about them was the *dirt*."[170] After telling of an acquaintance who had fallen in battle, Waddell remarked with a mixture of honesty and fear: "What a change has come over the feelings of the people since the early months of this war! We hear of the wounded and slain, almost without emotion."[171]

On April 17, 1862, the first anniversary of Virginia's secession, Waddell offered a meditation: "Just a year ago to-day, the two companies left this place for Harpers Ferry. Then the war began, so far as our community was concerned. What events have taken place since then! How many battles in Virginia, . . . how many lives lost in battle and from sickness! At this time there are nearly a million of men in the field, on both sides; the enemy are coming nearer and nearer to us at Staunton; large portions of the State are devastated."[172] Waddell agreed with a newspaper from down the Valley in its bleak assessment of the situation. It argued that "conquest of the South by the North is impossible, that success on either side is impossible, that peace is impossible, that a continuation of the war as at present and restoration of the Union are both impossible, and the only possibility is that we shall have a military dictator before many years."[173] Waddell, like many other people, simply could not imagine how the vast machinery of war could be stopped once it began.

THE MENNONITE FARMER Jacob Hildebrand watched the war from his farm near Fishersville ten miles to the east of Staunton. A cavalry unit passed through Augusta on April 19, Hildebrand noted, along with "about 300 Confederate Horses and a great many cattle and sheep belonging to Refugees from down the valey. was in Staunton persons are leaveing in large numbers The road from Staunton to Waynesboro is lined with wagons, cariges &c, are continually passing down. Gen. Johnson has orders to fall back to Staunton with his army. Rain and mud The roads are almost impassable."[174] Hildebrand worried about his son Benjamin, posted on the western side of Augusta with the 52d, and noted every night that the cold rain poured down on the army. Jacob visited Benjamin on May 2 to take him a pair of shoes but "had Dificulty to through Pickets The Army is under marching orders it is likely to leave in the morning I suppose to join Gen Jacksons."[175]

People in Augusta, including soldiers themselves, were mystified by the Confederates' movements because they were supposed to be mystified. Those movements were in large part determined by a military struggle hundreds of miles away, where the Confederates were trying to find some way to keep the Union from concentrating its forces and seizing Richmond. Lee, coordinating the Confederate efforts from Richmond, thought that the key to protecting the capital actually lay on the other side of the Blue Ridge, with Stonewall Jackson and his force of 17,500 men. Jackson, despite his nickname, was hardly a famous figure in the Confederacy at this point and had done little to distinguish himself since Manassas. His idiosyncrasies were well known, and not a few of his soldiers called him Old Tom Fool. But Lee was desperate and had more faith in Jackson than did some of those around Lee in Richmond. Jackson jumped at the chance to wage the aggressive strikes he believed the Confederacy needed.

Jackson wanted to attack the Union forces under Banks at Harrisonburg, only twenty miles north of Staunton. Banks's army of nineteen thousand men presented a tempting target, a slow-moving foe burdened with heavy wagon trains of rich stores. Before Jackson could tackle Banks, though, he first had to make sure that Staunton was secure. Thus the Confederates would first move against a Union force in the Allegheny Mountains to the west of Augusta. There John C. Frémont—Pathfinder to the West, "liberator" of California, and former Republican presidential candidate—commanded twenty thousand men. Only three thousand Confederates, Benjamin Hildebrand and the rest of the 52d Virginia Infantry among them, stood between Frémont and Staunton.

Jackson's plan was audacious. He would attack Frémont and then

Banks, both of whom had larger forces than Stonewall Jackson. And he would launch these attacks one right after the other, keeping the enemy off-balance and immobilized with indecision. Jackson posted General Richard Ewell near Banks with about half of the Confederates' total force and then set off on his improbable plan.

In the midst of this campaign, William Smith Hanger Baylor paused at Jackson's headquarters to write his wife, Mary, a long letter. They had a new child. Will Baylor did not think the Union troops in the Valley would move "very rapidly upon Staunton, for fear of being flanked by us—and we hope soon to be able to do so—that our force will allow us again to give them battle and by the blessing of Providence drive them from our homes." He laughed at the fear of the civilians in Staunton. He thought them "exceedingly ludicrous and amusing—women and children and negroes and especially the men and more especially the office-holding men—Quartermaster and Commissioner were seen running to and fro through rain and much begging and hiring passage to some other point of safety." He had heard that "the Virginia Hotel was so completely deserted as to require it to be closed up—and all this panic when the enemy was at least 30 miles from them." He had advised his parents to stay put, but they seemed intent on leaving Augusta.[176]

Baylor had fought the Yankees for a year and still waited for what he was convinced would be God's aid for the Confederacy. "I hope that it will be His pleasure to restore us all to our homes with liberty and peace and happiness smiling upon us and hearts full of gratitude for his mercy and kindness." Baylor admitted that "it is a hard matter to give up home" to an enemy "seeking our destruction and the wisdom of God can alone see why it is done. Let us submit and pray for his blessing to restore us to him soon again and in His own good time." In the meantime he would keep fighting.[177]

The 5th had just elected Baylor to the colonelcy by a unanimous vote. Will confessed to Mary that "it is no pleasant thought to have the care of the lives of 800 to 1000 men—I will use every effort to look after them—to be a father I hasten." Such responsibility was indeed great for a twenty-seven-year-old man to bear. "I beseech you and all to pray to Heaven to give me the ability and assistance necessary for so hard a task and so responsible a position—I will have a fine regiment—one that loves me and will do everything I can to make it a pride and noble defence of the country."[178] Jed Hotchkiss, apparently like everyone else who knew the young colonel, thought Baylor "a good fellow—first rate, good natured and accommodating."[179]

Despite his earlier laughter about the trepidation of the people back home, Baylor worried about his wife. "The enemy are fast drawing their coils about Richmond and within them I fear you may come—If so remain at home and act as many of our noble women have done and you need fear no harm for God will protect you." The brave face gave way once again to doubts of God's will. "Oh when will this avenging sword be drawn and wielded in the cause of the just—It cannot be that our cause is not just—It cannot be that we have so sinned as to be worthy of destruction—No it cannot be." Surely "if we rely upon God and do our duty the result will be our success."[180]

Joseph Waddell, watching in Staunton, tried to piece together what all the movement of early May meant. A rumor arrived that Jackson was crossing the Blue Ridge at Brown's Gap, going East, leaving Ewell at Swift Run Gap. "I thought the report too ridiculous to be credited," Waddell wrote, but it was confirmed by passengers on the cars, "and the express rider reports that the army began to cross the mountain last night. There persons are under the impression that Jackson will enter the Valley again by way of Rockfish Gap, and that the movement is a piece of strategy. It seems to me absurd, but I can scarcely believe the reports."[181] The reports were true: Jackson had left the Valley and wanted everyone, including Federal scouts, to know it. The enemy assumed Jackson was going to aid in the defense of Richmond. His men marched relentlessly up the steep mountain through driving rain and mud that mired their wagons. Dead horses lined the roads. When the troops finally made it back down to flat ground on the eastern side of the Blue Ridge after three days of brutal marching, they found trains waiting for them on the Virginia Central Railroad. Many exhausted, dirty soldiers were loaded on the cars and, to their surprise, headed west, back over the mountains they had just climbed, back into the Valley once again, back to Staunton. The men, who had thought they were on their way to Richmond, cheered.

Waddell could not believe his eyes when he saw "a long train, drawn by two engines," for it "was full of soldiers! A number of ladies were on the hill, to see." Waddell "was informed that Jackson's movements were intended to deceive the enemy. A large number of soldiers had arrived on the train, principally such as were more or less broken down by their march of yesterday. Many of them are badly clothed and almost destitute of shoes." Waddell noted that "pickets have been posted on all the roads leading from town toward Rockingham, to prevent information getting to the enemy. Gen. Jackson and staff have arrived in town, on horseback. One or two more trains with soldiers have also come. The main body are coming afoot. I fear that most of them will be utterly broken down. They have made a marvelous march of it."[182]

On Monday, "train after train has arrived to-day, bringing various regiments . . . all of which have been through this place once or twice before. But how different their appearance since last Summer! Many of the men are ragged and quite a number entirely without shoes. They also look dirty, and sickly. . . . The town was full of country people this evening, who were permitted to come in but not to got out. Pickets are posted on all the roads."[183] Jackson did not want word of his true position known to the Federals. The 5th Virginia was back in Augusta, camped two miles outside of town along with other Valley units that had fought there since the onset of the war. "It is said that when they found that the army was really leaving the Valley at Brown's Gap, they were greatly depressed; but when their faces were turned toward Rockfish Gap, every face brightened."[184]

Jacob Hildebrand, whose son would soon be involved in fighting, noted laconically: "Monday 5th planting corn, Gen Jacksons army is in Staunton."[185] Indeed it was. With Federal reports erroneously putting him in places all over the state, Jackson set up headquarters in Staunton's Virginia Hotel, his troops camped around him in Augusta County. When cadets from the Virginia Military Institute, where Jackson had been teaching barely a year before, arrived to join him, looking impressive in their sparkling new uniforms, Jackson decided to get a haircut and finally to don a uniform other than the U.S. Army coat he had worn since his days at VMI.[186]

After this brief rest Jackson and his troops set out to confront an advance unit of the Federals in the mountains. "I rode out to get a view of the army, but there was no point at which the whole column could be seen," Waddell wrote. "We are utterly at a loss to know the destination of the army, but presume that it will soon turn and move down the Valley." He was fooled, of course, just as Jackson intended. "Soldiers engaged in actual war present a very different appearance from those on holiday parades," Waddell observed. "There is no such thing as 'uniform'—all sorts of coats, pants, hats, and caps, but they are alike in dustiness, dirtiness, and general shabbiness."[187] Jacob Hildebrand merely observed that "yesterday Gen Johnsons army left camp valey mills for the west and also Gen. Jacksons force," including Hildebrand's son Benjamin. Hildebrand himself was ministering to a friend, M. A. Coiner, whose children were dying one after another in a scourge of scarlet fever sweeping through Virginia. First, their "little son William," then their daughter Fanny, "and there are 2 more not expected to get well."[188]

On the ninth Hildebrand "heard that Gen Johnsons Brigade had an engagement on Bull Pasture Mountain near McDowell in Highland County Va."[189] Highland touched Augusta's northwest border; McDowell was a small village tucked into the mountains. Jed Hotchkiss was with Jackson as they pushed into the mountains with 5,000 men. The engineer knew the area, as he was coming to know the entire Valley, and led Jackson to an overlook and to Confederate General Edward Johnson, who had been commanding the troops in the mountains throughout the war (Old Allegheny, his troops called him). The Union and Confederate troops plunged into desperate fighting on the rocky hillsides, the Northerners attacking uphill. The Confederates drove their enemies from the field, losing more men (75 killed and 423 wounded) than the Union (26 killed and 227 wounded) even though the Yankees retreated. The Confederates had pushed the Union back, but, Hotchkiss admitted, "our troops were mingled together in the greatest confusion imaginable, calling for comrades, command, &c. like a swarm of bees, no one able to distinguish another in the darkness."[190] Hotchkiss thought the result was "a sickening sight. God be praised that we won the day."[191]

When the sun came up the next day, Hotchkiss could see more clearly what had happened at the Battle of McDowell. "The Yankees abandoned a large quantity of stores here, baggage, etc—I got quite a number of things and enjoyed plundering them, retaliating for Rich Mtn," he wrote

Sara in a letter mailed in a captured "Yankee envelope." Despite the victory, Hotchkiss admitted that "this country is a scene of desolation. Living scarce."[192] Jacob Hildebrand, hearing of the fight, wrote a brief but relieved note. "Today self and Jno. Groove started for to go to the army to see our friends got to Staunton heard that my son Ben and his brother was not hurt he Returned home."[193] Joseph Waddell, though delighted to learn of the victory, quietly noted that "a number of the wounded in the late battle near McDowell arrived this morning. Also, the corpses of eight of the slain, which lay at the Depot, scarcely more noticed than bales of goods, so accustomed to such scenes have people become."[194]

As Hildebrand and his friend moved through Augusta to the west, they too saw somber sights. "Today met great maney Dead and woundet which were bro't home by their friends 12 o'clock we got to where a great maney were woundet and were left in care of their friends at Mr. Wilsons 30 miles from Staunton." The fighting had not ended. "Gen Jackson is still persuing the enemy towards Franklin in Pendleton County and Expects to engage them he has already captured many of their stores and bagage, and a great many of the Yank."[195] Jed Hotchkiss was given the job of taking cavalry to block the three main mountain passes that led into the Valley. Jackson did not want Frémont and Banks to be able to join forces. Hotchkiss rode to his home in Churchville and recruited the company of Major Frank Sterrett, his close friend and the husband of Hotchkiss's niece Alansa. The cavalrymen covered fifty miles and used boulders and trees to clog the ways out of the mountains.[196] Meanwhile Ewell, back in the Valley, wondered where Jackson might be.

Jackson, having done what he could to keep the two branches of the Union forces from joining, now began the second stage of his plan: attacking the Yankees far to the north in the Valley at Front Royal. He told his officers to prepare to march long and hard, fifty minutes out of the hour. Every man had to keep up, no matter how fast the line marched. The pouring rains made the march through the mountains even harder than it would have been otherwise. Shoes disintegrated and wagons mired. Despite the conditions, Jackson made sure the troops covered at least fifteen miles per day. They arrived back on the rolling ground of the Valley, near Harrisonburg. Jackson consolidated the troops under this command and headed north in the Valley.

The men's progress was crucial, for the news in the rest of the Confederacy was alarming. As Waddell noted, "This evening we heard that the Federal gun boats were only twelve miles from Richmond, at the obstructions placed in the river, and assailing our batteries on the banks. Much murmuring on account of the inefficient means of defence provided by the government."[197] Jefferson Davis, facing setbacks from Nashville to Norfolk to New Orleans, proclaimed a day of humiliation and prayer. Jacob Hildebrand welcomed it. "And thus may we be Reformed, and not destroyed," he prayed. "Thus may we be holy, that we may be a happy people, whose God is the Lord."[198] Despite the prayer, he admitted two days later that "Today I have felt a great deal concerned about our army. may God in his mercy save us from our enemy's is my daily prayer, yet thy will be done O God."[199]

Meanwhile Jefferson Davis and Robert E. Lee were afraid that Banks would abandon the Valley and head east to McClellan's aid. Jackson and Ewell must keep up the pressure. So Jackson decided to attack Banks, trying to drive him all the way north to the Potomac, removing him as a threat to Richmond. The 52d Virginia, now freed from its battles in the mountains, joined in the pursuit. Jacob Hildebrand took his eldest son, resting at home a few days after McDowell, to join up with Jackson in Harrisonburg, "to go down the valey with the army to drive out Abe Lincolns Hireling tools who are Invadeing our soil and desecrating our homes. I bid farewell to Benjamin probably for the last time God only knows Yet I know that God has been our help in ages past and is our hope in years to come, and that not even a sparrow falleth to the ground but by his will."[200]

Back in Staunton, no word came. They could not know that Jackson and Ewell were pursuing Banks by stealth and speed. The Confederates now had 17,500 men joined together. They deceived Banks into thinking they were attacking in one place and then attacked elsewhere. They overran one Union stronghold after another, taking back Valley towns lost earlier to the Federal forces. On May 25 they caught up with Banks at Winchester.

The battle went better for the Confederates than they dared hope. Jed Hotchkiss wrote a brief note to his wife, Sara, the evening after the battle, scrawled in big letters on a torn half sheet. "We have whipped Banks completely, our Cavalry are in pursuit—we have had a series of victories and hardly any loss, have captured immense stores—I am perfectly well & will write soon. God be praised."[201] The next evening he spent fourteen pages describing the victory in detail and with great relish. He wrote "after a day of enjoyment in which I wish you could have participated and enjoyed some of the good things they left behind in their hasty retreat, delicacies of every kind, in getting up which the Yankee nation seems to have surpassed itself." But he was ahead of the story. Jed wanted to tell Sara how the Confederates "drove the haughty and insolent foe back from our Valley." He laughed at how the Confederates' actions, in which the topographer had played a key role, were "completely puzzling everyone in regard to our movements."[202]

The young artist and engineer, the devout Presbyterian and schoolmaster, the tender father and husband gave himself over to bloodthirsty language, telling how "with pulled sabers our men" rushed upon the enemy, "over the fences, and scattered them to the four winds, causing many of them to bite the dust and inflicting horrible wounds upon others." A "perfect stampede" of Federal soldiers "occurred in every direction, seeking to escape from the dreaded 'horse and his rider,' but in vain, and hundreds of them were captured that night and the next morning." The New York–born engineer began to talk like his mentor, Stonewall Jackson, in cold-blooded language. A Confederate regiment "gained the crest of a low ridge, along one side of which the road ran"; as a Union cavalry passed, the Confederates "poured into them a deadly volley, and such a tumbling of men and horses, as the General afterward remarked, 'it looked too bad to see so many of them disposed of at once.' "

Hotchkiss lingered over the image of Jackson in the moment of victory, chasing Banks out of Winchester. "The intrepid leader, in front, amid the roar of musketry and artillery, devoutly raised his hands to heaven, as if for Divine aid, when the enemy's line wavered, fell back, and fled. 'Now,' says the General, swinging his plain gray cap, 'Let's shout,' and at his shout up went that of the host with him and all dashed forward in pursuit." Hotchkiss described the love Jackson's men displayed for the leader they had frequently cursed and whose sanity they had doubted. "For all, even the dullest, now was the consummation of the long marches, the short rations, the sleepless nights, interdicted furloughs—

victory had come from them, and as the hero of it turned back there was one shout of triumph, one spring up, one waving of hats from one end of the long line to the other, all murmurs were hushed, and 'Old Jack' was the greatest of warriors to them and the idol of the hour's affections."

Perhaps the sweetest experience of all for Hotchkiss was marching through Winchester, freed from "the foe that had gloried in its pride and power but two short days before, amid the huzzas, shouts, tears, thanks, looks of unutterable delight, waving of Confederate flags and handkerchiefs of its whole liberated population." Hotchkiss took pleasure in telling how the people of the Valley aided the Confederacy, rounding up the fleeing Union soldiers. "They were brought in from all sides by men and women and even servants." The Confederates captured three thousand Union soldiers in two days.

Hotchkiss emphasized that "even servants" helped capture the Yankees who fled in front of the cavalry, and that was the sort of act that Confederates cherished then and for generations after, supposed testimony to the loyalty of slaves to the Southern cause. But within parentheses Hotchkiss admitted that the servants who had done so were among "what few were left, for many preceded them in their flight and we captured many of them." The same Confederate army that had chased Yankees now chased slaves. Though the men on horseback captured "many of them," more slaves escaped.

The Confederates won more than a tactical victory in the Valley. They "sent Banks and his proud array in confusion and dismay across the Potomac and where we go now will be for our own choosing." The Confederates also captured "a vast store of medicines and hospital supplies, more I suppose than we had in the whole Confederacy, a large amount of valuable ammunition etc." They captured nearly 10,000 small arms, a half million rounds of ammunition, 15,000 pounds of bacon, 2,400 pounds of sugar, and 350 bushels of salt. The hospital supplies alone were worth a quarter of a million dollars. It took John Harman of Augusta, Jackson's quartermaster major, a week to drag all the supplies to Staunton.[203]

The day after the battle Joseph Waddell noted that "an order has come for 'all the wagons in the county' to go down to remove the captured stores."[204] Harvey Bear took time from his farming to "go round to hire teams to start to Winchester to morrow for stores taken by our army from

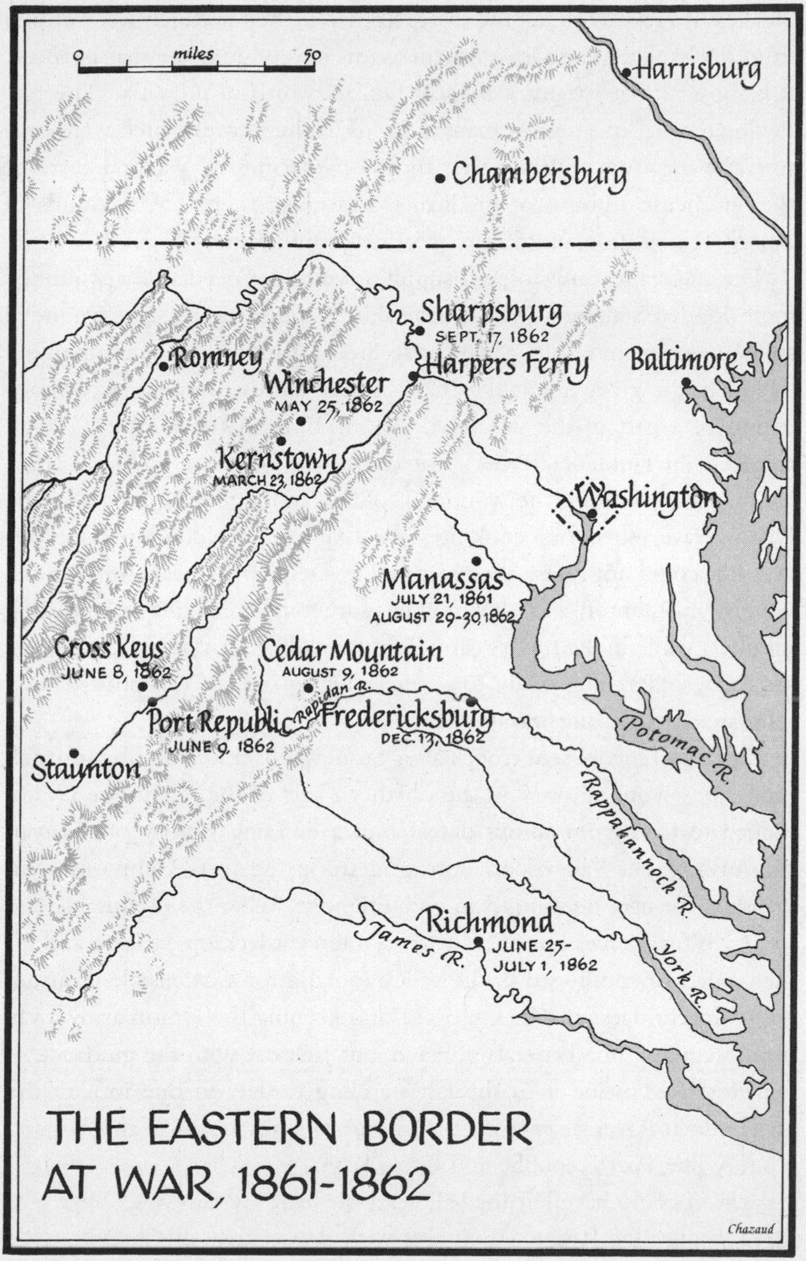
0 miles 50
Harrisburg
Chambersburg
Sharpsburg
SEPT. 17, 1862
Harpers Ferry
Baltimore
Romney
Winchester
MAY 25, 1862
Kernstown
MARCH 23, 1862
Washington
Manassas
JULY 21, 1861
AUGUST 29-30, 1862
Cross Keys
JUNE 8, 1862
Cedar Mountain
AUGUST 9, 1862
Rapidan R.
Port Republic
JUNE 9, 1862
Fredericksburg
DEC. 13, 1862
Potomac R.
Staunton
Rappahannock R.
Richmond
JUNE 25-
JULY 1, 1862
James R.
York R.
THE EASTERN BORDER
AT WAR, 1861-1862
Chazaud

enemy succeeded very well."[205] Jacob Hildebrand wrote that a neighbor's "team was pressed to haul the stores from Winchester which we captured from the Yankees The Government wants 400 wagons for that purpose. it is soposed that we got a million Dollars worth of property." The following day he "met a great many wagons hauling stores which were captured by the army at Winchester mostly medacines."[206] Waddell heard of the "immense amount of medical stores taken there—500 pounds of opium, several thousand dollars worth of quinine, etc."[207]

The medicines and hospital supplies would be needed, for wounded men flooded Staunton. "Great mortality among the sick and wounded soldiers—as many as 15 a day have died," Waddell sadly commented. "Tents in the grove about the R. R. Depot are used for the accommodation of a part of the wounded. About 1000 in the Hospital." A bit annoyed, the Confederate clerk noted that "the ladies are using my office for preparing food for the wounded soldiers in the tent hospital near the Depot. Have a shed for a cooking stove. Expect they will injure the property, but could not refuse the use of it."[208] Despite the best efforts of the people of Staunton and the military surgeons, men died in appalling numbers while in the town's care. "I counted 89 graves outside, and there are many others dug ready to receive the remains of the poor fellows who are dying in our hospitals."[209]

Abraham Lincoln sent troops after Stonewall Jackson, hoping to catch him exposed and unwary in the northern part of the Valley. The Union longed to turn ignominious defeat into a defining victory of the war, vanquishing the Valley, concentrating troops against Richmond, and bringing the ugly fighting to an end. Frémont, still in the mountains, had to march forty miles out of his way to intercept Jackson. Jackson and his men raced far southward in the Valley, looking for a defensible position, destroying bridges after they crossed, and keeping the Union army away from Staunton. The Federals pursued, but Jackson, with the guidance of Jed Hotchkiss, made it to the last standing bridge on one fork of the Shenandoah River, at two small communities just north of the Augusta County line, Port Republic and Cross Keys.

Jackson could have left the Valley. At his back lay Brown's Gap, a pass through the Blue Ridge Mountains with the security of Charlottesville on the other side. Instead he waited with fifteen thousand soldiers. And he almost lost them. The U.S. forces sought to attack at Port Republic and Cross Keys at the same time, and on June 8 a sudden rain of artillery surprised the Southerners at Port Republic. Only Jackson's destruction of the bridges in the area kept the Federals from coordinating the assault and overwhelming the Confederate forces in the Valley. Staunton was filled with fear and false reports. "The probability of Jackson's leaving the Valley is talked about," Waddell breathlessly noted. "Staunton will be occupied by the enemy, of course, in that event."[210]

The Stonewall Brigade, in which Augusta's 5th Regiment fought, came into the front of action at 7:00 A.M. on June 9. Artillery ripped into its ranks, and it appeared that the men from Staunton and Fishersville, from Stuarts Draft and Churchville would suffer a devastating loss within miles of their homes. Had it not been for the sudden arrival of reinforcements and the impossibility of the Northerners crossing the rivers without bridges, the 5th might well have suffered defeat or capture. As it was, the U.S. forces, unwilling to occupy indefensible positions and having lost many men, retreated down the Valley.

Jacob Hildebrand, down in Augusta, captured the situation with characteristic brevity: "Tuesday 10th The Yankees suffered very much on yesterday. Wednesday 11th The Yankees are falling back."[211] This time, despite rumors to the contrary in Staunton, Jackson did not pursue. Instead he rested his exhausted army in the shade of the Blue Ridge. They encamped at Brown's Gap for the next week, waiting for orders.

Staunton had been saved, but the county lost heavily, especially from the ranks of the 52d Regiment. Killed at Cross Keys were William Huff, a twenty-two-year-old farmhand with five brothers and sisters, and Clinton King a twenty-five-year-old merchant with little property but a wife and three children. At Port Republic, the next day, the losses were stunning: fourteen Augusta men died. Twelve of them, all privates, came from five different companies with the 52d. They bore different biographies in the military records that briefly recorded their deaths:

Jacob Craun, forty-five years old, left a widow and five orphaned children.

Charles Dinkel, George Fultz, and Jacob Greaver had just reenlisted the month before.

Samuel Harris had worked as a laborer on his father's farm, a farm worth less than three hundred dollars.

John McAnaway was only eighteen years old, one of seven children in a nearly propertyless household.

Josiah Plecker had been living with his folks and young wife on a farm worth more than fourteen thousand dollars and worked by two slaves.

Robert Thuma, with a wife and three children, had gone AWOL the preceding year and had been court-martialed and fined eleven dollars; so had William Via, a thirty-eight-year-old day laborer with six children at home.

Forty-eight men from the 52d Regiment received wounds at Port Republic. The bland words of the casualty list obscured the reality of shattered bones, dripping pus, and horrific disfigurement. The list merely listed the afflicted the body part: head, stomach, hand, foot, breast, arm, leg, thigh, shoulder, hip, wrist, neck, head, groin. Sometimes the description ran to greater detail, as when it told of Private James Curry's wound: a "ball entered one inch below right and lodged 3 inches above the ankle joint." Or of George Washington Kennedy's, in which the ball entered "through cheek under left eye and lost sight in eye." Thirty-three men from the 5th Virginia also took wounds away from Port Republic.

These losses hit Augusta hard. In just those two days nearly a hundred households in the county knew the horror of death or serious injury to a husband, father, son, or brother. But Joseph Waddell, like the rest of the Confederacy, tried to put aside the growing list of killed and maimed to think of what had been won by their blood. He did not exaggerate when he noted that "the whole country is ringing with the name of Jackson, or 'Stonewall,' as he is called."[212] Stonewall Jackson, thanks to his audacity and the speed and resilience of his men, had become the most popular leader in the Confederacy, the most feared enemy of the Union army.

7

THE "UNEXPECTED AND STARTLING news of the retreat of Gen. Banks' division" threw Franklin County "into a high state of excitement," the *Valley Spirit* admitted. "At an early hour in the morning the drums were out and large crowds of people were collected on all the corners, and at public places reading the extras, and circulating the order issued by the Governor calling out the militia and Volunteers." The Federal army appearing to have failed, "many of our most patriotic citizens at once commenced getting up volunteer companies to proceed to Washington for the protection of our National Capitol, or to march to any point for the defence of the border." Fifty deserters from Banks's division came through Chambersburg, some by train and some "on horseback having 'contrabands' along, and towards evening a number arrived on foot." The deserters escaped in the confusion.[213]

More significant than the deserters were the former slaves who streamed into Franklin in the wake of the battles. In an article titled "First Installment," for the newspaper expected many more black people to follow, the *Spirit* reported that "over one hundred 'contrabands' arrived in this place on Monday and Tuesday last and were added to our colored population already too numerous." The new arrivals "have mostly taken up quarters in Wolfstown," the black part of Chambersburg and the place where the lynching of a black man had taken place less than a year earlier. The paper expected no good to come from "this influx of tenants."[214]

The war in the Valley of Virginia pushed other victims into Franklin as well. A meeting convened in the courthouse in Chambersburg to devise some "means for providing for the sick and wounded soldiers who are daily passing through this place." A committee immediately "secured a large room in the lower part of the Masonic Hall which has been fitted up with beds, &c." and arranged with a hotel keeper to furnish meals.

"The expenses are to be paid by contributions from our citizens who will, we are sure, as promptly and generously respond to this call as they have to every other for the maintenance and comfort of our brave soldiers."[215]

The *Spirit*, like the rest of the North, tried to play down the astonishing defeat in the Shenandoah Valley. They had a story in place to explain why the setback did not matter. This "little flash of victory" by the Rebels only revealed "the desperation of their cause." The Confederates could not protect Richmond, and so they made "this push of offensive operations to avoid acknowledging a defeat." The desperate efforts of Jackson in the Valley "cannot in any way affect the operations of General McClellan or General Halleck. These Generals will move on with their victorious columns as though nothing of the kind had happened, and a very few days will give us the glorious news of the fall of the rebel Capital, and the defeat of Beauregard's army at Corinth, and we will then wonder at our excitement and laugh at our fears."[216]

Such a long-term perspective could only partially allay the pressing fears of Franklin. What if the arrogant Rebels should push across the border to wreak vengeance on whatever part of the North they could reach? "The idea of the rebel army coming northward is absurd, and our people need have no fears on that score," the *Spirit* assured them. "In the first place they have not the means of transportation sufficient to move a large army northward with such rapidity as would enable them to accomplish any important object and then make a safe retreat." Nevertheless, a fearful reader could protest, the Confederates might be satisfied with burning, ravaging, and plundering Franklin County and then fleeing back to Virginia before they could be captured. While that might not seem an "important object" in the larger picture, it seemed important enough to local people. Similarly, the threats that any invading army would be attacked after they were already in Pennsylvania, leaving "their bones to bleach upon our hill-sides," hardly offered a cheering image of safety.[217]

The Confederate victory in the Valley bore contradictory political implications. Northern papers might see the defeat as one more reason to support the Union cause even more fervently. "It has thoroughly aroused our people and convinced them that nothing but heavy blows, struck in rapid succession, can bring this rebellion to a speedy end," the *Spirit* roared. The Democratic paper was ready to support the Lincoln administration if it would rain those heavy blows on the South. But the surprising strength and resiliency of the Confederate army in Virginia also showed, the *Spirit* warned, that the Republicans could not afford to let their troubling attack on slavery interfere with the true and essential purpose of the war: "crushing out this wicked insurrection speedily and effectually, and restoring peace to the whole country and re-establishing the Union and Equality of States." The Southern victory was having its intended effect, instilling doubt into the North and diverting attention from Richmond, whose assault General McClellan continued to prepare.[218]

While the letters and reports from the 77th Pennsylvania on the victorious battlefields of Tennessee and Mississippi offered inspiring news, those from McClellan's troops in Virginia supplied mainly discouragement. They told of boredom, restlessness, and the constant frustrated expectation of a fight. Christian Geisel of Franklin wrote to his sister back home from the Peninsula of Virginia. "We hear canonading most every day in the direction of Yorktown, but no general battle has taken place yet, but i suppose they will begin before long. there are now about 250,000 men concentrated around Yorktown on both sides, and i expect there will be a hard fight there."[219] No fight came. Weeks later Nathaniel Dunn thought he saw the beginning of the end. "I think against they get Richmond and Yorktown (our troops I mean) it will be the ending of the war. I hope so anyhow."[220] Weeks later still, Bob Taggart wrote his brother from near Fredericksburg. "Nothing definite has yet been done towards our leaving this place."[221]

During the protracted waiting of early 1862 Northerners had ample opportunity to think over where they stood. A Joint Committee on the Conduct of the War, convened in Washington by Congress to examine the humiliating defeats of 1861, announced that the Rebels had committed "barbarities" at Manassas, barbarities, the *Chambersburg Dispatch* charged, "from which the roving Bedouin and the fiery Cossack would shrink with terror." The most sensational charge was that Confederate soldiers had made drinking cups of Union soldiers' skulls and formed jewelry from their bones.[222]

Reports from the field amplified Northerners' disdain for their opponents. A soldier in northern Virginia described what he called poor white trash: "They live in the poorest kind of log huts, are uneducated, know nothing, rent farms for little or nothing, and can scarcely pay the rent. They are gaunt, half-starved, dilapidated human beings, without religion, without knowledge, without morals, and without any comforts whatever." The Union soldier presented his interview with a woman whose husband was fighting for the Confederacy:

" 'You must have to work very hard?'

" 'Guess I does. No niggers work as hard as us poor folks.'

" 'You do not say that you are worse off than the negro slaves?'

" 'Worse! Guess we is. I'm hard at work every night after the nigger is gone to roost, an that's the way with all poor people 'round here. We're wus than the niggers. We gits no edication, dont know nothin', an has to work all our life for them that owns the sile. That's it. We has children, an they grows up an they aint no better 'an us. I guess we are wus 'an the niggers.' "[223] According to the Union soldier, this woman had no idea what the war was about. "She knew there was a Northern and a Southern army, but appeared to be puzzled as to what Northern and Southern meant." The damning portrayal of the Rebels did not stop here. "As an illustration of the morality of these people, I will state, the eldest daughter, a woman of about twenty, was trotting a baby on her knee.

" 'Is that your child?' I asked.

" 'Yass,' she replied.

" 'And has your husband gone to the war, too?'

" 'Laws, *I never done got one yet!*' "

Whatever the authenticity of this interview, its telling confirmed the North's belief that it faced a debased foe.[224]

The same sense of moral and material superiority emanated from the Northern interaction with Confederate prisoners. Four hundred such men passed through Chambersburg and the *Spirit* observed them closely. "To judge by the appearance of these men one would say that 'Secesh was pretty well played out.' How it is possible to hold an army together in such a degraded state is more than a northern mind can understand." Citizens of Franklin chatted with the prisoners while the train stopped at the station. "They are certainly the most deluded set of men we ever heard talk," the *Spirit* judged. "They profess to believe that they have gained all the battles, captured more arms and prisoners, and have had the best of the war in every respect." The editor thought the soldiers' appearance alone belied their delusion. "If the balance of the Southern army are like these they are hardly 'foemen worthy of our steel.' "[225] A nagging question haunted, though: How could such people be defeating us?

James McPherson, in his magisterial history of the Civil War, identifies the fighting in Virginia in the summer of 1862, along with simultaneous Confederate victories in Kentucky, as the first of "numerous critical points during the war [when] things might have gone altogether differently." The Southern success along the border "arrested the momentum of a seemingly imminent Union victory," assuring a "prolongation and intensification of the conflict." The battles of early 1862 were, McPherson argues, the first of four major points of possibility in the war, points of contingency. [226]

Momentous battles stand out as the most obvious forms of contingency in history. Stephen Jay Gould, in his best-selling book on the course of evolution, Wonderful Life, *used the Civil War as the clearest example he could think of to explain what he meant by contingency, "the central principle of all history." Arguing against scientists who see nature as the inevitable working out of determining laws, Gould insisted that the very evolution of life depended on "an unpredictable sequence of antecedent states, where any major change in any step of the sequence would have altered the final result." To drive home his point, Gould argued that "the South lost the Civil War with a kind of relentless inevitability once hundreds of particular events happened as they did—Pickett's charge failed, Lincoln won the election of 1864, etc., etc., etc. But wind the tape of American history back to the Louisiana Purchase, the Dred Scott decision, or even only to Fort Sumter, Gould pointed out, "let it run with just a few small and judicious changes (plus their cascade of consequences), and a different outcome, including the opposite resolution, might have occurred with equal relentlessness past a certain point."*

Gould found the war "an especially poignant tragedy because a replay of the tape might have saved a half million lives for a thousand different reasons—and we would not have a statue of a soldier, with names of the dead engraved on the pedestal below, on every village green and before every courthouse in old America."[227] *Gould could also have pointed out that slavery would have followed some other path in the absence of the battles of the Civil War. That is the great tension we feel when we consider contingency and the war: we do not merely mourn the loss of lives, or bemoan that things did not need to turn out as they*

ecause the end of slavery eventually emerged through all the contingency. We embrace the result that eventuated even as we regret the costs it exacted. We acknowledge contingency but still feel the pull of the inevitable.

Stonewall Jackson's Valley Campaign held within itself innumerable moments when events could have taken a different turn. To use Gould's metaphor, run the tape backward and play it again. This time, have the Fifth Virginia unable to slow the Union pursuit at Kernstown in March so that Jackson's men, already defeated, were decimated. Or have the Union army push the desperate Confederates off the rocky hillsides at McDowell. Or, even after the Confederate glory at Winchester, leave a bridge unburned at Port Republic or Cross Keys and see the trapped Rebels pinned against the Blue Ridge. Had any of these very real possibilities occurred, the entire campaign could have failed and Gould's "cascade of consequences" begun.

If the war had ended in 1862, before the Preliminary Emancipation Proclamation, the institution of slavery would have followed a different course. In retrospect, perhaps the best thing the Confederate army could have done for Southern slaveholders would have been to have lost in 1862. If they had, slavery might have lived on for generations in a different form, slowly passing through apprenticeship laws and phased-in freedom for people born after a certain date. Emancipation might have taken the form of compensation and colonization, the vast resources of the nation used not for soldiers but for ships and supplies to take freed slaves to Africa, the Caribbean, or Central America.[228]

Just as the war would not have occurred without slavery, so would the history of slavery—and of the United States and the world—been different had Stonewall Jackson, aided by Jed Hotchkiss and Will Baylor, not accomplished all that they did in the Valley Campaign of 1862.

This single campaign changed the lives of people of every description, radiating into thousands of homes North and South, its contingency cascading through generations yet unborn in 1862. Those who witnessed the events of that year thought and felt and acted differently about the war as a result of the battles on the spring landscape of the Valley. They understood the Confederacy and the Union in new ways, evaluated the essential characteristics of each side on a new calculus, weighed their chances of success and failure in a different scale. What has seemed inevitable before now seemed perhaps impossible; what had seemed foreordained now seemed inscrutable.

PART FOUR

THE PRESENCE OF MINE ENEMIES

FALL 1862 TO SUMMER 1863

Thou preparest a table before me in the presence of mine enemies: thou anointest my head with oil; my cup runneth over.

1

WHILE STONEWALL JACKSON and his men had been racing up and down the Shenandoah Valley, the U.S. Army under George McClellan had been massing for what Northerners felt certain would be the final campaign of the war: the drive up the Peninsula of Virginia to the Confederate capital at Richmond. Throughout April and May elaborate preparations and tentative movements proceeded. In late May Jackson's attacks in the Valley forced the Federals to dispatch troops to the west that could have aided the assault on Richmond. Nevertheless, McClellan commanded 105,000 men outside the city.

Hard fighting raged around Richmond as May turned to June. The Battle of Seven Pines (or Fair Oaks, as the Union called it), a few miles east of Richmond, exacted a cost of six thousand casualties on the Southern side and five thousand on the Northern, but accomplished little. The most important consequence of the battle came when Confederate General Joseph Johnston was seriously wounded and Jefferson Davis replaced him with Robert E. Lee. The Union registered no fear of the new leader. Indeed, McClellan professed himself happy to have Lee as his opponent, for he considered him "likely to be timid and irresolute in action."[1]

Lee proved to be more formidable than anyone expected. He pursued an aggressive strategy toward McClellan from the outset, sending cavalry under J. E. B. Stuart to conduct a reconnaissance of the vast Union army to the east of Richmond. The flamboyant young cavalry leader put himself on front pages across the country by riding with twelve hundred men all the way around McClellan's troops, taking prisoners and seizing supplies as well as headlines. Armed with the intelligence from Stuart, Lee began to plan his attack. He brought Stonewall Jackson from his brief rest to aid in a coordinated assault. In Augusta, Joseph Waddell noted the excitement but admitted: "I cannot tell how our cause comes on. No indications of a close of the war. Our people, however, seem determined to hold on."[2]

Two days later the uncertainty only increased when rumors arrived that Jackson had headed east. "Everybody wondering to-day the cause of Jackson's movement across the mountain. Some suggest he is going to Richmond, intending to fall upon McClelland's rear. Others that he crossed to meet Frémont's army, which, it is rumored, has left the Valley and gone East."[3] Thomas Smiley, writing his sister from Jackson's army, had no clearer idea. "Some think that we are going to the Valley and from there to Maryland and Pennsylvania, but I have no Idea myself where we are going."[4]

The uncertainty in Augusta grew in part because the *Staunton Spectator* finally succumbed to the shortage of paper and money and shut down in the spring of 1862. It was to remain out of commission until October. With no local newspaper, the people of Augusta were forced to rely on any scraps of news they could find. Telegraphic reports arrived at the train station, and whatever news they brought—as often as not erroneous—quickly spread by word of mouth. Passengers on the train from Richmond carried firsthand stories and recent newspapers from the capital, but those trains might or might not appear, depending on the demands of the army, which relied on the Virginia Central as a lifeline.

"Dispatches received by the telegraph operator here say that a battle began yesterday about noon at Richmond," Waddell recorded in his diary on the afternoon of Friday, June 27. "At least one hundred thousand men are arrayed on each side—what multitudes are now passing into eternity, and how many more are this moment writhing in pain on the bloody ground!" This was not merely one more battle for Waddell. "I have acquaintances, friends, and relatives there." Yet Waddell admitted a strange effect of the war: he had grown numb to the pain. "I do not feel the awful solicitude which in former times I would have anticipated." Despite his lack of feeling, he prayed that "May god in mercy spare the shedding of blood, and give us the victory!" As the telegraph dispatches continued to pour in over the next several days, the people of Augusta could hear the cannonading over the hundred miles and towering Blue Ridge that separated them from Richmond.[5] The messages on the telegraph reported that the enemy had been pushed back, but they also reported heavy losses to the Confederacy. There was no telling how things might turn out.

Day after day the cannon rumbled in an unseen distance. Day after day, for a week, the reports arrived tangled and contradictory; some had the Union army entirely surrounded and captured while others had the Union forces escaping. On June 27 a battle broke out at Gaines Mill, to the northeast of Richmond. Unlike the Valley, the land there was broken and confusing, and so was Confederate strategy. Stonewall Jackson stumbled and seemed perpetually late, only two weeks after the glory that was Cross Keys and Port Republic. The Union met Southern strength with strength, leading to horrific losses but no decisive victories.

Fifty-five men from Augusta, from both the 5th and the 52d, received wounds at Gaines Mill. Three men in each regiment had been killed. Four of those killed left short records in the census and on the rolls; they were privates, they owned little (none owned slaves), and they were too young to have families. They were, in other words, like most of the soldiers in the Civil War. But James Lucas was different. At thirty-eight years of age, he left his wife, Jane, with seven children, five of them younger than ten years old, to raise on her own. And William Henry Randolph was different for another reason. He had attended the Virginia Military Institute for six months back in 1856, and he served as an officer in the 5th Virginia, starting out as a second lieutenant and rising to captain three months before he died "at the head of his company," Company D. In his mid-twenties, Randolph was the only son of elderly parents. In normal times he would have inherited a large farm and seven slaves.

Only garbled word of Gaines Mill and the other battles of what became known as the Seven Days' Battles reached Augusta. "I am certain only of this," Waddell wrote on July 4, "that the enemy have been repulsed, losing several thousand men in killed, wounded and prisoners, and some cannon &c; and that our loss is also heavy." He decided the next day that "McClellan has, no doubt, at last reached a position on the James River, where his transports and gunboats are, his columns a good deal shattered, but not seriously reduced in numbers."[6]

That assessment was correct. But Waddell did not know that his neighbors from Augusta had been the targets of much of the cannonading. Men from the 5th, the 52d, and the Staunton Artillery all had been engaged at Malvern Hill, one of the few places the Federal army had dominated in the Seven Days'. Malvern Hill was not really a hill, but a long sloping plateau, more than a mile long and three-quarters of a mile across, gradually rising at just the right elevation for cannon to fire down. The Confederates tried to blast the Union cannon out of position but were annihilated before they could unlimber their guns, shattered and beheaded by the shells screaming in on them. Lee tried an assault of infantry up the hill, but the Northern guns ripped them apart. By the end of the day the Confederates had suffered more than five thousand men killed and wounded, twice as many as the North lost. That night rain fell on the Rebels strewn across the open ground, parts of their bodies often yards away, severed by some of the heaviest and most effective artillery fire the war would ever see.

Will Baylor, colonel of the 5th Virginia, described how officers had to lead in the midst of this deep confusion. He plunged right into the middle of the story, when his brigade found itself "partly cut in two" by another brigade, which "resulted in depriving me of some of my best men, who, in the confusion and rapid movement, lost their way and were unable to join me during the battle." Baylor and the 5th soon found themselves ordered forward and "made at a rapid pace through swamps and bogs and thick undergrowth, which made it exceedingly difficult to keep the proper alignment." He gave credit to his men, who fought "like veterans" and allowed him to keep his lines intact even though shells "fell around us thick and fast." After his men emerged from the woods, they confronted "an open and almost naked field, ascending by a regular inclined plane for almost 1,000 yards." The brigade was ordered to charge even though dusk was descending; Baylor operated more by sound than by sight.

Baylor's brigade charged up Malvern Hill, facing both artillery and infantry, until it found itself stepping on other Confederates, Georgians, who had thrown themselves on the ground because all their officers had been hit and because they had no ammunition. Baylor asked if they had bayonets. They did, and he ordered them to charge with him to the top of the hill. There they overran the Federals and "captured two Parrott pieces in battery, which, from their heated condition, evidently had been used very freely and with terrible effect upon our forces. The enemy retired slowly and sullenly, and, to the best of my knowledge, did not abandon the pieces and their position until our line had approached to within 75 yards of his." The Confederates stayed in that position as darkness fell. "My men got but little repose, as we had every reason to believe that the enemy intend to attack us during the night." As soon as he could, Baylor sent out men to find the wounded and bury the dead.

Will Baylor handed out praise to the officers, including one "killed at my side" during the charge up Malvern Hill and another, "the idol of his company and of the entire regiment," who was killed by an enemy shell after Baylor had removed the troops to the woods away from the worst fighting. Baylor found "it impossible to give too much praise to the non-commissioned officers and privates, who, without the hope of praise or the incentives of promotion, behaved like heroes."[7]

The struggles of the Augusta men were described in other official reports, with their language of romantic exposition mixed with a workmanlike accounting of losses. Brigadier General Charles Winder praised Colonel Baylor, who led his line "forward in handsome style through a swamp and thick undergrowth of laurel and bushes." Baylor and the colonel of another regiment "moved so rapidly they got in advance of the line, receiving a heavy fire, which thinned their ranks, depriving them of some of their best officers. Nothing daunted, they held their ground until the line came up, and moved on with that same impetuosity and determination." Baylor and the 5th, despite their heavy losses, "held the extreme left, and delivered to me two Parrott guns, a part of the fruits of his victory." The overwhelming rain of shells killed three men from Augusta—one each from the 5th, the 52d, and the Staunton Artillery—and wounded sixteen from the three units. The next day the Union army had disappeared, withdrawing to Harrison's Landing on the James River, eight miles away. The Confederates pursued McClellan in the rain and mud, but disease, exhaustion, and distance overcame them.[8]

All the fighting in what became known as the Seven Days' Battles ended in horrible losses on both sides: twenty thousand dead, wounded, and missing for the South; ten thousand killed and wounded for the North. Though Lee had lost nearly a quarter of his army, McClellan had fallen back. The meaning Waddell attached to the Seven Days' was the meaning others attached to it as well: "Although we have not routed the Federal army, we have a great success. The North had no expectation of a repulse" from Richmond.[9] Despite the massive army the Union had gathered in Virginia, despite the great expectations that accompanied McClellan, the Confederate capital remained safe. Lee and his fellow Confederate officers, for their part, might be relieved, but they could not be pleased with their performance, especially at Malvern Hill. As many had been killed and wounded in the Seven Days' as in all the battles of the West, even including the carnage at Shiloh. The fighting on the Peninsula was nothing like the glory of the Valley Campaign.[10]

Though Staunton grew quiet as the distant cannon calmed, the pain of the battle outside Richmond had just begun. "Yesterday a poor woman who lives in town not far from our house, heard that her husband, a member of the 52d Regiment, had been killed by a cannon ball," Waddell sadly recorded. "Her wailings were heard at our house for an hour or two. Alick was called in to see her. I met him to-day, and he seemed filled with disgust at war—horrified that rational human beings should thus slaughter one another, and fill the world with lamentation and wo." Waddell clearly felt the same way, though he abruptly ended his meditation with "we have no choice."[11]

The reports from the field were horrifying. "I suppose you have heard all about the fighting in the papers, better than I can tell you, it beat all the fights that I ever was in," James Gabbert wrote Mary Baylor in Augusta. "I could stand in place and count fifty dead yankees without moving out of my tracks some of them aren't buried for five days and some wasn't buried at all I don't believe." Gabbert was writing from the 5th Virginia's Camp Gordonsville, preparing for the next battle. As he waited, he recalled the struggle at Malvern Hill: "The Battle field was a horrible sight. To hear the wounded and dieing moaning and calling for water and for some one to take them away. We layed rite in amongst the dead & remained in the field that night it was the dreadfulest night I ever spent."[12]

Faced with losses and suffering all around them, women sometimes responded with bitterness. "Mrs. McClung, generally the personification of kindheartedness, has become bloodthirsty," Joseph Waddell observed, "and frequently sighs for Lincoln's head to be taken off."[13] While editorialists often leveled charges at men for their lack of devotion to the Southern cause, no article ever criticized the women of Augusta. Women were mentioned only to be praised for their sewing, cooking, or nursing. To read the newspapers, one would think that white women combined female nurturance and high-minded patriotism in a sort of elevated way all the more potent for its lack of vengefulness. But their letters and diaries reveal women to have been as bloodthirsty as men.

Nancy Emerson certainly felt the war deeply. She lived with her brother Luther, his wife, and three children in Augusta. Fifty-five years old in 1862, Nancy Emerson turned to her diary to express her outrage at the Yankees. She and her brother, a Presbyterian minister and the owner of two slaves, both had been born in Massachusetts, but by the time the war arrived, the Emersons had been longtime Augusta residents. Nancy began a "Memoranda of Events, Thoughts &c" in 1862. On June 30 she noted: "Firing has been heard in the vicinity of R[ichmond] for several days, & intense anxiety has been felt to learn the result." She heard the same rumors that Joseph Waddell heard, perhaps at the same place: "Tidings was bro't to church that our armies have been victorious thus far, that many prisoners, & cannon had been taken—heavy loss on both sides. Public thanks were offered for their deliverance. Our help is in God & in him alone. The battle still rages." Though partially deaf, she could still hear the cannon "several times on this occasion. Sister C. counted 25 reports in one minute by the watch."[14]

When a copy of the *Richmond Whig* arrived, Nancy Emerson "devoured it eagerly." She could not read about the battle itself, "as they are not permitted to publish yet," but she did read that "some Louisianians advanced to the charge with the name of Butler as their war cry, fought desperately." General Benjamin Butler had occupied New Orleans and in May issued a famous order decreeing that women who insulted Union soldiers would be treated as "women of the town plying her avocation"—as prostitutes, in other words. Nancy Emerson accordingly deemed Butler "the best man for our cause within the limits of the S[outhern] C[onfederacy]. He has given a union to the Southern heart, and a nerve to the Southern cause as one that none among ourselves could possibly have done." Abraham Lincoln had "performed a similar operation for us at the commencement of the struggle by his proclamation for 75,000 men, insulted Va. almost to a man & drove her out of the Union as by a thunderbolt." It was the "insults" that animated Emerson and that she assumed animated in the men in the field.[15] She noted with satisfaction that the English denounced Butler for his insult and nodded with approval when she read that a Montreal paper predicted that New Orleans "will yet take frightful vengeance for these bitter wrongs."[16]

Nancy Emerson could not understand what "the people in Yankeedom" must be thinking as they waged war against the South. "They have not got the truth yet & are still hugging the delusion that Richmond will soon be theirs. McC will get up a battle of falsehoods as usual, but truth will out sometime, & how astounding when it comes. Pity, pity, that the Northern people should have been made the dupes of such a set of knaves." Emerson felt confident that "this judgment from God has fallen upon the North because of their declension from him." Though the war's sufferings "have come upon us, & more heavily thus far," she admitted, "the end is not yet." The Confederacy too had "cause for deep humiliation, but we shall achieve our independence, & if guided aright, shall fulfill a high destiny & be far more prosperous than ever before."[17]

Emerson, despite her Northern origins, did not doubt the Southern cause. "Never for one moment since this struggle commenced, has my mind wavered as to the final result. Never could I for one moment believe that a righteous God would suffer us to be trodden down as the mud of the streets, whatever our cruel and insolent invaders might threaten." She could not doubt because "too many prayers have been ascending to heavens night & day for such an event to come to pass." Retribution might "possibly be delayed a short time but it will most assuredly come. The violent dealing of the wicked will acrue down upon his own head." There could be no uncertainty about where the wickedness lay. In fact, so certain was Nancy Emerson that she begged God for mercy on the evil foe and for reconciliation in His name. "May heaven lighten the blow, & turn the hearts of both nations to him & to one another."[18] She wrote these thoughts on the Fourth of July, when the two nations had begun as one.

2

THE *VALLEY SPIRIT* worried about the Fourth of July. "We never like to see an American citizen make a beast of himself on the fourth of July. If there is one day in the whole year that he should respect and observe decently it is this day." Unfortunately Franklin County had a tradition to the contrary, for "this day has been given up pretty much to drunkenness and riotous jollification by quite too large a portion of our community." Surely the war would impart a greater feeling of solemnity to the occasion in 1862.[19] When the day of national celebration arrived, however, the newspaper was disappointed. "We never knew as much rioting and drunkenness on one night as was put through on the night previous to the Fourth." Even ministers "who are not apt to tread on the toes of our fashionable vice" felt compelled to bring it up the next Sunday in church. "Unless something is soon done for the morals of this community—and that speedily—a catastrophy like that which befell Sodom and Gomorrah may be looked for almost every day."[20]

Partisan politics ate away at Franklin County in the summer of 1862. The fight with the South exacerbated the contempt the Republicans and Democrats held for each other. They squabbled in every issue of the *Valley Spirit* and the *Dispatch*, fighting over the conduct of the war, the role of slavery in the Union effort, the limits of legitimate dissent, and the degree of one another's despicability. "It does not surprise me," one letter to the Republican paper proclaimed, "that the *Valley Spirit*—a sheet notorious for its traitorous proclivities—should attempt to screen rebel sympathisers by a suppression of facts, in order to cast odium upon the brave soldiers of the Union army."[21] The *Spirit* responded in kind: "These negro-worshiping abolition traitors must not think that because they hide the meanest political bigotry under the mask of patriotism other men do the same."[22] Things would only get worse when election time approached.

Deserters hid out in Chambersburg. Some shirked duty, hidden behind uniforms. A squad of cavalry descended on the town in July and "arrested quite a number of persons dressed in soldiers clothes, who have been keeping up a military reputation on their three months shoddy." The *Spirit* urged that no one be able to wear a U.S. uniform who was not in active service. "These stay-at-home patriots who are so fond of aping the soldier, would have their vanity brought down a peg by such a wholesome regulation."[23]

The Federal government stepped up its demands for men to fight in the summer of 1862. On July 2, after the bloody Seven Days' Battles outside Richmond ended, President Lincoln put out a call for three hundred thousand men who were to serve for three years or as long as the war lasted. Units that fought for only nine or twelve months demanded much training and outfitting and still put green troops into battle. The United States needed men who would dedicate themselves to the war for the duration. It almost immediately became clear, however, that not enough volunteers were going to step forward.

The United States did not resort to a direct draft but rather gave each state a quota of men it had to supply to the Union cause. In turn each state mandated that its congressional districts provide their fair proportion of soldiers. The threat of a national draft hung over the entire process, as did inefficiencies and perceived injustices. States and districts argued that their quotas, extracted from imprecise numbers, were too high. Democratic partisans charged that the Republicans discriminated against Democrats' districts, demanding more men for the army and leaving fewer voters behind. Since communities suffered when men with critical skills or roles left for war, they expected the government to supply bounties to compensate soldiers' families for the economic sacrifice enlistment meant. This decentralized system did not work well. The new three-year term exacerbated all these problems, as did the recent record of Federal defeat in Virginia.

Governor Curtin of Pennsylvania, encouraged by much popular opinion, declared that he would provide men for nine months or a year but not for three years. That was demanding too much; Pennsylvania men would fight, but not for so long. The Union faced a desperate situation with these divisions over the draft. "Only the few who had accurate knowledge of the situation had any conception of the grave peril that confronted the administration," Franklin's Alexander K. McClure, the chairman of Pennsylvania's Republican party, recalled. "Our great army in the East had been defeated in repeated battles, its numbers were greatly reduced, and only by speedy and large reinforcements could the tide of disaster be turned to victory."

The federal government called on the governors of the Northern states to help them mobilize this massive number of men without triggering the resistance they rightly feared. Mayors of leading cities made no secret of their opposition to a draft. The governors met and issued a unified call. McClure deemed this "the turning point of the war." Had the governors not educated "the loyal sentiment in the North up to the point of accepting the fearful sacrifices necessary to sustain the Union, it is doubtful whether the government could have been successful in replenishing the broken lines of our army." As it was, the national government continued to threaten a national draft if the local efforts did not succeed.[24]

Faced with a shortfall in recruiting, the U.S. War Department upped its bounty rate, paying men to enlist, and localities added bonuses on top of that. The leaders of Franklin County drummed up support with direct pleas for local safety. "The people of the towns throughout the county are holding War Meetings and using every means to encourage enlistments," a local paper reported. "Should this rebellion be allowed to go on much longer our neighborhood cannot escape the horrors of war if the threats of the rebels mean anything." The editor felt certain that "there are scores of men ready and willing, in every section of the county, to serve their country but they are waiting to be asked. That is not the way to show their patriotism—they must come forward voluntarily at the tap of the drum."[25]

A soldier in the field was not so sure. James Carman of the 107th told his father that he feared "very much whether Pennsylvania can make up her quota of troops without drafting. I only hope she can for her own credit." Even Carman, an officer, admitted that he had "been tempted to resign before this when I look and see how things are going." But he reminded himself and his father, who was encouraging his son to resign, that "I have taken an oath to support the Constitution of the U. States and obey the President and assist in him in carrying out and administering the law." By August, Lincoln's call for troops had produced 421,000 men for three years and another 88,000 for nine months. Pennsylvania never quite attained its quota but still supplied more than 60,000 new soldiers.[26]

Many who had waited eventually came forward. In August, Franklin began the formation of the 126th Pennsylvania Volunteers, a nine-month unit. It took three weeks to gather eight companies, eight hundred men, from throughout Franklin, with two more companies coming from a neighboring county. Chambersburg contributed Companies A, D, and G, Mercersburg supplied Company C, Antrim manned Company B, and Waynesboro Company E. "From the highlands of Path Valley" came Company H, and from Greencastle Company K. Men from St. Thomas, Greencastle, and Chambersburg were elected colonel and major. "The towns and hill-sides of the Conococheague sent their best youth," an officer of the regiment bragged. The 126th could be "regarded with pride by her people as her peculiar contribution to the war."[27]

More than a hundred men joined the Chambers Infantry within the 126th. "The company is composed of the very *elite* of the young men of this community, and are as respectable, intelligent and fine looking a body of men as can be found anywhere. They left in fine spirits and seem to have entered upon the life of a soldier with a hearty good will." Indeed, "almost the entire population of the town had collected around the depot to witness the departure of the company, and take leave of the gallant young men who have volunteered so promptly at their country's call." The fact that they had waited for well over a year to enlist, and had done so only when dictates from Washington forced their hand, did not seem to cloud the glory. "They were the first company to arrive in Harrisburg under the late call for additional troops," the *Spirit* proudly noted. "Well done for Chambersburg."[28]

A member of the Chambers Infantry filed reports with the *Valley Spirit* as the unit headed to Camp Curtin in Harrisburg, describing the conversion of the civilians into soldiers. A young man who signed his name Kennedy sent the reports from the unit back home from the very beginning of their service. He was probably Private William Kennedy, a twenty-three-year-old editor from Chambersburg with gray eyes, black hair, a florid complexion, a stature of five feet five inches, and a charming sense of self-deprecation. His letters made it sound as if the war had just begun, as if tens of thousands of young men had not already died, as if the war were any closer to a conclusion. Everything seemed new and exciting. "Their whole route was a complete ovation—at all the way-stations where large crowds had assembled cheers welcomed the volunteers, and the air was filled with fluttering cambric." After walking over a mile in the "broiling hot sun," the "infants" were examined and equipped. As they pitched their tents, they "all congratulated ourselves on doing very well for the first attempt."[29]

Thousands of soldiers poured into the camp every day, bolstering the confidence of one another. "The kind friends at home should not picture to themselves dreary scenes of the camp, and imagine that their 'brave soldier boys' are in the least low-spirited or discontented, for a more jolly set were never seen. Wit and pleasantry rule the hour."[30] A week later these young men found themselves on the "sacred soil" of Virginia, as they sarcastically called it. The 126th had traveled, "after innumerable unpleasant delays," to Baltimore and then to Washington, where they had an hour to see the sights before they were marched out of the city.[31]

The addition of nearly half a million new soldiers and the change of leadership in Virginia infused the Union army with confidence in the summer 1862. The men who joined the cause in the late summer and fall of 1862, despite having done so only after much talk of quotas and drafts, did not differ very much from those who had enlisted in the first year of the war.

Nor did the Franklin recruits differ from their counterparts in Augusta. The similarities were striking in age, in occupation, in birth order. Most striking of all was the similarity in class background: in Franklin as well as in Augusta, men in the bottom ranks of the property order were represented twice as heavily as those of any other property category. Moreover, since Augusta whites held more property than those in Franklin, the poorer soldiers from the Northern county were, as a whole, poorer than those from the Southern county. The Civil War was disproportionately a poor man's fight.

The experience of Franklin County with enlistment typified that of the North in general. Just over a third of the eligible white male population in Franklin was to fight for the U.S. Army, nearly the same as for the North as a whole. Augusta, like the South as a whole, sent a higher proportion of its men into the service at each step of the war. By the end of 1862 Franklin had recruited 2,585 men for the cause; in the same time, Augusta had sent 2,304 men to the Confederacy, about double the rate relative to population. Also, most of the Augusta men had gone to war more than a year earlier than their Franklin counterparts, the great bulk of whom signed on in the fall of 1862.[32]

In the wake of the Seven Days' losses, the president brought Henry Halleck from the Western theater to serve as general in chief, a role that Lincoln himself had been playing. The president also transferred John Pope from the West and put him in charge of a new army, the Army of Virginia, forged from those that Jackson had defeated in western Virginia and the Valley. Pope found the three corps under his command dispirited and in disarray after the defeats of the preceding months.

At the same time that it tried to bolster the ranks and leadership of its Eastern armies, the Union also declared harsh policies against the civilian population that sustained the rebellion in Virginia. Pope, with the blessings of the Lincoln administration, issued new general orders in July, each order establishing a far harder line than the Federal army had pursued before. One decreed that "the troops of this command will subsist upon the country in which their operations are carried on." The army would take what it needed, giving vouchers to repay those who could show, at the end of the war, that they were loyal citizens of the United States. Another general order notified "the people of the valley of the Shenandoah, and throughout the region of the operations of this army, living along the lines of railroad and telegraph" that they would "be held responsible for any injury done to the track, line or road, or for any attacks upon trains or straggling soldiers by bands of guerrillas in their neighborhood." Civilians would be held responsible for abetting those who would hinder or endanger the Union cause. Moreover, "if any soldier or legitimate follower of the army be fired upon from any house, the house shall be razed to the ground and the inhabitants sent prisoners to the head-quarters of this army."[33]

FRANKLIN SOLDIERS IN THE FIELD approved of new harsh measures instituted by the Federal leadership. James Carman, a lieutenant in the 107th Pennsylvania, stationed near Warrenton, Virginia, told his father back in Franklin that "this war must be conducted on different principals than what it has been or our case will be in danger." What had to be done? "Slaveholders must not look for their property or negroes to be protected they must either be for us or against us." Carman had seen enough deception by the Virginians by whom he was surrounded. "They who are loyal must come out and them who are rebels must swear allegiance to the country or be taken as prisoner of war." The Union simply could not win "if we alow rebels to run lose carry all information to the enemy. They can, we must stop these things, and start out on the new."[34]

Upon taking command in Virginia, John Pope bragged to his new units about his performance in the West, "where we have always seen the backs of our enemies," and promised to wage a harder war in the East. He authorized the confiscation of Confederate property without compensation and the expulsion from occupied territory of all civilians who would not take an oath of allegiance. He also declared that captured guerrillas would be shot. He justified his action by quoting papers captured from John Imboden, commander of the Confederate 1st Partisan Rangers, papers that told of Imboden's plans to blend into the local population by day and wreak terror by night, to "shoot down every sentinel, picket, courier and wagon driver we can find." Pope's orders would fight fire with fire.[35]

His fellow Union generals did not hold Pope in high regard, and he reciprocated with equal disdain. Nevertheless, Federal soldiers in Virginia welcomed the change and admired Pope's hard line. "We are now in Pope's great army of Virginia," William Kindig wrote his friend Henry Bitner in July. "The men have great belief in him and his energetic policy, and all desire and expect that he will soon give us a chance to distinguish ourselves. We all regard his late stringent orders as just the thing." Kindig and his fellow soldiers "all are down on slow coach McClellan, who marched his army into the swamps of the Chickahominy, and kept them intrenching and digging, while they were dying by the thousand, and all this time made no attempt on Richmond."[36]

The Union soldiers felt a growing hatred for their foes. "The Rebels are wors then a set of heathren," J. B. Sweigert wrote home to his cousin. "They take our men and pin them up aganst treas with their buynetts and fire upon our hospitals wheir the sick are. An they have fired on severails of our flag of truth and whe it comes to that roust i thik it is time to du somthig it rais my blud evry time i see sutch things." Sweigert had grown weary of the war, for "i have seen more then i ever expect to see and more then ever i want to see again." He approved of Pope's harsh measures: "General pope has gaven orders to take evry thing Whe want of the farmers and whe will du so." After the Union soldiers had picked the land clean, "i think the rebels will not get mutch on the ground." Many Federal soldiers used the orders as an excuse to take everything they could from the local population, appropriating so many animals to kill for fresh meat that their camps looked like slaughterhouses. Officers, disgusted with the looting, warned that the unrestrained destruction was eroding discipline in the Army of Virginia and feeding a growing hatred of the occupying army as word of the spoliation spread across the South.[37]

Union soldiers could see the effect the war was having on Virginia slavery. Although the land was fertile and "grain and potatoes, in profusion" had been planted throughout central Virginia, a soldier in Pope's army wrote to the local newspaper, "Nearly all the best of the slaves who were not sent South have run off towards our army." On one plantation, 170 women and children remained, but only "eleven men fit to work in the field; most of them had run away." "Several thousand able bodied men can yet be gathered up" in surrounding counties, this soldier believed, and the Union army was eagerly doing so. The boundary between coercion and persuasion was not always clear. A group of enslaved men came " 'to see the sojers,' and the Provost gathered them up and put them into the service; all seemed pleased at the change." During a march "one of the mules gave out; on the side of a hill was discerned a darkey ploughing, over goes a cavalry man, and soon the 'dark' was on his mule, coming across to the road; his mule now has his tail and mane cropped, the badge 'U.S.' upon his shoulder, and the dark was set to carrying the knapsacks of some weary and footsore soldiers."[38]

When the men of Pope's army stopped "to get a drink of an old slave woman," they "asked her if she ever heard of 'old John Brown.' 'Yes, indeed massa, long while ago; de Lord sent him out to free de slaves, but de Virginians hanged him and now de Lord send down hosts of men.' " This enslaved woman "was firm in the belief that it was 'de contention of de Lord' to make all free. Although near a hundred years old, she seemed as highly delighted at the prospect of freedom as would a youth with the world before him." The soldiers discovered that many black

Virginians believed that "John Brown was merely out on a kind of reconnoissance, and that he was the originator of the present war."[39]

A white Virginian from the locality admitted to the Pennsylvania soldiers that "Virginia is ruined, and that she cannot recover from the losses she has sustained in 25 years. He says that slavery in Virginia is practically abolished; that the few they now hold will never be of any value, no matter if the war were ended today." This man, who "says he was a Union man while there was any Union men, but now there was none," was what the Federal soldier called a "religious rebel": " 'believes in foreordination,' and says it seems to be the will of God that slavery shall be wiped out; but for all his hatred of the Yankees is bitter in the extreme; he thinks that Virginia, or the South, will never submit to the North, and he will leave all—home, property, and all—before taking the oath."[40] The Union would have to overwhelm such men, break such men; the time for compromise had long passed.

Bob Taggart from Franklin told with relish of occupying the show plantation of the leading secessionist of Virginia, Edmund Ruffin. "I write this in 'Old Ruffin's' barn," Taggart boasted to his brother, also a Union soldier. Ruffin had "fired the first gun on Sumter, in return for which our boys are now subsisting on his place, and have appropriated to themselves his large library, and every article of house and kitchen furniture." Ruffin, Taggart noted, "was a man of note here. Editor, Agriculturist, Senator, Doctor, etc. etc. His plantation is large and supplies our Brigade right handsomely with corn potatoes, apples, peaches and such like."[41] Ruffin had written widely on agricultural reform, and now the Northern men he hated so bitterly harvested his bounty.

As the Union shifted troops from the Peninsula and consolidated command under Halleck, commanders worried about what the Rebels might do during the period of instability. The 126th Pennsylvania, full of Franklin men and formed only weeks earlier, found itself on the move toward Gordonsville, where the United States maintained a large supply base. "Indications are that the severest battle of the war will be fought in this vicinity, in a very few days," the young correspondent from Franklin wrote back home. "There seems to be great need of men, and in all probability we will take an active part in the approaching engagement." Though the men "are all in the highest spirits and anxious to have their courage put to the test," the correspondent admitted with considerable understatement, "there seems to be a general regret that they are not better drilled. Yet all have confidence in their officers and each other. If the worst must come, you may rest assured Franklin County will never be disgraced by the 'One Hundred and Twenty Sixth.' " Artillery rumbled in the distance, and ambulances continually passed carrying sick and wounded soldiers. "We nearly all came to the conclusion that it begins to look very much like war in this vicinity."[42] The Franklin correspondent had already mastered the laconic understatement that soldiers used to make the horror bearable.

3

ROBERT E. LEE, like his fellow Southerners, saw in John Pope the very embodiment of Yankee hypocrisy, greed, and incompetence. Lee wrote to the U.S. government in the summer of 1862 to announce that Pope and his men were no better than "robbers and murderers"; any captured officers of that command would not treated under the same rules as other prisoners of war but would instead be held in "close confinement." Moreover, if Pope's men killed any unarmed Virginians, the Confederates would hang a corresponding number of Union officers captured by the Southerners. The United States refused to accept the letter.[43]

Throughout July 1862, Lee watched the Union forces in northern Virginia and on the Peninsula, worrying about both Pope and McClellan. The Federals might follow several plans to overwhelm the Confederates. The Northerners might cut off the rail connection to the vital Shenandoah Valley and then push to Richmond against a weakened Confederate force, or they might coordinate their armies and launch simultaneous attacks on Richmond and the Confederates in northern Virginia, forcing Lee to sacrifice one for the other. A third possibility was that McClellan would leave the Peninsula, where he had failed to seize Richmond, and join with Pope in northern Virginia, crushing the heavily outnumbered troops under Lee while protecting Washington.

It appeared in the blazing days of midsummer that the Federals were pulling back on the Peninsula at the same time that Pope was occupying Culpeper and posing a threat to the railroads to the Shenandoah Valley. The Confederates, running low on supplies of every sort, depended on the railroads that ran into the interior of the Confederacy to keep them alive. "I am well and in good spirits except now and then, when we run short of rations, which is very often," Tom Smiley wrote his sister Mary back in Augusta. "The sound of the rail car whistle is a great relief to men whose appetites are sharpened by hunger it betokens more to eat and of a better quality." Lee dispatched Stonewall Jackson and fourteen thousand men to stop Pope and protect the railroads.[44]

Pope massed his troops for an attack on the crucial stations, towns, depots, and rail lines of northern Virginia. More than a hundred thousand men, equally divided between the two sides, prepared for a confrontation midway between Richmond and Washington. Confederate troops were glad to be in this part of Virginia, away from the trenches of Richmond and the quagmires of the Peninsula. "This is a fine country down here it looks like old Augusta," John Wise of the 5th Virginia told his sister. "The wheat crops and corn crops are very fine in this country. Culpepper is a fine county as far as I have been."[45] Jed Hotchkiss thought their current base of operations "a very pleasant rolling country, on the slopes of the South West Mountain, in full view of the Blue Ridge." The view "reminds us of our homes, the General says."[46]

As the armies prepared for a confrontation, fighting erupted at the fords of rivers, at railroad stations and bridges, and at gaps in the mountains to the west. Cavalry raced among scattered units of the enemy; patrols confronted one another in surprising places. John Wise had been "sent up on a little mountain to stand picket while the wagon were loadening. We could see the yankeys riding about the camp very plainly with a glass. They have a large force down in Culpepper." Jackson's "whole army moved forward on yesterday. There will be a large battle down here on a few days," Wise and his fellow soldiers believed. "I think Jackson will give Pope a good grubbing."[47] Hotchkiss, intimately involved in reconnaissance and planning for Jackson's wing of Lee's army, was not so sure. "I do not know what is to be done—There are all sorts of extravagant stories in circulation—some say that Jackson is to have 80000 men and go to Pennsylvania by the way of Harrisburg—and some that he is to go to Washington &c &c," he wrote his wife, Sara. "But I do not presume to know anything about it as yet—though I doubt not he will be allowed to have his own way—You will see all the news there is, in the papers."[48]

The news in the papers brought little encouragement before the looming battle. Joseph Waddell in Staunton noted that the draft for the Union seemed to be going well, and the lesson was clear: "The feeling at the North is more vindictive than ever, and the war will be waged more ruthlessly." Pope's new orders struck Waddell as "savage." He listed their provisions in detail, including one that decreed confiscation of "the negroes employed for our subjugation (they do not *say* as soldiers)." The Yankees were clearly preparing to convert slaves into soldiers, whether in name or not. Waddell was sure that Pope's harsh orders would backfire. "Wherever the Yankees go, therefore, the men will fly from their homes, thousands will take arms who otherwise would have remained quiet, and Gen. Pope will find the number of his enemies increased at every step."[49]

While the North grew stronger, the South showed signs of distress. A "poor serving woman," a white woman, of Staunton visited Virginia Waddell. She told Mrs. Waddell that prices had grown so high that "she would have to work several weeks to make enough money to purchase one dress." The woman wanted to know if she could "get an old dress and pay for it in work. She said the women of her class generally are suffering greatly, both for want of the means of living and from mental anxiety in regard to the war." Waddell could see why such people worried. "They read no papers and are without correct information, and are therefore exposed to all the thousand reports which fly through the community." Though it was only July, "next winter is dreaded by many besides the very poor."[50]

Waddell, while devoted to the Confederate cause, did not shrink from recording its moments of weakness. "This morning I heard from my office a sound of lamentation" outside the window. "Going out I found the noise proceeded from an upper room in the Court house. A negro woman informed me that it was a soldier crying because he had to go to the war!" He had been drafted from lower Augusta. "Poor fellow! Although I pitied him, there was something very ludicrous in his wailings. Several men and women stood in the street, some laughing and others denouncing the recruit."[51] A number of deserters from the Union army appeared in Staunton, reporting that "there was great dissatisfaction in the Yankee army, many of the soldiers having deserted and many more intending to do so at the first opportunity."[52] But the North had many soldiers, more every day.

In the field Hotchkiss reported that "we are all very much incensed at Pope's atrocious orders, and hope the day of retribution may soon come to him & his vile crew." Fortunately for the Confederates, "our ranks are filling up with conscripts from the Carolinas, Ga, &c, and we have some reinforcements, so we are safe from any force that may be sent against us, and may take the offensive if the powers that be shall so ordain." Throughout late July and early August the two armies maneuvered for the vast confrontation that was sure to come.[53]

The Union sought to keep Stonewall Jackson's men from joining with those of Lee to the east. Though heavily outnumbered, Union General Banks, still angry at being beaten by Jackson two months earlier in the Valley, drove against Jackson's forces at Cedar Mountain on August 9. The 5th Virginia Infantry, along with the rest of the Stonewall Brigade, met the Yankee attack on a day when the temperature raged at a hundred degrees. The brigade anchored the Confederate line for one assault after another as many thousands of artillery rounds flew from both sides. The 5th fought ferociously, surging out onto the field, capturing enemy troops by the hundreds along with three highly treasured regimental and national flags. Eight men of a Connecticut unit were killed one after another while carrying their unit's flag at Cedar Mountain. The 5th Virginia ended the battle with the trophy in its hands.[54]

The 52d Virginia was not as fortunate. It was trapped by Union forces and fought until darkness halted the firing. Between them, the two Augusta regiments lost seven dead and thirty-two wounded. The Confederates punished Banks for his audacious attack, inflicting casualties on a third of his men. "We had a bloody day yesterday—as desperate a fight as I ever saw," Hotchkiss wrote Sara that evening from a church near the battlefield.[55] Waddell saw the wounded flow into Staunton from the battle. "These sights give us a horrid view of war. Men without arms and legs and shot in the head, body &c." One "poor woman" examined each face, "looking for her husband, who, she has heard, was wounded or killed."[56]

The battle at Cedar Mountain, a glorious moment for the 5th Virginia and the Stonewall Brigade, ironically brought political squabbling. Among those killed was General Charles Winder, mangled by a cannon shot. His death unleashed a bitter debate within the brigade. "There is quite a commotion in the 1st Brigade as to who shall command it now that poor Winder is no more," Hotchkiss wrote home. The officers had earlier recommended prominent Augusta resident William Harman for the promotion to brigadier general, but after Winder's death those same officers claimed to have supported Harman "from mere charity they say, of course not expecting him to command them." Despite their resistance, Harman's friends "press his case at Richmond & produce this recommendation as evidence that the 1st Brigade wants him." Unwilling to put their lives in the hands of a man they did not trust, "the officers back out & send a counter petition that they do not want him—& ask to have Baylor made Brigadier." The Baylor to whom Hotchkiss referred was William Smith Hanger Baylor, the longtime colonel of the Augusta militia, leader at Harpers Ferry, and hero at Malvern Hill. With no particular stake in the matter, Hotchkiss viewed the conflict with distaste but no real feeling. He ended his story with a shrug of the shoulders of a man who had seen much in the last year: "& so it goes."[57]

Hotchkiss did not have time to dwell on military politics. At the same time that Jackson and the Augusta men fought at Cedar Mountain in mid-August McClellan's men were moving from the Peninsula. With the threat to Richmond removed, Lee immediately began to shift men west to join with Jackson to confront Pope. Lee himself left the capital on August 15. "We are now again on the move," Hotchkiss wrote. "Gen Lee is with us & Gen. Longstreet & a host of men & I suppose we shall make a big move now." There was "no telling where we shall go to," Hotchkiss admitted, "but our faces are Northward & we are moving."[58]

Over the next two weeks Jackson's men never stopped moving. "I have never known a more active campaign," Hotchkiss observed, "but it is the only kind to protect us from the movements of the Yankees—we must keep them busy all the time or their roving dispositions will cause them to annoy us."[59] The twenty-four thousand men of Jackson's corps marched more than fifty miles in two days.

Jackson, Hotchkiss, and the Augusta men were after John Pope. Pope in turn was after the Confederates, and soon he would have reinforcements from McClellan's enormous army pulling away from the Peninsula. Pope thought that Stonewall Jackson and his troops were heading into the Valley after Cedar Mountain, but the Confederates pivoted and headed along the Orange and Alexandria Railroad to Manassas. There the Union maintained the main supply base for Pope's army. The Confederates planned to hit the Federals hard while they had the chance, launching dangerous maneuvers that separated the Southern forces in order to surprise Pope. With the U.S. Army undergoing confusing changes in leadership and location, it proved to be a good time for the Confederates to attack.

On August 26 Jackson's men took apparently limitless Union stores at Manassas after only token resistance. James E. Beard, a thirty-eight-year-old soldier in the 5th Virginia, gave an understated account of the situation: "We had some Yankees to contend with here, but they hurt none of us. We got plenty of provisions here which came in very good indeed for we were all very hungry." They marched again that night, heading out at eleven, "when we started for the old battleground of Bull Run."[60] Pope pursued Jackson, and they met on August 28 and 29—at Manassas Junction, the scene of the opening battle of the war a little more than a year before. Now there would be a Second Bull Run in the Federal terminology, and a Second Manassas in the Confederate.

In that battle the Stonewall Brigade, with Augusta's 5th Regiment, was to play a central role. Famous throughout the Confederacy and beyond for their remarkable record under Stonewall Jackson in the Valley, in the Seven Days', and at Cedar Mountain, the brigade had suffered greatly. Twenty-five hundred men had enlisted in the 5th and the other four regiments that composed the Stonewall Brigade. By August 1862, however, only eight hundred remained to fight John Pope.

At the head of the brigade now stood Will Baylor of Augusta County, the new brigadier general. Though he had long experience as captain of the Augusta militia and as a colonel under Jackson, Baylor's pending promotion brought him great anxiety. He had told General Jackson he did not want to be promoted, but his men had signed a "most complimentary petition" insisting that he be given the post. Will was honest with his wife, Mary, admitting that "of course my ambition is like everybody's." He was grateful to his men and to General Jackson. "To know that I am considered worthy of so high a position is certainly a compliment long to be cherished." Baylor prayed: "May God give us a great victory and preserve me to you & my child."[61]

Battle came soon after Baylor's letter, on August 28. The first day Baylor and his brigade chased a Wisconsin unit at a run, only to have the Union men find cover, turn, and launch a furious fire. The Stonewall

Brigade surged forward, taking refuge, such as it was, behind a rotten rail fence less than a hundred yards away from the Federals. "Within one minute all was enveloped in smoke," one witness wrote, "and a sheet of flame seemed to go out from each side to the other along the whole length of the line."[62] Reinforcements rushed to the U.S. forces and then to the Confederates. The close-range firing raged long after it seemed possible that anyone could still be alive, even after darkness fell. Finally the fighting stopped from sheer exhaustion. With all the killing, each side had barely moved from its first position. When the guns stopped, men from both sides moved with lanterns among the thousands of wounded, dying, and dead, trying to save those they could, stumbling over the bodies strewn around them.

When the Confederates gathered back in camp the next day, with the Yankees having retreated but surely preparing to strike again, Will Baylor asked for a prayer meeting. "I know the men are tired and worn but I cannot rest tonight without asking God's mercy on us for tomorrow," he said. A chaplain led the meeting, attended by most of the brigade's four thousand men. "It was a tender, precious season of worship," one in attendance wrote. "Colonel Baylor entered into it with the burning zeal of the young convert—he had found Christ in the camp only a short time before."[63]

The next morning, August 30, General Jackson rode by Baylor's position. "Well, Baylor, it looks as if there will be no fight today; but keep our men in line and ready for action." It was not until four that afternoon that the Union struck against the five hundred remaining men in the Stonewall Brigade. "The Federals came up in front of us suddenly as men rising out of the ground," wrote a man from the 5th, "showing themselves at the old railroad line opposite our line in double battle phalanx and coming forward in slow time, pouring their shot into our ranks in unmerciful volume." The Union men outnumbered the Confederates five times over, and the Federals marched forward with flags flying over their many regiments. Color bearers fell as the Confederates opened fire with muskets and artillery.

As the battle shifted its intensity from one place to another across the landscape, the Stonewall Brigade found itself first on the margins and then suddenly in the midst of some of the heaviest fighting in the entire

Civil War. Confederate regiments went down as they tried to secure a position at the end of Jackson's front lines, in a cut created for an unfinished railroad. Finally the job fell to Will Baylor and what remained of the Stonewall Brigade. To get to the cut, they had to run across two hundred years of open field, where a wall of Federal fire awaited. When the men from the Valley hesitated, Baylor seized a flag from one of his regiments and yelled, "Boys, follow me!" His men moved forward. "It was a splendid sight," one of those who survived recalled. "We did follow him, shouting and firing, out into the field, only to see the brave man shot down, wrapped in the flag he carried, pierced by many bullets and dead."

The Stonewall Brigade retreated into the woods from which they had emerged. Outraged at the death of his friend, Captain Hugh White, who had helped lead the prayer meeting the day before, rushed to Baylor and picked up the flag that had fallen with him. White rushed ahead, commanding the men to follow even though they were in no position to do so. He vanished in the dense smoke. The few who followed White found him down, his hands on his face, tangled in the flag, dead. Yet another officer, Colonel Andrew Jackson Grigsby, ordered the men forward, and this time they stood the fire, made it to the cut, and held the line. Knowing they could not hold it long, Grigsby sent a messenger to Jackson to ask for reinforcements. Jackson could hardly make out what he was told; when he learned that it was the Stonewall Brigade that needed his help, his first response was merely to "give my compliments to them and tell the Stonewall Brigade to maintain her reputation." The messenger turned to leave, only to have Jackson reconsider. He would send reinforcements in ten minutes. Before that could happen, General Longstreet turned artillery on the Federal soldiers and took the pressure from the bleeding remnants of the Stonewall Brigade.[64]

The immense battle went on for another day, for thousands more deaths. Only a few generals had a chance of understanding the horrible choreography of the battle, so intricately staged for a brutally simple purpose. The men who did the fighting could see only what lay before them, their own wounds, their own friends shattered or dead. The 5th Virginia lost fourteen killed and ninety-one wounded, far greater casualties than it had suffered at any fighting at First Manassas, in the Valley Campaign, or in the Seven Days'.

So many of the dead, like so many who lived to fight again, left nothing in the bureaucratic records to distinguish them. Their characteristics were those of the mass of men on both sides: they were mere privates, in their early twenties, not yet married and not yet propertied. A few men had made a mark in the preceding year of fighting. Narcissus Finch Quarles, a twenty-two-year-old carpenter, with no father and no money, had, his family believed, been recognized by no less than General Jackson himself. Only two weeks before Second Manassas, at the Battle of Cedar Mountain, Quarles had captured three flags and nineteen prisoners in the glorious victory. In recognition and in gratitude, Quarles received a sword. Another young carpenter, also living without parents and without property on the eve of the war, Thomas Supple was to be buried at Manassas, where his gravestone read "A Faithful Soldier."

Some men had made a mark back home before they were killed. Charles Swoope, born in Bavaria, had moved to Staunton to become superintendent of the gasworks, one of the signs of progress of which the town was most proud. He and his wife, Mary, had a three-year-old child, Henry. Though he held property worth only seventy-five dollars, Swoope had a profession and a future before the war.

The 52d Virginia Infantry suffered almost as much at the 5th. Eight men died from the regiment in that battle. Edward Valentine Garber, a native of Augusta, had moved to Missouri before the war but returned home to join the Confederate army when Virginia seceded. A twenty-five-year-old mechanic, Garber began his service as a first lieutenant but was elected captain in May 1862. In his military record, someone took the trouble to make sure that those who read the documents would know what kind of man Garber had been: "In all relations of life he uniformly bore himself with rare and undeviating faultlessness. He approved himself to his comrades brave, generous, self-sacrificing. He encountered all the vicissitudes of the trying service in which he was engaged with unwavering fortitude. He discharged all the duties of this office with signal ability and fidelity—he met all the difficulties with unshaken equanimity." The records told too of men who had not been as devoted to the cause yet died in its service. Thomas Humphrey, a laborer, twenty-six years old, had gone AWOL in the winter of 1861 and then again in the spring of 1862, more than likely to see the wife soon to be his widow.

Humphrey had returned to the 52d in time to fight at the terror that was Second Manassas. He died with a shot to the face.

One loss among the Augusta men stood out more than the rest. Will Baylor's body was recovered and, accompanied by many more bodies and the wounded, was put on a train back to Staunton and his wife. "If we were not so used to it," Joseph Waddell wrote sadly as the men arrived, "the sight of multitudes of wounded and suffering soldiers constantly arriving would be shocking."[65] While the people of Staunton might grow accustomed to the dead and wounded in general, individuals were another matter. Mary Baylor, Sara Hotchkiss wrote her husband in the field, had been inconsolable upon news of Will's death. Hotchkiss gave a soldier's reply, sounding like the Stonewall Jackson he so admired: "I am very sorry that Mrs. Baylor takes to heart so much the loss of her husband. It is well to grieve for the dead, but half the pang is removed when one dies as Baylor died, at the head of his troops—bearing the colors & cheering them on when he was met by a volley from a whole regiment of the enemy."[66]

More comforting, certainly, was a letter to Mary Baylor from Edward P. Walton, chaplain of the 5th Virginia. He wrote two weeks after the battle, just having been released from imprisonment in Washington. Walton told Mary of Will's character in camp and in battle. "On the fatal day of his immolation upon the altar of Patriotism, I was guarded by hireling Yankees, in full view of our forces," the chaplain wrote the widow, "compelled to witness their heroic sufferings, without being able to offer aid or consolation to my wounded and dying companions." The Reverend Walton had heard of Will's death from a fellow prisoner, who told him that Colonel Baylor had been "mortally wounded that day, while lifting the Colors of his Regiment from the ground where they had fallen with the gallant color-bearer of the 5th."[67]

When the chaplain heard the news, "I felt as if my own brother had been stricken from my side. I rebelled at the Providence that denied me the privilege of being by his side and following his remains to their final resting place." Walton had shared a tent with Baylor. As they lay on their beds, they had talked of the progress of religion in the regiment. "How he cheered up, as I would tell him of one and another of his men, who come to converse wh. me, on the subject of religion," Walton wrote

Mary Baylor, "and said with earnest emphasis 'I would rather a revival of religion in my Regiment than to realize any temporal advantage whatever.' " Such was a sign, surely, of Baylor's conversion, and so was his abandonment of his old habit of swearing. "I never knew a man addicted to swearing that could refrain from profanity when provoked, without Divine assistance," the chaplain assured the young widow, "and yet I have seen Col. Baylor under the most harrassing provocation, without yielding to the promptings of his old habit." Baylor, commonwealth attorney for Augusta County, had even expressed interest in becoming a minister after the war. The last words the young colonel said to his friend were " 'Walton, I do hope that Christians are praying for us at home.' "[68]

Walton ended with the highest secular praise he could offer, the blessing of Stonewall Jackson. "It is well known that the General indulged the warmest feeling of esteem and affection for your Husband." During one battle the general did not see Colonel Baylor on the scene and worried out loud that the Stonewall Bridge "would not maintain its reputation; but when he was told that your Husband was at his post, he replied 'all is right, they will prove worthy of their commander.' "[69]

The Confederates could take satisfaction in the outcome of Second Manassas: they had inflicted sixteen thousand casualties while suffering ten thousand. The Southern army had proved itself as never before, with Lee, Jackson, and Longstreet bringing their capacities and their men into concert. Pope retreated toward Washington. Jackson's soldiers luxuriated in the gratitude of the residents of northern Virginia. "The people here are perfectly wild with joy all true—the ladies come out to shake hands & feed all," Hotchkiss wrote his wife.[70]

Second Manassas changed the face of the war. The border with the North lay, unprotected, tantalizingly nearby. In about two months Southern troops had managed to push and pull a Federal army, a force twice their size, from Richmond all the way to the doors of Washington. "Everybody greatly elated; many think the war will soon terminate," Waddell exulted. "There are certainly some hopeful signs. The tone of the Northern papers, so far as we have heard from them, is depressed." Rumor had it that Lee had "slipped a part of his force into Maryland. What is to be done there is a mystery." Lee threatened a victory on Union soil, a victory that could bring the conflict to a sudden end.[71]

The ruins of Manassas

"IMPORTANT AND STIRRING NEWS from the seat of war in Virginia" announced the *Valley Spirit* in Franklin County. "A severe engagement took place on Friday between Gen. Popes forces and the rebel forces under Gen. Jackson, on the old Bull Run battle ground, between Centerville and Manassas."[72] A week later the reports of what had happened were still broken and unreliable. "Of two things, however, there can be no doubt—our army has fallen back within range of the cordons of Forts that guard the approaches to Washington from the Old Dominion—and, during the recent engagements, we have lost most severely in killed, wounded and prisoners, as well as guns, ammunition and stores captured by the enemy."[73]

News from what was later known as Second Bull Run trickled in, all of it bad. "It is useless for me to attempt to describe the scene," read a letter from a Franklin soldier in the field. "Every available vehicle from Washington was used to carry the wounded, and still there were thousands of wounded walking. Thousands of soldiers who were lost or their regiments were cut up, with any quantity of negroes, all trying to get to Washington."[74]

Manassas lay close to the Maryland border, and Maryland lay on the Pennsylvania border. Franklin, resting on that boundary line, roused itself after the Confederate victory. The "insolent foe" threatened the nation's capital, and "our own beautiful valley may at any hour become the victim of a similar invasion. Citizens of Franklin county, the enemy is at the very threshold of your homes, your altars and your firesides. Will you not instantly respond to the call of your Government in this the day of your country's peril?" The *Spirit* begged men to enlist in one of the companies forming in Franklin and do so before a draft law could tarnish their patriotism.[75] Meanwhile the county should "keep cool." Though the enemy threatened, "Let there be no dismay, no panic among us."[76]

The fact remained, however, as the *Valley Spirit* put it, that "we are apparently no nearer the end of this struggle than we were a year ago." The lessons of the last few months seemed clear: of all the mistakes the Union had made, "the first and greatest in our opinion, was underestimating the strength and resources of the South."[77] The notion that the South could be beaten with one hand tied behind the North's back had proved mistaken.

That fundamental error led to others. Had the Union mobilized two hundred thousand more men at the outset, the Democrats claimed, McClellan could have taken Virginia. "But unfortunately for the country, Congress was in session at the time, both branches controlled in a great measure by men of one idea—miserable charlatans, abstractionists and theorists, devoid of common sense and lacking in everything necessary to constitute practical statesmanship." These Republicans "had other ends to accomplish than the saving of the country. They had a *party* programme to carry out. Slavery had to be abolished in the District of Columbia and the Territories. Confiscation and emancipation bills were introduced and urged with a persevering energy and fanatical zeal, regardless of Constitutional objections or their injurious effect upon the Union cause in the Slave States." So great was the "clamor and 'pressure' of these men" that President Lincoln had been forced to "tinker at the slavery question" rather than drive the war to the quick and certain conclusion it deserved.[78]

The Democrats had warned the Republicans that their words and actions would bring on war. Now the Democrats wanted "the whole power and resources of the loyal portion of the country thrown into this struggle, in order to suppress this unholy, terrible and damning rebellion at once." Everyone could see that if the war continued until the North was "exhausted we shall have anarchy in the country as certain as tomorrow's sun shall rise; and after anarchy we will have despotism as its legitimate and logical sequence." The recent orders by General Pope and the recent acts of Congress "proposing confiscation, emancipation, and the employment of negroes" were "desperate expedients to supply the lack of power. If they had called for the whole power of the country the rebellion would have fallen without any of these desperate expedients, and it will never be put down with them." The Democrats wanted "no new laws with hard penalties leading to barbarous results. We want soldiers, soldiers, soldiers in countless multitudes—legions, that there is no power in this conspiracy to resist."[79]

A soldier in the 126th Regiment, stationed in Virginia, heard rumors of Jackson's invasion of Pennsylvania. Reports already put the rebel army in Chambersburg, Gettysburg, and Hagerstown. The soldier doubted the rumors were true, but he did not doubt that the Confederates would do all they could to invade Pennsylvania. His advice was not to "keep cool," but to fight. "Make every hill top a fortification, and every valley a rebel burying ground before you yield your Liberties and your Government. Think of your brothers already in the field, think of your families, your properties and your lives, and, under the sacred impulse of all these ties, strike a deadly blow at your powerful and desperate enemy."[80]

The plea was compelling, even to a young man who had just returned weeks before to Franklin County after several years' absence. Samuel Cormany had grown up on a farm eight miles north of Chambersburg but had left in 1859 for Otterbein University, a United Brethren school in Ohio, using his inheritance from his recently deceased father for tuition. There he met Rachel Bowman from Ontario, Canada. Her mother had set up a boardinghouse in the college town while Rachel was in school, supporting her daughter in the unusual pursuit of a college education by a woman. Samuel and Rachel married in November 1860 and headed to Canada for their honeymoon and to live with Rachel's family. They found themselves unhappy there and decided to return to Franklin County despite the war raging just to the south of its border. They arrived in August 1862.

When the Cormanys came to Franklin, they were twenty-four and twenty-six (Rachel the elder), with a new daughter, Cora. They were not sure what Samuel would do for a living, but they enjoyed the warm reception they met. Samuel described his feelings as he took Rachel (Pet, he called her in his diary) and Cora (Baby) to the Old Salem Church, where his father had been a lay minister and was now buried. "A great time shaking hands with old acquaintances and introducing My Rachel and our Baby—I was simply proud of my Wife and Baby—and rec'd many congratulations from very nice people."[81] After several more days of pleasant visiting, in which Samuel discovered that his old dog Tippy still recognized him and that "memories of boyhood days and pranks, their toils, and amusements come scampering along," he realized he could not ignore the war.[82] He would have to decide what to do.

On September 9 "I went to see about enlisting." In Chambersburg, Cormany heard all the discussion about the draft that would come in the spring, and he wanted to enlist before it took effect. "The air is full of calls for men who are patriotic to enlist—I really inwardly feel that I want to go and do my part—as a Man—as a Volunteer—leaving others to wait and

Samuel and Rachel Cormany, with Cora

be drafted." Fortunately Rachel agreed. "That is, she is loyal and true—and wants to see the South subdued—and however hard it would be to be alone here amongst strangers—and to have me exposed—and away. She calmly consents." The two young people spent "a great deal of time on our knees, before our God." Samuel ended his explanation for his enlistment with a touch of humility and honesty: "The fear of being drafted, if I did not volunteer—had possibly some weight in inducing decission."[83]

The next day Cormany enlisted in Captain W. H. Sollenberger's cavalry company. Sollenberger, a master carpenter in town before the war, had already served three months. Now he had been given a captain's commission and was organizing a company to become part of the 16th Pennsylvania Cavalry. Cormany persuaded his friend Adam Yost to enlist and began recruiting more members. The recruiting may have been easier because people expected the Confederates to appear in Franklin at any moment. "People are awfully scared—Many are leaving town." Cormany laughed at such folks but found that "brave cool men are somewhat scarce."[84] He located rooms for Rachel and the baby in Chambersburg. Four days later he and his new company left for Camp Curtin in Harrisburg.

One piece of news cheered the Federal troops in Virginia during these weeks: President Lincoln had removed Pope, sending him to Minnesota to fight Indians, and reinstalled McClellan. The same men who had cheered Pope and his hard approach to the South a few weeks earlier now cheered his departure. A correspondent to the *Spirit* trusted that Pope would be better qualified for fighting Indians "than for commanding a grand army, opposed by a most cunning, wiley and determined enemy." McClellan had the complete faith of his men, if not the leaders in Washington. "I always believed 'little Mac' to be popular with his men, but had no idea the enthusiasm for him was so intense as it is until I learned it from the mouths of the very men who have served under him, and who have shared with him his trials and his triumphs," a Franklin soldier reported from the field. "Many of them declared, on their way to Manassas, that they would fight under no one else; and the sequel of those disastrous engagements gives occasion to say had he been in command, as he was justly entitled to be, the result might have been different."[85] McClellan would now have another chance to show what he could do.

McClellan believed that the Confederates might well attempt to take the war to the north. He wrote to Governor Curtin of Pennsylvania late in the evening of September 10: "You should concentrate all the troops you can in the vicinity of Chambersburg, not entirely neglecting Gettysburg. I will follow them up as rapidly as possible, and do all I can to check their movements into Pennsylvania. Call out the militia, especially mounted men, and do everything in your power to impede the enemy by the action of light troops; attack them in flank, destroying their trains and any property which must inevitably come into their possession." He reassured the governor, albeit in typically cautious language: "You may be sure that I will follow them as closely as I can, and fight them whenever I can find them. It is as much my interest as yours to preserve the soil of Pennsylvania from invasion, or, failing in that, to destroy any army that may have the temerity to attempt it."[86]

Two days later Pennsylvania did what it could, posting cavalry on the line between Chambersburg and the Maryland line. Although such meager forces could not stop a Confederate invasion, they could "give some degree of confidence to the inhabitants, as well as to prevent a panic, which was rather imminent among the more easily frightened portion of the people in that neighborhood."[87]

THE CONFEDERATES, flush with victory after Second Manassas but exhausted, hungry, and ravaged by losses, could not stay where they were. Northern Virginia had been stripped bare by both armies. Even though harvest time approached, the desolate farms could not provide enough food to support an army. Lee and Jackson might have returned to Richmond to regroup, but Lee longed to take the war to the North, to bring the same despoliation and deprivation that Virginia had experienced to those over the border. The Confederacy was finally doing better in the West, with major strikes planned in Kentucky and Tennessee. A well-timed and successful blow at the North might bring European recognition of the Confederacy and help the Democrats in the North turn out Republican officeholders. It might even end the war. "What a change since six months ago or less!" Joseph Waddell exulted in his diary.[88]

The carnage at Second Manassas remained long after the exhilaration had passed. "The Yankees were burying their dead on Sunday last,"

Waddell somberly wrote, "more than a week after the battle." An officer had described the battlefield: "Their faces blackened and their postures in some cases horribly ludicrous. The buzzards had torn the entrails of some." In a note of reassurance after this disturbing passage, Waddell quietly observed that "our dead were buried soon after the battle."[89]

Jed Hotchkiss visited the battlefield the day after the guns had fallen silent. "I thought I had seen war & bloodshed in its worst shape at Port Republic & elsewhere, but that was nothing," he wrote his young wife in what could not have been a comforting letter. "Their dead were strewn over a space 5 miles long and three wide—piled up in many places—sometimes in long lines as they stood in the ranks, and then one on another where they attempted, seven times, to break Jackson's line, and were as many times repulsed." The Confederates had captured many men and then paroled them. "Gen. Lee told them to come and bury their dead, but they did not come and they lie in thousands over the battle field, rotting & enriching the soil they vainly boasted as their own."[90]

When Lee turned toward the Potomac River, "our troops knew for the first time that they were surely going to cross into Maryland, so completely had our movements been kept from all the officers and men of our command—all were joyous at the prospect and marched with a light step—fewer straggling than I almost ever saw," Hotchkiss wrote Sara. "The passing of the Rubicon was not more memorable for we were really advancing—we had driven an exultant foe, in less than two months 150 miles, far away from our own capital, and were now threatening his, were taking our army where it had never been before." Hotchkiss did not mention the many men who straggled, falling by the side as their feet, or their hearts, failed them at the prospect of another battle so soon. The Confederate army had never been in more desperate shape; thanks to the relentless fighting and poor logistics, the Rebels marched into Maryland hungry, dirty, shoeless, and exhausted.[91]

Hotchkiss preferred to notice how Maryland sparkled as the troops crossed the Potomac, flags waving in an unclouded sky and the band playing "Maryland, My Maryland." "The news of our coming spread rapidly, and young men & old flocked to see Gen. Jackson, whom they look upon as their deliverer," Hotchkiss proudly wrote. People brought "anything they had for the use of our army." After the poverty of war-torn Virginia, "our men were in a paradise to them, and those that would take Confederate money could not hand out goods fast enough—especially such things as boots, shoes &c—and especially eatables." Hotchkiss could see that not everyone welcomed the Rebels. "Many of the Unionists left before we came, and in much terror." But he emphasized the positive: "About half the population is strongly with us & they are willing to do anything." The visit to Maryland had whetted his appetite for more. "We are only some 15 miles from Pa. and I do hope we may go there."[92]

After crossing the Potomac, Lee sent Stonewall Jackson's troops to capture Harpers Ferry on September 10. Lee knew he incurred a risk in separating his army, since McClellan had left Washington on September 7, heading west. In one of the great improbabilities of the war, a Union soldier had found a copy of Lee's orders separating his armies, the paper wrapped around three cigars. With that information, McClellan had what he needed to strike Lee while his command was divided. McClellan waited, however, and in the meantime a Southern sympathizer who happened to be nearby when the Federal general received the news rushed to the Confederates to let them know their plan had been discovered.

It was too late to stop Jackson's attack on Harpers Ferry, but fortunately for the Rebels the green Federal troops there could not resist the artillery and positioning of the Confederates. The near-bloodless victory there gave the Confederates more than confidence. The raw Union troops, Hotchkiss reported jubilantly and accurately, "surrendered unconditionally 11000 men, over 1000 horses, any quantity of wagons, tents, ammunition, 60 pieces of artillery, 7 splendid guns, about 15000 stand of arms, all new &c &c—one of the greatest captures of the war & we hardly lost anything." Ebullient, he dared express his deepest wish: "If victory keeps with us, as heretofore we shall end this war soon & may God grant it that we may soon get home. Read the news to the neighbors & thank God for our victory." At the end of the letter, Hotchkiss added an exultant, if incongruous note: "Love to all—& kisses for Nelly and Anna—We got about 1500 slaves back."[93]

McClellan attacked the Confederates at several mountain passes and took almost a quarter of the troops with Lee. The Little Napoleon reported a glorious victory to Washington. Lee thought about abandon-

aryland. But when he heard of the coup at Harpers Ferry and that he would soon have reinforcements coming from seventeen miles away, he decided to stay and fight, taking shelter from the hills around Sharpsburg, anchored on either end of his lines by the Antietam Creek. The two armies threw themselves into the struggle on September 17 with a desperate desire to conclude the conflict once and for all. The Northern troops had been disparaged; now they would prove themselves. It was "the bloodiest & hardest fought battle of the war," Jed Hotchkiss wrote Sara the day afterward. "The enemy began the attack and we repelled them and drove them back with great slaughter." The battle "raged from 4 in the morning until 9 at night."[94]

The Stonewall Brigade fought desperately in a cornfield that became the center of the battle at Antietam. The brigade was shredded by artillery and suffered an assault by ten thousand Union men. Jackson lost 40 percent of his command to death or wounds at Sharpsburg. The Confederates would likely have been routed had reinforcements from Harpers Ferry not arrived at a desperate juncture. In this, the bloodiest single day of the Civil War, twenty-three thousand men were killed or wounded, evenly distributed North and South. Augusta lost thirty-seven men to wounds and five to death. The Confederates steeled themselves for an attack the next day, but it never came. That night they retreated across the Potomac in a thunderstorm. John Harman, Jackson's quartermaster and an Augusta man, led the fording of the river, swearing at the mules that carried the supplies and the wounded back to Virginia. "Both parties were too much exhausted to renew the fight," Hotchkiss wrote. "We spent Thursday in collecting our wounded, burying our dead &c & that night we quietly left Maryland, avoiding the plan of McClellan for fighting us."[95]

The Confederates had invaded the North without being destroyed and had gained a mountain of crucial supplies at Harpers Ferry, but the U.S. Army claimed a crucial victory. The invasion of the North had been thwarted, the threat of European intervention prevented, Lee's army saddled with enormous losses. McClellan thought he had won a great victory; Lincoln and the leaders of the government in Washington thought he had wasted a perfect opportunity to crush Lee's army completely and end the war. Nevertheless, Lincoln used the opportunity to announce the Preliminary Emancipation Proclamation, which had sat in his drawer for

In the wake of Antietam

two months awaiting something he could call a victory. The proclamation decreed that unless the Confederates came back to the Union by January 1, 1863, their slaves "shall be then, thenceforward, and forever free."

Joseph Waddell, so cheerful only two weeks earlier, recognized what the Confederacy had lost at Sharpsburg. "Every arrival confirms the impression that we have been worsted in Maryland, on the whole. Rumored that our army was reduced by 20,000 men, in one way or another."[96] The losses did not stop with the sobering body count. "News from Europe not favorable for intervention," he wrote a week after the battle. "Thos. Carlyle says of the American war that it is 'the foulest chimney that's been afire this century, and the best way is to let it burn out.' "

Waddell recognized that "unless European powers do interfere in some way, at least by acknowledging our independence, the war must go on interminally. We cannot go on as at present many months longer—exhaustion must soon come, and a state of guerrilla warfare will ensue."[97]

The battle had disillusioned the Confederates about Maryland. Lee had hoped and expected the people there to rush to the Southern flag, but they had not. "I dont think Maryland will go with the south," Thomas Garber, a young Augusta Man in the 12th Virginia Cavalry, wrote his sister on the day of the battle in Sharpsburg. "I think more than two thirds of the people are Union anyhow they were in the part I was in it is true as we passed along we would meet a Secesh family here and there but they were scarce." Garber, dejected, admitted: "I never want to go back again. I would like to go through Pennsylvania but I dont want to stop in Maryland five minutes longer than I can help."[98]

As the soldiers stumbled back south, wounded Confederates filled Staunton, trying to get back home. "Many look very forlorn," Waddell recorded, "hand and arms hurt, faces bound up, badly clad, barefooted and dirty. We are afraid to offer them shelter, lest they fill the houses with vermin." When nearly five hundred Union prisoners marched through town two days later, Waddell could not help noticing that the Yankees were "better clothed than our poor fellows."[99]

Only days passed until Abraham Lincoln issued "a proclamation declaring slaves in the 'rebel' States free after the 1st of January." In response, Waddell nervously noted, some in the Confederate Congress had proposed "to wage a war of extermination against the Yankee invaders, to take no prisoners, and ask and give no quarter." Waddell thought "the war must come to this. There is no prospect of an end. Civil liberty is nearly gone in this section, as well as among the Yankee States, and a military despotism will finally prevail." The weary people of America "will be ready to accept any authority which may restore peace." Waddell feared that Lincoln's proclamation would only make the chaos worse, for it seemed "calculated and intended to excite servile insurrections in the South—to such a pitch of ferocity have our enemies arrived."[100]

"THE NAME GIVEN to this battle is the 'Antietam,'" a letter to the *Valley Spirit* breathlessly reported of what the Confederates called Sharpsburg.[101]

"It is acknowledged on all hands to have been the greatest battle of the war." The carnage had been "most terrific," but "the rebels sought the first opportunity to beat a hasty retreat across the Potomac into 'Dixie.' Though the war is not yet over by any means, we think the rebels have received such a drubbing as to cause them to think long and consider well, before they again attempt the invasion of 'Maryland, my Maryland!' "[102]

The battle had threatened Chambersburg. As the battle formed, George McClellan had written Washington that "the whole force of the enemy in front. They are not returning to Virginia. Look well to Chambersburg."[103] In the midst of the battle McClellan had wired to headquarters the request that it "take military possession of the Chambersburg and Hagerstown Railroad, that our ammunition and supplies may be hurried up without delay. We are in the midst of the most terrible battle of the war—perhaps of history. Thus far it looks well, but I have great odds against me. Hurry up all the troops possible. Our loss has been terrific."[104]

But the U.S. Army had stopped the Confederates in Maryland. As the wheat grew full and ripe in the fields of Franklin County in the autumn of 1862, people hoped that the hardest fight of the war had come and gone.

The 107th Pennsylvania Infantry had been right in the middle of the Battle of Antietam. Captain James MacThompson described the unit's experience in what became known simply as the Cornfield. "We entered the field and pushed rapidly through to the other side. Here we found, in different positions, three full brigades of the enemy. We opened fire immediately upon those in front, and in fifteen minutes compelled them to fall back." It looked as if the Franklin County men had taken the field, but reinforcements arrived for the Confederates, who regained the ground they had lost, "and an unequal conflict of nearly three-quarters of an hour resulted in forcing us back through the corn-field. Our brigade had, however, done its work. We had held at bay a force of the enemy numerically five times our superior for considerably more than an hour, and at one time driving them." This hour or so blurred into the others of the battle, just as the blood of the nineteen killed and forty-five wounded out of the 107th Pennsylvania mingled with that of men from the rest of the country at Antietam. But the people of Franklin knew what their men had done, so close to their own border.[105]

The *Spirit*, thrilled with the result of the battle, was disappointed that President Lincoln used it as the occasion of his Preliminary Emancipation Proclamation. "This new policy is to be the great panacea for all our ills, and is to kill the rebellion at one blow. We shall soon see the fruits of the policy and know from practical experience, what abolition philosophy is worth." The Democrats expressed doubts, of course, about the legality and strategic wisdom of the proclamation. The conservative men of the North had hoped that the president "would eventually see the true ground of his position, discard the mad counsels and revolutionary teachings of the radical men of his party, plant himself firmly upon the pillars of the Constitution, and make an earnest effort to save the country." Instead he had buckled under the pressure. The entire white South would now be unified as it had never been unified before. Jefferson Davis, the paper claimed, "would have given the last dollar in the Confederate Treasury to have just such a proclamation emanate from the President of the United States."[106]

Antietam could be seen as the turning point of the Civil War, the beginning of the end of the Confederate cause. Not only did the Union army repulse the invasion of the North by Lee's forces, but the battles provided Abraham Lincoln a plausible opportunity to announce the Preliminary Emancipation Proclamation and to turn England and France away from recognition of the Confederacy. More decisively than the Valley Campaign and Seven Days Battles of that spring helped the South, the eminent historian James McPherson believes, the thin victory at Antietam seemed to turn the tide in favor of the North. With this defeat the South lost its best chance at gaining credibility in the eyes of the world.

This portrayal of Antietam as the "crossroads of freedom," as McPherson calls it, is a strong argument, one that would seem to support the notion of deep contingency that underlies this book. But deep contingency, working on levels throughout the societies of the North and the South, was not so easily turned after all these months of war. The Confederacy, assimilating its transformation into a new nation-state built around slavery, proved more durable than Lincoln, the British, or the French foresaw in September 1862. The Preliminary Emancipation Proclamation may have given some in the North a new sense of purpose and resolve, but it did the same thing for the white South. The Confederacy saw its suspicions of Lincoln confirmed: he would unleash a race war rather than let Southern states leave the Union.

Turning points in the Civil War, in other words, did not merely turn in one direction. For the foreseeable future, the Confederacy would not be dissuaded or discouraged by a greater clarity of purpose in the United States. And even in the North, Lincoln's new declaration of principle led to an immediate counteraction by the Democrats, who seized on the opportunity to build greater strength than they had held before. They did not want a war against slavery and Lincoln had taken a crucial step toward that end. The Democrats did not see how Lincoln could fulfill the promise he made in the proclamation without prolonging the war indefinitely and without loosing former slaves on the North. From the Democrats' point of view in the fall of 1862, Antietam might have been a turning point against Abraham Lincoln. Everything would depend on whether Lincoln, the Republicans, and the generals would be able to convert the narrow victory in Maryland into the first of a series of victories in Virginia and across the rest of the South. That was by no means obvious as another winter at war began to settle over the exhausted nation.

THE LOCAL AND STATE ELECTIONS that waited just weeks away would give voters across the North a chance to express their opinions on Lincoln's policies. Many agreed with the Democratic paper in Franklin that the election would be "the most important one that has occurred in the history of our country." The issue now was clear: "Abolitionism threatens the overthrow of the Constitution, the disruption of the Union and the elevation of the negro to an equality with the white man." The true men of the Democracy thus had to fight two evils at once. "Whilst the army of the Republic is crushing out Secessionism in the field, do not forget that you have a duty to perform by voting down Abolitionism at the Polls."[107]

In the field the hero of the Democrats, General George McClellan, forbade discussion of the president's proclamation. Though Democratic Union officers and soldiers declared that they would never fight to end slavery, McClellan reminded his men that the boundary between political decisions and military power must be jealously protected. "The remedy for political errors, if any are committed, is to be found only in the action of the people at the polls." Everyone knew what McClellan wanted the "people at the polls" to say: the war should be for reunion, not for emancipation. Voters should repudiate the president, his party, and his policy by voting for the Democrats.[108]

Even as the political heat rose in Franklin, the county prospered. "Our town has greatly changed by the events of the war—business is so good, our small town is taking on a city appearance of activity," sixty-six-year-old merchant William Heyser noted in his diary in early October. Though the movement of dead and wounded through town was discouraging, "the engines and cars are very busy taking supplies to McClelland on the Potomac. They are running night and day."[109] The trains brought prosperity to Chambersburg. "Business good at the bank," Heyser noted. "We declared a 5% dividend on the past 6 months business. The stock is $10 above par. We have a surplus of $42,000."[110]

Amid the relative quiet and prosperity, an astonishing thing occurred: Confederate General J. E. B. Stuart, accompanied by more than twelve hundred cavalrymen, thundered into Chambersburg early one rainy evening in October. A company of the Rebels "appeared in the Public Square carrying a flag of truce and demanding a surrender of the place," a dejected and embarrassed *Spirit* reported. "No military force being here, able to resist, the town was surrendered on the terms that private property would be respected and citizens be unmolested. They then took full possession of the place." The Confederates burned a number of buildings that held supplies and machinery. The paper would have said more, but "we are hurried in getting to Press and can give no extended notice of this humiliating Rebel invasion of Pennsylvania soil."[111] Stuart rode all the way around the Union army and returned safely to Virginia after stealing horses, guns, and pride from southern Pennsylvania.

William Heyser viewed the raiders dispassionately. "They immediately took possession of the bank and telegraph office," he wrote the night of the raid. "Also requisitioned provisions, clothing, etc. as to their needs." They "all look well fed and clothed, and so far, conducted themselves orderly. They will be busy stripping our stores and gathering up horses," he predicted.[112] The next morning the elderly merchant watched as the Confederates did just that. "Broke open Isaac Hutton's shoe store, helped themselves freely. Then to the depot and confiscated a large shipment of arms and clothes." They set fire to a building "used as a storehouse for government ammunition. The succeeding explosions of shells and powder was tremendous. The loss must be very great. All the machinery and present locomotives destroyed at the shops."[113]

Rebels raid Chambersburg

Heyser was not afraid. "The troops were well disciplined and polite. Not a single house or person injured. They were more orderly than troops of ours that have passed this way. Outside of their plundering of Isaac Hutton's shoe store, nothing else occurred to criticize them." As word of the raid spread, "many people from the country came into town in search of news and carried home relics of the Rebel Invasion, as shells, balls, saberparts, parts of musquets, etc. Nearly every man and boy had some souvenier."[114] Several days later Heyser added a chilling footnote: "They did take eight young colored men and boys along with them, in spite of their parents pleading. I fear we will never see them again, unless they can escape."[115]

Alexander K. McClure had just been commissioned assistant adjutant general of the United States and was on a list of twenty men to be arrested and taken prisoner by the Confederates. "While walking across the square that was then filled with the raiders I was suddenly slapped on the back, and when I turned around I recognized Hugh Logan, who had lived in the South Mountain before the war, but who joined the Southern army immediately after the war began." Fortunately for McClure, "Logan had been a client of mine, and I had successfully defended him in a kidnapping case." McClure went to his home outside town and waited on the porch for the troops to come to his farm, the same porch where, a year and a half earlier, he had sat with Union officers before the catastrophic battle at Bull Run. Ten of his horses had already been stolen.[116]

About midnight more than a hundred cavalrymen arrived at the McClure place. They took corn and started to burn his fences, but McClure walked up to them and offered firewood instead. They cheerfully took it and left the fences alone. A Confederate officer, unaware of McClure's importance, asked for coffee. McClure told him he had coffee, but "had no way to make it, as my servants were colored and had escaped. He said that they were not hunting negroes, and that if I could find my servants and get them coffee he would assure absolute protection to all of them and to everything in the house. . . . I told him that I could find my servants," and six officers came inside. "There was a bright fire burning in the library and the New York and Philadelphia papers were on the table with my name on them, and the officers seized upon them at once to see what was told about the war. They were not a minute in the room until they discovered that they had asked for hospitality and were about to receive it from one whom they were ordered to arrest as a prisoner and take to Richmond. They had no opportunity for conference, as we were scattered around in a single well-lighted room, but they intuitively took in the situation and acted in perfect accord." They did not give their names or ask his.[117]

The Union political leader and the Confederate officers talked for an hour "with the highest measure of courtesy on the various questions relating to the war. I shall never forget the earnestness, the eloquence and pathos of one of the officers who reminded me that their command was then armed with the best cavalry weapons captured from our forces, that the second year of the war was drawing to a close and we had not yet fought a successful battle with the Confederate army of Virginia. He inquired how we could hope to prosecute a war that in nearly two years had won no victories, and that even under the most favorable conditions the North could never conquer the Southern people. There was no trace of bombast or arrogance."

McClure gave him a surprising answer: the North had to fight to protect itself from itself, regardless of what happened to the Confederacy. "There was no hope for the unity of the North unless it asserted its military mastery over the South," McClure observed. "To be defeated by inferior numbers would simply demoralize and disintegrate the North, and instead of having a Northern republic it would break into a series of petty principalities and practically anarchy." The North simply could not allow the South to leave. The Confederate officer "bowed his head in sadness and said that it was the only forceful reasoning he had yet heard for the continuance of this cruel war. He spoke of the emancipation measure, and asked whether I favored it. He insensibly shuddered when I told him that I did." McClure, initially reluctant for Lincoln to proclaim emancipation because of the political costs it would exact, now stood behind the decision. At daybreak the men shook hands, and the Rebels left.

Word of the Chambersburg raid quickly reached Franklin County troops stationed only a few dozen miles away in Maryland. They proclaimed themselves humiliated. "Strange to say, we of the army of the Potomac, who had gone forth, with so many loud words about protecting our firesides from the ruthless tread of the invader, first learned of the Rebel occupation of Chambersburg, through a stray copy of the Philadelphia *Inquirer* which reached camp by way of Harper's Ferry," a correspondent from the 126th Infantry wrote three days after Stuart's men had left. "A hundred men wanted to read at once, and those who read aloud were only greeted with cries of 'louder! louder!' from the unfortunate ones on the outer circles of the crowd that assembled almost in the twinkling of an eye." Despite protests of disbelief, there could be no doubt: "Chambersburg was part and parcel of the dominions of Jefferson D." Finding that no one had been hurt, the correspondent laughed at the situation; the Franklin soldiers treated "the affair as a very good joke, as it certainly is upon us, who marched to the Potomac to defend our homes." In spite of the light tone, make no mistake, "We felt the mortification and disgrace keenly, anxious countenance could be seen amongst us for many dreary and uncertain days, and we now sympathize deeply with those who have suffered by this daring movement."[118]

Samuel North, a nineteen-year-old tanner who had enlisted in the 126th only two months earlier, did not find the raid funny at all. "We have been most crazy on account of the rebel raid into Franklin Co. The idea of 2500 Cavalry passing through one end of our lines, capturing Horses & clothing, passing around the whole army and then unmolested, going back into virginia at the other end of our lines is the most ridiculous Slur on our Generals and army ever heard of." Sam North came from Mercersburg, the southernmost township in Franklin, and knew the people whose horses the Confederates had stolen. "It would be hard to describe the effect it has had on the 126. the chambersburg boys were wild. they say they dont blame the rebels but give them credit for the way the thing was accomplished and for the way they treated our people. but they curse our officers and the way the army is commanded."[119]

The *Spirit* reprinted the detailed Confederate record of the raid, from Robert E. Lee's order authorizing the endeavor to J. E. B. Stuart's final report. "You are about to engage in an enterprise which, to insure success, imperatively demands at your hands coolness, decision and bravery," the young general had admonished his men. Stuart's orders showed the Confederates in a flattering light: "Individual plunder for private use is positively forbidden, and every instance must be punished in the severest manner, for an army of plunderers consummates its own destruction."[120]

The report did not reflect well on Chambersburg. "The officials all fled the town on our approach," it said, "and no one could be found who would admit that he held office in the place." The "prominent citizens" who did come forward were told that they had three minutes to surrender or see their town shelled. They surrendered. The 275 wounded soldiers in town were paroled—captured, disarmed, and released on the promise that they would not fight again. "The wires were cut, and railroads obstructed." The Confederates discovered five thousand small arms and ammunition in the railroad buildings. What the Rebels could not carry they demolished. "The extensive machine shops and depot buildings of the railroad, and several trains of loaded cars, were entirely destroyed."[121] Stuart did not mention that a primary purpose of the raid, the burning of the railroad bridge in Chambersburg, had failed. In fact, aside from acquiring horses and columns of newspaper coverage, the Confederate raid into Pennsylvania gained little.

The raid unleashed recrimination and backbiting in Franklin rather than fury against the enemy. "A great deal has been said about the 'cowardice' of the Chambersburgers," quaked the *Spirit* in response to a snide article from a paper in a neighboring county. "It is said they might have repulsed and routed this attacking force of one thousand cavalry with very little trouble, or at least scared them away, as did the farm[ers of] Adams county." Adams lay directly to Franklin's east, with the town of Gettysburg as its seat, and the Chambersburg paper could barely stand the insinuation that its town had somehow let down the Union cause. "It would have been an act of madness to have made resistance under the circumstances, and would have involved the total destruction of the town." Only forty-eight members of the Home Guard had been in Chambersburg, and the Confederates had managed to take the storehouse where the Guard's guns were stored before anyone knew they were in town. If the Rebels came again, the *Spirit* sarcastically promised, "we intend organizing a Brigade of Scarers to operate in case of future raids, and would like to get those 'Farmers of Adams county' as veteran scarers to join."[122]

In the meantime, in the fall of 1862, the elections for state and local office came; the result was stunning. "The election is over and has resulted gloriously for the Democracy," boasted the *Spirit*. "We have elected our candidate for Congress in this district, the State Senator and both members of the Legislature" as well as many local offices.[123] "The People Speak in Favor of the Union as it was, the Constitution as it is and the Negroes where they are," the paper claimed, with "Fanaticism, Abolitionism and Niggerism Repudiated."[124] Pennsylvania as a whole went the same way. "We have elected a majority of members of Congress and a majority of eight or ten of the lower branch of the State Legislature, which gives us a majority on joint ballot and secures the election of a Democrat to the United States Senate in place of Hon. David Wilmot." Wilmot had long been a leading voice against slavery's expansion, and his defeat was cherished by the Democrats. Though soldiers in the field could not vote in this election, reports from Franklin units suggested that the Republicans barely triumphed there.[125] Their votes would not have been nearly enough to make a difference.

From the very day of the Preliminary Emancipation Proclamation on September 22, Alexander McClure later recalled, "those who had intelligent understanding of the general conditions had little hope of carrying any of the debatable Northern states at the fall election of that year. The Republicans of New England and of the far West were fully up to the high-water anti-slavery mark, and ready to sustain the destruction of slavery by any practicable method," but the states of the border and the Midwest remained dubious. McClure declared himself "earnestly anti-slavery in conviction" but very positive in opposition to the Emancipation Proclamation" on political grounds. "I looked at the greatest of all the questions ever presented to the ruler of the Republic from the mere standpoint of political expediency, and I predicted that an Emancipation Proclamation would defeat the administration in all the great States of New York, New Jersey, Pennsylvania, Ohio, Indiana and that political disaster was possible." That disaster "was more than fulfilled." All those states elected Democratic governors and sent Democratic delegations to Congress."[126] Democrats gained thirty-five congressional seats.

The *Spirit* thought the reason clear: men had voted "against the unconstitutional proclamation of the President, proclaiming freedom to 3,000,000 negroes in the South, to be turned loose upon the country, to enter into competition with white men and eat out their substance, and against fanaticism, bigotry, tyranny and despotism in all their different phases and forms."[127]

Though the Republicans remained in control of the House of Representatives and the Senate for the time being, the tide seemed to be turning. If the war continued to go badly, there was no reason to expect a Republican resurgence. The Union-loving white men of the South could now see that "the people of the free States are not all Abolitionists and that there is yet hope of a re-construction of the Union upon the broad principles of the Constitution." There would be no more talk of emancipation, the Democrats hoped, and more talk of peace.[128]

William Heyser viewed the situation with the cool eye of the banker he was. "Our national debt is staggering, some 640,000,000 dollars. The expenditure of a million and a quarter a day to keep this war machine going."[129] In the meantime "we all feel those at Washington are doing little to protect its citizens. Too much inactivity by our military leaders. They seem to not know what to do."[130] Heyser blamed the Republicans. "They must play politics first, and then decide the course of their plottings." He and his friends considered Lincoln "but a tool in his party's hand."[131]

The Democratic papers portrayed the consequences of Republican attacks on slavery in graphic stories. The *Spirit* passed on one such tale from another southern Pennsylvania county. "Three big, ugly, black female niggers came to a farm house in his neighborhood and asked to stay all night. But they were told they could not stay." The black women's request denied, "there came a second lot, consisting of four big, ugly, black male niggers." The white family, supposedly in favor of Lincoln's emancipation policy, "became still more frightened at this new feature in 'politics,' said they could give them their supper, but could not possibly accommodate them through the night." The black people supposedly challenged the sincerity of such white Northern friends. " 'O yes, dat's de way we am served; you white people in de Norf told us to run away from our masters, an' would treat us like brudders an' dis am the way we am treated.' "The former slaves supposedly took the meal and spent the night anyway, without "so much as even 'thanky.' " The Democratic paper thought the moral clear: "This is only the beginning. Before a great while these runaway blacks will be among us as thick as five in a bed."[132]

The Democrats worried about the interest black people displayed in politics and the war. Always eager to lampoon the Republican *Dispatch*, the *Spirit* related what it considered a funny story. The editor of the Democratic paper had supposedly seen people in the black part of Franklin, Wolfstown, reading the Republican paper. One "remarked that 'dis is de best newspaper printed in dis town.' A venerable darkey of that locality informs us that the articles in that paper, abusive of aged and respectable white citizens, and those detractive of General McClellan, are highly applauded by the intelligent community of that classic region." The Democrats were undoubtedly correct that Franklin blacks found more to admire in the Republican paper than in their own.[133]

Despite the emboldened political confidence of the Democrats across the North, Lincoln and the Republicans did not back down. Only weeks after the election the president removed George McClellan from command of the Army of the Potomac. The reports from Franklin's companies in Virginia expressed fury at what many saw as a political purging. "Officers and men unite in denouncing the order as an outrage upon the army," one correspondent charged. "Many have prepared their resignations, and distinguished officers of rank assert that they will no longer serve in the army if the order be not rescinded." Soldiers argued that "upon every occasion when General McClellan was upon the eve of a decisive battle—one which would to a great extent settle the whole question now in issue between the Government and the rebels—he has been prevented from striking the blow by the interference of the government."[134] The Democrats saw the darkest motives behind the Republicans' action: because "a general and decisive engagement must occur very soon, and may take place at any moment," the Republicans wanted credit for the victory.[135]

Thanksgiving Day brought some comfort to Franklin and the North. William Heyser helped decorate his church for the holiday, blending religious and secular purposes. "The gallery and pillars ornamented with spruce," he wrote with satisfaction. "The pulpit lamps and walk behind the pulpit beautifully ornamented. Two flags handsomely draped in the background. The whole effect enhanced when the gas lights turned on. Our efforts were a huge success in that all were surprised as well as delighted with our arrangements."[136] People seemed to behave themselves better in Chambersburg than they had during past Thanksgivings, when drunkenness was all too common. Moreover, "through the efforts of the ladies connected with the different churches, the sick and wounded soldiers in the Hospitals, were provided with a sumptuous thanksgiving dinner, and it was pleasant to behold the way in which the gallant defenders of our country disposed of the good things furnished."[137]

The Union army presented an imposing spectacle in the late fall of 1862. The impressive fighting at Antietam offered the first encouragement in months, and the Federal ranks grew stronger as hundreds of thousands of recruits trained and flowed into Union regiments. A Franklin member of the Army of the Potomac described the scene as units massed in northern Virginia. "For miles around one sees hill and valley covered with tents." Drums, trumpets, and popular songs filled the air. "Flags, national and State, float proudly to the breeze from the headquarters of every regiment." Officers in fancy dress and privates in plain uniforms passed one another in the crowded camps. "Orderlies with big envelopes, sealed orders perhaps of grave import, speed over the road and through the camps with telegraphic rapidity. Wagoners are cursing, mules kicking, whips cracking, trains creaking." A young man could not help being proud to be a part of such an army, which "in discipline, numbers and appointment, this world has seldom seen."[138] The army, its men thought, rested halfway between two victories: Antietam and the taking of Richmond. "All that we hear goes in our favor and it is expected that the war don't last long any more," young Peter Boyer wrote his father. "I don't think that I or any of us will get into battle which gives me great courage."[139]

4

THE PRELIMINARY EMANCIPATION PROCLAMATION drove the South to distraction. The *Staunton Spectator* saw it as an invitation for "the servile population of the South to enact the bloody scene of St. Domingo throughout the limits of the Southern Confederacy." The Haitian Revolution, seventy years earlier, stood as the example for Southern whites of what would happen with black freedom: rampant bloodshed and chaos. Only the devil could be responsible for such a ghastly plan, and that devil had spoken to Lincoln at a weak moment, "when he was writhing under the mortification of a succession of defeats." The proclamation, the paper reassured its readers, would "strengthen the South and weaken the North, and bring down upon the Lincoln Administration the condemnation of the whole civilized world." Surely the world would see that "the Lincoln Government is now the most tyrannical military despotism which has ever existed upon the earth."[140]

Yet neither England nor France expressed outrage or aligned itself with the Confederacy as the weeks dragged by. The battle at Antietam seemed to buy the Union new credibility with the European powers, who showed less interest in the Confederacy than they had earlier in the year. "It is apparent that they wish the war to go on till both sections are hopelessly broken down, but won't interfere to prevent a reunion," complained Joseph Waddell in his diary. "They desire the ultimate success of the 'rebels' in *dissolving* the old Union, but want to see the country ruined first."[141]

Jeb Stuart's raid into Pennsylvania provided momentary amusement and encouragement. "This distinguished and gallant cavalry officer has again astonished and electrified the public by another dashing 'circum-bendibus' entirely around the enormous army of Gen'l. McClellan," Staunton's paper gushed. "Now take the map and trace the route of his glorious and triumphant gallopade around the large and boastful army of the enemy." Exactly what the "gallopade" had accomplished remained unclear, but "it is sufficient for us to know that it was done for a purpose.—What that purpose was will be developed at the proper time."[142]

In praising Stuart, however, the reports of his raid gave suffering Southerners a disheartening glimpse of the wealthy North. The main towns through which his troopers passed, Mercersburg and Chambersburg, "are situated in Franklin, a county which contains a population of more than 40,000." The Richmond papers portrayed the wealth of Franklin County in tantalizing detail: "Most of the country is a rich limestone valley, well watered. The productions in 1850 were 837,000 bushels of wheat (the greatest quantity produced by any county of the State, except Lancaster), 539,976 of Indian corn, 393,447 of oats, 33,591 tons of hay, 67,546 lbs butter, and 44,192 of wool. The number of horses and mules in the county in 1850 (in round numbers), was 9,000, neat cattle 22,000, sheep, 14,000, swine 35,000." The county seat of Franklin, the town of Chambersburg, was a "thriving place" of about five thousand. "The houses are mostly of brick or stone, and the general appearance of the town is neat and comfortable. There are manufactories of cotton, wood, flour, paper, and iron in and near the town." In such a portrayal, the people of Augusta could remember their own county as it used to be.[143]

By contrast, unmistakable signs of want and deprivation appeared throughout the Valley of Virginia. War and weather had combined in a demoralizing assault on the farms. "The short crop of wheat and corn for the past year, the fatality that has attended the hog crop; the waste superinduced by large standing armies; the drought which has retarded the Fall operations of farmers in getting their wheat sown, and the embarrassments that the agricultural portion of our citizens have suffered, in consequence of the presence of the enemy, and the demand made upon them by our Governments, State and Confederate, will we fear, be manifest in a short supply of bread and meat next year," the local paper lamented. The money saved from richer years mattered little, for the people of the Valley found themselves "excluded from the markets of the world, and are compelled to rely upon what we have within ourselves. Money cannot produce one grain of corn, or increase by one pound, our quantity of meat." Though harvest season had come to the

Valley, this was a time for "earnest self-denial, and abounding patriotism and charity."[144]

Augusta County struggled to feed itself. As early as October, Joseph Waddell confided worries to his diary: "Provisions of all kinds scarce and prices high." Flour was fourteen dollars per barrel. "Serious apprehensions for the future. Clothing very difficult to get. Great demoralization among the people. Rights of property not respected as formerly."[145] A few weeks later Waddell experienced at first hand the erosion of those "rights of property" when someone stole wood from his lot. He tried to see things in a dispassionate way, pointing out that "the extortion practiced by those who have anything to see adds greatly to the hardship of the times," but the fact remained that his family would miss the wood during the long winter ahead.[146]

Though Waddell noted with some hope the Democratic victories in the Northern elections, he admitted that the Confederates had "more to fear from the scarcity of foodstuffs and clothing than from the Yankee armies. The drought continues unabated—the fields are perfectly barren—the wheat must perish soon. Farmers are unwilling to sell the produce they have on hand." As a town dweller Waddell knew that "many persons who have money can scarcely procure necessary food, even this early in the Fall, usually the most abundant period of the year."[147]

When the county court purchased "12,000 bushels of salt for equal distribution among all the citizens giving to each individual 20 lbs.," many families did not get their share. "Now we, as tax-payers, and good and loyal citizens of the Confederacy, want to know, nay, we have a right to know, how the salt received, and being received has, and is being distributed, and why so many families have not been able to get a pound," "Independent" wrote in fury to the local paper. "We also wish to know, whether or not, the horses, cattle, sheep, &c., of the sub agents of Mr. Davis were counted as inhabitants."[148] Suspicion and anger flourished in the hard times.

Virginia had borne more than its share of sacrifice for the Confederacy. The people of the Valley bridled at reports that the residents of deep South states, instrumental in bringing secession and war, resisted the efforts of the new nation to recruit men and supplies. The *Spectator* printed a speech from a Confederate congressman from Georgia attesting to Virginia's selflessness and loss. "The people of Virginia have lost their property, their negroes, their food, their all. Their houses, their barns and fences have been burnt before their eyes, their wives and children insulted and driven from home and themselves carried away captives, and still they are true. You know nothing of the ravages of war." The lesson was clear: Georgia should quit whining and instead contribute to the cause. "Had you not better do all you can to keep the war away from your borders? Is it well for you to be squabbling about State Rights and who shall appoint captains and colonels when the enemy is thundering at your doors?"[149]

The Confederate army did its share to despoil the Valley, especially the lower Valley, the broad area where the forks of the Shenandoah River flow into the Potomac. "It was doubtless the policy of our Generals to leave that unfortunate section utterly unavailable to the enemy for occupation for any purpose," a soldier from Jackson's corps commented in early December. "Hence all the railroads leading into it—the Baltimore and Ohio—the Winchester and Potomac, and the Manassas Gap, have been effectually destroyed. All the surplus forage and provender for man and beast have been consumed by our army, which literally spread itself by brigades and regiments all over the region, and subsisted off it entirely. So the enemy will now find it a section hard to get in, hard to stay in, and hard to get out of." This Augusta soldier made no apologies for the strategy but did express sympathy. "The abomination of desolation" had swept the northern Valley: "Houses are closed and deserted; forests and even orchards are demolished for fuel, or in wantonness by the enemy; bridges burnt; the once beautifully cultivated fields are scarred all over with the marks of encampments, and all so changed from the fair and fruitful appearance it presented when we first marched into it."[150] Of course the slaves were long gone.

For all its destructive foraging, the Confederate army remained desperately impoverished. The men had worn out their clothes and shoes with hundreds of miles of marching, sleeping on the ground without tents, and the loss of equipment in one battle after another. An observer told of "men on the march whose miserable outfit was not sufficient to cover their nakedness. Some were without shirts, others had on only the dirty remnant of a pair of pants, without shoes, and almost without caps or hats. Some were barefooted, others had on ragged socks but no shoes."[151] A visitor sadly reported that "many of the men are yet without shoes in some of the regiments, and it is most piteous to see them painfully picking their way along through frost and ice. Many are without blankets, and how they stand it, is more than can be imagined by those of us who are so fortunate as barely to escape freezing under two blankets by lying out in these frosty nights." Despite all this, the soldiers somehow remained "wonderfully cheerful. They live, too, in hopes of seeing an end of the war, when they will return home with renewed zest for the pleasures of peace." Sitting around a fire in early December, a group of men fantasized over the question 'supposin peace was declared, what would you do?' One said, 'I'd get up right here, and go across that field, over that stone fence, straight home.' "[152] But a soldier who came home in the winter of 1862 would not find peace and plenty.

Smallpox, a "dangerous and loathsome disease," broke out in Augusta. The *Spectator* begged every family to "have all of its members vaccinated as soon as possible." Reports had come of the spread of the disease in rural communities in the county, and the people of Staunton requested "our country friends to be careful not to bring it here, for, as soldiers are passing daily through this place to the army, it may in this way get into our army and do us more harm than all the soldiers Lincoln has been able to bring into the field against us."[153] Joseph Waddell noted the outbreak of smallpox as well but thought it had "spread from the Hospital into the town." The litany of miseries inflicted upon the South finally led him to cry out, "War, pestilence and famine! Oh for the faith of Habbakuk! Alas, we never know how little faith we have till the day of trial comes."[154]

A captured Union spy came through Staunton in November 1862. Upon his release he sent a report back to headquarters describing his journey through Virginia. "Approaching Staunton from the north side, with the mouths of cannons pointing toward you, one might suppose the rebels were occupying the same in force. Enter, and you feel surprised," Joseph Snyder wrote in a passage that must have been tantalizing to the Federal leadership. "The manufactories for boots, shoes, and clothing for army use, the extensive hospital preparations for thousands of sick, the general supply depot, the place of safe-keeping of all the captured Harper's Ferry plunder," all was defended by a single company of infantry, twenty-four field pieces, and a mixture of cavalry and artillery, although small in number. If that were not reason enough for the U.S. Army to focus on Staunton, "the Virginia Central Railroad has been in fine running condition, and has been the main line of nearly all supplies sent to the Army of Northern Virginia. The only direct telegraphic communication from Winchester to Richmond is via Staunton, along this road." The longer the war went on, the more important Staunton and the Valley became.[155]

Faced with such challenges and threats, people in Staunton seemed to become more selfish. "What has become of the Soldier's Aid Societies of our county?" asked "A Farmer." "One year ago they were doing good service by furnishing our soldiers with many essential and indispensable articles of clothing, and no doubt made glad the hearts of us brave men who were in the tented field, exposing their health and lives for the sake of the dear ones at home, and for all that is dear to them and us, our National Independence." Augusta County had prided itself back then on its selfless aid for their families of fighting men. But "Alas! I am pained to say that with many or all of these societies, apathy and indifference seems to have taken the places of effort and kind feelings." People needed to rouse themselves from their lethargy and "enter into the obligation due our brave men without delay."[156] Residents continued to sacrifice, of course. "I went to Preaching this morning and the Preacher wants the people here to cut up their carpets to make blankets for the soldiers," Kent Langhorne reported from up the Valley. "They are going to give the carpets in the aisles of the churches here to them."[157]

Some soldiers dreamed of buying a substitute, although only about twenty Augusta men were to fight for the Confederacy as substitutes. A. W. Kersh, the cabinetmaker from Staunton, told his brother George of conditions in his camp near Winchester: "We have no tents now. some have little Yankee tents. The officers all have tents. We build little shanties and cover them with Oil cloth cedar and brush." He confirmed the stories about the soldiers' lack of clothes, reporting that "some of the boys are barefooted in our regiment now and their cloths are very dirty and ragged Marching so much."[158] He asked his brother to look into getting a substitute, but he had no luck. Kersh had been thinking about securing a substitute since the spring, but the odds against getting out of the fighting worsened as the battles dragged on. "Our Captain wont except none boys from sixteen to seventeen or good men born in the South unless the Colonel is agreed then he will take them in." Kersh was willing to pay considerable money. "I will go fifteen hundred if you can get one for that bring him if not dont." According to the census, A. W. Kersh only had $2,150 in total property. He would pay almost all of it to get out of the army, even if it meant hiring a sixteen-year-old boy to suffer in his place.[159]

Short of hiring a substitute, there seemed little prospect of escaping war. In early December the *Spectator* published a persuasive and dispiriting list of signs from the North that the war would not end soon. The list included the arming of 450,000 new men who had enrolled in September; the rapid expansion of the U.S. Navy, including river gun-boats; the fortification of all the places the Union had occupied in the South; "their avowed intention of conquering every seaboard city and blockading up all access to the sea"; and the "inhuman and iniquitous proclamation of President Lincoln, looking towards the utter destruction of our country," the proclamation against slavery. The final bad sign was "the unity of the people of the North on the war. The Democratic party is coming into power again, but that party declares it will prosecute the war to our certain and entire subjugation and the restoration of the Union."[160]

Faced with such odds, the Confederacy drew more heavily on one resource that it had relatively neglected in the first two years of war, its enslaved population. Slaves had been put to work from the very beginning on fortifications, and slaves had produced much of the food consumed by the Southern army, but the government had treated slaveholders gingerly, asking little of them as a class. In the winter of 1862, however, Virginia's Governor Letcher issued a proclamation calling for the use of slaves by the state. "The slave population is a large one, nearly one-third of the population of the whole State," he noted somewhat defensively. "The slaves are exempted from serving in our armies, they are freed from all military duty, and it is but reasonable that a small portion of their time and labor should be devoted to the prosecution of works conducive to the public defence." It also seemed only fair that the earthworks of the Confederate fortifications should be "constructed by laborers who are inured to such service."[161]

With apologies out of the way, the governor eased into the proclamation. "The act is a liberal one to the owners. It allows sixteen dollars per month as a compensation for the labor of each slave" besides rations and medicine. Just as important, "it provides that all such slaves that may escape" or be killed by the enemy or die "shall be paid for by the Confederates States." The governor ordered the county courts to decide the best way to meet their quota of slaves and to do so in "such manner as to be least onerous upon their fellow-citizens, particularly as there is no appeal from the decision they make."[162] Augusta's share was two hundred slaves. Slaveholders would have to bring their slaves to the courthouse at the end of the year to have them appraised by a special committee appointed by the county court and then "drafted" and some sent off to the Confederacy.[163]

The governor had one other thought on his mind about Virginia's enslaved population: "Our slaves have hitherto been contented and happy, peaceable and trustworthy, and I doubt but they will remain so, notwithstanding the disgraceful proclamation of the President of the United States, and the shameful attempts of abolition emissaries and armies to render them discontented and insubordinate. But in times like these it is proper to be ever watchful, ever on the guard." He recommended that the counties establish patrols to keep watch over "all negro quarters and other places suspected of having unlawful assemblies or such slaves as may stray from one plantation to another without permission."[164] The slaves could be a crucial resource for the Confederacy; they could also bring its sudden downfall from within were they not kept under control.

In the meantime the war only made slaves more valuable. The government and army competed with private citizens for slaves' services, driving up prices and fueling competition for hired slaves. Jed Hotchkiss traveled to Staunton trying to find "a servant to come to the army, but it was of no avail, there are so many to go to Richmond & so many that want substitutes, to send to Richmond, for their servants that they want to have stay at home." The cars on the Virginia Central Railroad were crammed with black people. "The servants of course had it almost to themselves, so many going & coming—as this was the hiring day—I never saw so many slaves along the R.R."[165] War made white people depend even more on the black people in their midst.

5

LINCOLN PRESSED MCCLELLAN to move toward Richmond after Antietam, even visiting him in camp. McClellan wanted to make sure everything was in order before he ventured back into Virginia, however, and more than a month passed before the U.S. Army finally began to head south. When it did move, it did so quite slowly, as McClellan squabbled with Lincoln, the cabinet, and the military leaders in Washington. The Union soldiers' confidence remained high after Antietam, and they enjoyed taking what they wished from farms large and small along the way in the season after the harvest and the butchering, but they began to grow discouraged as winter settled in early that year. The first days of November, often a mild time in Virginia, brought freezing snow and rain in 1862. With clothes and shoes worn, typhoid fever raced through the ranks.

Lincoln, disgusted with McClellan's delays and excuses and complaints, removed him from command of the Army of the Potomac on November 7. In his place Lincoln appointed Ambrose Burnside, a former employee of McClellan's in civilian life and his subordinate in the army. Burnside, an affable and popular man, insisted that he was not up to the job, but he received the job nevertheless. It would be up to him to take the Union force of 110,000 to Falmouth, across the Rappahannock River from Fredericksburg, a beautiful town of 5,000 (about the size of Chambersburg) midway between Richmond and Washington.

From Falmouth, the U.S. forces would be able to march on Richmond, using the Union's command of the rivers for supply, before the Confederates could catch them. The only challenge was crossing three rivers between Falmouth and Richmond, but the Union had devised excellent pontoon bridges. As the soldiers piled up on the northern banks of the Rappahannock, however, the pontoons, to be shipped down from Maryland, failed to arrive for a week.

During that week Lee arrived in Fredericksburg from northern Virginia and established his troops there behind heavy fortifications on the southern side of the Rappahannock, above the little city. He put up a line four miles long, command-

ing the river and the fields below from behind rock walls. He called Jackson to Fredericksburg from the Valley. Jackson's men raced east, marching twelve days straight, often barefoot on the freezing ground, and arrived just in time for the fighting. The Confederates now had seventy-five thousand men in place. Most of the people of Fredericksburg fled to refuge in Richmond or Charlottesville. Lee read the newspapers of the North, depending on them for reports of troop size and positioning as well as for signs that the North's resolve might be breaking.

THE TWO ARMIES watched each other. A Franklin soldier in the Army of the Potomac reported on the strange situation. "From the hills on this side of the Rappahannock we can look down upon the ancient place, and wonder that our leaders did not move to its possession when we first came here." On this Sunday morning, "the ringing of the church bells can be distinctly heard and people seen repairing to their respective places of worship." In fact, "there seems to be no cessation from the usual routine of business and altogether there is an apparent unconcern as to our presence or future movements."[166]

The Confederate army too seemed complacent. "Along the river bank fortifications have been thrown up and are hourly strengthened without molestation, and Rebel Cavalry come down to the streams to water their horses and converse with our pickets on this side. Under the circumstances our position seems a very queer one." President Lincoln and the wife of General Burnside visited the Union forces at Fredericksburg. General Burnside was "rendering himself very popular by his unassuming manners and free social intercourse."[167]

By December 11 the bridges had finally arrived at the Union outpost. Workmen labored in ice and fog to lay the boards across the pontoons, Rebels firing on them from the other side of the river. With their progress slowed and several men killed, Burnside ordered his artillery to shell the positions of the Confederates firing down on them. The shelling turned into a barrage, as the Union artillerymen rained down hot metal on the houses, streets, businesses and churches. Buildings toppled, crashed, and burned. Few remained untouched by the artillery fire, the heaviest soldiers on either side had ever seen. In the wake of the firing, their bridges completed, Union soldiers rushed into Fredericksburg.

The *Valley Spirit* and letters home told the story of the battle. "Gen.

Burnside's army has made a decisive and victorious movement," came a breathless report. "The city of Fredericksburg is now occupied by his forces after a terrible bombardment, which lasted nearly all day yesterday, and resulted in the partial destruction of the city by the heavy fire of our artillery."[168] After the guns had stopped, Union soldiers flooded into the city. "The town was all ransacked. books, chairs and every kind of furniture was lying in the Streets," Sam North wrote. "Some of the boys got books and some other things. Haze Boyd got Milton's complete works lying in the Streets." The Federals sacked Fredericksburg, taking out on the city their months of frustration. "There was abundance of flour fish pork and in short every thing but salt," North reported, but "the story of the South starving is all a Hoax. they had things just as plenty as we have at least in Fredericksburg. our soldiers helped themselves as well as they could."[169] Men stole everything from toys to women's clothes to the communion sets from churches. They feasted and drank among the bodies of their Confederate enemies.

On December 13 the Union soldiers surged from the streets of Fredericksburg, bayonets fixed, to rush Confederates fortified behind stone walls on Marye's Heights. Fourteen brigades—fifty-six thousand men—ran

Federal soldiers in Fredericksburg

across ravines, ditches, and sunken roads. Unceasing fire from thousands of protected Confederate guns shattered one line after another. "The roar of the cannon and the sharp cracking of the musketry was awful, beyond description," wrote a Franklin correspondent. "As night approached the blaze from the cannons appeared through the smoke like forked lightning in a howling storm." At the very end, "just as the Sun was lowering behind the distant hills, the gleam of thousands of bayonets, and the double quick of the men became visible. It was a gallant but desperate charge on a line of battle." Yet "the work could not be accomplished."[170]

"The long line of stone wall was a sheet of flame," an officer from the 126th reported. It looked as if the men of the Franklin unit, charging with bayonets but not pausing to fire their guns, might reach the top. But men of other regiments, who had fallen to the ground and been passed over by the charging Franklin soldiers, "began to fire at the enemy through our advancing lines. Immediately there was a stop. The fire in the front, the fire in the rear, every flash visible in the twilight, astounded the soldiers. Bewildered, they stood for a moment irresolute; then in their excitement began to fire at the rebel line. This was fatal. The charge was over. All its momentum was lost." Although the officers "urged" their men along, suffering wounds as they tried to lead, the "feeble fire against the stone wall was futile." The men of Franklin fell back to where they had begun. "Probably the whole of the advance and the retiring did not occupy fifteen minutes," a participant reported. Out of the 4,000 men who had been sent up the hill, 1,760 lay there when the charge ended.[171]

The dead and wounded piled up at the stone wall at the bottom of Marye's Heights. "I have heard of the horrors of the battle field but the reality is terrible," Sam North told his brother. "It is not realized but the thoughts and impressions seem to be burned in my brain. the still pale faces of the dead and the shrieks and groans of the wounded and dying, oh! it is awfull." He admitted with a shudder that "we could hardly step without tramping on them."[172] James Carman, a lieutenant in the 107th Pennsylvania, wrote his father that "I never want to get into another battle it is terrible persons falling all around me if ever I trusted in God I did that time."[173]

When darkness finally came, thirteen thousand Union men had been lost—as many as at Antietam three months earlier. Unlike that battle, however, the Federals had nothing at all to show for the sacrifice. The Rebels remained in place; they had lost five thousand men, most on Jackson's end of the line away from Marye's Heights. "The ill-advised precipitation of our troops upon the almost impregnable position of the rebels having resulted in a bloody repulse, and being now acknowledged as such, the Army of the Potomac has marched back over the Rappahannock, and taken up its old quarters at Falmouth," read the next week's summary of war news.[174] A soldier reported sadly but honestly: "I have just been among our wounded. Our Regiment has been terrible decimated, those who were not killed or wounded are entirely exhausted, and suffering from excitement and general debility. Some of the wounded are greatly lacerated in all parts of the head, body and limbs."[175] The 126th had made the last charge against the Confederate guns.

On the fourteenth, men from both sides began to tend to the wounded. They traded tobacco for newspapers and even shook hands. Soldiers scavenged among the bodies for overcoats or boots; bodies were stripped bare, left white and naked. The next day, after a formal truce, burial crews came out to wrap bodies in thin blankets and throw them into two shallow trenches hacked out of the frozen earth. That night a rare aurora borealis hovered in the sky above the two armies, illuminating the contorted dead who yet lay exposed on the killing ground.

The *Spirit*, like papers all over the North, could hardly stand the news. "The people have thus far borne patiently the burdens that have been imposed upon them by the necessities of the times. They never murmured as long as they saw any hope for the country, but when they see their treasure wasted and the resources of the country exhausted in fruitless expeditions around the outskirts of the rebellion, and their brothers and sons murdered in cold blood through the incompetency of imbeciles at the head of the Government, they begin to cry enough." The *Spirit* blamed the Lincoln administration, not General Burnside and certainly not the thousands of men who rushed into almost certain death.[176] Lieutenant Carman admitted that "if my resignation would be exceped I would resign right away but there has been some half dozen sent in from our regiment but there were all sent back but one."[177]

On the day before Christmas the *Spirit* published column after column of the dead and wounded from the 126th Pennsylvania. Of its 632 men,

12 had been killed, 57 wounded, and 14 were declared missing. The more serious wounds afflicted every part of the body: "severely in left fore arm; severely in right knee and both hands; severe flesh wound in right thigh; in heel by shell; in right shoulder; in spine, lower part of the body paralyzed; in breast severely; in forehead severely; in face, ball; in left side by concussion of shell producing paralysis; in back with shell seriously; in stomach and bowels by being run over and trampled; knocked down and trampled, and spine injured; in right ear; left arm, since amputated."[178]

Franklin's soldier correspondent allowed himself to dwell on the meaning of the list of dead and wounded that he had mailed back to Chambersburg. "Many a mother's cheek is even now bedewed with tears and her heart ready to break as the intelligence comes to her of the death of her cherished son on the gory field of battle. The father's pride is gone and he bows his head in grief. The joyous spirits of the sisters have forsaken her." "Shenandoah" permitted himself to imagine "the agony of the loving wife as she hears 'among the killed' her husband. Husband, father, protector gone and forever, his life a sacrifice upon the altar of his country." Multiply the losses of Franklin County by hundred of times, and "we can partially realize the desolation and distress which prevail through the land."[179] Ten thousand of the wounded men lay in Washington, D.C., where Abraham Lincoln grieved.

THE SLAUGHTER AT Marye's Heights filled Franklin County's soldiers with determination to redeem themselves. "We will have another fight in the neighbourhood of Fredericksburg before long," Christian Geisel of the 6th Pennsylvania Cavalry predicted to his sister back home as 1863 began. "Our men have been at work for the last three nights making a corderoy road through the field just below us in a field to the river." Other crews worked elsewhere along the Rappahannock, but "where they are going to cross is yet a secret. I hope and pray that if our army makes another attack, we may be successful rout the rebels out of their strongholds."[180]

Samuel Cormany narrowly missed the battle at Fredericksburg. He was on his way through Washington to join General Burnside's troops in Virginia as the new year began, full of faith in his unit: "New Men of 3 months training—New Arms and Accoutrements—Bright Flags & Guidons."

The scene in Washington was everything Samuel had imagined when he had enlisted in Chambersburg back in September. "Proudly and bravely our Regiment moved along Pennsylvania Avenue," he wrote in his diary, "uproariously cheered by the populace and saluted by Soldiers singly and in squads enroute." He felt deeper excitement when he drew his first ammunition, for it "brings up the idea of going into ACTUAL WARFARE, and makes one feel the importance of the situation—Life is at Stake."[181] Back in Chambersburg, his wife, Rachel, tried to busy herself but worried as she watched townsmen bury an anonymous soldier in the church graveyard across the street from the dingy rooms she shared with their infant daughter, Cora. "I feel sad all day. The thought that next I hear from my Samuel may be that he was killed rings in my ears continually."[182]

Everyone expected combat. The situation in Virginia seemed perfect for a Union counterattack after the Fredericksburg debacle. "Such splendid weather as we have had for this time in the season, has no parallel in the memory of the oldest inhabitant," read a public letter from a soldier in the *Valley Spirit*. "The roads are in as good condition as they possibly can be and the organization and condition of the army can scarcely be made better." This veteran would not speak with the childish enthusiasm of the preceding year—"None of us are 'spilling for a fight'—that exclamation in an earnest tone has had its day"—but he did want General Burnside to do something "to convince the country and the world that the Grand Army of the Potomac, the most splendid military organization of modern times, is capable of doing its full share in speedily ending the Rebellion."[183]

Burnside heard the demands of his countrymen. Still determined to take Fredericksburg despite the horrific losses of the last assault only weeks before, the Union general wanted to hit Lee from the flank, driving the Confederates from behind the twenty-five miles of trenches and stone walls that protected them. An unusually dry January made it possible to contemplate such a complicated maneuver in the dead of winter, when armies usually dug in and waited for spring. Burnside began to move his men across the Rappahannock River, which separated the Federal and Confederate armies.

"Their is a move at the presant and at this time they are moving by thousands towards the Rappahack River and whe are at this time furnish with 3 Day Rasions and 60 rounds of cartridge to move at an airely hour to morrow morning," Thad Donely wrote breathlessly to his friend Henry Bitner back in Franklin. "Before 48 hours more their may be a very heavy Battle fought." The memory of the recent debacle at Fredericksburg overshadowed the effort, Donely admitted, for "the Men are some what Depressed in spirits owing to the last defeat at the River but yet they will go." He soberly told his friend that this "may be the last letter I shall write to you but whe hope for the best if their is a fight and I shall do my duty."[184]

As the vast force began its move, rain fell from the Virginia skies for two days and nights. An officer in Franklin's 126th Pennsylvania described the scene: "Pontoon trains, wagons, guns, ammunition trains, encumbered the roads. Horses and mules were everywhere floundering in the mud. The soil, though tenacious, was without bottom." The Union army, despite all the desperate hopes for redemption, despite all the preparation, was forced to turn back.[185]

The soldiers had to build their own roads for the retreat. "Regiments could be seen coming across the country like moving groves," the Franklin officer reported, "every man carrying a tree top"; behind them came others bearing fence rails to lay on top of the branches. "Whole woods were cut down and thrown into the road," the work fueled by an unusual whiskey ration.[186] The mud was of an "almost unfathomable depth," a soldier wrote home. As mules and horses struggled in the mire, "such swearing and cursing, pulling and tugging, was never heard or witnessed before." Finally, after four days of what immediately became known as the "mud march," Confederates jeering across the river, the Union army made it back to where it had started, exhausted and humiliated.[187]

In the wake of this fiasco Burnside resigned. General Joseph Hooker took command of the Army of the Potomac, his task to rebuild the strength and morale of the devastated troops. Hooker had strong ties to the Lincoln administration and to the radicals in the Republican Congress. He could be counted on to push the Union offensive; his nickname was Fighting Joe. "With the assumption of command by Gen. Hooker, a new era in our existence begins. We enter upon it full of hope for the speedy and complete success of our army," enthused a Franklin soldier. The Army of the Potomac certainly needed a "new era," for desertions were "enormously on the increase" and "a large number of vacancies caused by resignations, deaths and dismissals, now exist in every Army Corps."[188]

In October state-level conscription finally arrived in Franklin County. The commissioner set up a table in the courthouse in Chambersburg and announced the names of those who would serve for nine months in the 158th Pennsylvania Militia. According to the *Valley Spirit*, "Those in attendance who were drafted seemed to receive the announcement with equanimity." Pages of the paper were filled with the names of men who had to leave from every township in the county.[189] Added to the thousand or so whom the 126th had brought in a few months earlier, Franklin had now contributed twenty-two hundred men to the federal army by January 1, 1863.

More than two hundred Franklin County men deserted in 1862, the most who did so at any time in the war. Some simply disappeared from camp, blending into the civilian population as they moved west or into some city where they were unknown. A few deserted while the army was in Virginia or Maryland. But two-thirds of those who deserted did so at one time. The men of the 158th, the unit formed in October 1862, when the threat of quotas and drafts—and the allure of bounties—hung over their heads, were sent to Camp McClure in Chambersburg to train. There, in December, a heavy storm descended on men who had not been provided adequate shelter. As the *Valley Spirit* described the scene, "they broke guard and fled in every direction."[190] Officers had to post a battalion of the provost guard to "guard the camp and prevent further desertions." Even counting this group desertion, Franklin County troops generally stayed with their units.

While the army drilled and consolidated, Samuel Cormany received a furlough to go to Chambersburg to visit Rachel and the baby. "Praise the Lord," he wrote, "and thanks to Uncle Sam." When he got back home, though, he was confronted with the body of a friend whom his unit had left behind in Washington; there the young comrade had become sick and then died. The uncle of the dead young man "acted real meanly to me as tho I was the cause of it all," Samuel admitted. Usually softhearted, the religious Cormany callously brushed aside any guilt. "Sure I was desirous

'Will' should go with me—become a soldier good and true—but he n't the stuff in him—and for lack of it, colapsed." Samuel forgot the hard feelings during his warm reunion with Rachel and Cora. "How delightful to lie in the embrace of one so good, so dear, so true, and to have our little one climbing all over and about us before going to sleep."[191]

William Heyser, the elderly banker who viewed matters through the eyes of a practical businessman, coolly assessed the situation in Franklin and the North at the beginning of 1863. On the positive side: "the war years profitable to our bank, as our deposits growing. We have a surplus to invest." On the debit side: "Rapid rise in stocks, much speculation, fortunes will be made, but many will be ruined. An unhappy time for our nation, for it will never be the same again. Greed and power transcends all." Heyser blamed Abraham Lincoln for ruining things. "The war is going badly. President Lincoln has a fearful account to render to the country and posterity for his unfaithful stewardship." The costs lay close to home, for when Heyser went to the farm he rented, he found "my tenant rather distressed that Lincoln's draft plans will take all the men, leaving the females to run things. They are convinced all the real criminals are in Washington, and Lincoln-the ring leader."[192]

The federal government, realizing how widespread such opinions were, acted to strengthen the shaky Union cause in the early winter of 1863. The Republicans enacted a banking act to stabilize the currency, producing all the greenbacks the Union cause needed to outfit itself as no army had ever been equipped before. They cracked down on Democratic dissidents across the North from New York to the Midwest, chasing the leading Copperhead—what Republicans called an antiwar Democrat—from Ohio and charging him with treason. They issued the Emancipation Proclamation, freeing slaves in all territory held by the enemy and advertising the Union cause to the world as a fight for freedom. Facing a shortage of new men eager to enlist, they still pushed for a conscription bill, offering threats of a draft and inducements of bounties to join the army. With the spring and summer likely to determine the outcome of the war, the Union could afford no less.

6

THE NEW YEAR of 1863 began with disconcerting boredom for the Confederates in and around Fredericksburg. "Our camp is still under the hill, by the side of the run, under the shade of the oaks, cedars and hollys," Jed Hotchkiss wrote home to his wife, Sara, one relaxed Sunday night in January. "We build our fires, eat our meals, read the papers, talk & work in the most humdrum way imaginable." Such an experience was strange, "a sort of trance after our perpetual motion, unending variety-way of doing ever since last spring, with an occasional night mare rumor."[193] Sitting in their camps, the soldiers dreamed of one thing only: "We must pray our merciful Heavenly Father that these days may be shortened and that neither we nor our offspring may see any more of the like."[194]

Hotchkiss wrote his young daughter Nelly to tell of recent battles around Fredericksburg, translating the killing into words he thought she could comprehend. "I will make a little map for you to look at and see how the armies were located when they fought. Look at the map I have made for you," he instructed, teaching her cartography along with tactics. "The roads are put down: red lines, our troops in black lines and the Yankees in blue ones." Jed told of the pontoon bridges and the Yankee crossing of the river. "When they came up towards the woods where our men were we fired a great many thousand guns at them and they fired at us, and so we did for a long time and we drive them back, having killed a large number of them and wounded many more—we had a good many killed and wounded too, but not as many as they did, for we were protected by the woods." The father drew out the moral of the story: "Now they have gone away across the river, and we must thank the good Lord that he enabled us to whip them and drive them away, for they would come and destroy us and our country if they could."[195]

Hotchkiss rode into Fredericksburg in late January to see what the Yankees had done with their shelling and occupation a few weeks earlier. "I had no idea before how a bombarded sacked city would look and I do not wish to see it again, unless it would be right to sack Washington, that sink of iniquity, after bombarding it with all 'old Abe's' horrid crew in it." In the meantime "we must nobly endure and suffer, for the boon we seek is a priceless one, but O how much it costs."[196] Fredericksburg had become a ghost city, its citizens refugees, its buildings blasted. The town's treatment at the hands of the occupying Yankees confirmed the Confederates' perception of their enemies as marauding vandals.

The people of Staunton and Augusta recognized that Fredericksburg's fate could have been their own. They gave Stonewall Jackson the credit for saving them during the Valley Campaign. A group of leading citizens, including Alexander H. H. Stuart, sent Jackson a beautiful horse and equipment to show their gratitude. "The people of Augusta are deeply sensible of the important services which you have rendered," their resolution announced, "in protecting their homesteads from desolation, and themselves and their families from insult and oppression." They prayed that General Jackson "may pass safely through the perils of the great contest for liberty and independence in which we are now engaged, and be speedily restored to the enjoyments of peaceful life."[197]

Though the town had been spared devastation, the costs of the war appeared all too obvious in Staunton. The hospital and burying grounds would never let citizens forget the dying that went on throughout the winter even while the guns remained silent. Joseph and Virginia Waddell took a walk one Sunday afternoon and, passing by a military cemetery, were appalled "to see the rows of graves recently dug, waiting with gaping mouths for still living victims who are to fill them," Waddell recorded in his diary that evening. "The sight brought before us visibly the sufferings of the soldiers dying in military hospitals, far from home and kindred and all the horrors of a time of war."[198]

Death soon came home to the Waddells. Joseph received a dispatch about his seventeen-year-old nephew Addison Waddell Stuart, "stating that Addy was dead, that his remains would be brought to Staunton, and requesting me to meet Sister in Lynchburg on Friday. I felt that I had received a staggering blow, and oh! the overwhelming sympathy for his heart-broken mother—he her only son.—And such a son!—So obedient, affectionate, sympathizing—so upright, truthful and brave." As Addy had moved with his unit from Kentucky to Petersburg, Virginia, "from every point he wrote to his mother, cheering her up, and assuring her that he would be happy if he only knew she was not in trouble about him." But Addy caught pneumonia along the way and died in less than twenty-four hours.[199]

The only consolation was the most important consolation of all: "Long ago, he came forward, of his own accord; and made a profession of religion," Joseph gratefully observed. Addy had written the words that mothers across the nation longed for: " 'I go cheerfully, trusting in God.' " Addy was a popular boy among his comrades as well as a model son. "But he is gone from us—God has ordered it so, and oh let us bow to His will. His stricken mother broke forth into praise when she received the dispatch this morning, stating that in his last moments his mind was unclouded and hopeful."

The next day Joseph helped his sister bury her only son. "Just as the light of day was departing, we laid Addy Stuart's remains in the grave, by the side of his sister, little Cornie, who two years ago died in the triumphs of faith." Addy's mother heard of her son's last words, spoken to a friend who accompanied the body home. " 'It will kill Ma,' he said, 'but tell her that I trust in God, and am willing and not afraid to die.' "

Religion flourished in this second winter of the war. People looked for signs, translating their history into biblical terms. A long article in the Staunton newspaper, through elaborate exegesis, proved to its author's satisfaction that the rise and fall of the North had been prefigured in the Bible and that Abraham Lincoln was the Antichrist, preparing for the End of Time.[200] Jed Hotchkiss too thought the North was violating God's will. "His wide designs are frustrated by man's evil machinations that destroy the peace of families, states and empires." Southerners such as Hotchkiss saw Northerners as invaders, the instigators of the war who awaited God's judgment. "O may the happy days come when the Prince of Peace, the Son of Righteousness shall make his advent again to the world, proclaiming the coming of the days when war shall be no more and every man may sit under his own vine and fig tree with *none* to *molest* or make him afraid."[201]

Stonewall Jackson set a high religious standard for the men who served under him. He "devoutly prayed for all classes orders & conditions of the Confederate States," Hotchkiss told Sara, "for success to our arms at all times, for confusion & defeat to our enemies." Even the apparently bloodthirsty Jackson could raise himself above prayers for vengeance and ask God to help their enemies, "blessing to them in all right & proper things, especially that they might have the blessings of peace." Jackson "very earnestly prayed that this 'unnatural war' might speedily be brought to a close." General Lee too spoke easily and frequently of God in the Confederate encampment. At prayer meetings and church services Lee reminded the soldiers straining to hear him that "no portion of our people have greater cause to be thankful to Almighty God than yourselves. He has preserved your lives amid countless dangers; He has been with you in all your trials; He has given you fortitude under hardships, and courage in the shock of battle; He has cheered you by the example and by the deeds of your martyred comrades; he has enobled you to defend your country successfully; against the assaults of a powerful oppressor." With such leaders, Hotchkiss thought, the advantages of the North seemed to matter little: "Numbers, equipments, treasure—all disappear as did the fretwork of this morning's frost before the glorious sunshine that now gladdens the earth." The young father asked his family's help in invoking divine favor. "Pray for our country's cause, my wife & children, pray for the ceasing of these evil days & for the coming of those of peace."[202]

The South took heart because the triumph at Fredericksburg had shaken the confidence of the North. Hotchkiss had been "along the river yesterday & spoke to the enemy's pickets." He read the *New York Herald* from January 22 and believed that " the peace party is gaining ground rapidly and if the 300000 nine months men whose time expires in about 90 days, shall go home then, as they say they will, I should not be surprised if an armed armistice took place and there were no more fighting but a year of diplomacy." As it was, "one of the enemy's pickets yesterday proposed to ours to throw the arms into the river and all go home." The idea sounded good to Hotchkiss.[203]

The Confederates could see the Union army moving about on the other side of the Rappahannock, marching fruitlessly in the relentless and bottomless mud. Southerners worried less that the Federals would launch a counterattack at Fredericksburg than that the panicked Northerners would instigate race war as their only hope of salvaging a semblance of victory. What else could the Emancipation Proclamation be, they asked, since it would not actually free any slaves in areas controlled by the Union army? Abraham Lincoln, "feeling that he cannot cope with the Southern Army in fair battle," charged the *Staunton Spectator*, "seeks to excite servile insurrection and deluge Southern soil in blood."[204]

White Southerners considered the Emancipation Proclamation a cynical political maneuver. "The first of Jan has come & gone, & Lincoln's proclamation has brought no desolation," Nancy Emerson sarcastically noted in her diary. "What awful disappointment will be experienced by our friends the abolitionists." The Massachusetts-born Emerson could barely contain her disgust with the North. "This whole agitation about slavery which has prevailed at the South these years, is the most monstrous humbug ever got up since the flood." In fact, she declared, "I am if possible a thousand times better satisfied of the propriety of slavery than I was before the war." Emerson thought Yankee words against slavery were blasphemous, an attempt "to be wise above what is written." She believed "that the infatuation which has precipitated the North into this war, is a judgment from God upon them for their deep declension from him manifested among other ways by their fanaticism and every other ism." Emerson had to admit that "this whirlwind" of war "has spent much of its force upon *us* thus far, but if this is the end of the matter, I have miscalculated this eclipse altogether. Both nations may have to make a long sojurn in the wilderness before they reach the land of Canaan."[205]

Confederates reassured themselves that the desperate Northern strategy would have no effect. "Lincoln's Proclamation, liberating the slaves, which was recently approved, creates no sensation," Joseph Waddell wrote. "He chooses to consider all Southern territory in possession of his armies as 'loyal,' and proclaims freedom to the negroes only in the regions where he has no control!"[206] Soldiers in the field also shrugged. "Lincoln's Proclamation, proclaiming freedom to the slaves, excites no attention, hardly affords a subject for conversation in the army," Hotchkiss noted in his diary.[207]

Slave prices offered a more concrete index of Southern confidence. "We feel curious to know what the deluded people of the North think of the present unprecedented high prices of slaves in the South," asked a paper in Augusta. "Just at the very time when Lincoln declares that they are to be emancipated, they command higher prices than ever before. Could anything demonstrate more satisfactorily the futility of his infamous proclamation?" To prove its point, the *Spectator* listed recent prices, showing that even "defective" slaves and children were selling at high rates, sometimes at twice the prewar rate—albeit in Confederate currency. "The people of the South never felt that the institution of slavery was ever safer than at the present time," the paper bragged.[208]

Slave hiring too flourished in the midst of war, with high demand and high prices. "The town was full of negroes to-day; as usual on New Year," Waddell noted on January 1. "A negro woman hired at auction for $140!" The bidding was driven up by the competition of the Confederate government, which levied a call for slaves to work in the defense of the capital. "Aunt Sally's Tom goes to Richmond with other hands to work on the fortifications," he observed. "They leave on Saturday night—about 250 from this county. The hands were drafted like soldiers, and are to be employed for sixty days."[209] The Confederacy, already mobilizing virtually every able-bodied white man for military duty, would be in trouble without the enslaved workers. The slaves were happy in Richmond, officials reported. "Let the owners of slaves know that they are all well, near Drewry's Bluff. In fine spirits and cheering for Jeff Davis and the Southern Confederacy," a telegraphic message told Augusta owners. As with soldiers in the field, of course, even happy slaves could use some support from home. "Their rations are short—new corn meal sifted and bacon. Owners should join and send enough for one ration a day to the respective overseers."[210]

The enslaved people could have no better friends than white Southerners, these Confederates told themselves. "The Southern people *build* churches for the colored population, and the Yankees *destroy* them," argued an Augusta paper in a report of Northern soldiers dismantling a black church for firewood. "The Yankees pretend to be their friends, whilst they are really the only enemies they have."[211] Hotchkiss noted the sadness a fellow officer felt upon the death of one of his slaves. "Dr.

McGuire buried his servant today and he is very sad, mourns for him as a brother."[212]

Hotchkiss, like many Confederate officers, relied on slaves in camp; he also secured another slave to send back home to his wife. "I have got William hired, expect him here now every day, got him very low—and in the Spring I will hire Allen out to some farmer & send William to you and he can make garden & do anything you want done." William's arrival improved Hotchkiss's quality of life, for the hired slave "washed me some flannels and made them soft white and nice and he looks after everything finely." Soon the engineer depended on William for care of the horses crucial to his work. "I am sorry I cannot let William stay up for some time," Hotchkiss wrote home, "but we have 4 horses and no one but him to see to them if we should move, as Boswell has not yet found a servant, so I can only let William stay long enough to get my trunk home & the box back." The enslaved man even became a carrier of sentiment between husband and wife. William returned from a trip back to the farm in Augusta with the things he carried "all safe, everything right & nothing broken." The hired slave, Jed proudly told Sara, "had faithfully attended to every errand I sent by him—he gives glowing accounts of the beauty of your yard, the condition of your wood pile and the air of 'Comfort' that pervades all things 'at home' & almost made me homesick with the recital."[213]

While they reassured themselves about the loyalty of their slaves, white Southerners thought they saw a loss of will and fragmentation in the North. "Volunteering in the North is now dead, and the Western States will not submit to another draft," asserted the *Spectator*. The critics of the Lincoln administration were gaining strength across the North as people "are beginning to appreciate the fact that the South cannot be conquered, and that the continuance of the war will only have the effect of destroying all hope of liberty at the North."[214] The South seized on dissent and anxiety in the North as evidence of an impending crisis above the Mason-Dixon Line. Southern people loved to read warnings from leading Northerners to other Northerners, telling them that "we have more danger to-day from conspiracies against the Union in the Free States than in the Slave; I think the danger is greater from these than from those."[215]

Joseph Waddell could afford to be more honest with himself in the quietness of his diary. "Much talk for several days past about the supposed opposition to Lincolnism and the war, in the North and West." It was true that "there is a growing discontent in those regions; but a victory or two, especially the capture of Vicksburg by the Yankees, would bring the whole '*nation*' together again."[216] During these weeks Union General Ulysses S. Grant worked relentlessly to seize Vicksburg, the last Confederate holdout on the Mississippi River. Everyone in the North and South waited for word on whether Grant's frantic efforts to dig canals and launch a siege would succeed before the blazing and deadly Mississippi summer began.

To the Confederate soldiers in the freezing fields of Virginia in January and February, the collapse of Yankeedom and the end of the war could not come soon enough. "We had a great variety on the table for our christmas dinner," Tom Smiley of the 5th Virginia wrote sarcastically to his young sister back in Augusta. "The breakfast consisted of beef steak and bread, diner was bread and Roast Beef, and supper out of what was left at breakfast."[217] Things only got worse over the rest of January and February, as General Lee worried about how he would feed his army. As it was, soldiers received only eighteen ounces of flour and four ounces of bacon each day. Their horses suffered greatly. The Confederacy had food ready to ship from farther south but could not get it to their men in Virginia because of inept administration.

Soldiers dreamed of substitutes to take their place on the hard ground. Adam W. Kersh wrote his brother to complain that "Harris had gone to Richmond to try for a substitute for me and that he had been bothered very much this trip on account of us being he had sold out before he got to us." With the draft in place and competition stiff, Kersh expected to pay " two thousand dollars for a substitute as I dont think that I could get one for less now."[218] The standards for acceptable substitutes had risen. Kersh's captain said "that I might have bring five or six before one would please him." Faced with such odds, Kersh decided to give up the idea of hiring someone to serve in his place. He kicked himself for not having acted sooner.[219]

Hundreds of men, after making similar calculations, deserted. More than two hundred—a fifth of the entire regiment—had fled the 5th Virginia in 1862. A hundred had deserted from the 52d. Colonel Michael G. Harman published a plea in the newspapers of the Valley requesting any "information in regard to any of the members of my Regiment who are at home without leave, as every man is needed now and should be at his post."[220]

Desertion from the Confederate army reached its peak in 1862. Some deserted while fighting in West Virginia or Maryland; others in Augusta itself. Some later appeared fighting for other Confederate units while others went over to the Union army; some left hospitals never to return. James Riddel, Jr., of Mount Solon was shot in August for attempting desertion near the Rapidan River. The *Spectator* filled a long column with a humiliating list of names of Augusta men who had deserted from the 5th or the 52d Virginia.[221] The names of 10 officers followed those of 154 enlisted men. The Confederacy promised a twenty-dollar bounty for each man returned.

While most men who deserted did not advertise their intentions beforehand, Joseph Wilson admitted to a friend that "I have got enough of the foot Cavalry I don't think it would be just to tell you how I do like it & therefore I will put it off & say nothing about it but I Think I will play quits with Old Jeff."[222] Wilson had grown disgusted with the conditions he faced. He sent his friend a sarcastic advertisement that he wanted to "have published in Spectator if you please & charge me with the bill": Wanted: "Five Hundred (500) hound puppies in the 14th Reg VaCal for the purpose of devouring the Rotten Beef rancid to the men as rations."[223]

Despite such disgust, many soldiers did not consider merely leaving camp to be desertion. During the winter months the prospect of fighting was slim, conditions in camp were miserable, and families relatively close by. Men who could not win furloughs decided to leave for quick visits back home to see the children, check on the farm, and lie in warm beds with their wives. Their fellow soldiers were often tolerant of such unauthorized leaves and looked out for their compatriots. "I wish you would tell Sam Thomas if he does not hurry down here that he will be published as a deserter tell him he has been absent long enough," Thomas Garber wrote his sister in Augusta as the spring arrived.[224]

Officers could not afford to be so lenient with deserters. In early 1863 Generals Jackson and Lee clamped down as they waited along the Rappahannock. The Confederates relied on many different kinds of punishment. One man of the 52d "received 39 lashes and then sent to richmond to do hard labor for 12 months with ball and chain fastened to his foot and all of his wages and 39 more when he is released," Jesse Rolston wrote his wife, Mary. "I say that is hard," but he had "went home three times" and "in times of a fight would run off til it was over." Other men "has to ware a flower barrel for ten days one hour each day and from 2 to 6 months pay deducted." Rolston would not pass easy judgment on either the soldiers or their officers. "I think that is hard on some of them and some deserves it."[225]

Officers had to take an analytical view of desertion. "Yesterday a deserter was shot in the Brigade encamped quite near to us—he wept bitterly, wishing to see his family," Jed Hotchkiss sadly reported to Sara. "He fell dead, pierced by five balls—poor fellow—it seems hard, but in no other way can the discipline of the army be maintained." People back home had to be careful what they wrote to the men in camp. "One fellow was shot who had been contented in the army until his wife wrote to him with constant complaints until the poor fellow could stand it no longer and as he could get no furlough he deserted & went home, was caught and suffered the penalty of death." Not all deserters were shot; Hotchkiss had seen "some whipped, some drummed out of camp and then put to labor with a ball and chain, some branded on the backsides with the letters D. or C. for desertion or cowardice &c &c."[226]

As the spring thaw began, all the soldiers realized that fighting must come soon. "I don't think well stay heare many more days until we move," Jesse Rolston told Mary in early April. Rumor had it that "we are to go out back in the mountains west of Stanton but I don't know whare we will go for they take us whare they please." The Yankees who talked with the Rebels along the river told their foes that "they don't want to fite if they can help. they say there is a great many of them will go home the first of May or rebell against oald Abe. if they do that the war cant last much longer."[227]

Waddell thought it unlikely that the war would end soon. "Lincoln has full control of the men and money of the United States—he is absolute dictator—Unless there should be popular rebellions he may carry on the war indefinitely." Even more dangerous was news that "the Yankees are mustering *negro regiments* at various places."[228]

7

WHILE ITS ARMY waited for the spring battles to begin, the North debated the role of black people in the conflict. Banker William Heyser glumly began his diary for 1863 on a sober note: "This day Lincoln issued his Emancipation Proclamation. I think it will do more harm than good. Little can be done with it, but to make more enemies."[229] The *Valley Spirit* remained true to its principles as it kept up its assaults on black character and, like Democratic papers across the North, denounced President Lincoln's Emancipation Proclamation as "unwise, ill-timed, outside of the Constitution and full of mischief." The proclamation would do no good but only "unite and exasperate the whites of the South in their resistance to the National Government, and to make the war still more prolonged, bloody and bitter."[230]

Frustratingly for Franklin Democrats, Thaddeus Stevens, a mine and foundry owner in the county as well as a leading radical Republican in the U.S. Congress, led the fight for the recruitment of black men in the Union army. He aggressively pushed a bill providing for 150,000 black soldiers. "Yes, there is a God," he thundered to his many critics, "an avenging God, who is now punishing the sins of this nation for the wicked wrongs which for centuries we have inflicted upon a blameless race and which many of you wish to make perpetual."[231] Stevens demanded that the Union enlist, train, and arm former slaves and Northern free blacks to turn against the secessionists and slaveholders of the South.

Democrats, predictably, would have none of it. They saw the initiative to arm black men as a sign of white men's failure. "Unsuccessful in saving the Constitution and hope of liberty on this Continent," one Democratic congressman protested, Republicans would admit "that the negro was now our only hope of salvation." Another Democrat warned that "prejudice cannot be eradicated," that white men would not alongside black, that the creation of black soldiers would only bring disaster to the Union.[232]

The Republicans had perverted the Union cause, the Democrats charged. "Had the war been prosecuted with the one undivided object of restoring the Union and maintaining the Constitution, we might today have been able at least to see 'the beginning of the end,' " the *Valley Spirit* complained. Instead Union armies failed in Fredericksburg and slogged pathetically and pointlessly through mud. A " 'Union with slaveholders' had become so unrighteous a thing in the eyes of the radicals" that Congress "rushed madly on from one wild, impracticable, revolutionary scheme to another, without regard to constitutional obligations or natural, inevitable consequences."[233] The talk of arming black men threatened to bring radicalism to its logical conclusion: race war, insurrection, unending struggle between North and South.

Radical Republicans dismissed such warnings as so much political nonsense. They looked on the Emancipation Proclamation and the arming of black troops as harbingers of victory. A white soldier from Franklin, William Barnitz, wrote a series of lengthy and effusive letters for newspapers back home from his camp on the North Carolina coast, where he had witnessed the effects of emancipation firsthand. Things had been discouraging in the North, he admitted, because Democrats had tried to "deceive the masses and array them against the Government, spreading discontent and sowing disaffection broadcast." But now, with more aggressive words and acts coming from Washington, the Union army "increased, inspirited, jubilant will march on from victory to victory, crush the last stronghold of rebellion and show to the world that a republic has with in itself a self-sustaining power."[234]

Barnitz had seen with his own eyes the longing for black freedom. "There are about 8,000 contrabands here, working on the railroad, cutting wood, and raising a regiment of volunteers." Nothing offered more inspiration than the eagerness of the black children to learn in the schools opened by Northern philanthropists. "The avidity and ease with which they study and learn, is truly surprising," Barnitz told readers back in Franklin, "how their eyes glitter with every new discovery, with what satisfaction they enter the school room, how attentive, as if they feared something beautiful would escape their notice; it humbles one to see the efforts these youth put forth to attain knowledge, and it is a grand omen for the amelioration of the race."[235]

Black soldiers, former slaves, displayed heartening talents. They were "attentive, active, quick to learn, ambitious, and, above all, courageous." Barnitz guaranteed that "when put in the field, they will surprise even the cowardly copperheads, whose superiors they are, in everything constituting manliness, worthiness and honor!" Unlike the croakers back home, who saw the black soldiers as evidence of Union weakness, the transformed slaves in fact stood for strength. "The rebellion will be crushed in six months, and these unchained people, fierce under the stings of recent goads, will dash down before the nabobs, who have kept them in eternal bondage, ignorance and degradation, for their own gratification." Barnitz could hardly wait for the punishment of the slaveholders, who, "like satan, dissatisfied with prosperity, with a government the most benignant ever known, with civil immunities and privileges, unknown to other nations, and with an enslaved race to produce the necessaries of life," in their arrogance attempted "at one fell blow to dash down their government." In its place they elevated the so-called Confederacy "with nigger heads and hearts for foundation, pillar, and dome."[236]

In other letters Barnitz attacked Northern Democrats as vociferously as public print would allow. "*How are you, Copperheads*? I really *do* hope that *these few lines* may find you in the highly gratifying condition of a Jackass turned out to die." Just as he had seen with his own eyes the possibilities of black freedom, so had Barnitz seen who the Democrats really were: "the lowest, meanest, dirtiest, draggle tailed, whisky drinking, card-playing, horse-racing, hell-defying" people in the North.[237]

No letter could have infuriated the Democrats any more. Although Barnitz had been born in Texas, he had settled in Waynesboro in southern Franklin County, a confidant told the *Valley Spirit*. There he "soon became known as a blatant and slanderous abolitionist, and wrote dirty, contemptible articles" in a little local paper, "assailing and villifying many of the oldest and most highly respected inhabitants of that vicinity." Moreover, despite his claims of bravery, the Democrats pointed out, Barnitz "was the very first in the town to 'skedaddle' when the rebels entered Maryland, and the very last to come back, after the enemy had been driven back into Virginia" the preceding year. Despite his claims of patriotism, Barnitz "could never be induced to enlist in defence of his country, and would not now be in the army had he not been drafted and found himself unable to procure a substitute."[238]

Once he was in the army, Barnitz's Republican political connections had allowed him to rise to the rank of captain, but he remained a pathetic soldier nevertheless. Crossing a river in a recent skirmish, the informer to the *Valley Spirit* serving with Barnitz gleefully reported, with "no enemy in sight, the Captain suddenly became inspired with ecstatic valor, and, brandishing his bloodless sword in the air, wanted immediately to cut several hundred rebel throats in cold blood." Barnitz's sword flew out of his hand while he waved it "and sunk into the river, amidst the jeers and the hootings of all who saw the knight's mishap. 'And, there,' says our informant, 'it is yet, and it is a matter of very little importance whether he ever gets it or not; for he would be the last man to use it, even if he does get into a pinch, which, in my opinion, he will take very good care not to.' So much for William Tell Barnitz." With all his blustering about hanging Copperheads, the Democrats warned, "we suggest to the Captain to modify his views before he returns to Franklin county, or during one of his valiant sallies, he may find a considerable quantity of copperhead boot-leather inserted somewheres about the lower end of his spinal column." Whether or not the story of Barnitz's military ineptitude was true did not matter to the Democrats, of course.[239]

To judge from the election returns of spring 1863, most Franklin whites agreed with the *Valley Spirit* on the issues of the war and black freedom. "In the face of the bitterest denunciation and most unscrupulous misrepresentation, the Democracy, with scarcely an effort, have carried nearly every district in the county, and in those they have not carried, have reduced the Republican majorities to a merely nominal figure," the *Valley Spirit* crowed in an article titled "The 'Copperheads' Victorious!" Although the elections were for relatively minor offices, they reflected the ongoing national struggle, in which the Democrats steadily gained power in early 1863. "This seals the fate of Abolitionism in our midst. Franklin county is now largely Democratic beyond the peradventure of a doubt."[240] A correspondent from Barnitz's town of Waynesboro crystallized matters in the characteristic language of the Democrats: white voters believed that "the white man is better than a nigger, and that if Father Abraham, under the pretext of prosecuting the war for the restoration of the Union, is willing to sacrifice the lives of white men to liberate slaves, he would as well not look to Washington Township to furnish him soldiers."[241]

Down in the battlefields of Virginia, meantime, the Union army grew stronger and prepared for the final battles. "The boys live well now; having plenty of bread, coffee, tea, sugar, onions, potatoes, beans, rice, &c. Fresh beef is issued four times a week," a cheerful soldier reported to the local paper in late March. "The excellence of the Commissariat has done much to establish General Hooker in the confidence and esteem of his army. They feel that he cares for them and is doing all he can to promote their comfort."[242] The fighting men of Franklin would be ready.

The situation of the South, by contrast, could not be more heartening for the Union, according to the Northern press at least. The Confederacy, everyone knew, confronted the spring with "a bankrupt treasury, with a starving population, with scarcely any means of rapid transportation, and with no hope left of foreign armed intervention." It could "not withstand a defeat." The Union strategy of pushing on the South everywhere at once was finally paying off. "At last they are beginning to feel the coils of the anaconda tighten around them," even the Democrats could see. "In the Gulf, at Charleston, at Savannah, in North Carolina along the Blackwater, the Rappahannock and the Shenandoah, at Vicksburg, Port Hudson, and Murfreesboro, and along the line in Kentucky, our forces are prepared for a general advance. Soon we will 'hear the thunder all around the sky.' "[243]

Should the Lincoln administration fail to crush the rebellion with all these advantages, "the Democratic party will, when it gets hold of the reins of Government, use all power, and all the statesmanship it can muster to its aid, to restore the Constitution in its ancient spirit and vigor." Many white Northern men simply would not sustain the Republicans much longer in the face of inactive or ineffectual armies combined with Republicans' growing demands for emancipation and black recruitment. Given another loss or two, the Democrats would seize power and then "reunite our shattered and bleeding Union, as it was before the reckless fanaticism and uncompromising, revengeful spirit of the present day severed the holy bonds which bound us in one brotherhood." The crusade against slavery would come to an end.[244]

Even as white men fought with one another in Franklin and other counties in the North, black men were joining the Union army. African Americans had rushed to enlist from the outset of the war but had been turned away until the summer of 1862, when they joined in Union-occupied Louisiana, Kansas, and South Carolina. While Congress debated the recruitment of black troops in early 1863, Massachusetts acted on its own, receiving authorization from its governor to create black regiments officered by white abolitionists.

The 54th Regiment of Massachusetts Volunteer Infantry formed in Boston. At its head stood Robert Gould Shaw, young son of a leading antislavery family in Boston and a veteran of another Massachusetts unit. Leaders of the abolitionist movement, black and white, raised more than a hundred thousand dollars and began a vigorous recruitment campaign across the North from Massachusetts to Ohio. Everyone involved was determined to show that African American men were eager to fight for Union and abolition, eager to put their lives on the line against a foe that decreed that any black man captured fighting against the South would be hanged for instigating insurrection. "The paper proclamation must now be made iron, lead, and fire," Frederick Douglass declared.[245]

In March, Franklin's Democratic paper noted with relief that "in this neighborhood, there has, so far been no effort to procure negro recruits, that we have heard of, and it is currently said that such an effort, if made, will be useless. They will have to be drafted, if obtained at all." White men in Franklin County and throughout Pennsylvania were already being drafted to fill the state and local quotas. Certainly black men would not be braver.[246] Only a week later the *Valley Spirit* reported that "a negro recruiting officer visited this place last week and of course was quite a 'lion' among the 'free Americans of African descent;' but, as far as we know, he did not obtain a single recruit." Rather than join in the fight, the paper said, "it is rumored that one of the 'sable brethren' retorted to the urgent appeals of the recruiting officer in favor of his cause: 'Nigger has nuffin to do with dis war. Two dogs fight over a bone—did you ever see de bone fight?' "[247]

The newspaper could not have been more wrong. Only four weeks later, in late April, it ruefully noted that "some forty or fifty black recruits for the Massachusetts Regiments, left this [community] for Boston, on Monday morning last." The paper, clearly surprised, blustered that "we are only too glad to get rid of these worthless negroes." Always eager to find something wrong with anything black people did, the editors whined that "we scarcely like the idea of their being credited to Massachusetts, and thus filling up her quota under the last draft, while Pennsylvania was compelled to fill her quota, under that same draft, with free white male citizens."[248]

The black men of Franklin would not wait for Pennsylvania. They seized the first opportunity they found to join the fight. Apparently a recruiter from the 54th Massachusetts, perhaps based in Harrisburg or Philadelphia, decided that Franklin County offered a promising field in which to recruit free black men. The details of his decision have been lost. Maybe the large percentage of African Americans in southern Pennsylvania attracted his attention; or allies on the Underground Railroad passed on word of the active community there; or leading black abolitionist Martin Delany, a former Franklin resident, led the campaign; or Frederick Douglass recalled his visit there three years earlier, when black men had helped John Brown. In any case, forty-five men living in Franklin County enlisted in the 54th, and another thirteen signed up in the 55th, the regiment formed by the overflow from the first regiment. Eleven men born in Franklin County whose residence was listed elsewhere also enlisted with the 54th. These numbers made Franklin County perhaps the greatest contributor to these early African American regiments, on a per capita basis, of any place in the United States. Overall, Pennsylvania produced more black soldiers than any other Northern state, including Massachusetts.[249]

Ten of Franklin's recruits came from Chambersburg, and ten came from Mercersburg, the small community in southern Franklin where a large portion of the free black population lived. The Burgess family contributed two brothers and a cousin, the Christy family four brothers, the Demus family three, the Krunkleton family four, the Rideout family two, and the Watson family two. Almost all these men were young, between eighteen and twenty-five. They owned almost nothing, and they worked as laborers and farmers, by and large, though Joseph Burgess was a teacher, Thomas Burgess a carpenter, and Joseph Christy a woodcutter. George Orford worked as an engineer, Jacob Watson as a butcher, and Hezekiah Watson and Thomas Cuff as quarrymen.[250]

About a third of Franklin's black recruits signed up on the same day, April 22, 1863, almost exactly two years after Fort Sumter. The recruiting officers offered each a fifty-dollar bounty, thirteen dollars a month in pay (the same as white soldiers received), and eight dollars a month for the family left behind. Others joined throughout May as the 54th gathered in Massachusetts, about a hundred men a week arriving at the gray and muddy camp outside Boston. After an especially rigorous physical examination to choose the most fit, the new recruits were immediately put to drill and training. Supporters saw to it that all equipment and food were first-rate. Visitors, male and female, came to view the novel sight of black soldiers drilling. Among the visitors were William Lloyd Garrison and Frederick Douglass, whose son joined as sergeant major.

From Mercersburg the four Christy brothers—Samuel, William, Joseph, and Jacob—joined up with David Demus. The young Christy men lived with their father, Jacob, a widower of fifty-four who owned a small farm worth two hundred dollars, and their sister, Mary Jane, a twenty-year-old domestic worker. Demus had grown up a quarter of a mile from the Christys and married Mary Jane Christy in 1860. All the men, in their early twenties, worked as laborers and held no property. The census taker categorized the Christys as black and Demus as mulatto. All of them had learned the basics of writing and sent letters back to Mary Jane about their experiences as they headed to Boston for training.

Jacob wrote first: "i take my pen in hand to inform to you that I am well and all the rest of them are well we are very well pleas with soildieren." He knew "we wont have it so easy when we leave Boston we spect to leave about the first of June and it may be sooner for what we know for the rigiment is nearly fill out." The Christys arrived first, but soon David Demus and his brother George appeared and "we was all very glad to see them boys coming." David sent word back to Mary Jane that "we didant no when we would get any money but i dont think it will be very long." The young husband was eager to send his wife money from his first pay draw.[251]

The training was hard, and punishment came quickly. "Two of the boys was made go and get there knacksack and they had to wear them to punish them for looking aroung wile thay was in ranks when we are in ranks we are not aloud to look around or spite or to raise our hand." The discipline was worth it, though, for "we also gut our arms this day they are springfield rifles wich we have they are aloud to kill a great disants." The Pennsylvania men "dont like the climent atoll for it is very cold out here now we heft to wear our over coats all day it that cold." They knew that when they finished their training and "we go down south it will be worm enough and wormer then we wish."[252]

David Demus shared some of the same opinions of Boston in early May—"it is very cold here it snow and rain on the day that we lander"—but proclaimed himself "very well satify" and "very well pleas." He was glad to see that "we got in the nix Camp that sam and them other boys is in that left mercersburg." Like all soldiers, Demus longed for letters from home; he asked Mary Jane to "rite as soon as you can and let me no how mother is and all the rest of the friends."[253] Samuel wrote his sister the next day to let her know that "we expect to move soon to north carlina" because "the rigment ar ful now and we gut ar unform and arms." He planned to send a likeness "as soon as i can git it taken" and asked Mary Jane to "tel father that i will send sum monney home to pay Clark for my boots as soon as we git ar buntey that will be soon."[254]

At the end of May the troops gathered to hear the governor of Massachusetts address them in inspiring terms and then to march before cheering crowds through Boston. They boarded steamships to head for the Sea Islands off the coasts of Georgia and the Carolinas. Whites had abandoned the islands, among the wealthiest plantation areas of the South. "We was on the sea seven days befor we gut to Camp," Samuel Christy wrote home, "and after we weas thear one day we went out to put up ar tents." After filling their canteens and loading their haversacks, "we was March to the river and gut on the ship and went a but fifteen mils thear was thee guns bots with went be for us and at last we Came to a little town."[255]

The little town was Darien, Georgia, up the river from the coast. The 54th walked into the wealthy and nearly deserted town of about one hundred houses. At their officers' orders, they stripped it bare. The men

African American soldiers prepare to fight

got out "of the ship and went in to it and took every thing that was good," Samuel told Mary Jane. "We gut sum sheep and sum cattl and hogs and chickens and meny others things."[256] David Demus calculated that the "the hole amont Was a boat a milion of dollars."[257] Officers' tents were soon equipped with rich furniture, carpets, and mirrors.

After taking what they wanted, Samuel noted matter-of-factly, the soldiers "set the town on fier and burnt it down." A white officer, James Montgomery, told Colonel Robert Shaw, "with a sweet smile," that he wanted to destroy Darien because "Southerners must be made to feel that this was a real war." The white South was "to be swept away by the hand of God like the Jews of old." Montgomery had been an associate of John Brown's in Kansas and shared Brown's belief in vengeance. He argued that the Confederacy did not recognize the legitimacy of the black troops, and so "we are outlawed, and therefore not bound by the rules of regular warfare." Montgomery lit the blaze in Darien himself. Driven by the wind, it soon destroyed everything but a church, a few houses, and a lumberworks owned by a Northerner.[258]

Shaw admitted in a letter home that "in theory it may seem all right to some; but when it comes to being made the instrument of the Lord's vengeance, I myself don't like it." He protested the burning to his superiors, fearing that it would reflect badly on the black soldiers under his command. He had no doubts about burning a town occupied by Rebels, but the "wanton destruction" of Darien seemed "dirty business." As the weeks passed, however, he came to admire Montgomery and adopt some of his ideas about conducting war.[259]

The men of the 54th retired to camps on St. Simon's and St. Helena near Hilton Head. The camps were pleasant, cooled by the breezes off the Atlantic. The black soldiers continued to train and drill, awaiting orders for further movements. In the meantime, orders from Washington cut their pay from thirteen dollars a month to ten dollars, below that of white soldiers in the Union army. They heard rumors that their rifles would be taken away and replaced with pikes. The political pressure against the black soldiers remained strong in the North. Many whites doubted black men would fight when faced with enemy resistance.

Slaves across the South seized their freedom while the Christy brothers and the Demus brothers prepared to fight for the 54th Massachusetts. By the middle of 1863 slavery had been undermined by the United States army in places throughout the Confederacy. Enslaved people in eastern Virginia, where North American slavery had first taken root two hundred years before, were among the first to use the presence of Union troops to flee bondage. Enslaved people near Washington, where the slave trade had long scandalized visitors to the nation, were freed with the support of the federal governement. Enslaved people in northern Virginia, where armies and battles dislocated the entire society, fled to safety and security. Slavery further south in the Shenandoah Valley had yet to be dislodged, but everyone knew the arrival of the Union army would quickly change that.

Meanwhile, slavery had been dealt hard blows in Kentucky and Tennessee, occupied for over a year now by the United States forces. Slavery had dissolved along the Mississippi River between Memphis and New Orleans, where many slaveholders had fled and were replaced by Northern soldiers and civilians. The same thing happened in the Sea Islands of South Carolina and Georgia, where male and female reformers from the North came to create a showcase for free labor and free minds. All of these places had been strongholds of plantation slavery, with large black populations and rich lands. And in all of these places African American men enlisted in the army and navy of the United States by the tens of thousands.

Yet slavery remained a crucial weapon of the Confederacy. The institution had not been touched throughout most of South Carolina, Georgia, Alabama, and Mississippi by the middle of 1863. Across the vast black belt, the richest land with the richest plantations, slaves produced the supplies that sustained the Confederate forces. The labor of enslaved people allowed the South to put a remarkably high proportion of its white men into uniform and into battle. Despite all the damage that had been done to slavery in the first two years of war, its importance to the Confederacy not only remained undiminished but actually grew as white Southerners saw their men killed, maimed, and lost in the battlefields of the border.

Slavery's meaning in the North changed as well. On one hand, as Union soldiers fought to destroy an enemy which drew its power from slavery they grew to hate slavery itself. Meeting enslaved people turned many soldiers into willing allies of those eager to see slavery destroyed. Republican newspapers finally began to define a consistent abolitionist ideology. The North as a whole was far more willing to bring the end of slavery in 1863 than it had been two years earlier.

On the other hand, many white Northerners would have ended the war in 1863 if they could have brought their sons and husbands home in return. Seeing enslaved people in the South confirmed many white men in their belief that slavery was the best situation for black people. Even in 1863 a considerable number of Republicans would have colonized freed slaves if they could. The white definition of black freedom remained elusive even after two brutal years of war.

WHITE SOUTHERNERS SAW the efforts of radical Republicans to create 150,000 black soldiers as the greatest example of Yankee hypocrisy and desperation. "There is not a man in the South who will not rejoice at this action of the Lincoln Congress," defiantly claimed the *Spectator*. "It furnishes the most conclusive evidence that they have despaired of conquering the South." The irony lay right on the surface: "The negroes will now see that instead of the Yankees fighting for them, as they professed to be, they are about to make the poor negroes fight for the Yankees."[260] Indeed, "the negroes will find that the Yankees, instead of being their friends, as they profess, are their worst enemies. They induce them to leave good homes to go into the army to be slaughtered."[261]

Confederate soldiers would not, could not treat invading black men under the same rules of war accorded white soldiers. "The Yankees know that every negro who is caught with arms in their hands will be hung, and yet they insist on putting them in the service," the *Spectator* warned. "This shows that they care nothing for the life of their deluded victims."[262] The white South took no share of the blame, for "according to the laws of every Southern State, the penalty for inciting insurrection is *death by hanging*." And what did black soldiers signify if not insurrection? The Yankees had "fair notice" of the fate that awaited black soldiers. "If they come upon our soil and are taken, the *officers* know their doom. They will be certainly *hanged*."[263] If they were not hanged, they would be reenslaved. "As soon as they come within reach of the Southern army they will be captured, and be restored to the condition for which Providence designed them."[264] Free black soldiers "shall be sold into perpetual bondage, for the purpose of raising a fund to reimburse citizens of this confederacy who have lost their slave property."[265] The North stood forewarned.

With the prospect of critical battles ahead, Augusta County took stock in the spring of 1863. The Confederacy seemed a miracle; its "stupendous and rapid growth" in "power and influence, is almost beyond conception, and unequalled in the history of nations." All the odds had been stacked against the survival of the new nation. Its enemy had possessed an army, a navy, modern weapons, manufactories, everything necessary to win a war. The South had had only "patriots burning with the wrongs their aggressors had heaped upon them." Two years later "we now behold an army extending from the rolling banks of the Old Potomac, to the sandy shores of the lone star State" and a navy of "bold privateers scouring the ocean in quest of the enemy, pouncing down upon him when he least expects it." The Confederate flag, "once considered by our enemies as the standard of a few insolent and rebellious States, [is] now floating in triumph over a hundred hard fought battles, on land and water." God obviously smiled upon the new nation, so "let then our promising position in the world awaken in us the warmest emotions of gratitude to the Supreme Being."[266]

Grateful though they might be to God, people in Augusta, Virginia, and the Confederacy struggled with problems closer to home. With armies in the field that had to be fed, with inflation consuming the savings of lifetimes, and with planting season upon them, people in the Valley felt victimized. "Her sons were the first to rush to arms, after the secession of Virginia, and the most liberal, in their gratuitous, voluntary and bountiful contributions to the cause of the Confederacy," the *Vindicator* reminded the authorities in Richmond. "The mothers and daughters emulated, proudly emulated, the determination of their husbands and brothers, . . . conjuring them not to return to the comforts of home, until the foot of the invader had been driven from the historic and sacred soil of Virginia." The battles of 1862, which had brought both the Union and Confederates armies through the Valley, had left the region devastated. "From Staunton to Harper's Ferry the hand of desolation and carnage mark every acre of her fertile valleys, fields laid waste, fences burned, dwellings razed to the ground, hearts stricken and universal blight and mildew prevailing."[267]

People would have to take care of themselves. "Whatever may have been indulged in and tolerated in other days, the time has now come, when all must work or starve," a farmer wrote to the *Spectator*. "Some useful employment must be followed by rich and poor alike. Let no food be sold to those who are able bodied and will not work, while any of the industrious and helpless are in want." The citizens of Staunton would have to do their part. "The farmers are in great need of help and the time is growing short for getting out the crops. Send out the idlers and loafers from the towns to the country, to toil with the farmers from day light till dark and help to make bread for all. This will be far better for them, than standing about the streets prating about the high prices of living."[268]

The farmers needed help in part because so many slaves had run away. The newspapers admitted to the erosion of slavery not in their editorial pages but in their classified advertisements, where ample testimony to runaways appeared. In February, eighteen-year-old William Hamilton "ran away (or escaped from the cars at Charlottesville)" from none other than Michael G. Harman, quartermaster general. The runaway was "18 years of age, 5 feet 10 1/4 inches high, has a pleasant face, very square across the shoulders, and not a mark or scar on him. He had an overcoat with a cape, a brown Janes frock Coat, no Vest, dark Janes Pants, and wore an old Fur Cap. He speaks very slowly when spoken to."[269] In later weeks an enslaved man named Nelson escaped in Augusta, as did Ezekiel. Townsfolk should keep an eye out for both these runaways, for "they may perhaps be lurking in the neighborhood of Staunton, as one of them has a wife near town, who is free."[270]

Women escaped too. George Talbot offered the high reward of two thousand dollars for four slaves who had run away, including two attractive young women: "Nancy Ashby, a mulatto girl, fine looking," and "Sarah Gaskins, brown skin, fine looking."[271] Another reward appeared for "Caroline, and her two negro children: Mary Adaline, about 7 years old, Armistead, about 4 years old. Caroline is black, tall and straight, with the thumb off the left hand. They are probably on their way to Winchester."[272] Many of the runaways were thought to be "making their way down the Valley." Down the Valley—toward the North, where they could find the Union army and perhaps freedom.[273]

While their slaves ran away, Augusta farmers found the Confederate government impressing their food and other goods to feed the army, taking what they needed and offering in return whatever the army thought fit. John Baldwin, a longtime political leader of the county, wrote to Secretary of War James A. Seddon, protesting the government policy in which property was taken "against the will of the owners, and at prices fixed without consulting them, and without regard to market rates." Baldwin leveled a long and legalistic attack, but the secretary responded flatly: "The department does not consider it important to enter into a discussion of the legality of impressments, or the doctrine of what is a 'just compensation' under the extraordinary and anomalous conditions that now exist." Legalities did not matter; the army had to be fed, and the food had to come from somewhere.[274] There was no use in complaining. "If the army be not sustained, we all fall back into the power of the Federal enemy," an editorial pointed out, "all our lofty aspirations to national independence sink and vanish forever, and we subside again, whipped rebels, into the hateful old Union." Lest all the grumbling lead people to forget, "it is the Yankee Government, not our own, that is hateful to this people."[275] Sacrifices of corn and horses were nothing compared with the sacrifices of manhood and freedom that would come if the Confederate army could not be fed.

Augusta people could see what resulted when people succumbed to deprivation a hundred miles to the southeast, in Richmond. There a riot, led by desperate women, erupted in early April 1863. Grocery bills had increased by a factor of ten in the Confederate capital since the war began as the army competed with civilians for supplies. The women broke into stores and took all they could, turning to items other than food when that was exhausted. It required Jefferson Davis himself to quell the riot, threatening to fire on the women if they did not disperse. Officials promised to do more to help the poor and ordered the Richmond press to keep the event quiet, but Joseph Waddell immediately heard rumors from people on the railroad "of a fearful bread riot in Richmond—more alarming news than the report of a defeat. The papers are silent on the subject."[276]

By the next week, however, word had spread throughout both the North and the South. The papers made their reports and offered their interpretation. The *Vindicator*, relying on eyewitness accounts of prominent Augusta people in Richmond, viewed the episode with disgust and no sympathy for the rioters. "It was not a food riot as pretended, but simply a villainous, wholesale robbery," the paper argued, echoing the line of the Southern government and press. Not only did some of the rioters own houses and other property, but "the charitable associations had distributed supplies to all the needy who had applied for them, and still had a sufficiency on hand." The rioting women did not go after food, the paper reported, but instead were "trudging along under heavy loads of harness and hardware, books and boots."[277] "It was not a 'bread riot'—it did not proceed from want, but crime," agreed the *Spectator*. It seemed that the riot may even have been a Yankee plot, "with the view of encouraging the North to prosecute the war by making the impression that the South is approaching a starving condition."[278] The eruption of twelve other riots across the South that spring, all of them directed at the exorbitant prices charged by speculators, only confirmed the suspicion that they must have been somehow inspired and coordinated by the enemy.

The Yankees would do anything to win, make up any lie, Southerners told themselves, for the North simply could not lose many more battles. The North was all the more dangerous for being so desperate. "Success, and that speedily, is the agonizing cry of all Abolitiondom," the *Spectator* charged. "Success, or else conscription fails—success, or the financial bubble bursts—success, or the three hundred thousand go home in May—success, or the demoralized ranks will grow skeletons by disease and desertion—success, or no new armies can be levied—success, or the copperheads will strike." The Confederates had even more riding on the coming battles of spring 1863, the paper reminded its readers in Augusta. "Everything we have and are and expect to be is at stake. National independence, personal liberty, property, honor, fame, home, wives, children—all depend on the hazard of this fearful struggle."[279]

Jed Hotchkiss could see the battle building from the headquarters of Stonewall Jackson, eleven miles from Fredericksburg. For more than four months the Confederates and the Yankees had watched each other across the Rappahannock River.

8

*A*FTER THE BLEAK DAYS *of January, when things had been bad in the Union ranks—desertion rampant, squabbling incessant, food scarce, and memories of Marye's Heights and the Mud March haunting—April brought hope. Joseph Hooker, handsome and confident, had restored discipline and confidence. A buoyant St. Patrick's Day celebration sponsored by the Irish regiments, complete with horseracing, pole climbing, and punch drinking, lifted the spirits of everyone from general to private. The Northern troops were eager to redeem themselves. There was another reason to hurry as well: dozens of regiments would see their terms of service expire in April, May, or June 1863. Hooker needed to fight before those soldiers went home and even less experienced troops took their place. Franklin County's 126th volunteer Regiment was one of the twenty-five nine-month regiments counting the days until their terms expired.*

More important, Hooker had a plan to move Lee and the Confederates out of the Union's path across the Rappahannock. No more assaults on fortified defensive positions. Instead the Federals would send cavalry to cut the single line of the Richmond, Fredericksburg, and Potomac Railroad, which supplied the Rebel troops from the south, and then wait for Lee to "ingloriously fly" from the heights he occupied. With the Rebels flushed from behind their stone walls they would face "certain destruction" from the much larger Union troops. Lee and Jackson out of the way, the Army of the Potomac could then march into the capital of the Confederacy.[280]

Robert E. Lee held Joseph Hooker in the same disregard he held the other men he had faced. Indeed, Lee and his troops, though hungry, ill supplied, and outnumbered, were confident and ready for a fight themselves. They had enjoyed one victory after another since June 1862, the march into Maryland the only disappointment. With the grass and corn greening around them in the Virginia spring, the Confederates were eager to take whatever the Federals had in mind. One more blow might destroy the Union effort in Virginia enough to turn the North against

Lincoln. As Lee wrote to his wife, the Confederates simply needed to hold on "manfully" and "baffle" his Union opponents in the field until "the friends of peace" in the North could push the Republicans out of power.[281]

UNCHARACTERISTICALLY LEE had to wait for the enemy to make the first move. The United States had to get across the Rappahannock and past the Confederates at some point. In late April the signs of battle began to stir across the river. "I must write to you again upon the eve of an expected battle, that must be one of the most sanguinary of the whole war," Jed Hotchkiss wrote Sara on April 29. All day long thousands of enemy troops had been crossing the Rappahannock and massing in front of the Confederates. "O! tomorrow, Death will hold high carnival—but I am sure, with God's blessing, we shall whip them."[282] Hotchkiss reassured his wife that he would be safe, for no one on Jackson's staff had ever been wounded. The general seemed to be protected by the Almighty, whom he so freely invoked.

Hooker launched three movements. He sent thousands of cavalry on a raid to cut Confederate supply lines thirty-five miles south, left part of his army at Fredericksburg, and marched the bulk of his 134,000 men west along the Rappahannock River to cross it at a relatively unprotected area and flank Lee. The elaborate plan worked beautifully, surprising the Rebels and getting the Northern soldiers where they wanted to be, south of the river and on strategic ground at Chancellorsville, a crossroads and tavern nine miles west of Fredericksburg. Lee had no choice but to move his men from behind the fortifications they had occupied for months and fight on the open ground.

One problem did confront Hooker and his army: the battlefield he had chosen lay in what the locals called the Wilderness, an area cut over so many times to supply a nearby iron furnace that it had become covered with choking brambles. Its ravines and bogs made marching difficult; its dense trees obstructed the views for artillery, reconnaissance, and signaling. This battlefield did not offer the vistas and freedom of maneuver of the corn and wheat fields of earlier battles in Virginia and Maryland. Instead it provided cover for stealth and surprise.

The Wilderness offered another advantage for the Confederacy. While Hooker and his generally effective military intelligence units had little knowledge of this complicated landscape, Jed Hotchkiss had mapped it for Lee and Jackson. Even though the Federals called the shots at Chancellorsville, the Confederates were prepared to fight there on short notice because Hotchkiss could tell them of the lay of the land and the opportunities it held. Working with a local man who had helped cut new roads through the Wilderness, Hotchkiss raced between Jackson and Lee as the battle developed, carrying word and offering advice of ways to use the landscape to their advantage. Hotchkiss had long been an invaluable and trusted member of the Confederate command. Chancellorsville proved his worth once again.

Lee surprised Hooker by going on the offensive as soon as the Confederates learned that the Federals had crossed the river. Rather than wait for Hooker to flank him and pin him against Fredericksburg, Lee went right at the Union strength at Chancellorsville. Adding to the surprise, Lee divided his already outnumbered forces and on May 2 sent Jackson on an audacious twelve-mile march on a narrow road through the Wilderness to hit Hooker on his flank. Protected from Union eyes by the heavy growth, the thirteen brigades with Jackson, including the 5th Virginia Regiment from Augusta, suddenly burst on unsuspecting Union troops late in the afternoon while they cooked their dinner. With the Federals running before them, Jackson's troops pushed right at Hooker's headquarters at the tavern at Chancellorsville. Confederate artillery fired at the building too, and one shot knocked a wooden post on the porch against Hooker. The resulting concussion left the general dazed and immobilized.

The Union forces, larger and better equipped than the Confederates and occupying ground they had chosen, found themselves overwhelmed in one part of the battlefield after another. Lee and Jackson drove the Federals back across the river to where they had begun days earlier. Union troops in Fredericksburg had taken Marye's Heights during the days of the battle in Chancellorsville, but Hooker waited in vain for the cavalry to cut the Rebel supply lines to the south.

Hotchkiss, at the center of the struggle start to finish, summed it up for Sara: "The Yankees have just gotten over the river again—after 4 days fighting one of the most severe & bloody battles of the war in which our loss has been very heavy as could have been expected." Fortunately, "the enemy's has been much greater & he has been completely beaten—in his own chosen & fortified position his forces routed & demoralized." The much-vaunted Fighting Joe Hooker had discovered that "human efforts are unavailing when in a wrong cause."[283]

As an engineer Hotchkiss could understand what had happened better than most in the battle, fought in heavy woods and brambles. "The smoke of battle has cleared away and we now see what we have done." The results could hardly have been better. "We have severely punished Hooker & his immense army—his loss in killed, wounded, & prisoners, can not be much less than 20000, we fought him over a space of country 15 miles long & 5 wide, having some 5 or 6 distinct battles with him & he did not gain an advantage in one of them, though we had many valuable men killed & wounded." Hotchkiss was not far wrong: at the end of the Battle of Chancellorsville, which stretched from May 1 to May 4, the North had lost seventeen thousand dead, wounded, and missing; the South had lost thirteen thousand. Even though the Southerners had taken the field and driven the Northerners back across the Rappahannock, the Confederate casualties represented 22 percent of their army to the Union's 15 percent. Five hours at Chancellorsville on May 2 had seen losses higher other than anywhere other than at Antietam, and that battle had spanned twelve hours.

Despite their enormous losses of soldiers and officers, Confederate confidence had soared, Hotchkiss wrote, when the Southerners discovered that "as soon as we flank them they become panic stricken & no amount of leadership can avail them—they have been so often whipped that they always begin half whipped, and give up at light reverses—though they bray and bluster and are going to do wonders." Lincoln had supposedly called out the "militia of the North, fearful of an invasion, now that his 'best army on the planet,' has been demoralized."[284] One Augusta soldier noted with amazement and relief that "the Yankees just went like chaff before the wind."[285]

Letters back to Augusta carried bits and pieces of the great battle. Adam Kersh had not been hurt; in fact, "none in our Company got hurt our regiment did not get to fire gun the whole eight days the Yankees had all went back on the other side of the river when we left and said they did not intend to fire on us."[286] His regiment, the 52d, posted back near Fredericksburg, had missed most of the fighting but did find itself under fire from the Union artillery. "One thing I must acknowledge fighting is not very Pleasant work the worst is going to it but when one is in to it once and fires a few rounds he becomes less excited I hate these infernal bums that the Yankees throw at us they make such dreaded, noise they make one believe they are going to hit him if they dont come near him." Hooker had not performed well, Kersh had heard through the rumor mill. "They say he is very much depressed Well he ought to bee I wish he would dry up and go in his hole."[287]

Tom Smiley, fighting with the 5th Virginia and marching with Stonewall Jackson on the flank march through the Wilderness, had a quite different experience. He had come close to being killed, he wrote his sister, but had "made a very narrow escape indeed. There was a shell exploded a few yards from me one of the pieces of which struck in the ground by my side throwing the dirt and gravels over me my eyes were blackened and bruised up and my right hand was struck bruising and swelling it so that I could not do duty for a couple of days." After he recovered, he could see that the fighting had been glorious: "We charged them they breaking and running like frightened sheep."[288]

Other accounts of the Stonewall Brigade at Chancellorsville told a fuller story, a more harrowing one. Jeb Stuart ordered ten regiments to move forward to a log barricade, where hundreds of men who had already fought, and exhausted their ammunition, cowered. The Stonewall Brigade pushed over those men, "some of them saying, with not very pleasant levity, that they would show us how to clear away a Federal line," a South Carolina man recalled. The commander of the Stonewall Brigade, Frank Paxton, had recently become more devout and carried a Bible with him at all times, over his heart. Pushing forward past the huddled men and through the tangle and snarl of the Wilderness, Paxton was shot through the chest. The Stonewall Brigade stumbled forward until they were sixty yards from the Northern troops but finally could stand the fire no more and fell back among the men they had passed over before. The 5th Virginia saw 9 men killed and 116 wounded at Chancellorsville.[289]

Even hardened troops shuddered at what they had seen at Chancellorsville. "This last battle is one among the most terrible we have had lately," Tom Smiley admitted. "A great many of the wounded Yankees being burnt to death. The large brick house at Chancellorsville took fire and burnt up with about two hundred wounded Yankees who were so badly hurt that they could not move and their own soldiers did not help them any. Later in the day the woods took fire and a great many more helpless men perished." Wounded men watched the fire engulf them. "I seen some of these buried and it was truly sickening to see their burnt and charred bodies and their burial was not much better as there was so many that our men could not dig graves for them but just threw a few shovelfuls of dirt over them and passed to the next remarking as they did so that if they had staid at home as they should have done they might have gotten a decent burial."[290] Terror, disgust, and exultation piled on one another, with no time to separate the emotions or give them proper names.

Jesse Rolston wrote the day after the battle to tell his "deare and affection companion" that he remained "amongst the live whilst many of my fellow soaldier has falen and gon never to return." His unit was glad to be back in their camp, "altho if I could be in oald Augusta o how much better satisfyed I would bee whare I could be with you and the children and heare them pratel." Rolston thought this last battle should show everyone that battles were useless. "I do think that this ought to do for all men to quit fiting boath north and south, east or west and setel it up some other way. fiting never will setel it." He had talked with some of the wounded Yankee prisoners, and they agreed. There are "40 thousand of them that their time is out may and they wont volentear for no prise nor they wont fite no more. hoame is their place. if all men would do that what a joyful time it would be."[291]

Henry Dedrick of the 52d Virginia wrote his father with a line that must have occurred to many soldiers as they read about the exploits of the great generals: "You said that you heard that Gen. Jackson had a fight. It was not only him it was all of the troops."[292] But General Jackson was on everyone's minds, for he had been wounded, accidentally shot in the arm by one of his own men as he rode out in the dark to check on troop positions after the glorious flanking exploit on May 2. He was carried to an ambulance and then a hospital on a bruising journey, with his litter bearers, under fire, dropping him heavily on his wounded shoulder. After amputation of his left arm, Jackson seemed to rally. His wife joined him, and characteristically, the general lamented that the Confederates had not been even more aggressive at Chancellorsville. "If I had not been wounded, or had an hour more of daylight, I would have cut off the enemy from the road to the U.S. Ford," a paper reported in its detailed accounts of Jackson's convalescence, "and we would have had them entirely surrounded and they would have been obliged to surrender, or cut their way out; they had no other alternative."[293]

In words that immediately grew into Confederate legend, Jackson used his days in the hospital, where he seemed to recover quickly from his wounds and amputation, to encourage his men. "I consider these wounds a blessing," he insisted, "they were given me for some good and wise purpose, and I would not part with them if I could." He praised the men of the Valley. "The men who live through this war will be proud to say 'I was one of the Stonewall Brigade to their children'—he insisted that the term 'Stonewall' belonged to them, and not to him." One of his last wishes was to be buried at home, the scene of his greatest victories, "in the Valley of Virginia."[294]

Rumors swirled while Jackson lay in a plantation office used as a sick-room. "They say that Jackson was wounded one arm was taken off and two fingers of the other hand," Adam Kersh wrote.[295] Henry Dedrick had heard a few more details: "General Jackson has lost one of his arms and [has] now got the pneumonia. He is not expected to live. He was shot by our own pickets. He got out side of our pickets after night and he come up in a gallop and they fired on him and wounded him and all of his guard but one." By the time Dedrick finished the paragraph the bad news had been confirmed. "I have just heard that General Jackson was dead. If he is it is a great loss to the Southern confederacy."[296] Kersh echoed the judgment when he got the word. "One great loss to our Country is our beloved Jackson he died on the 10th being wounded then taking the pneumonia it soon took him off."[297]

Jed Hotchkiss saw the events of Jackson's wounding and death at close range. Hotchkiss had loaned Jackson his saddle blanket for a bed on the night before the flank march. After Jackson's wounding, Hotchkiss watched day by day as disease took the once apparently invincible general. "The charmed circle in which General Jackson and his staff moved is broken & the break was a heavy one," he told Sara. "I do pray Heaven to spare him, unless in the wise counsels of eternity, he has accomplished the end for which he was created—he said himself that he did not doubt but it was for the wisest of purposes that he lost his arm as the revelations of Eternity would show,"[298] Jackson died that evening. In Staunton, Joseph Waddell had heard all the rumors but still was not prepared for the news. "The Telegraph Operator stepped into the room where I was writing, and handed me a dispatch from the War Department at Richmond, to be sent to Lexington, announcing the fact.—I could scarcely control my hand so as to write my name. Universal lamentation. Jackson was to us like Elijah to his people—'the chariot of Israel and the horsemen thereof.' "[299] The news hurt the more it sank in. "Never was there a more universal lamentation among any people than this event has caused. He was a man of remarkable singleness of purpose, fearing God and naught else.[300]

Jackson was carried back to the Valley to be buried. All along the canal and railroad route people gathered to pay their respects. "He is gone and sleeps in the Valley he loved so much," Hotchkiss wrote. "We miss him all the time & a void is made here which time can hardly fill." General A. P. Hill had been appointed in Jackson's place, an encouraging replacement "in a purely military point of view, but he is not a 'man of God' like & wears not the sword of the Lord and of Gideon, but still we have Gen. Lee, a *good* man & true, faithful in all things & we trust Gen. Jackson 'still lives' to plead our cause." Hotchkiss tried to be philosophical about the loss he felt so heavily. "I am sorry the people despond. I see no reason to do so, but, on the contrary, much to cheer and gladden—true lives have been sacrificed, but such is the price of liberty and without it there can be no redemption—*all* will mourn, I doubt not, but the days must come when sorrow shall be turned into joy."[301]

Hotchkiss hated what the war had done to his beloved Virginia. "The conduct of the enemy is horrible in the Valley, but I hope our day of retribution will come soon." He had met a woman whom the Yankees had "robbed" three times. "They had taken everything she had laid up to eat—she said she prayed & she hoped it was not a wicked prayer 'That there might never be another Yankee child born & that not one of the race might be left on the face of the earth by the first day of next June'— & as she spoke the tears ran down her cheeks."[302] The Confederates had done their share of hurting Virginia as well. "We have left many a scar on the face of the once lovely valley of the Rappahannock to tell of our long occupancy." In addition to all the miles of fortifications, "wide forests have been swept away, many an old mansion has fallen a victim to the flames or been torn away piece meal by the destroying hand of war—whose business is, surely 'devastation & destruction'—O! that this might come to an end."[303] Adam Kersh and several friends walked over the battlefields around Fredericksburg while the Confederate army rested. The ground barely covered the dead. "We could see plenty of old half decayed Yankees some with their heads sticking out arms hands and feet sticking out it was awful sight to behold."[304]

Many Confederates dreamed of taking the war to the North, showing the enemy what war meant. Hotchkiss knew that such talk was not crazy, for since February he had been drawing a detailed map of the Valley in Pennsylvania all the way to the capital in Harrisburg and on to Philadelphia. General Lee had wished "the preparation to be kept a profound secret."[305]

THE FIRST REPORTS by telegraph of the battle at Chancellorsville were all that the people of Franklin County could hope for, especially since the largest single unit of county men, the 126th Pennsylvania Volunteers, would be involved. "The victory of Gen. Hooker's army is more complete than was at first supposed. All that the most sanguine could hope for has been realized, though the losses are very heavy."[306] But later reports told the hard truth: "Our gallant army of the Potomac has again been repulsed, with heavy loss."[307]

Franklin County's men had been left "hanging in the air" at Chancellorsville, positioned on the extreme flank, with no support to keep them from being overwhelmed by the enemy from the side or rear. Confederate General J. E. B. Stuart came right at the 126th, "pouring down his troops on the right and rear, filling all the woods." Two other Federal regiments had peeled away under the pressure, leaving the 126th exposed. An officer from the regiment explained: "To change front in that dense thicket was impossible, even if the impetuous charge which the regiment was now sustaining in front would have permitted. The line was held, however, till the last minute—till the rebels on the flank were within forty yards; then, from right to left, the line melted away in the thick woods." The Franklin men clung to their position as long as they could, their ammunition nearly gone, but then had to give up and retreat in good order. That night was a "hard and gloomy one. It rained violently. They burned their commissary stores to keep them from capture. The army was falling back across the river. Again all sacrifices had been in vain." The men waited all night in the rain for the order to move to the rear; it came at daylight. They passed over the river and marched in the mud twelve miles back to where they had started several days earlier.[308]

Samuel W. North of the 126th Pennsylvania described for his father the unit's role in the Battle of Chancellorsville, using borrowed paper and pencil: "Our brigade was ordered to support another then ahead & advancing into the woods when it came near the enemies lines. they tried a few shots & then fell back & left us to stand it our selves. we were engaged about 2 hours. the amunition began to run out & there was neither support nor relief coming so we had to fall back & they followed us yelling like indians. I fired 30 rounds. some fired more, but my gun was so hot I was afraid to load any faster." North concluded with two observations: "The result is a failure so far as I can hear," and "you need not fear that I will enlist again." The 126th lost four dead, thirty-two wounded, and six missing at Chancellorsville.[309]

Samuel Cormany, in a related cavalry unit, put the situation in a better light. "Seems we are falling back—whipped—But an occasional defeat makes a good soldier a better fighter, and knocks a coward out." Three days later he added that "our move accomplished a lot in the way of information, experience"; the optimistic young soldier added a more elaborate rationalization the next day: "Of course a company—a squadron, a regiment or a brigade may seem to be whipped—and may retreat—and not even in the best of order—when in fact such movement gives way for another, resulting in decided success." Indeed, the Union army had not been routed so much as its commander had lost nerve and direction.[310]

The Franklin men at Chancellorsville had fought well, just as they had at Fredericksburg several months earlier. But in both battles leadership had been dreadful. While some papers tried to call it by other names or offer excuses, "the painful experience of the last two years has taught us that it is far better to look these stern realities in the face, than to try and captivate the ears of the people with the syren songs of victory and glory, when we know that defeat and disaster follow close after the retiring footsteps of our national armies." The *Valley Spirit* admitted that it would have preferred George McClellan at the head of the army, but it had supported the Republican Hooker. "A victory gained by him would have been a victory for the nation; his defeat is the nation's defeat; his humiliation is the nation's humiliation. The men who fought and bled and died under him were our friends and brothers and sons." The paper had "only our most sincere sorrow to offer the President and his advisers for the terrible disasters they are visiting upon the nation, and for which the people and history will hold them responsible; and to express the hope that in the good Providence of God they may be instrumental in bringing upon us no greater evils than we will be able to survive."[311]

Family members waited for the roll of dead and wounded to be published. "The last week was one of terrible anxiety and suspense in this community—such as we have only known on one or two occasions before, and such as we pray God we may not know soon again." Word of a "great battle" in Virginia arrived, but days passed before "we heard any definite or reliable news. And then we learned for the first time, that our brave boys had participated in the bloody conflict and that many of them were among the killed and wounded." When word did come, it only added to the confusion and misery. "Names were so wretchedly misspelled as to be scarcely recognizable—and numbers of regiments and companies were confused and unintelligible." Family members, desperate for information, gathered around town; "anxious and careworn faces could be met with every place there was a probability of getting news."[312] The report finally listed the deaths and the dozens who had been wounded from every Franklin community.

The pain was ameliorated by the knowledge that the 126th was coming home, its nine-month term of service expired. The regiment took a train to the Potomac, a steamboat ride up the river to Washington, another train to Baltimore and then to Harrisburg. Once back in Pennsylvania, "the comrades, free from restraint, gay and happy, enjoyed themselves about the town or in the camp, for several days, while the officers were busy with the preparation of the muster-out rolls." Finally receiving their pay and discharges, the men of the 126th, "with cordial hand-shakings," separated and started to Franklin on the train.[313]

The unburied at Chancellorsville

Even as the soldiers made their way home, the people there squabbled over the ceremony for the reception. The Democrats worried that the Republicans were using the moment of glory for partisan gain, associating the men's return with Abraham Lincoln and Union Leagues, Republican organizations that mobilized support for the war and the party that led it.[314] The Republicans lamented that the Democrats' *Valley Spirit* still existed at all, for its death would "spare many good men who are deceived by its misrepresentations, falsifications and incendiary dictums!"[315] Good times as well as bad brought out the hatred between the Democrats and Republicans.

Such petty bickering was set aside, however, on the day of the soldiers' arrival, when "the people from the country began pouring into town from every direction. The Hotels were soon filled to overflowing, and their yards and the neighboring streets lined with vehicles of every description," the Democrats' paper cheerfully reported. "And then the towns-people began to run out their flags and close their places of business, as the Court House bell announced that the train was on its way from Harrisburg, bringing home the loved ones whose coming had been so anxiously awaited." Signals came when the train passed Shippensburg and again when it went around the big curve three miles north of Chambersburg; people jammed together at the depot. Thirty-four little girls dressed in white, representing all the states of the Union, marched in a parade that also included young cadets from the town's academy. The 126th marched throughout the town, wending through streets decorated with flags and bunting, and ended up in the Diamond at the center. The wounded from Chancellorsville rode in a wagon of honor.

Everyone met at the Town Hall, prepared by the ladies, "beautifully decorated with evergreen and flowers; the walls were adorned with the national colors and many such inscriptions as: 'Welcome to our brave defenders.' " Food abounded. "Seven long tables, running the entire length of the Hall, . . . groaned under a profusion of all the substantials and delicacies the country could afford." After this banquet the companies from Greencastle, Waynesboro, and Mercersburg got back on the train to head to their home communities, where they celebrated all over again.[316]

9

CHANCELLORSVILLE OCCURRED two years after the war had begun. Those two years had seen hundreds of battles and hundreds of thousands of young men killed. They had seen the Republican government turn against slavery in both hope and desperation. They had seen the Federal army push deep into Confederate territory and control the seacoast and major cities yet fail to dislodge the largest, most powerful, and most symbolically important Confederate army, that of Robert E. Lee.

People in the North and South had grown to hate each other, but many still spoke of stopping the fight and going home. Slaves had rushed to freedom at every opportunity, the Emancipation Proclamation had decreed the end of slavery in Confederate territory, and African American men in both the North and the South had enlisted in the Federal army, but large numbers of white Northerners still spoke of ending the war and restoring slavery as soon as they could seize office. The vast majority of slaves remained firmly bound, with no hope of freedom in sight.

Everything turned on the unity of the North. The South did not have to win; it only had to hold out until the North lost the will to drive the war forward. Battles and politics grew ever more tightly implicated, home front and battlefield ever more entwined.

Union soldiers found support for the Confederacy strong and defiant wherever they went in Virginia. By 1863 Southerners did not speak of states' rights or of slavery as the cause of their fighting; rather, they spoke of Yankee marauders, vandals, "heshens," despoilers. Even the mild Jed Hotchkiss and Joseph Waddell, strong Unionists before the war, now saw the Yankees as heartless invaders. Alexander H. H. Stuart and John Baldwin, desperate holdouts against secession in Virginia's convention, offered gifts to Stonewall Jackson for protecting the homes of Augusta, advertising their loyalty to the Confederacy in word and action.

Despite the brutal impact of the war on its farms and cities, white Virginia had not lost the will to fight. In fact, the war had forged Virginia into far greater unity and identity with the Confederate cause than ever before. Everything had become simple. Complicated debates over the Constitution, the Bible, and the Founding Fathers had collapsed into elemental emotions. War's emotions—sentiment and heroes and denial—flourished. White Virginians refused to acknowledge that slavery dissolved wherever the Union army approached; they did not talk of slavery at all if they could help it, preferring to think of themselves as victims and valiant defenders of black and white alike from the hypocritical, relentless, yet hapless Yankees. They explained away inflation as the result of individual greed, bread riots as the result of a few weak women. They looked with pride on the Army of Northern Virginia, victorious over larger and better-equipped opponents. So long as that army could be fed and armed the Confederacy would live.[317]

In 1863 the North seemed far more likely than the South to break from within. Although Southerners exaggerated the degree of dissent above the Mason-Dixon Line, partisan conflict did lie on the surface. Whereas the South smothered its political divisions, the North paraded its differences in one election after another. The Democrats refused to let up on Abraham Lincoln and the Republicans, refused to soften criticism of generals and their many failures, refused to accept that the fundamental purpose of the war had become emancipation or that the war should be prolonged to bring slavery to an end. The Democrats filled newspapers with their denunciations and attracted voters to the polls in undiminished numbers.

The unity of the white South and the division of the white North drove Abraham Lincoln to make the war a war over slavery. The worse the war went, the more he and the Republicans pushed antislavery. The South appeared far harder to defeat than Northerners had anticipated, and slavery, it became clear, offered the Confederacy a great advantage. But the more Lincoln focused on slavery and the arming of black men, the more he alienated Democrats, immigrants, and potential recruits. These opponents already hated the idea of occupying the South; the turn against slavery and toward black soldiers incensed them. Lincoln gambled that the South would be defeated before the North abandoned him and his party, support for which had weakened after Fredericksburg and Chancellorsville.

That was the balance in 1863: a race between the destruction of the Southern army and the fracturing of the Northern home front. It was this calculation that made Lee decide to invade Pennsylvania.

ROBERT E. LEE had wanted to take the war to the North since at least February, when he ordered Jed Hotchkiss to draw a map of southern

Pennsylvania. With his army hungry, the farms of northern Virginia stripped bare, and the news from Vicksburg and Tennessee threatening Confederate losses, Lee longed to shift the costs of war to the Union. From southeastern Pennsylvania, the Southern army could threaten Washington, Baltimore, Philadelphia, or Pennsylvania's capital at Harrisburg. The Federals would be pulled away from Richmond, giving Virginia desperately needed time to recover from the occupation. The Confederate leadership gently asked Lee about going to the aid of Vicksburg or to the Confederates in Tennessee, but Lee deflected any such suggestions. Capturing or cutting off the vast stores and political leadership of Washington would, he calculated, bring the war to a close faster than any other strategy.

John Imboden of Staunton, recently named brigadier general after arduous labor in building up his guerrilla fighters into a regular unit, helped Lee in crucial ways during these months. Imboden's forces, now grown into more than a thousand men and including infantry, cavalry, and artillery, relentlessly harassed the Unionist civilians and Federal troops of West Virginia. The guerrillas' capture of two trains, destruction of two dozen bridges, and cutting of telegraph lines of the Baltimore and Ohio Railroad and the Chesapeake and Ohio Canal disrupted key Union supply lines. Their capture of five thousand head of cattle and twelve hundred horses provided essential food and transport for the Confederates. Their burning of oil fields and capture of cannon and a thousand small arms led many Unionists to fear that the partisan guerrillas would invade Pittsburgh or Wheeling; the guerilla threat kept the Federal troops from massing more men farther east, where they expected Lee to strike.

Hooker had forced the Battle of Chancellorsville on Lee, diverting him from taking the war north. Although Hooker had been driven from the field in the battle, he had inflicted grave damage on the Confederate army and succeeded in keeping his troops between the Confederates and Washington afterward. As Lee reorganized his army in preparation for the march northward, he worried about finding a general to replace Jackson, about desertion, about mounts for his cavalry, and about what the still-strong Union army across the Rappahannock might do. In late May he finally decided the time had come to push the fighting into the North. He successfully disguised his intentions from Hooker, who watched him

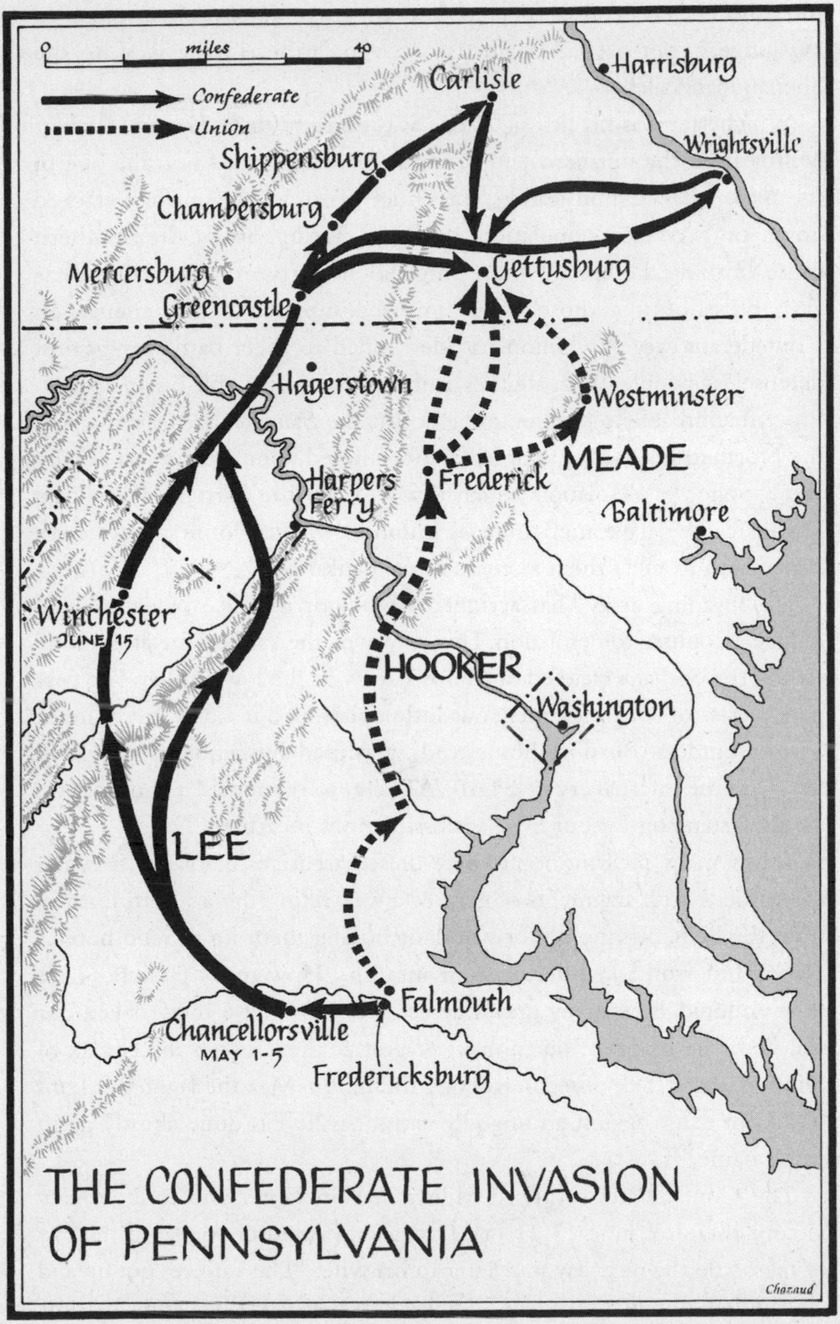
0
miles
40
Confederate
Union
Harrisburg
Carlisle
Wrightsville
Shippensburg
Chambersburg
Mercersburg
Greencastle
Gettysburg
Hagerstown
Westminster
MEADE
Harpers Ferry
Frederick
Baltimore
Winchester
JUNE 15
HOOKER
Washington
LEE
Falmouth
Chancellorsville
MAY 1-5
Fredericksburg
THE CONFEDERATE INVASION OF PENNSYLVANIA
Chazaud

ntly. The Federals expected Lee to cross the Potomac close to Washington, but he had decided to sweep farther to the west, to the Shenandoah Valley.

Winchester was his first goal; Lee was eager to drive General Robert Milroy from the northern end of the Valley. Milroy had become one of the most hated Union leaders, for under his orders troops had cracked down on a civilian population strong in its support of the Southern cause, burning the homes and seizing the property of Rebel sympathizers and shooting those who actively supported the enemy. In Confederate eyes, the Union had descended to sheer barbarism against defenseless people. With neither military force nor the Emancipation Proclamation able to overcome the South, the *Staunton Spectator* charged, the Northerners had "as their last resort entered upon a course of cruelty and a policy of desolation which throw down the barriers of civilized hostilities. We have met them as enemies of our country—we have henceforth to meet them as enemies of mankind."[318]

No invading army "has a right to blot out the face of nature, and reduce a country to desolation. This, however, the Yankees are attempting to do," the *Spectator* charged of Milroy's army in the lower Valley. The desperate cries of "our aged men, our little children, our ladies, are heard in all our borders. Burning homesteads, a ruined husbandry, a desolated land, and the infernal cry of 'STARVATION to the rebels!' tell us that we are now standing for our lives, against demons incarnate."[319]

"How many pleasant homes have these barbarians desolated, strewing the gardens with fragments of glass & china, filling the air with feathers from the beds, hewing up for wood, or boxing them up to send home," Nancy Emerson asked her diary in anguish. "How many churches have they polluted, how many graves desecrated. How have they soaked our soil with the blood of our noblest & best & then to cap the climax of injury & insult, talk of reconstructing the union. May the righteous Lord plead our cause against an ungodly nation, as he has done already, glory to his name."[320]

The Confederates surprised Milroy in Winchester and took an easy victory there on June 13. Henry Dedrick of Augusta conveyed the gist of the battle the next day in a letter to his wife: "The yankees got up and scadaddled out of that place." Dedrick was especially happy to hear rumors that "we have got old Gen. Milroy. If we have got him it is a fine thing for he has treated some of our people very bad. I think we have got about four thousand of them. Our loss is not very heavy. We only lost one man out of our Regiment."[321] Jed Hotchkiss quickly scribbled a note to Sara: "This has been one of the most complete successes of the war, our men behaved splendidly. Milroy's surprise was complete." The Union general had not been captured, but his army was "scattered far & wide."[322]

In the wake of the Confederate assault on Winchester, Staunton once again became "a great thoroughfare for the army." More than four thousand captured Federals passed through, eliciting sharp commentary from Waddell: "The Yankees seemed to be very cheerful . . . . They seemed to have none of the feelings of captured robbers as they are." Waddell refused to talk with them himself, "feeling too much detestation of the vandals. These are the wretches who would have come to invade our homes."[323]

At the same time, many Southern soldiers were "passing through to join their commands," all heading north toward Maryland.[324] "Passengers from Winchester state that our army had crossed the Potomac into Maryland, at three points," noted Waddell, excited and mystified by the news. "Gen. Lee, with another portion of our army, has disappeared somewhere, and it is not known when or where he will turn up. . . . These movements are wonderful—so rapid and secret."[325] Maybe the magic of Chancellorsville still hovered over the Confederate army.

NEWS QUICKLY ARRIVED in Chambersburg about the disaster in Winchester. "Our town in an uproar," William Heyser glumly noted the day after Milroy's defeat. Even though the residents could not believe everything they heard, "we all feel Pennsylvania will be invaded. Many families are hiding their valuables, and preparing for the worst. . . . The stores are packing up their goods and sending them off, people are running to and fro."[326] Alexander K. McClure wrote a leading Republican: "If the Rebels come they will come much stronger than before, and I doubt not with a much more destructive purpose. Our raiders south have been wantonly destructive with private property. . . ."[327]

Philip Schaff, a theologian who taught at the Mercersburg Seminary, viewed the looming Confederate invasion through the lens of Scripture. "It seems to me that I now understand better than ever before some passages in the prophetic discourses of our Savior, especially the difference between *wars* and *rumors of wars*." Schaff could see the effect of rumors, "conflicting, confused, exaggerated, and frightful." The "whole veteran army of Lee, the military strength and flower of the Southern rebellion is said to be crossing the Potomac and marching into Pennsylvania. We are cut off from all mail communication and dependent on the flying and contradictory rumors of passengers, straggling soldiers, run-away negroes and spies." As a result, "all the schools and stores are closed; goods are being hid or removed to the country, valuables buried in cellars or gardens and other places of concealment."[328]

With the pending invasion, the worst in people came out. Pennsylvanians, Schaff regretted to say, turned against one another. "Political passions run high; confidence is destroyed; innocent persons are seized as spies; the neighbor looks upon his neighbor with suspicion, and even sensible ladies have their imagination excited with pictures of horrors far worse than death." With these effects of the rumors of war, Schaff found himself thinking that "it would be a positive relief of the most painful suspense if the rebel army would march into town."

The next day the Confederates did arrive in Mercersburg, a dozen miles south of Chambersburg. "They rode into town with pointed pistols and drawn sabres, their captain (Crawford) loudly repeating: 'We hear there is to be some resistance made. We do not wish to disturb private citizens; but if you wish a fight, you can have it to your heart's content. Come out and try.' " The Rebels had already been to a nearby town, where they took 200 cattle and 120 horses "of the best kind," Schaff noted, worth perhaps eleven thousand dollars. They also carried with them two or three "negro boys." None of the citizens resisted.

Schaff, a brilliant scholar born in Switzerland and educated in Germany and destined to emerge in a few years as a leading American and European theologian, talked with the officer in charge of the raid, Colonel Ferguson. The Southerner spoke with "great decision, though courteously." The Confederate officer told the professor: "I care nothing about the right of secession, but I believe in the right of revolution. You invaded our rights, and we would not be worthy the name of men if we had not the courage to defend them. A cowardly race is only fit for contempt." Ferguson thought the North lived "under a despotism; in the South the

Habeas Corpus is as sacredly guarded as ever. You had the army, the navy, superiority of numbers, means, and a government in full operation; we had to create all that with great difficulty; yet you have not been able to subdue us, and can never do it. You will have to continue the war until you either must acknowledge our Confederacy or until nobody is left to fight. For we will never yield. Good-by, I hope when we meet again we will meet in peace." Schaff thought the officers of the Confederate army "intelligent and courteous, but full of hatred for the Yankees."

Schaff had to admit that he "felt deeply humbled and ashamed in the name of the government." The Union had apparently decided to abandon southern Pennsylvania. "The authorities concluded to fortify Harrisburg and Pittsburgh, and to leave all Southern Pennsylvania exposed to plunder and devastation, instead of defending the line and disputing every inch of ground. No forces of any account this side of Harrisburg, and the Rebels pouring into the State with infantry and artillery. The government seems paralyzed for the moment. We fairly, though reluctantly, belong to the Southern Confederacy, and are completely isolated."

Mercersburg saw a succession of Confederate units, ranging from the most disciplined and orderly to the most rapacious. Days after Colonel Ferguson's men left "the town was occupied by an independent guerrilla band of cavalry, who steal horses, cattle, sheep, store goods, negroes, and whatever else they can make use of, without ceremony." Mercersburg was home to a large proportion of the African American population of Franklin, and "the poor negroes, the innocent cause of the war, are trembling like leaves and flying with their little bundles 'to the mountains,' especially the numerous run-away slaves from Virginia, from fear of being captured as 'contrabands' and sold to the South."[329]

The guerrillas went "on a regular slave-hunt, which presented the worst spectacle I ever saw in this war," Schaff bitterly recorded in his diary. "They proclaimed, first, that they would burn down every house which harbored a fugitive slave, and did not deliver him up within twenty minutes. And then commenced the search upon all the houses on which suspicion rested." A number of white households hid black people they knew and risked everything they owned as a result. Schaff asked one of the Confederates rounding up the women and children, " 'Do you not feel bad and mean in such an occupation?' He boldly replied that 'he felt very comfortable. They were only reclaiming their property which we had stolen and harbored.' " Under the threat of the search, Schaff sadly observed "all the contraband negroes who are still in the neighborhood, fleeing about like deer. My family is kept in constant danger, on account of poor old Eliza, our servant, and her little boy, who hide in the grain-fields during the day, and return under cover of the night to get something to eat." Eliza's daughter and her children had already been captured and returned to Virginia.[330]

Even in Chambersburg, miles from the border, the "colored people are flying in all directions," William Heyser noted. First "a number of contrabands entered our town, fleeing from Martinsburg with the Rebels not far behind. These were followed by a wagon train, many on three wheels, and less being dragged and pushed as fast as possible. The street is crowded with horses and wagons, all in the wildest state of confusion. Upon asking one of them as to their plight, said the Rebels are not far behind."[331] The *Repository* spoke of "dark clouds of contrabands" who rushed into town. The black people of Franklin could not afford to take chances, and "the Negroes darkened the different roads Northward for hours, loaded with house hold effects, sable babies, &c and horses and wagons and cattle crowded every avenue to places of safety."[332]

Rachel Cormany watched as "contrabands on ahead coming as fast as they could on all & any kind of horses, their eyes fairly protruding with fear—teams coming at the same rate—some with the covers half off—some lost—men without hats or coats—some lost their coats as they were flying, one darky woman astride of a horse going what she could. There really was a real panic. All reported that the rebels were just on their heels."[333] Jacob Hoke wrote on the same day of the "large number of colored persons, men, women, and children, bearing with them huge bundles of clothing, bedding, and articles of house-keeping. Many of these had come from the valley of Virginia, while a few were residents of our own county and the neighboring county of Washington, in Maryland."[334]

"MD. & PA. looked pretty much alike," L. M. Blackford, a young officer with Pickett's Division, blandly observed as Lee's army crossed the

Mason-Dixon Line. Things got more interesting in the village of Greencastle in Franklin County, Pennsylvania, where "the people swarmed about doors and windows and sullenly gazed on our troops passing by. Several women wore the U. S. flag on their bosoms, where it was seen by our men." The Union women apparently imagined that their patriotic displays would infuriate the Confederates, but "such natural and innocent indications of loyalty to their government, our soldiers would of course *scorn* to object to. It would be a matter of indifference to me if every woman in Pa. had one on her person, and every house one floating from its roof."[335] The Confederates expected nothing else.

On the other hand, at least one young man from Franklin decided to join the Rebels. Cephas Richey Hallar of Mercersburg was the youngest of five brothers, all the rest of whom were already fighting for the Confederacy. His mother had recently returned to Mercersburg, her hometown, from Missouri when her husband died. Barely sixteen, Hallar watched for an opportunity to go to the Southern army. The raid provided that chance. After sharp questioning, the Confederates decided the boy's loyalties to the South were genuine, and they took him in. His nickname became Pense, short for "Pennsylvania."[336]

The march up through Franklin County proved "interesting enough" to L. M. Blackford of Staunton. "It is fertile and highly cultivated, and more like our Valley than anything else." Despite the similarity of the landscape, Blackford could not help noticing the differences. "It is 2 or 3 times as thickly settled," he observed, "the fields are much smaller, the houses more frequent & handsomer; (generally of stone or brick) and the barns bigger and more complete than any I have ever seen." In fact, Blackford admitted, many of the barns were "of stone and brick, and have glass window sashes. An indifferent building of this sort is hard to find, and the average of the most inferior is better than that of the best in Eastern Virginia." One barn in particular caught his eye, "on the premises of a Mr., or Judge McClure, this side of Chambersburg." Anyone in town could have told him about McClure, but the barn itself was impressive enough: it "was not only of very large size, but really elegant: painted snow-white, with ornamented eaves, pendants. The house and whole property of this individual however are beautiful and complete beyond description."[337]

The Confederate invasion, just beginning, was already having one of its intended effects. The Northern papers, Joseph Waddell noted with satisfaction, "show a wild excitement in Yankee land on account of Lee's anticipated invasion. Lincoln has called for 100,000 six months men. New York, Philadelphia +c are in a blaze." Rumor had "large numbers of men hastily off to Harrisburg, which is presumed to be the point aimed at by 'the rebels.' " One report seemed undeniably true: "Some of our cavalry have certainly been at Chambersburg, Pa." The mild Waddell could not hide his delight with the prospect of Confederate occupation of Pennsylvania. "Oh that the Yankee advocates of this war may experience at their own firesides and in their own persons some of the horrors they have inflicted upon us! Perhaps they will then be more disposed to desist from their attempt to subjugate or devastate our country."[338]

Waddell did not seem to know whether to be proud or frustrated that from all accounts, "our cavalry at Chambersburg respect private property."[339] Even the Northern papers admitted that "our soldiers now in Maryland and Pennsylvania, offer no ill treatment to any one—What a contrast to Yankee depredations on this side of the Potomac!" He knew the North would "anticipate and dread retribution; but our troops are restrained by rigid orders, as license to pillage would soon demoralise the army. Horses and beef cattle and whatever else is needed by the army are taken, and paid for as far as possible. Apple butter is so abundant in Pa, that as one of our Staunton boys writes, they called their camp 'Applebutter Spread!' "[340]

Hotchkiss found himself, with most of Lee's army, in Chambersburg, the county seat of Franklin, a rich place on the southern border of Pennsylvania. The Confederates, he wrote with amusement and a clear sense of satisfaction, had "invaded the old 'Keystone,' frightening the Dutch out of their senses." The Yankees "confidently expected us to burn every thing and lay waste the country and they thought we would be justified in so doing," Hotchkiss reported with amusement, but the Southerners prided themselves on their restraint. "When they found us doing all things decently & not disturbing them except to supply our army with everything it needed to eat &c &c and furnish any number of big horses & wagons, all sorts of supplies, leather saddles &c all called for by a polite officer, & no pillaging, they were rejoiced to get off so well &

set before our men any quantity of the good things they have so abundantly." In Hotchkiss's eyes, the natives of Chambersburg seemed almost glad to have the Rebels in their midst. "It was one of the most amazing sights I ever saw to see the broadclothed gentry coming in & bringing saddles, bridles &c & making a pile of them in the square for the use of the Rebels." Respect mixed with wonder in Hotchkiss's patronizing air, for "this land is full of every thing."[341]

Lee seized the opportunity to show how an army should behave on enemy soil. The Confederates would not act like the invading hordes of Pope and Milroy, but rather like Christian soldiers. From Chambersburg, Lee issued Order No. 72, the script for the invasion, widely distributed and printed in newspapers North and South. It decreed that "no private property shall be injured or destroyed by any person belonging to or connected with the army, or taken except by the officers" officially designated to do so. The officers would follow strict rules of payment and receipt. If any Northerner hid property "necessary for the use of the army," he or she lost the protection and the officers could take all property. General Ewell, commanding Augusta men, issued an order that went even further: "All struggling and wandering from the ranks, and all marauding and plundering by individuals are prohibited, upon pain of the severest penalties known to the service."[342]

The high-minded rules both excited and disappointed Southerners. "This invasion follows the overrunning of parts of several States of our Confederacy by the enemy, in all of which they have committed outrages so far wanting in humanity that they could scarcely be pardoned in the most heathenish and savage people of the earth," the *Staunton Vindicator* declared. "This inhumanity, mostly exhibited to defenseless women and children, in the burning of their houses, barns, and granaries, the plundering and destroying their property generally, and sending them as exiles from their homes, for the crime of a husband, father, brother or son" created a longing for retribution. But those who wanted an eye for an eye would be disappointed. "Could our people divest themselves of the feelings excited by the wrongs they have suffered they would agree to the propriety of this course," the paper reluctantly admitted. As it was, "we are satisfied that our able Generals know what is the proper course to pursue and in pursuing it will meet with the hearty concurrence of those even whose disappointment may be greatest."[343]

Despite Lee's order, the line between fair dealing and retribution remained unclear. After all, the Pennsylvania merchants "had to sell goods at their old prices for Confederate money." And Confederate money, everyone knew, held little value in the Confederacy and no value at all in the North; Lee's army simply carried printing presses to print all the money it needed. The fiction of payment permitted the Southerners to imagine themselves gallant and generous. As a member of the generals' staff, Hotchkiss won a chance at goods that enlisted men would be denied. "I bought about $100 worth of calico, wool delaine, bleached cotton, hoops, gloves, thread, gingham, pins &c &c which I hope to get home in due time if we stop short of N.Y," he happily wrote Sara. Such sundries were in short supply in Staunton, and Hotchkiss knew his wife would be thrilled at the valuable but light and portable gifts.[344]

"I spent some hours in Chambersburg, which is a pretty town of 5600 inhabitants," L. M. Blackford wrote back to Virginia. "The stores were all closed when we entered the place, but many of them were opened by threats of violent entrance by armed force if it was not done quickly. When opened, guards in most instances—not all—were posted at the door and but a limited number allowed to enter at a time. When we did get in we bought what few things we could find that we wanted with C.S. money." The merchants raised their prices a little, "but at this no one complained." It was true that "at some of the stores the soldiers got in, and not being restrained by a guard, took a good many things without pay. There was, in short a good deal of lawlessness, but not as much as might have been expected under the circumstances. I did not know of more than 6 or 8 stores in all being opened." Blackford bought himself " a handsome black felt hat"; indeed, "our whole party re-hatted themselves."[345]

There could be no doubt in late June that the Confederate invasion was a brilliant maneuver in every way. "Providence has abundantly blessed our movement, few casualties of any kind—and our success wonderful—we shall get nearly a million dollars worth of horses, supplies of all kinds &c from this county," Hotchkiss wrote with satisfaction. Who could have imagined that invading the rich and powerful North would have been this easy? "The people are very submissive and comply, meekly, with the demands made on them—I think we shall be able to do a good deal towards bringing about an honorable peace."[346] "The army is in splendid condition: marches almost wholly without straggling, and is in the highest spirits," Blackford assured his family back in the Valley of Virginia. "Lee is making a bold stroke for peace. Pray that it may succeed."[347]

Joseph Waddell soon saw the results of the Confederate occupation of Pennsylvania down in Staunton. "A number of wagons loaded with hardware, stationery +c *purchased* by our Quartermasters in Chambersburg, Pa., arrived to-day." The underlining of "purchased" conveyed irony rather than emphasis, as the next sentence made clear. "The benighted Yankees have been excluded by the blockade, from Southern market for so long, that they are away behind the times in regard to prices."[348] A file that cost three dollars in Staunton cost only twenty cents in Chambersburg.

Waddell grew philosophical. "The vicissitudes of the war are very strange—Just two months ago (May 7th) we thought the Yankees were advancing upon Staunton—now the war is raging a way off in Pennsylvania. Two months hence the Yankees may be around us again." Like all his neighbors, Waddell had learned not to expect anything other than the unexpected from this war. "When I read of wars in my boyhood, I thought of them as belonging to the dark ages of the world, and never expected to witness horrors of the kind."[349]

CHAMBERSBURG'S REPUBLICAN EDITOR portrayed the behavior of General Albert G. Jenkins, leader of a brigade of J. E. B. Stuart's cavalry, in mock-heroic language. "The women and children having been sufficiently frightened by the threatened booming of artillery," the paper noted, "the most desperate charge ever known in the history of war—in Chambersburg at least—was made. Down the street came the iron clatter of hoofs like the tempest with a thousand thunderbolts." A gun went off somewhere, "and the column recoiled before it reached the Diamond." Discovering that one of his own men had fallen and accidentally discharged his gun, Jenkins regained his momentum and seized undefended Chambersburg. "Having won it by the most determined and brilliant prowess, Jenkins resolved that he would be magnanimous, and would allow nothing to be taken from our people—excepting such articles as he and his men wanted."[350]

The Confederates went through the motions of buying things from the local stores. "True, the system of Jenkins would be considered a little informal in business circles," but the merchants of Chambersburg had no choice. Jenkins "didn't stoop to haggle about a few odd pennies in making a bargain. . . . Doubtless our merchants and druggists would have preferred 'green-backs' to confederate scrip that is never payable, and is worth just its weight in old paper; but Jenkins hadn't 'green-backs' and he had confederate scrip, and such as he had he gave unto them." In true gallant Southern fashion, the paper continued in its sarcastic tone, Jenkins, "to avoid the jealousies growing out of rivalry in business," patronized "all the merchants, and bought pretty much everything he could conveniently use and carry." The Rebels wanted horses more than anything else, but "sore was the disappointment of Jenkins at the general exodus of horses from this place. It limited his booty immensely. Fully five hundred had been taken from Chambersburg and vicinity to the mountains."[351]

The Republican paper would not waste an opportunity to throw doubt on the loyalty of the Democrats in Franklin. It gleefully told of a citizen who acted the part of "the genuine Copperhead," approaching the invading Confederates with offers of help and support, but who was rebuffed by the invaders. " 'Well, if you believe we are right, take your gun and join our ranks!' " Jenkins supposedly told a Democratic sympathizer. "To another he said—'If we had such men as you in the South, we would hang them!' "[352] Nothing could have pleased the Republicans more.

The people of Franklin sometimes disappointed one another with their cowardice and greed during the Confederate raid. Local authorities had stored a large amount of government supplies in a warehouse undiscovered by the Rebels. Rationalizing that the goods would soon be discovered by the invading army, "men, women, and children came running in crowds, and a general scramble took place." The townspeople broke into the warehouse, and "upon every street and alley leading from the warehouse persons were seen carrying bacon and rolling barrels of crackers and beans. In the general *melee* some came in contact with others, when scolding, kicking, and fighting ensued." Two women, each rolling a barrel, collided and fell into a fierce fight.[353]

Franklin residents had to admit that the Confederate officers had some principles. Merchant Jacob Hoke told of a Southern soldier who strode into a store and "seized a number of remnants of ladies' dress goods," merely tucking them under his arm and walking out. As the soldier passed General Jenkins, however, the officer "caught the fellow by the back of the neck and ran him back into the store on the double-quick, saying to us as he rushed him up to the counter, 'Did this man get these here? and did he pay for them?' Upon hearing the truth, "the General drew his sword, and flourishing it above the man's head and swearing terribly, said, 'I've a mind to cut your head off.'" Turning to the merchants, Jenkins told them to report any other such failures to pay, for "we are not thieves."[354] The Confederates did not live up to Northern fears. Demolitions of a railroad bridge and roundhouse "were the only acts of real destruction attempted," Hoke acknowledged. "True, many horses, cattle, and other things were taken, but all was within the rules of war."[355]

One great exception to the "rules of war" marked the Confederate behavior: "the carrying away of free negroes." The Confederates' actions toward black people proved to be even worse than the white residents of Franklin had anticipated. "One of the revolting features of this day was the scouring of the fields about the town and searching of houses in portions of the place for negroes," Hoke lamented. "These poor creatures—those of them who had not fled upon the approach of the foe—sought concealment in the growing wheat fields around town. Into these the cavalrymen rode in search of their prey, and many were caught—some after a desperate chase and being fired at." Philip Schaff, down in Mercersburg, saw the capture of black people he knew "to have been born and raised on free soil."[356]

Rachel Cormany anguished over the raids. The Confederates, on the second day of their occupation of Chambersburg, "were hunting up the contrabands & driving them off by droves. O! How it grated on our hearts to have to sit quietly & look at such brutal deeds—I saw no men among the contrabands—all women & children." Like Hoke and Schaff, Rachel Cormany could see that "some of the colored people who were raised here were taken along." She could do nothing, only watch "on the front step as they were driven by just like we would drive cattle. Some laughed & seemed not to care—but nearly all hung their heads. One woman was pleading wonderfully with her driver for her children—but all the sympathy she received from him was a rough 'March along'—at which she would quicken her pace again." Rachel could not imagine what the Rebel soldiers "want with those little babies—whole families were taken." She assumed that the black men "left thinking the women & children would not be disturbed. I cannot describe all the scenes."[357]

The white people of Franklin did not always stand by and watch the kidnapping by the Confederates. Hoke interceded for two of his kidnapped neighbors, and down in Greencastle "a few determined men, armed with revolvers, captured a squad which had in charge a number of these poor frightened creatures, and released them from the unhappy fate which threatened them."[358] A prominent Reformed Church theologian, Benjamin S. Schneck, went directly to Confederate headquarters to testify on behalf of Esque Hall, a "well and favorably known colored man," as well as for two repairmen on the Cumberland Valley Railroad.[359]

Jemima Cree took things in hand as well. She heard that the Rebels had been "scouting around, gathering up our Darkies, and that they had Mag down on the court house pavement. I got my 'fixens' on, and started down," she wrote her husband. "There were about 25 women and children, with Mag and Fannie. I interceded for Mag, told them she was free born, etc. The man said he could do nothing, he was acting according to orders." Fannie was indeed "contraband," so Cree could have done nothing for her. In any case, the Confederates left before the Franklin woman could take her complaint higher up.

"They took up all they could find," Cree wrote with terror and disgust, "even little children, whom they had to carry on horseback before them. All who could get there fled to the woods, and many who were wise are hid in the houses of their employers." Despite such efforts by white patrons, the numbers and guns lay with the Confederates, who captured "about 250 people . . . into bondage," Chambersburg merchant William Heyser estimated. Amos Stouffer sadly observed that Confederates "are scouring the country in every direction about Waynesboro, Greencastle, Mercersburg [and] Finkstown for horses and cattle and Negroes."[360]

Wagons left Chambersburg with thirty to forty black women and children, heading for Virginia under the control of a Confederate chaplain and four soldiers. A group of local whites, led by the owner of a local inn, stopped the wagons, disarmed the soldiers, took them prisoner, and set the women and children free. The Greencastle residents decided that they risked the destruction of their town if they did not release the soldiers, and so they did so. But the chaplain demanded fifty thousand dollars to pay for the loss of the people he claimed as his slaves. Though he lowered his demands by half, the townspeople still did not have that much money. After threatening to return and burn the town, the chaplain left. A local reporter met thirteen of the captured African Americans voluntarily returning to Greencastle after they had heard of the threatened burning. They were going to turn themselves over to prevent retaliation against their friends but were delighted to hear that the man who claimed to own them had departed.[361]

On June 17, Rachel Cormany "thought the Reb's had left—but they are still here. All forenoon they were carrying away mens clothing & darkeys." She stood in the window with her baby watching the Confederates. "Some of the officers tipped their hats to us I answered it with a curl of the lip. I knew they did it to taunt us. The one after he had tipped his hat most graciously & received in answer a toss of the head & curl of the lip took a good laugh over it." She could not help noting that "there were a few real inteligent good looking men among them. What a pity that they are rebels." Rumor came that Union soldiers were on the way, and the Southerners fled. "Among the last to leave were some with darkeys on their horses behind them. How glad we are they are gone—None of our Soldiers came."[362]

Out in the countryside, where officers were scarce and soldiers could do as they please, farmers felt the brunt of the invasion. Michael Hege wrote an account of his experiences in German, "not wanting to make for myself a name or an honor, only to tell what happened." The poem told of a harrowing encounter:

It was a nice morning, but we were fearful and afraid of what would happen that day, and who would be able to keep his life.

It was between eight and nine when three rebels came to the house. They asked, with a curse, for our money and I gave them the book right away.

After he had emptied it out he gave it, flattened, back to me. Then they said more to me: "Open the door and we won't break it down."

One of them roughly took my wife and children right away, at gunpoint, and set them along the wall.

They were mute with fear, not knowing at what moment they would all be shot, and when their lives would end.

So that my family would not help me, as they would have liked, they took me into the bedroom. I went trembling, fear and lamentation.

I opened up the chest. They took the money and cursed me that there wasn't more. They asked me where the rest was.

I took them into another room. Then it was more lamentation. They set down their guns and began to hunt for it.

I sat on the bed because fear had overtaken me. After I had opened the chest one of them sat down in front of me.

They dug through my papers to see if I had hidden anything in them, such as bonds and money. That was what he wanted.

The one to my left took the clothes from the wall, then he grabbed his gun again and hurried back to the bed.

He said, not joking, to me: "You shall die now!" He aimed at me and put his hand on the trigger.

Holding the gun to my side, everything was ready. Only one step. Only a hair between death and life.

I turned my head, not wanting to see him fire. I closed my eyes and thought, "This is it."

Then I pled to the Lord Sebaoth in my need, and as soon as I had prayed he let me go.

One of them sprang to his feet and said, "Don't shoot." He jumped between me and the gun. He did it very suddenly.

Then they let me go again, and when I turned I found myself all alone. My murderers were gone.

I felt like I had never felt before in my life. It was as if I were dreaming, but I was sitting on the bed.

Then I quick got up to see about my wife and children. I discovered them all free as well.

Nothing had been done to them. The murderers were gone. It was an hour that cannot be described.[363]

The proximity of the border made itself felt in other ways. Rachel Cormany was visiting a neighbor when a young Confederate came up and introduced himself as a relative. "He was raised here—His mother is burried here." The neighbor "told him he ought to go & kneel on his Mothers grave & ask for pardo[n] for having fought in such a bad cause. against such a good Government." The Rebel, whose brother was also fighting for the South, tried to explain himself. "Tears almost came, he said he could not well help getting in, but he would not fight in Pa. he told his officers so, he was placed under arrest awhile but was released again. Now he said he is compelled to carry a gun & that is as far as they will get toward making him fight." His conversion did not seem complete to Rachel, for he says "Jackson was a christian & means it honestly & earnestly." She doubted any real Christian could fight for the Confederacy.[364]

Moments of tenderness mixed with the disdain. After a day in which the Rebels pulled up crossties on the railroad and prepared to burn warehouses, Rachel observed, "Quite a number of the young folks were in the parlor this evening singing all the patriotic & popular war songs. Quite a squad of rebels gathered outside to listen & seemed much pleased with the music—'When this cruel war is over' nearly brought tears from some.

they sent in a petition to have it sung again which was done. they then thanked the girls very much & left—they acted real nicely."[365]

The Confederates stayed day after day, their purposes unclear. But on the twenty-seventh, Rachel noted, thousands more suddenly arrived. "A body would think the whole south had broke loose & are coming into Pa." She saw between thirty and forty pieces of cannon and "an almost endless trail of waggons. While I am writing thousands are passing—such a rough dirty ragged rowdyish set one does not often see—Gen's Lee & Longstreet passed through today. It makes me feel too badly to see so many men & cannon going through knowing that they have come to kill our men." Rachel, like other Northerners, thought the invasion might be for the best. "Many think this the best thing in the wor[l]d to bring the war to close—I hope our men will be strong enough to completely whip them—Now it is on our side." For years soldiers like her Samuel had been fighting "in the enemys country & citizens kept the rebels posted in our army movements—now they are in the enemys country. Scarcely any are willing to give them anything—in fact none give unless the have to except perhaps the Copperheads."[366]

"The great preponderating impression" made by the Confederates, Jacob Hoke thought, "was its *immenseness*. No idea of its magnitude can be formed by any description which can be given." If the army, artillery, wagon trains, ambulances, and the rest "had all been placed in a line in usual marching order, it would have extended nearly from Chambersburg to Harrisburg—fifty miles." He saw one wagon train fourteen miles long and another twenty-five miles long. "Like a huge serpent, it slowly and cautiously made its way into our State, turning its head now in one direction and then in another. . . ."[367]

Alexander McClure raced from Chambersburg to Philadelphia to help organize troops to defend his state. Desperate, he wrote President Lincoln a telegram pleading for help. "Our people are paralyzed for want of confidence & leadership & unless they can be inspired with hope we shall fail to do anything worthy of our State or Govt." McClure's suggestion for leadership could not have been pleasing to Lincoln: "I am fully persuaded that to call McClellan to a command here would be the best thing that could be done." George McClellan had long lost the confidence of Abraham Lincoln but not of the people of the border, McClure thought. "Unless we are in some way rescued from the hopelessness now prevailing we shall have practically an inefficient conscription & be powerless to help either ourselves or the National Govt." The facts were simple: "Without military success we can have no political success."[368]

Lincoln rejected McClure's plea, arguing that reappointing McClellan would be like "opening one leak to stop another." But McClure would not give up. The next day, July 1, he told Lincoln that McClellan "would be earnestly sustained by thousands of loyal men in the Democratic ranks who are poisoned against the government." Moreover, should the unthinkable happen and Pennsylvania be lost to the invading Rebels, the Democrats would have their "just share of responsibility in defending our State & sustaining the government. If then disaster should be the issue of battle between Lee & Meade, instead of revolution threatening us with anarchy," all would share the blame. McClure knew that some members of Lincoln's cabinet hated McClellan, but those men were not on the border. The simple fact was that "with the shadow of disaster growing still heavier" under the series of failed generals the Union had put forward, "the people sympathize with our exiled generals." Despite his plea, McClure recognized that the moment had passed, if it had ever existed. The Union would have to fight with the men it had and take the consequences. The battle could not be far away.[369]

Even after most of the Confederates had moved through Franklin, some desperate outfits still arrived. The men of General John Imboden came into Pennsylvania in their usual way, as foragers, guerrillas, and avengers. A band of Imboden men swept across the Mason-Dixon Line into the counties around Franklin, leaving with nearly a thousand head of livestock. They came to Jacob Stouffer's mill and "took, or stole, all the corn the others had left me," Stouffer wrote with disgust in his diary. "They took all the bags they could find—emptying flour, feed, and chop from the bags and taking the bags along—carrying the oats and corn off on their horses, what they did not waste and feed on the ground." Imboden's men had been guarding the rear and flank of the great invasion; by the time they arrived, they found almost none of the fabled riches of Pennsylvania. "They were hungry and troublesome—wanted bread, milk, butter, and almost anything when these were gone." After climbing through the "corn in the crib and over the wagon shed, and at the hay in my barn and mill stable, they camped for the night, using Stouffer's "two timothy fields and 2 clover fields—30 acres—as camp and pasture." They broke into beehives and the springhouse.[370]

Philip Schaff wanted to know what sort of person the famous partisan ranger, the famous guerrilla, Imboden was. The professor got his chance when the "large, commanding, and handsome officer" told the people of Mercersburg what drove him as he led the most destructive force in Lee's army. "You have only a little taste of what you have done to our people in the South," Imboden told the Northerners. "Your army destroyed all the fences, burnt towns, turned poor women out of house and home, broke pianos, furniture, old family pictures, and committed every act of vandalism. I thank God that the hour has come when this war will be fought on Pennsylvania soil." Schaff noted that every Southern soldier with whom he spoke "has his tale of outrage committed by our soldiers upon their homes and friends in Virginia and elsewhere. Some of our soldiers admit it, and our own newspaper reports unfortunately confirm it. If this charge is true, I must confess that we deserve punishment in the North." Imboden went further than most in his longing for vengeance, saying that "if he had the power he would burn every town and lay waste every farm in Pennsylvania."[371]

Rather than burn the towns of Franklin, John Imboden stripped them of all he could. He presented a long list of items for the people of Mercersburg to gather for his men: 5,000 pounds of bacon, 20 barrels of flour, 2 barrels of molasses, 2 barrels of sugar, 2 sacks of salt, and 150 pairs of shoes. As men gathered these items, a Confederate messenger rode into town "on a dead run," bearing a message from General Robert E. Lee to John Imboden. After quickly reading the message, the partisan leader commanded his men to march immediately. They left the piles of provisions gathered by the citizens in the middle of the street.[372] The Confederates were heading to a nearby town, a town of the border, Gettysburg. "Somewhere near there is a heavy engagement," William Heyser had heard.[373]

The outcome of the Civil War remained profoundly uncertain as the Confederates threw themselves into the culminating battle of the great invasion. It seemed to many in both the North and the South that the Confederacy might tri-

umph in the looming struggle, might occupy the capitals of Pennsylvania and the United States, might win the recognition and support of England or France to establish the dominion of the new nation across a large part of North America.

The people of Augusta and Franklin had paid enormous costs by the middle of 1863. Beyond all the sadness, dislocation, and economic hardship lay the service of men who might lose their lives any day. Augusta had sent 2,761 men to the Confederacy by the time of Gettysburg; Franklin had sent exactly 100 fewer, out of a white population twice as large. Augusta had put over 75 percent of all the white men in the county between the ages of eighteen and forty-five into the service, and Franklin had mobilized 40 percent of its eligible male population in the first two years of the war.

In one hard battle after another from First Bull Run to Second Bull Run, Augusta had seen 619 men wounded; in fewer but costly battles such as Fredericksburg and Chancellorsville, Franklin had 143 men wounded. Some of those wounded men died or went home forever disabled or psychologically shattered; others returned to the ranks, often to be captured or wounded yet again or killed in battle.

In the two years of fighting before Gettysburg, Augusta saw 106 men killed in action, Franklin 25. The bodies of some were sent back home to be grieved over and buried in church or family graveyards. Others were among the thousands thrown into trenches, naked, and barely covered with frozen soil, or left for the hogs that wandered the battlefields, or burned to death in woods, frantically pushing aside brush with their last energies.

Even more men died of diseases than died in action. Of Augusta's soldiers, 149 were killed by the illnesses that attacked them in the iron cold of the mountains or the melting heat of the Tidewater. Of Franklin's soldiers, 69 died from disease they contracted while sitting in the muck of the Peninsula or shivering along the Rappahannock. In an especially cruel calculus, the young tended to die from disease more often than the older men among whom they fought, prey to diseases such as mumps or chicken pox they missed when they were children a few years before. In addition, about 200 Augusta men had been captured, compared with 42 from Franklin. Capture did not yet carry the terror it would later, for prisoner exchanges were still common before Gettysburg.

Altogether, the casualties in the first two years of totaled 1,074 for Augusta County. About 4 of 10 men who went to the Confederacy suffered capture or injury, wound, or disease serious enough to be recorded and preserved in the scat-

tered records of the would-be nation. The Franklin numbers were less daunting only by comparison: In the months of war before Gettysburg, 359 men—over 13 percent of those who enlisted—were killed, wounded, captured, or died of disease. To gauge what these losses meant to their communities, multiply these numbers by 4 or 5, the average size of families in the Valley, and calculate their costs to widows and orphans, to bereaved parents and siblings.

The poor, as in all wars, suffered disproportionately in both Augusta and Franklin. They sent a larger percentage of their boys and men to the army, and their families had less money, food, and resources to fall back on when they did so. Poorer soldiers especially resented the speculators and malingerers who profited from their families' vulnerability, the militiamen who stayed home and the conscription officers who enforced quotas, the rich who bought substitutes and won exemptions.

Despite these inequalities, both counties had demonstrated more unity than division by the middle of 1863. They mobilized rapidly and thoroughly. Many wealthy men enlisted, and many died. The rates of desertion, while certainly significant and troubling at times, were not remarkably high, considering how close to home men fought, how many hardships they suffered, and how many battles they were thrown into. More officers than enlisted men were killed, for officers often stood before the ranks, leading men into battle on foot or on horseback, carrying flags and waving swords in the full view of the enemy.

African Americans too demonstrated remarkable support for the war effort in Franklin and throughout the North, especially as the Northern purpose began to turn against slavery. Black men enlisted at a speed and with a spirit that surprised their white neighbors. The forty-nine Franklin County African Americans who signed up at the first opportunity in 1863 foreshadowed a massive enlistment of black men throughout the United States over the next two years.

The aspirations and strategies of black people in Augusta were much less obvious from the written record, for as always, the white people of the county did not like to acknowledge any problems with slavery or enslaved people. Slave prices remained high, and markets in the hiring and purchasing of slaves remained active. The number of runaways did seem to grow, but trying to escape when the Valley was filled with tens of thousands of Confederate soldiers eager to capture runaways was as daunting as in peacetime. Augusta masters were fortunate that the U.S. Army did not come any closer than it did, for everywhere in Virginia and the South slaves risked everything to escape when they knew the haven of the Northern army awaited.

Women in Augusta and Franklin proved ardent patriots in the first two years of the war. To judge from their letters and diaries, from their service as nurses and seamstresses, and from their actions when confronting the enemy, women saw themselves as crucial parts of their nations' military struggle. They showed little evidence of halfheartedness. If anything, they may have been even more vociferous than their male relatives or neighbors in their hatred of the enemy.

Up to the middle of 1863 the North had managed to channel the bitter partisan warfare of party, ethnicity, class, and locale that threatened to end the war. The South had managed to hold slavery in place everywhere the U.S. Army had not reached, and slaves continued to produce essential food and supplies for the Confederates in the field. But both sides realized the potential for division and explosion from these sources. Abraham Lincoln knew that without victories on the battlefield he was likely to be turned out of office in the election of the following year. White Southerners knew that slaves used every opportunity to escape slavery, risking their lives to gain any kind of freedom. Both sides realized that poor men and women would decide at some point that they had given enough. Both sides raced to seize victory before these weaknesses overwhelmed them.

The coming and fighting of the Civil War had demonstrated the overwhelming power of nationalism, even a new nationalism, to define people's understanding of themselves. It demonstrated the ability of war and violence to recast identities, to submerge the self in the thrill of tribal belonging. It demonstrated that events could fundamentally change deep structures of interest and belief. War turned out not merely to be policy by other means, but a force all its own, carrying people to places otherwise impossible and unimaginable.

In the middle of 1863, though they would not have believed it, the people of Augusta and Franklin had not yet confronted the most dramatic events that the war would bring. The outcome of the fighting would remain undecided for incomprehensibly vast battles yet to come, for hundreds of thousands of lives yet to be lost. Slavery, the great engine of power and suffering that drove the war, would continue to turn.

CODA

WHAT CAN THE EXPERIENCES of two counties tell us about the vast American Civil War? Some things were obviously unique to these places. There was only one Jed Hotchkiss, mapmaker for Stonewall Jackson and Robert E. Lee. There was only one Alexander K. McClure, confidant of Abraham Lincoln and architect of Republican ascendancy on the border. There was only one raid by John Brown and only one Great Invasion by the Confederates, one Stonewall Brigade and one final charge on Marye's Heights.

In Augusta, however, Maria Perkins faced being sold away from her child just as millions of enslaved people faced separation. Just at Alexander H. H. Stuart pleaded for Union on the very day Virginia seceded, thousands of Unionists swallowed their principles for the new Confederacy. Just as John Imboden raged at the head of his partisan rangers, thousands of loving fathers and civic-minded leaders became vengeful soldiers. Just as the *Staunton Spectator* lowered the American flag, formerly Unionist papers throughout the upper South became staunch supporters of the Confederacy. Will Baylor's death at Second Manassas may have been better noted than most of the 620,000 deaths on the battlefields and in the hospitals of the Civil War, but his wife and child missed him no less for all the glory.

On the other side of the Mason-Dixon line, David Demus enlisted in the 54th Regiment of Massachusetts Volunteer Infantry just as 180,000 black men would enlist for the Union. Rachel Cormany waited at home along with millions of women who participated in the war at a physical remove but with a passionate engagement. The *Valley Spirit* sneered at black Americans and Republicans just as Democratic newspapers throughout the North criticized Abraham Lincoln and African Americans. The *Repository and Transcript*, like other Republican papers, helped redefine the purpose of the war in the face of setback and disaster.

While every American and Confederate county experienced the war in its unique way, they all knew the same faiths, fury, anxiety, regret, self-righteousness, and uncertainty. People across the North and South explained the war to themselves much as the people of Augusta and Franklin did, for proximity to the border did not mute passion and conviction. Augusta proved itself as committed to slavery and the Confederacy as any county in the deep South. Franklin supplied more Republican voters and leaders, and more white and African American troops, than many counties in New England.

If Augusta and Franklin stood out, it was because they so fully experienced the fundamental transformations of the Civil War. More rapidly than in most places in the Confederacy, Augusta converted itself from a proud member of the Union to a proud member of the Confederacy. More than most places in the North, Franklin moved from sympathy with the South to hatred of their former friends. Earlier than most Southern counties, Augusta learned what it was to live with war, with the relentless hunger of its own troops and with bodies stacked on its sidewalks. Franklin knew more than many other Northern counties what it was to live in the presence of its enemies and to see its African American population rise to fight against slavery.

Together, the stories of Augusta and Franklin tell of a war both simpler and less straightforward than general accounts reveal. The Civil War was like all wars in that it elevated the worst human emotions and called them virtues. People let themselves be driven by arrogance and revenge as well as by ideology and principle. People watched themselves descend into rage and numbness, knowing themselves unworthy of their feelings. People invoked the Constitution and Declaration of Independence against enemies invoking the same icons. People enlisted God in their cause and anxiously awaited signs of His approval for the blood they shed.

At its core, the Civil War grew from a struggle over the meanings of black slavery for white Americans. But that struggle came wrapped in layers of evasion, symbolism, and calculation. It continually changed form.

Confederates used language and ideals other than the mere defense of slavery to justify their abandonment of the United States, but they ultimately allowed black slavery to stand as the measure of all their political rights. They persuaded themselves that they must secede to protect not only slavery itself but also white property, autonomy, equality, and respect. Without this rationale, white men of all classes and of all parts of the South would not have given their lives for the new Confederacy. But without slavery the rationale would not have been invoked in the first place.

The white North, for its part, did not go to war to destroy slavery. Democrat and Republican alike fought to deny the right of the South to leave the Union, though the majority of Northern whites thought that abolishing slavery neither possible nor desirable. White Northerners fought incessantly over the meaning of slavery even as they waged a war against the slave South. Emancipation grew from the demands and opportunities of war, from African Americans' words and acts, from insistent efforts by the radical Republicans in Washington, and from Lincoln's tortured and lonely leadership, not from an imperative outside the deep contingency of history.

The military events of the Civil War redefined the societies that waged them. Battlefield and home front, political decision and military strategy bled together. Lincoln openly made political decisions for military reasons and vice versa, all the time mindful of the large numbers of dissenters and doubters in the North. Robert E. Lee too moved his army according to calculations of the effect on the home front and on his soldiers' morale as well as for military advantage. Hungry for a fuller understanding of enemy and ally alike, both men eagerly read the newspapers. They knew military success was contingent on people far removed from the battlefield.

It eventually became clear that the Union could not be saved without the aid of black Americans North and South. With that recognition of need, whites in the North finally began to imagine a South where black Southerners would live as a free people, as a people who had helped save the Union, who helped win the cause for which whites had gone to war. In July 1863, however, as thousands of guns began to echo on the border, any such deliverance lay uncounted years and lives away.

NOTES

A Note on the Documentation

Each primary source for this book is identified so that it can be found in its original archival location. Usually those sources can also be examined in the Valley of the Shadow website at http://valley.vcdh.virginia.edu; in some cases, as when private individuals loaned us papers and images to include in the digital archive, those sources are available only on-line. Though I have attempted to write from primary sources available on-line whenever possible, I have also drawn quotations from a number of secondary accounts, which I gratefully acknowledge.

The literature on the American Civil War is rich in its mass, complexity, and pace of production. I have focused on the most relevant and recent works in the notes. Some of the generalizations that follow are based on statistical patterns presented in tables on the Valley of the Shadow website.

Manuscript Collections Consulted

Albert and Shirley Small Special Collections Library, University of Virginia, Charlottesville, Virginia

Augusta
- Blackford Family Letters
- Brand Family Letters
- Casper C. Branner Letters
- Nancy Emerson Diary
- Fackler Family Letters
- John Hartwell Cocke Papers
- John T. Blake Papers
- Joseph Addison Waddell Diary
- McCue Family Papers
- McGuffin Family Papers
- Michael G. Wise Papers

Smiley Family Papers
Stuart Family Papers
Thrift Family Papers

Franklin
Henry A. Bitner Letters

Archives and Special Collections, Waidner and Spahr Library, Dickinson College, Carlisle, Pennsylvania

Franklin
John Andrew Jackson Creswell Collection
Slifer-Dill Collection
Thomas Creigh Collection

Augusta County Historical Society, Staunton, Virginia

Augusta
Garber Family Letters

Berkeley County Historical Society

Franklin
Robert P. Bryarly

Fredericksburg and Spotsylvania National Battlefield Park, Fredericksburg, Virginia

Augusta
A. H. Byars Letters
A. W. Kersh Letters
James Cadwallander Diary
James E. Beard Diary
James H. Skinner Letter
P. H. Powers Letters

Gilder Lehrman, Pierpont Morgan Library, New York, New York

Augusta
Sue Carter Letters

Historical Society of Dauphin County, Harrisburg, Pennsylvania

Franklin
Simon Cameron Papers

Kittochtinny Historical Society, Chambersburg, Pennsylvania

Franklin

Abraham Essick Diary

William Heyser Diary

George C. Traxler Papers

Library of Congress, Manuscripts Division, Washington, D.C.

Abraham Lincoln Papers

Augusta

Jedediah Hotchkiss Papers

Franklin

Alexander K. McClure Papers

Edward McPherson Papers

Simon Cameron Papers

Thaddeus Stevens Papers

National Archives and Records Administration, Washington, D.C.

Franklin

Compiled Military Service Records for the Civil War, RG 94

Pension Files, RG 15

Pennsylvania Historical and Museum Commission, Harrisburg, Pennsylvania

Franklin

Bloss Family Collection

Christian Geisel Collection

John Taggart Papers

Franklin County Wills

David D. Hougham Papers

Nathaniel Dunn Papers

Potter Family Papers

Personal Papers Collection, Library of Virginia, Richmond, Virginia

Augusta

Evans-Sibert Family Papers

Southern Historical Collection, Wilson Library, University of North Carolina at Chapel Hill

Augusta

Achilles J. Tynes Papers

Hubard Family Letters
Marguerite E. Williams Papers

Franklin
David Hafer Letter in the Federal Soldiers Letters

Special Collections Department, William R. Perkins Library, Duke University, Durham, North Carolina

Augusta
Edward Flood Papers
Eli Long Papers
Houser Family Letters
John Jarrett Papers
Lauramann Howe Russell Papers
Marshall Clayton Stoner Papers
Matthew Pilson Papers

Special Collections, James G. Leyburn Library, Washington and Lee University, Lexington, Virginia

Augusta
John P. Dull Letters
James B. McCutchan Papers
Michael Reid Hanger Diary
Rockbridge Historical Society Collection

Special Collections, Virginia Polytechnic Institute and State University, Blacksburg, Virginia

Augusta
A. M. Chacky Letter
Cochran Family Letters
Harvey Bear Diary
John N. Hull Letter
John N. Snider Letter
William S. H. Baylor Letters

State Historical Society of Wisconsin Archives, Madison, Wisconsin

Augusta
William Smiley Papers

Sterling Memorial Library, Yale University, New Haven, Connecticut

Augusta
Maria Perkins Letter

Stuart Hall Alumnae Association, Staunton, Virginia

Augusta
Sarah Cordelia Wright Diary

U.S. Army Military History Institute, Carlisle Barracks, Pennsylvania

Franklin
Civil War Miscellaneous Collection
Alvin H. Alexander Papers
David Wagner Papers
Foster Family Papers
Franklin Rankin Papers
James Carman Papers
Lucius P. Mox Papers
Reynolds Laughlin Papers
Samuel W. North Papers
Samuel Z. Maxwell Papers
Sylvester McElheney Papers

Harrisburg Civil War Round Table Collection
Henry C. Metzger Papers
John and Samuel Hamer Papers
Peter Boyer Papers

Ronald D. Boyer Collection
Henry M. Erisman Papers
Jonah Yoder Papers

Virginia Military Institute Archives, Lexington, Virginia

Augusta
Henry H. Dedrick Papers
Jacob Kent Langhorne Papers
Michael G. Harman Papers

Waynesboro Public Library, Waynesboro, Pennsylvania

Franklin
William B. Gallaher Letters

York County Heritage Trust, York, Pennsylvania

Franklin
Miller Family Papers

Private Collections

Augusta
- Andrew Brooks Diary
- Downman Family Papers
- James Poage Papers
- Nelly Clayton Letter
- Wilson Family Letters

Franklin
- Anna Mellinger Diary
- Stouffer Family Papers

Published Documents

Augusta

Gallaher, DeWitt Clinton. *A Diary Depicting the Experiences of DeWitt Clinton Gallaher in the War between the States while Serving in the Confederate Army.* (Waynesboro, Va: Reorganized Co. E, 1st Virginia Cavalry, 1961)

Miller, Joyce DeBolt, ed. *"Until Seperated by Death": Lives and Civil War Letters of Jesse Rolston, Jr., and Mary Catharine Cromer* (Bridgewater, Va.: Good Printers, Inc., 1994)

Perdue, Charles L., Jr., Thomas E. Barden, and Robert K. Phillips. *Weevils in the Wheat: Interviews with Virginia Ex-Slaves* (Bloomington: Indiana University Press, 1980)

Hildebrand, Jacob R., ed. *A Mennonite Journal, 1862–1865: A Father's Account of the Civil War in the Shenandoah Valley* (Shippensburg, Pa.: Burd Street Press, 1996)

Franklin

Mohr, James C., ed. *The Cormany Diaries: A Northern Family in the Civil War* (Pittsburgh: University of Pittsburgh Press, 1982)

Preface

1 I discuss these issues at some length in an essay, "Worrying about the Civil War," in Karen Halttunen and Lewis Perry, eds., *Moral Problems in American Life: New Perspectives on Cultural History* (Cornell University Press, 1999).

Part One: Green Pastures and Still Waters

1 *Staunton Vindicator*, July 8, 1859, p. 2, column 2.

2 *Staunton Vindicator*, July 15, 1859, p. 2, column 4.

3 Letter by Governor Henry Wise, dated June, 30, 1859, reprinted in the *Staunton Vindicator*, July 15, 1859, p. 2, column 4.

4 *Franklin Repository and Transcript*, July 6, 1859, p. 4, column 5.

5 *Valley Spirit*, July 20, 1859, p. 5, column 2.

6 Ibid.

7 *Valley Spirit*, August 24, 1859, p. 5, column 2.

8 Ibid.

9 Congressman Owen Lovejoy, quoted in the *Franklin Repository and Transcript*, April 20, 1859, p. 5, column 2.

10 *Franklin Repository and Transcript*, August 24, 1859, p. 5, column 3.

11 Ibid.

12 *Valley Spirit*, August 31, 1859, p. 5, column 2.

13 Frederick Douglass, *Life and Times of Frederick Douglass* (London: Christian Age, 1882), p. 276.

14 *Franklin Repository and Transcript*, August 24, 1859, p. 5, column 2.

15 Alexander K. McClure, *Old Time Notes of Pennsylvania* (Philadelphia: J. C. Winston Company, 1905), pp. 360–62.

16 Douglass's account of this episode, here and below, comes from his *Life and Times*, pp. 276–79.

17 Charles L. Blockson, *The Underground Railroad in Pennsylvania* (Jacksonville, N.C.: Flame International, 1981), pp. 142–44.

18 Quoted in James M. McPherson, *Ordeal by Fire: The Civil War and Reconstruction* (New York: Alfred A. Knopf, 1982), p. 114. For an introduction to the role of religion in both the North and the South during this era, see Randall M. Miller, Harry S. Stout, and Charles Reagan Wilson, eds., *Religion and the American Civil War* (New York: Oxford University Press, 1998), and Steven E. Woodworth, *While God Is Marching On: The Religious World of Civil War Soldiers* (Lawrence: University of Kansas Press, 2001).

19 *Staunton Spectator*, April 29, 1857, p. 2, column 2.

20 *Staunton Spectator*, May 29, 1860, p. 2, column 1. For a helpful overview of the Valley of Virginia, see Kenneth E. Koons and Warren R. Hofstra, eds., *After the Backcountry: Rural Life in the Great Valley of Virginia, 1800–1900* (Knoxville: University of Tennessee Press, 2000). Most directly useful is the essay by J. Susanne Simmons and Nancy T. Sorrells on the centrality of slave hiring in Augusta County; suggestive are the essays on other places by Ellen Eslinger on free blacks in Rockbridge, Kenneth

Koons on wheat, Stephen Longenecker on antislavery, and Michael J. Gorman on politics in Frederick County.

21 *Staunton Vindicator*, September 28, 1860, p. 2, column 5.

22 Register of Free Blacks, Augusta County, Listing No. 467, June 27, 1859.

23 *Staunton Spectator*, December 6, 1859, p. 2, column 1.

24 *Staunton Spectator*, September 13, 1859, p. 4, column 4.

25 *Staunton Vindicator*, November 16, 1860, p. 2, column 1.

26 Letter from Maria Perkins to Robert Perkins, October 8, 1852, Yale University.

27 Melinda ("Roty") Ruffin, WPA Slave Narratives, quoted in Charles L. Perdue, Jr., Thomas Borden, and Robert K. Phillips, *Weevils in the Wheat: Interviews with Virginia Ex-Slaves* (Bloomington: Indiana University Press, 1980), pp. 243–44.

28 Mrs. Mary E. ———wsey, WPA Slave Narratives, ibid., p. 346.

29 Letter from John D. Imboden to John McCue, September 26, 1859, McCue Family Papers, University of Virginia.

30 Letter from John D. Imboden to John McCue, July 22, 1859.

31 Diary of Joseph Waddell, entry dated October 15, 1856, Joseph Addison Waddell Diary, University of Virginia.

32 Ibid.

33 Letter from Lydia Hotchkiss to Jedediah Hotchkiss, December 13, 1859, Library of Congress.

34 Memoir of Alansa Rounds Sterrett, undated, summer 1859.

35 *Staunton Vindicator*, July 22, 1859, p. 2, column 1.

36 *Staunton Spectator*, September 13, 1859, p. 1, column 6.

37 Ibid.

38 Some historians have argued that North and South were fundamentally alike: capitalist, racist, democratic for whites, largely Christian, largely British in culture. Other historians have argued that the regions were fundamentally different: capitalist, democratic, and modern in the North and anticapitalist, undemocratic, and antimodern in the South, even of different British ethnicities.

Readers who would like to orient themselves in the ongoing scholarly discussion may trace its outlines in Edward Pessen, "How Different from Each Other Were the Antebellum North and South?," *American Historical Review*, vol. 85 (1980), pp. 1119–49, and the discussion that follows and in Drew Gilpin Faust, "The Peculiar South Revisited: White Society, Culture, and Politics in the Antebellum Period, 1800–1860," *Interpreting Southern History: Historiographical Essays in Honor of Sanford W. Higginbotham*, ed. John B. Boles and Evelyn Thomas Nolen (Baton Rouge: Louisiana State University Press, 1987), pp. 78–120.

One reason I have focused on the border is to see more clearly the differences slavery made. Several books have suggested the importance of the border for understanding the Civil War. D. W. Meinig, *The Shaping of America*, vol. 2, *Continental America, 1800–1867* (New Haven: Yale University Press, 1993), pp. 475–89, emphasizes the "complicated geopolitical structure" along the border. Kevin Phillips, *The Cousins' War: Religion, Politics, and the Triumph of Anglo-America* (New York: Basic Books, 1999) also emphasizes the scale and importance of the border. William Freehling, in *The South vs. the South: How Anti-Confederate Southerners Shaped the Course of the Civil War* (New York: Oxford University Press, 2001), argues that the upper South did not fully share in the devotion to slavery evinced in the lower South. While the upper South did take a more circuitous path to secession, I believe it did so as another route to preserve slavery.

39 Diary of Reverend Abraham Essick, June 6, 1857, Kittochtinny Historical Society.

40 *Staunton Spectator*, October 18, 1859, p. 2, column 1.

41 Ibid.

42 *Staunton Spectator*, November 22, 1859, p. 2, column 4.

43 *Staunton Spectator*, December 6, 1859, p. 2, column 1.

44 *Staunton Spectator*, November 29, 1859, p. 2, column 4.

45 Ibid.

46 Robert J. Driver, *The Staunton Artillery—McClanahan's Battery* (Lynchburg, Va.: H. E. Howard, 1988), p. 1.

47 *Staunton Spectator*, November 1, 1859, p. 2, column 1.

48 *Staunton Spectator*, December 13, 1859, p. 3, column 1.

49 McClure, *Old Time Notes of Pennsylvania*, pp. 32–33, from which the following account comes.

50 *Valley Spirit*, November 2, 1859, p. 4, column 2.

51 *Valley Spirit*, October 26, 1859, p. 5, column 1.

52 *Valley Spirit*, November 2, 1859, p. 2, column 2.

53 *Franklin Repository and Transcript*, November 2, 1859, p. 8, column 1.

54 The literature on the politics of sectionalism and the coming of the Civil War is one of the most highly developed fields in U.S. history. An excellent overview and sampling of the evolution of that field can be followed in Michael Perman, ed., *The Coming of the American Civil War*, 3d ed. (Lexington, Mass.: D. C. Heath, 1993). As in the debate over regional distinctiveness, scholars have divided into schools. One group emphasizes intrinsic economic and cultural conflict and the projection of that conflict through ideology and a politics built around that ideology. Leading exponents of this view are Eric Foner's *Free Soil, Free Labor, Free Men: The Ideology of the Republican Party before the Civil War* (Oxford: Oxford University Press, 1970), Eugene Genovese's *The Political Economy of Slavery* (New York: Pantheon, 1965), and James McPherson's *Battle Cry of Freedom: The Civil War Era* (New York: Oxford University Press, 1988).

Other historians take the opposite view, emphasizing the complexity and relative autonomy of the American political system, its internal drives, divisions, and personalities. In the eyes of these historians, the twists and turns of the 1850s can be understood only by understanding the political system itself, which was not merely a reflection of social divisions. The leading exponent of this view is Michael F. Holt. See his *The Political Crisis of the 1850s* (New York: W. W. Norton, 1992) and *The Rise and Fall of the American Whig Party: Jacksonian Politics and the Onset of the Civil War* (Oxford: Oxford University Press, 1999).

Other historians have emphasized the interaction between social relations and political history. Models of this reflexive model are William Gienapp, *Origins of the Republican Party, 1852–1856* (New York: Oxford University Press, 1986), Daniel W. Crofts, *Reluctant Confederates: Upper South Unionists in the Secessionist Crisis* (Chapel Hill: University of North Carolina Press, 1993), and William G. Shade, *Democratizing the Old Dominion: Virginia and the Second Party System, 1824–1861* (Charlottesville:

University Press of Virginia, 1996). These books show the complex role politics played in the mid-nineteenth-century United States.

My own interpretation tries to take the contextualization of politics to an even more specific level, measuring not aggregate statistical tendencies but the behavior of individuals on the county level. Other examples of this approach are Daniel W. Crofts, *Old Southampton: Politics and Society in a Virginia County, 1834–1869* (Charlottesville: University Press of Virginia, 1992) and Paul Bourke and Donald Debats, *Washington County: Politics and Community in Antebellum America* (Baltimore and London: Johns Hopkins University Press, 1995). Such studies, including this one, show there was no easy correlation between individual attributes and political behavior, either in the North or in the South. This finding leads me to emphasize the interaction between relatively stable local identities and a swirling context at the state and national levels. Political loyalties and decisions came at the intersection of these various levels of political behavior. Only a dynamic model that pays close attention to language as well as voters' and counties' material characteristics, to interaction over time, to institutional boundaries and pressures, and to events and passions can account for the political behavior that brought on the Civil War. Politics was neither a passive reflection of a general ideology nor a self-contained system.

While his work did not descend to such empirical efforts, David M. Potter, more than any other scholar, has influenced my approach. His essay "The Historian's Use of Nationalism and Vice Versa," in his *The South and the Sectional Conflict* (Baton Rouge: Louisiana State University Press, 1968), pp. 34–83, helps us set aside the easy assumptions we often make about the way the Civil War evolved.

55 A recent book argues that the role of politics in this era has been exaggerated, and it is true that many men seemed relatively disengaged from the daily workings of the system, though turnout remained impressively high on election day. See Glenn C. Altschuler and Stuart M. Blumin, *Rude Republic: Americans and Their Politics in the Nineteenth Century* (Princeton: Princeton University Press, 2000).

56 The essential work on this subject is that of Michael Holt, cited above.

57 *Staunton Vindicator*, February 19, 1859, p. 2, column 3.

58 Diary of Joseph Waddell, entry dated May 27, 1858.

59 On the Republicans, see Foner and Gienapp from above. Also useful is Robert William Fogel, *Without Consent or Contract: The Rise and Fall of American Slavery* (New York: W. W. Norton, 1989).

60 See Foner and Fogel, cited above.

61 *Franklin Repository and Transcript*, March 7, 1860, p. 4, column 1.

62 Ibid., column 2.

63 Alexander Farish Robertson, *Alexander Hugh Holmes Stuart, 1807–1891: A Biography* (Richmond, Va.: William Byrd Press, 1925), pp. 176–77.

64 *Staunton Spectator*, May 17, 1859, p. 2, column 4.

65 *Staunton Vindicator*, May 14, 1859, p. 2, columns 3, 5, and 6.

66 *Staunton Spectator*, December 6, 1859, p. 2, column 1.

67 Ibid.

68 Letter from Lydia Maria Childs to Governor Henry Wise, October 26, 1859. Text as printed in the *Staunton Vindicator*, November 11, 1859, p. 2, column 4. The rest of this account is drawn from the exchange printed in this issue.

69 "Memorial to William Smith Hanger Baylor," by Bolivar Christian. This sketch

appeared first in *The Collegian*, of Lexington, Virginia; from an undated copy in Alderman Library, University of Virginia.

70 *Staunton Spectator*, December 13, 1859, p. 3. column 1. The remainder of this description comes from the same article.

71 *Staunton Vindicator*, December 16, 1859, p. 2, column 2.

72 *Staunton Spectator*, November 29, 1859, p. 2, column 2.

73 Diary of Joseph Waddell, entry dated November 9, 1859.

74 *Republican Vindicator*, January 13, 1860, p. 2, column, 1.

75 *Staunton Vindicator*, April 6, 1860, p. 2, column 4.

76 On John Brown, see the collection edited by Paul Finkelman, *His Soul Goes Marching On: Responses to John Brown and the Harpers Ferry Raid* (Charlottesville: University Press of Virginia, 1995).

77 The classic overview of this story is David Potter, *The Impending Crisis: 1848–1861* (New York: Harper & Row, 1976).

78 *Staunton Vindicator*, April 27, 1860, p. 2, column 2.

79 Ibid.

80 Ibid.

81 Ibid.

82 *Staunton Vindicator*, May 11, 1860, p. 2, column 4.

83 *Staunton Vindicator*, May 18, 1860, p. 2, column 6.

84 *Valley Spirit*, May 9, 1860, p. 4, column 3.

85 *Franklin Repository and Transcript*, May 16, 1860, p. 4, column 2.

86 *Franklin Repository and Transcript*, June 20, 1860, p. 3, column 1.

87 *Franklin Repository and Transcript*, July 11, 1860, p. 4, column 3.

88 Letter from Alexander K. McClure to Abraham Lincoln, June 16, 1860, Abraham Lincoln Papers, Library of Congress.

89 Letter from Alexander K. McClure to Abraham Lincoln, July 2, 1860.

90 *Valley Spirit*, May 16, 1860, p. 4, column 1.

91 Letter from Alexander K. McClure to Abraham Lincoln, August 21, 1860.

92 Letter from Alexander K. McClure to Abraham Lincoln, September 27, 1860.

93 Letter from Alexander K. McClure to Abraham Lincoln, October 19, 1860.

94 *Staunton Spectator*, July 17, 1860, p. 2, column 1.

95 Ibid., column 3.

96 Ibid.

97 Ibid., column 1.

98 *Staunton Vindicator*, July 20, 1860, p. 2, column 2.

99 *Staunton Vindicator*, September 7, 1860, p. 2, column 2.

100 Ibid.

101 *Staunton Vindicator*, October 5, 1860, p. 2, column 3.

102 Ibid.

103 *Staunton Spectator*, October 9, 1860, p. 2, column 1.

104 Ibid., column 2.

105 *Staunton Spectator*, October 23, 1860, p. 2, columns 2 and 3.

106 Ibid., column 4.

107 Letter from Lucas P. Thompson to John Howard McCue, November 1, 1860, McCue Family Papers, University of Virginia.

108 *Staunton Spectator*, November 6, 1860, p. 2, column 2.
109 Ibid.
110 *Staunton Vindicator*, November 2, 1860, p. 1, column 4.
111 *Staunton Spectator*, November 6, 1860, p. 2, column 2.
112 *Franklin Repository and Transcript*, September 5, 1860, p. 5, column 3.
113 *Franklin Repository and Transcript*, September 12, 1860, p. 4, column 1.
114 *Valley Spirit*, September 5, 1860, p. 2, column 1.
115 *Valley Spirit*, October 24, 1860, p. 2, column 4.
116 *Franklin Repository and Transcript*, September 19, 1860, p. 4, column 2.
117 *Franklin Repository and Transcript*, September 26, 1860, p. 4, column 4.
118 McClure, *Old Time Notes of Pennsylvania*, p. 427.
119 *Valley Spirit*, September 12, 1860, p. 4, column 1.
120 Ibid.
121 Ibid.
122 *Franklin Repository and Transcript*, August 8, 1860, p. 4, column 4.
123 *Valley Spirit*, April 11, 1860, p. 5, column 2.
124 *Valley Spirit*, August 8, 1860, p. 4, column 3.
125 Ibid.
126 *Franklin Repository and Transcript*, August 1, 1860, p. 4, column 3.
127 Tom M'Lell [illegible] to Edward McPherson, February 11, 1860, Edward McPherson Papers, Library of Congress.
128 *Franklin Repository and Transcript*, September 12, 1860, p. 4, column 1.
129 *Staunton Spectator*, November 6, 1860, p. 2, column 1.
130 Letter from Simon Cameron to Abraham Lincoln, August 1, 1860, Simon Cameron Papers, Library of Congress.
131 *Franklin Repository and Transcript*, November 14, 1860, p. 4, column, 3.
132 Fogel, *Without Consent or Contract*, pp. 382–86; Phillips, *The Cousins' Wars*, p. 417.
133 Fogel, *Without Consent or Contract*, p. 382.
134 McClure, *Old Time Notes of Pennsylvania*, pp. 385–86.
135 *Staunton Vindicator*, November 9, 1860, p. 2, column 6.
136 Ibid., column 2.
137 *Staunton Spectator*, November 13, 1860, p. 2, column 1.
138 *Staunton Vindicator*, November 9, 1860, p. 2, column 1.
139 Henry Thomas Shanks, *The Secession Movement in Virginia, 1847–1861* (Richmond, Va.: Garrett and Massie, 1934), pp. 121–23.
140 *Staunton Vindicator*, November 23, 1860, p. 2, column 2.
141 Ibid., column 4.
142 Letter from Alexander Rives to Alexander H. H. Stuart, November 20, 1860, Stuart Family Papers, University of Virginia.
143 Letter from John D. Imboden to John McCue, December 3, 1860.
144 The following paragraphs are based on ibid.
145 *Franklin Repository and Transcript*, November 14, 1860, p. 4, column 3.
146 *Franklin Repository and Transcript*, August 8, 1860, p. 4, column 3.
147 *Valley Spirit*, November 14, 1860, p. 4, column 1.

Part Two: Paths of Righteousness

1 The following account is drawn from the Memoir of Alansa Rounds Sterrett, undated entry, Fall 1860.

2 *Staunton Vindicator*, January 4, 1861, p. 1, column 3.

3 Memoir of Alansa Rounds Sterrett, undated entry, January 1861.

4 *Staunton Vindicator*, January 4, 1861, p 2, column 2.

5 Ibid., column 3.

6 Ibid., column 2.

7 Ibid., column 5.

8 *Staunton Spectator*, January 15, 1861, p. 2, column 1.

9 Letter from Alexander H. H. Stuart to Frances Stuart, undated, Stuart Family Papers, University of Virgnia.

10 Letter from Alexander H. H. Stuart to Frances Stuart, January 1861.

11 *Staunton Spectator*, January 22, 1861, p. 2, column 3. The following account is drawn from this article.

12 Letter from Alexander H. H. Stuart to Frances Stuart, undated.

13 *Staunton Spectator*, January 22, 1861, p. 1, column 5.

14 Ibid.

15 Letter from Casper Branner to his father, January 10, 1861, Casper C. Branner Letters, University of Virginia.

16 Letter from Andrew Brooks to his sister, January 23, 1861, private collection on the Valley of the Shadow website.

17 Letter from J. H. Cochran to his mother, January 26, 1861, Cochran Family Papers, Virginia Polytechnic Institute and State University.

18 *Staunton Vindicator*, January 18, 1861, p. 2, column 3; January 25, 1861, p. 2, column 3; *Staunton Spectator*, January 22, 1861, p. 1, column 6; p. 2, column 4.

19 *Staunton Vindicator*, January 25, 1861, p. 2, column 6.

20 *Staunton Vindicator*, January 18, 1861, p. 2, column 3.

21 Ibid., column 4.

22 Ibid., column 5.

23 *Staunton Vindicator*, January 25, 1861, p. 2, column 1.

24 *Staunton Spectator*, January 29, 1861, p. 2, column 3.

25 *Staunton Vindicator*, January 25, 1861, p. 2, column 3.

26 *Staunton Spectator*, January 29, 1861, p. 2, column 1.

27 Entry by Frank Sterrett in memoir of Alansa Rounds Sterrett, February 4, 1861.

28 *Staunton Vindicator*, February 8, 1861, p. 2, column 1.

29 Letter from John Imboden to Greenlee Davidson, February 15, 1861, quoted in Daniel Crofts, *Reluctant Confederates: Upper South Unionists in the Secessionist Crisis* (Chapel Hill: University of North Carolina Press, 1993), p. 154.

30 *Staunton Vindicator*, February 8, 1861, p. 2, column 1.

31 Crofts, *Reluctant Confederates,* p. 175.

32 *Staunton Spectator*, January 22, 1861, p. 1, column 3; *Valley Spirit*, February 27, 1861, p. 2, column 3.

33 Abraham Lincoln to John A. Gilmer, December 15, 1860, in Michael P. Johnson, ed.,

Abraham Lincoln, Slavery, and the Civil War: Selected Writings and Speeches (Boston: Bedford/St. Martin's, 2001), pp. 97–98.

34 Letter from Abraham Lincoln to William Seward, February 1, 1861, in ibid., pp. 101–2.

35 Speech by Abraham Lincoln, delivered in Cleveland, Ohio, February 15, 1861, in ibid., p. 106.

36 Abraham Lincoln to Lyman Trumbull, December 10, 1860, in ibid., p. 97.

37 *Richmond Dispatch*, February 9, 1861, quoted in Crofts, *Reluctant Confederates*, p. 153.

38 Letter from William Garvin to Simon Cameron, January 24, 1861, Simon Cameron Papers, Historical Society of Dauphin County, Harrisburg, Pennsylvania.

39 *Valley Spirit*, January 2, 1861, p. 4, column 4.

40 *Valley Spirit*, January 16, 1861, p. 4, column 2.

41 Address by J. McD. Sharpe to Franklin County Democrats, delivered February 13, 1861. Text printed in *Valley Spirit*, February 20, 1861, p. 4, column 1. The remainder of his quotations are drawn from this article.

42 Letter from John Berryhill to Simon Cameron, January 11, 1861.

43 *Staunton Vindicator*, February 8, 1861, p. 2, column 7. The *Vindicator* reprinted comments originally printed in the *Staunton Spectator*.

44 Letter from George Imboden to John Howard McCue, February 12, 1861, McCue Family Papers, University of Virginia.

45 Letter from J. H. Cochran to his mother, February 14, 1861.

46 Letter from Casper Branner to his father, February 9, 1861.

47 Robert J. Driver, *The Staunton Artillery—McClanahan's Battery* (Lynchburg, Va.: H. E. Howard, 1988), p. 2.

48 *Staunton Vindicator*, March 1, 1861, p. 1, column 6.

49 Henry Thomas Shanks, *The Secession Movement in Virginia, 1847–1861* (Richmond, Va.: Garrett and Massie, 1934), p. 158.

50 *Staunton Vindicator*, March 1, 1861, p. 1, column 6.

51 *Staunton Spectator*, March 5, 1861, p. 2, column 1.

52 Shanks, *Secession*, pp. 161–62; Charles B. Dew, *Apostles of Disunion: Southern Secession Commissioners and the Causes of the Civil War* (Charlottesville: University Press of Virginia, 2001), pp. 59–73, quote from p. 62.

53 George Reese, ed., *Proceedings of the Virginia State Convention of 1861, February 13–May 1* (Richmond: Virginia State Library, 1965), vol. 1, February 28, 1861, pp. 271, 273, 282, 283, 284, 285, 286, 289, 291.

54 *Staunton Vindicator*, March 8, 1861, p. 2, column 5.

55 Quoted in Johnson, *Lincoln*, pp. 108–15.

56 *Staunton Spectator*, March 12, 1861, p. 2, column 3.

57 *Staunton Vindicator*, March 15, 1861, p. 2, column 3.

58 Ibid., column 4.

59 Dew, *Apostles*, p. 73.

60 Reese, ed., *Proceedings of the Virginia State Convention*, vol. 2, March 21, 1861, pp. 138, 140, 142; March 23, 1861, pp. 210, 213, 216.

61 *Staunton Vindicator*, March 15, 1861, p. 2, column 4.

62 *Staunton Vindicator*, March 29, 1861, p. 2, column 6.

63 Ibid.

64 Ibid., p. 3, column 4.
65 Letter from John D. Imboden to John H. McCue, February 24, 1861.
66 Letter of John Cochran to his mother, March 3, 1861.
67 *Staunton Vindicator,* April 5, 1861, p. 1, column 5.
68 *Staunton Vindicator,* April 12, 1861, p. 2, column 2.
69 This account is based on John B. Baldwin, *Interview between President Lincoln and Col. John B. Baldwin, April 4, 1861: Statements and Evidence* (Staunton, Va.: Spectator Job Office, 1866).
70 Crofts, *Reluctant Confederates,* pp. 301–07. Crofts, the closest student of this encounter, believes that "a strong case can be made for the integrity of Baldwin's testimony and that of his corroborative witnesses," even though much about the episode is confusing and contested.
71 *Staunton Spectator,* April 9, 1861, p. 2, column 4.
72 *Staunton Vindicator,* April 12, 1861, p. 2, column 2.
73 *Staunton Vindicator,* April 12, 1861, p. 2, column 3.
74 Ibid., p. 1, column 4.
75 Letter from John Cochran to his mother, April 14, 1861.
76 *Staunton Spectator,* April 16, 1861, p. 2, column 1.
77 This episode is related in Driver, *Staunton Artillery,* pp. 2–3.
78 On Wise, see Craig M. Simpson, *A Good Southerner: The Life of Henry A. Wise of Virginia* (Chapel Hill: University of North Carolina Press, 1985), p. 249.
79 Alexander Farish Robertson, *Alexander Hugh Holmes Stuart, 1807–1891: A Biography* (Richmond, Va.: William Byrd Press, 1925), pp. 188–92.
80 Reese, ed., *Proceedings of the Virginia State Convention,* vol. 4, April 16, 1861, p. 9.
81 Harold R. Woodward, Jr., *Defender of the Valley: Brigadier General John Daniel Imboden, C.S.A.* (Berryville, Va.: Rockbridge Publishing Company, 1996), pp. 23–24.
82 Ibid.
83 *Staunton Spectator,* April 16, 1861, p. 2, column 2.
84 Driver, *Staunton Artillery,* pp. 3–4.
85 Shanks, *Secession,* pp. 18–21.
86 Proclamation quoted in Johnson, *Lincoln,* April 15, 1861, p. 123.
87 See Kenneth Stampp, "The Concept of Perpetual Union," *The Imperiled Union: Essays on the Background of the Civil War* (New York: Oxford University Press, 1980) and Phillip S. Paludan, "The American Civil War Considered as a Crisis in Law and Order," *American Historical Review* 77 (October 1972), pp. 1013–34.
88 *Valley Spirit,* April 10, 1861, p. 4, column 4.
89 *Semi-Weekly Dispatch,* April 19, 1861, p. 2, column 1.
90 Ibid., column 2.
91 Ibid., column 5.
92 Ibid., p. 3, column 1.
93 Ibid.
94 Ibid.
95 Correspondence from W. E. Camp to Thaddeus Stevens, April 19, 1861, Thaddeus Stevens Papers, Library of Congress.
96 *Valley Spirit,* April 24, 1861, p. 2, column 1.

97 Ibid., p. 2, column 1.
98 Ibid., column 1.
99 Diary of Reverend Abraham Essick, entry dated May 8, 1861, Kittochtinny Historical Society.
100 An excellent book that has influenced me as well as many others is Drew Gilpin Faust, *The Creation of Confederate Nationalism: Ideology and Identity in the Civil War South* (Baton Rouge: Louisiana State University Press, 1988). Faust shows how Confederates quickly assembled some of the main building blocks of national identity. A complementary account for the North is Susan-Mary Grant, *North over South: Northern Nationalism and American Identity in the Antebellum Era* (Lawrence: University Press of Kansas, 2000).
101 See James M. McPherson, *For Cause and Comrades: Why Men Fought in the Civil War* (New York: Oxford University Press, 1997).
102 *Staunton Spectator*, April 23, 1861, p. 2, column 1.
103 *Staunton Spectator*, April 30, 1861, p. 1, column 5.
104 Ibid.
105 *Staunton Vindicator*, May 3, 1861, p. 1, column 4.
106 *Staunton Spectator*, May 14, 1861, p. 2, column 3.
107 *Staunton Vindicator*, April 26, 1861, p. 2, column 3.
108 Driver, *Staunton Artillery*, pp. 4–6.
109 See James I. Robertson, Jr., *Stonewall Jackson: The Man, the Soldier, the Legend* (New York: Macmillan, 1997), p. 226.
110 *Staunton Spectator*, May 14, 1861, p. 2, column 7.
111 *Staunton Vindicator*, May 17, 1861, p. 1, column 3.
112 *Staunton Spectator*, May 14, 1861, p. 1, column 5.
113 *Staunton Spectator*, May 21, 1861, p. 2, column 2.
114 *Staunton Vindicator*, May 17, 1861, p. 2, column 2.
115 *Staunton Vindicator*, February 15, 1861, p. 3, column 2.
116 Letter from Mary Smiley to Thomas Smiley, May 23, 1861, Smiley Family Papers, University of Virginia.
117 *Staunton Vindicator*, May 24, 1861, p. 2, column 4; May 31, 1861, p. 1, column 3.
118 The following account is drawn from the diary of Alansa Rounds Sterrett, entries dated April 4, 11, 23, and 27, 1861.
119 Letter from unknown correspondent in Chambersburg to the editor of the *Pennsylvania Daily Telegraph*, dated April 30, 1861.
120 Ibid.
121 The following account is drawn from a letter from Alexander Cressler to Henry Bitner, May 17, 1861, Henry A. Bitner Letters, University of Virginia.
122 *Semi-Weekly Dispatch*, May 21, 1861, p. 2, column 1.
123 Ibid.
124 Broadside Portfolio 7, number 10, Rare Book and Special Collections Division, Library of Congress.
125 *Staunton Spectator*, September 3, 1861, p. 1, column 3.
126 Ibid.

127 *Valley Spirit*, May 1, 1861, p. 4, column 2; *Semi-Weekly Dispatch*, May 10, 1861, p. 3, column 2.

128 *Semi-Weekly Dispatch*, May 10, 1861, p. 3, column 2.

129 *Semi-Weekly Dispatch*, May 17, 1861, p. 3, column 2.

130 *Semi-Weekly Dispatch*, May 31, 1861, p. 3, column 2.

131 *Semi-Weekly Dispatch*, May 17, 1861, p. 2, column 1.

132 *Valley Spirit*, June 26, 1861, p. 1, column 4. Reprinted from the *Newark Journal*.

133 *Valley Spirit*, June 26, 1861, p. 2, column 1.

134 *Semi-Weekly Dispatch*, May 14, 1861, p. 2, column 1.

135 *Semi-Weekly Dispatch*, May 10, 1861, p. 2, column 2.

136 *Semi-Weekly Dispatch*, May 17, 1861, p. 3, column 1.

137 *Valley Spirit*, June 5, 1861, p. 2, column 2.

138 Ibid.

139 *Semi-Weekly Dispatch*, June 4, 1861, p. 3, column 2; *Valley Spirit*, June 5, 1861, p. 2, column 2.

140 *Semi-Weekly Dispatch*, May 14, 1861, p. 1, column 5; May 21, 1861, p. 3, column 1.

141 *Semi-Weekly Dispatch*, June 4, 1861, p. 2, column 2.

142 *Semi-Weekly Dispatch*, June 28, 1861, p. 2, column 4. Reprinted from the *Washington Republican*.

143 *Semi-Weekly Dispatch*, May 14, 1861, p. 2, column 2. Reprinted from the *New York Tribune*.

144 *Semi-Weekly Dispatch*, May 17, 1861, p. 2, column 1.

145 *Semi-Weekly Dispatch*, July 12, 1861, p. 3, column 2.

146 *Staunton Spectator*, September 3, 1861, p. 1, column 1; September 10, 1861, p. 1, column 1; p. 2, column 1; October 8, 1861, p. 1, column 1; column 5.

147 *Staunton Vindicator*, January 11, 1861, p. 2, column 3.

148 *Staunton Vindicator*, February 1, 1861, p. 2, column 4.

149 *Staunton Vindicator*, January 11, 1861, p. 1, column 3.

150 Augusta County Free Black Registry, entered by John D. Imboden, county clerk, January 28, 1861, Augusta County Court House, transcribed by Katherine Bushman.

151 *Staunton Vindicator*, January 11, 1861, p. 1, column 3.

152 *Staunton Spectator*, October 1, 1861, p. 2, column 2.

153 Diary of Michael Reid Hanger, entries dated April 19, 20, and 22, 1861, Hanger Diary, Washington and Lee University.

154 William Francis Brand to Amanda Catherine Armentrout, April 25, May 25, June 23, 1861, Brand Family Letters, University of Virginia.

155 Mary A. Smiley to Thomas M. Smiley, April 26, 1861; second quote is Ellen Martin to Thomas Smiley, April 28, 1861, Smiley Family Papers, University of Virginia.

156 Letter from Mary Smiley to Thomas Smiley, April 26, 1861.

157 Ibid.

158 Letter to Thomas Smiley from his cousin Maggie, July 12, 1861.

159 Letter from Mary Smiley to Thomas Smiley, May 30, 1861. For the notion of "vicarious war," see Charles Royster, *The Destructive War: William Tecumseh Sherman, Stonewall Jackson, and the Americas* (New York: Alfred A. Knopf, 1991).

160 Letter from Mary Smiley to Thomas Smiley, July 13, 1861.

161 Letter from Mary Smiley to Thomas Smiley, May 7, 1861. Junkin was the father of Stonewall Jackson's first wife.

162 Letter from Mary Smiley to Thomas Smiley, May 30, 1861.

163 Letter from Mary Smiley to Thomas Smiley, July 13, 1861.

164 Letter from Mary Smiley to Thomas Smiley, May 23, 1861.

165 Letter to Thomas Smiley from his cousin Hannah, [July] 1861.

166 Letter from John D. Imboden to John McCue, February 24, 1861.

167 Letter from Mary Smiley to Thomas Smiley, May 30, 1861.

168 Letter to Thomas Smiley from his mother, June 1861.

169 Letter from Mary Smiley to Thomas Smiley, July 13, 1861.

170 Letter to John McGuffin from his cousin, April 22, 1861, McGuffin Family Papers, University of Virginia.

171 Letter to John McGuffin from his mother, June 3, 1861.

172 Letter to John McGuffin from his mother, July 6, 1861.

173 Letter to John McGuffin from his mother, July 19, 1861.

174 *Staunton Vindicator,* April 26, 1861, p. 2, column 4.

175 Letter to Thomas Smiley from his aunt, Ellen Martin, June 4, 1861.

176 Letter to Thomas Smiley from C. Smiley, June 1861.

177 Memoir of Alansa Rounds Sterrett, copied from separate sheet, undated, probably early July 1861.

178 Diary of Michael Reid Hanger, entry dated July 7, 1861.

179 John P. Lightner to Amanda Catherine Armentrout, May 18, 1861, and June 29, 1861, in the Brand Family Papers, University of Virginia.

180 *Staunton Spectator,* July 16, 1861, p. 1, column 3.

181 Letter from William J. Willey to Alexander H. H. Stuart, dated May 7, 1861, Stuart Family Papers, University of Virginia.

182 Richard O. Curry, *A House Divided: A Study of Statehood Politics and the Copperhead Movement in West Virginia* (Pittsburgh: University of Pittsburgh Press, 1964), p. 7.

183 Ibid., p. 55.

184 Letter from Jedediah Hotchkiss to Sara Hotchkiss, dated June 27, 1861, Hotchkiss Papers, Library of Congress.

185 Letter from Jedediah Hotchkiss to Sara Hotchkiss, dated July 7, 1861. He had faith "in the God of justice to vindicate our cause." Letter from Jedediah Hotchkiss to Sara Hotchkiss, dated July 18, 1861.

186 David J. Eicher, *The Longest Night: A Military History of the Civil War* (New York: Simon and Schuster, 2001), pp. 82–86.

187 *Staunton Spectator,* July 27, 1861, p. 1, column 1.

188 *Official Records of the War of the Rebellion* [hereafter *OR*], M. G. Harman to Robert E. Lee, July 15, 1861, Series I, vol. 2, Serial 2, ch. 9.

189 Alexander H. H. Stuart to Hon. L. P. Walker, July 20, 1861, *OR*, Series 1, vol. 51, Serial 108.

190 *Semi-Weekly Dispatch,* July 2, 1861, p. 2, column 4.

191 *Semi-Weekly Dispatch,* July 19, 1861, p. 2, column 2.

192 Ibid., column 3.

193 Report of F. J. Porter, Assistant Adjutant-Gen, June 3, 1861, *OR,* Series I, vol. 2, Serial No. 2.

194 McClure, *Old Time Notes of Pennsylvania*, pp. 491–93.

195 Ibid.

Part Three: The Shadow of Death

1 For a useful overview of the large literature on the Civil War, see James M. McPherson and William J. Cooper, eds., *Writing the Civil War: The Quest to Understand* (Columbia, S.C.: University of South Carolina Press, 1998).

2 The following account is drawn from Robert J. Driver, *The Staunton Artillery—McClanhan's Battery* (Lynchburg, Va.: H. E. Howard, 1988), pp. 6–13, and Harold R. Woodward, Jr., *The Defender of the Valley: Brigadier General John Daniel Imboden, C.S.A.* (Berryville, Va.: Rockbridge Publishing Company, 1996), pp. 32–43. Also see Spencer C. Tucker, *Brigadier General John D. Imboden: Confederate Commander in the Shenandoah* (Lexington: University Press of Kentucky, 2003).

3 Diary of Michael Hanger, entry dated July 21, 1861, Hanger Diary, Washington and Lee University.

4 Ibid. July 22, 1861.

5 Diary of Joseph Waddell, entry dated July 22, 1861, Joseph Addison Waddell Diary, University of Virginia.

6 Ibid., July 26, 1861.

7 *Staunton Spectator*, July 27, 1861, p. 1, column 5.

8 Ibid.

9 Ibid.

10 Report of Brig. Gen. T. J. Jackson, C.S. Army, commanding 1st Brigade, Army of the Shenandoah, July 23, 1861, *OR,* Series I, vol. 2, Serial 2, ch. 9; Report of Col. J. E. B. Stuart, First Manassas, 1st Va. Cavalry, July 26, 1861, *OR*, Series I, vol. 2, Serial 2, ch 9.

11 *Staunton Spectator*, July 20, 1861, p 1, column 3.

12 *Staunton Spectator*, September 3, 1861, p. 1, column 7.

13 John Imboden, "Incidents of the Battle of Manassas," *Century Illustrated Monthly Magazine* (May 1885), pp. 92–98.

14 Alexander K. McClure to Eli Slifer, July 23, 1861, McClure Papers, Library of Congress.

15 *Valley Spirit*, July 24, 1861, p. 2, column 1.

16 Letter from Robert Taggart to his brother John, dated July 26, 1861, John Taggart Papers, Pennsylvania Historical and Museum Commission.

17 Letter from Alex Cressler to Henry Bitner, dated July 30, 1861, Henry A. Bitner Papers, University of Virginia.

18 *Semi-Weekly Dispatch*, July 26, 1861, p. 2, column 1.

19 *Valley Spirit*, July 27, 1861, p. 2, column 4.

20 *Valley Spirit*, July 31, 1861, p. 2, column 2. For a good overview of this topic, see Mark

E. Neely, *The Fate of Liberty: Abraham Lincoln and Civil Liberties* (New York: Oxford University Press, 1991).

21 *Valley Spirit*, August 3, 1861, p. 2, column 5.

22 *Valley Spirit*, August 21, 1861, p. 1, column 5.

23 *Semi-Weekly Dispatch*, July 26, 1861, p. 2, column 2.

24 *Semi-Weekly Dispatch*, August 27, 1861, p. 2, column 2.

25 *Semi-Weekly Dispatch*, July 30, 1861, p. 3, column 1.

26 *Valley Spirit*, July 31, 1861, p. 2, column 1.

27 *Semi-Weekly Dispatch*, August 20, 1861, p. 3, column 2.

28 Ibid.

29 Letter from Mary A. Smiley to Thomas M. Smiley, dated July 27, 1861, Smiley Family Papers, University of Virginia.

30 Letter from Jedediah Hotchkiss to Sara Hotchkiss, dated August 3, 1861; August 4, 1861, Jedediah Hotchkiss Papers, Library of Congress.

31 For examples of Hotchkiss's maps and a compelling portrait of the man, see William J. Miller, *Mapping for Stonewall: The Civil War Service of Jed Hotchkiss* (Washington, D.C.: Elliott and Clark, 1993). The Jackson quote appears on p. 52.

32 Letter from Jedediah Hotchkiss to Sara Hotchkiss, dated August 4, 1861; August 11, 1861.

33 Letter from Jedediah Hotchkiss to Sara Hotchkiss, dated August 3, 1861; August 11, 1861.

34 Letter from Jedediah Hotchkiss to Sara Hotchkiss, dated July 30, 1861; August 11, 1861.

35 Letter from Jedediah Hotchkiss to Sara Hotchkiss, dated August 16, 1861.

36 War Diary of Jedediah Hotchkiss, 1861, in the Papers of Jedediah Hotchkiss, Library of Congress. Letter from Jedediah Hotchkiss to Nelson Hotchkiss, dated September 18, 1861.

37 Letter from Adam W. Kersh to George P. Kersh, dated September 23, 1861, A. W. Kersh Letters, Fredericksburg and Spotsylvania National Battlefield Park.

38 Letter from Henry Dedrick to his wife, Lissa, dated October 4, 1861, Henry H. Dedrick Papers, Virginia Military Institute Archives.

39 Letter from Henry Dedrick to his wife, Lissa, dated September 29, 1861.

40 Letter from Henry Dedrick to his wife, Lissa, dated October 4, 1861.

41 Letter from Henry Dedrick to his wife, Lissa, dated October 4, 1861.

42 Letter from Henry Dedrick to his wife, Lissa, dated November 23, 1861.

43 Letter from Henry Dedrick to his wife, Lissa, dated December 9, 1861.

44 Letter from Henry Dedrick to his wife, Lissa, dated October 4, 1861.

45 Letter from Henry Dedrick to his wife, Lissa, dated November 23, 1861.

46 Letter from Henry Dedrick to his wife, Lissa, dated January 9, 1862.

47 Letter from Henry Dedrick to his wife, Lissa, dated January 22, 1862.

48 Letter from Henry Dedrick to his wife, Lissa, dated March 8, 1862.

49 *Staunton Spectator*, June 4, 1861, p. 2, column 2. For an overview, see Michael G. Mahon, *The Shenandoah Valley, 1861–1865: The Destruction of the Granary of the Confederacy* (Mechanicsburg, Pa.: Stackpole Books, 1999).

50 *Staunton Spectator*, July 16, 1861, p. 1, column 2. On the role of women in the war,

see Drew Faust, *Mothers of Invention: Women of the Slaveholding South in the American Civil War* (Chapel Hill: University of North Carolina Press, 1996); Catherine Clinton and Nina Silber, eds., *Divided Houses: Gender and the Civil War* (New York: Oxford University Press, 1992); and George Rable, *Civil Wars: Women and the Crisis of Southern Nationalism* (Urbana: University of Illinois Press, 1989).

51 *Staunton Spectator*, July 20, 1861, p. 1, column 1; column 2.

52 Diary of Joseph Waddell, entries dated July 20 and 24, 1861, in Joseph A. Waddell, *Annals of Augusta County, Virginia, from 1726 to 1871* (Staunton, Va.: C. R. Caldwell, 1901), pp. 285–86.

53 *Staunton Spectator*, July 20, 1861, p. 1, column 6.

54 Diary of Joseph Waddell, entry dated August 26, 1861, in Waddell, *Annals*, p. 288.

55 *Staunton Spectator*, July 20, 1861, p. 1, column 6.

56 Diary of Joseph Waddell, entry dated December 16, 1861, in Waddell, *Annals*, pp. 290–91.

57 John B. Baldwin to Judah P. Benjamin, October 16, 1861, *OR*, Series I, vol. 5, Serial 5, ch. 14.

58 *Staunton Spectator*, November 12, 1861, p. 1, column 3.

59 *Staunton Spectator*, December 10, 1861, p. 1, column 3.

60 Ibid.

61 *Valley Spirit*, September 4, 1861, p. 4, column 2.

62 *Semi-Weekly Dispatch*, September 10, 1861, p. 2, column 1.

63 *Semi-Weekly Dispatch*, September 13, 1861, p. 2, column 1; September 13, 1861, p. 2, column 3.

64 *Semi-Weekly Dispatch*, September 24, 1861, p. 2, column 2.

65 *Valley Spirit*, October 2, 1861, p. 4, column 1.

66 *Semi-Weekly Dispatch*, October 15, 1861, p. 2, column 1.

67 Ibid.

68 *Valley Spirit*, October 16, 1861, p. 4, column 1.

69 Alexander K. McClure, *Old Time Notes of Pennsylvania*, p. 496.

70 Ibid., pp. 496, 500–04.

71 *Valley Spirit*, September 11, 1861, p. 3, column 1.

72 Ibid.

73 *Valley Spirit*, November 27, 1861, p. 1, column 6.

74 *Valley Spirit*, December 4, 1861, p. 5, column 2; October 30, 1861, p. 4, column 5.

75 *Semi-Weekly Dispatch*, December 6, 1861, p. 2, column 1.

76 *Valley Spirit*, December 11, 1861, p. 4, column 1.

77 *Semi-Weekly Dispatch*, December 31, 1861, p. 1, column 5.

78 Ibid., p. 3, column 1.

79 Douglass quoted in James McPherson, *Battle Cry of Freedom: The Civil War Era* (New York: Oxford University Press, 1988), p. 354.

80 *Staunton Spectator*, October 8, 1861, p. 1, column 1.

81 *Staunton Spectator*, September 10, 1861, p. 1, column 1. Portions reprinted from the *Richmond Whig*. For similar comments see also *Staunton Spectator*, September 3, 1861, p. 1, column 1; September 10, 1861, p. 2, column 1.

82 *Staunton Spectator*, October 1, 1861, p. 1, column 4.

83 *Staunton Spectator*, November 5, 1861, p. 1, column 2. Reprinted from the *Richmond Whig*.
84 *Staunton Spectator*, September 3, 1861, p. 1, column 1.
85 *Staunton Spectator*, December 17, 1861, p. 1, column 1.
86 *Staunton Spectator*, October 1, 1861, p. 1, column 2.
87 *Staunton Spectator*, October 8, 1861, p. 1, column 5.
88 *Staunton Spectator*, October 1, 1861, p. 2, column 1.
89 Letters of Clinton Hatcher to Mary Ann Sibert, May 29, July 17, and September 24, 1861; Letter from Thaddeus Hatcher to Mary Ann Sibert, December 24, 1861. Evans-Sibert Papers at the Library of Virginia.
90 *Semi-Weekly Dispatch*, October 22, 1861, p. 4, column 1. Information reprinted from the *Evening Journal*.
91 *Valley Spirit*, October 30, 1861, p. 4, column 4.
92 Ibid.
93 *Valley Spirit*, September 4, 1861, p. 5, column 1; *Semi-Weekly Dispatch*, November 15, 1861, p. 3, column 1.
94 *Semi-Weekly Dispatch*, November 26, 1861, p. 3, column 2.
95 *Valley Spirit*, November 27, 1861, p. 2, column 4.
96 *Semi-Weekly Dispatch*, September 24, 1861, p. 3, column 2; *Valley Spirit*, September 25, 1861, p. 5, column 2.
97 Diary of Reverend Abraham Essick, entry dated September 26, 1861, Kittochtinny Historical Society.
98 The following paragraphs are drawn from the diary of Reverend Abraham Essick, entry dated December 31, 1861.
99 *Staunton Spectator*, January 7, 1862, p. 1, column 4.
100 Letter from George P. Kersh to Adam W. Kersh, dated January 29, 1862.
101 Letter from Thomas Smiley to Mary Smiley, dated January 10, 1862.
102 *Staunton Spectator*, January 21, 1862, p. 1, column 2.
103 *Staunton Spectator*, January 28, 1862, p. 1, column 3.
104 Ibid.
105 *Valley Spirit*, January 8, 1862, p. 4, column 1.
106 *Semi-Weekly Dispatch*, January 10, 1862, p. 2, column 1.
107 *Valley Spirit*, January 1, 1862, p. 4, column 2.
108 *Valley Spirit*, January 15, 1862, p. 4, column 2.
109 Ibid.
110 Ibid.
111 Ibid.
112 *Valley Spirit*, January 29, 1862, p. 4, column 1.
113 *Semi-Weekly Dispatch*, January 24, 1862, p. 2, column 1.
114 Ibid.
115 See two fascinating books: Michael Fellman, *Inside War: The Guerrilla Conflict in Missouri during the American Civil War* (New York : Oxford University Press, 1989) and Charles S. Royster, *The Destructive War: William Tecumseh Sherman, Stonewall Jackson, and the Americans* (New York: Alfred A. Knopf, 1991).
116 *"In Diesem Jahr . . . Deacon Michael Hege's Church Record Book, 1850–1896,"*

Mennonite Historical Association of the Cumberland Valley, Chambersburg, Pa.

117 *Valley Spirit*, February 19, 1862, p. 5, column 3.

118 Letter from Henry Erisman to his brother, dated March 12, 1862, U.S. Army Military History Institute.

119 *Valley Spirit*, April 16, 1862, p. 5, column 3.

120 Ibid., column 1. Reprinted from the *Pittsburgh Chronicle*.

121 *Valley Spirit*, April 23, 1862, p. 5, column 1. Reprint of letter from F. S. Stumbaugh, colonel, 77th Pennsylvania Regiment, dated April 9, 1862.

122 *Semi-Weekly Dispatch*, April 11, 1862, p. 3, column 2.

123 *Semi-Weekly Dispatch*, May 2, 1862, p. 3, column 2.

124 *Valley Spirit*, April 16, 1862, p. 5, column 1.

125 *Semi-Weekly Dispatch*, March 11, 1862, p. 4, column 1.

126 *Valley Spirit*, March 12, 1862, p. 4, column 1.

127 *Semi-Weekly Dispatch*, April 15, 1862, p. 2, column 2.

128 *Semi-Weekly Dispatch*, April 18 1862, p. 2, column 2.

129 *Semi-Weekly Dispatch*, May 6, 1862, p. 2, column 2.

130 Letter from John J. Miller to George Miller, dated May 15, 1862, Miller Family Papers, York County Heritage Trust.

131 Letter from Bob Taggart to Sam Taggart, dated June 24, 1862, John Taggart Papers, Pennsylvania Historical and Museum Commission.

132 *Valley Spirit*, April 9, 1862, p. 4, column 1.

133 *Valley Spirit*, April 30, 1862, p. 5, column 4.

134 *Valley Spirit*, August 6, 1862, p. 5, column 1. "F.F.V." refers to the First Families of Virginia, a title that linked contemporary white Virginians to the first settlers of the colony.

135 *Valley Spirit*, May 21, 1862, p. 5, column 1.

136 *Staunton Spectator*, February 18, 1862, p. 1, column 1.

137 Ibid.

138 Diary of Harvey Bear, entry dated March 15, 1862, Harvey Bear Diary, Virginia Polytechnic Institute and State University.

139 *Staunton Spectator*, February 25, 1862, p. 1, column 1.

140 Letter from James McCutchan to Kate McCutchan, dated February 20, 1862, James B. McCutchan Papers, Washington and Lee University.

141 Letter from James McCutchan to Kate McCutchan, dated March 13, 1862.

142 Letter from Adam W. Kersh to George P. Kersh, dated March 1, 1862.

143 Letter from Mary Dedrick to Henry Dedrick, dated February 1, 1862.

144 Letter from Henry Dedrick to Mary Dedrick, dated April 7, 1862.

145 Letter from Mary Dedrick to Henry Dedrick, dated April 15, 1862.

146 Diary of Joseph Waddell, entries dated February 10, February 22, and February 24, 1862.

147 *Staunton Spectator*, March 25, 1862, p. 1, column 1.

148 *Staunton Spectator*, April 8, 1862, p. 1, column 1.

149 *Staunton Spectator*, April 15, 1862, p. 1, column 2.

150 *Staunton Spectator*, April 1, 1862, p. 1, column 7.

151 *Staunton Spectator*, February 18, 1862, p. 1, column 3.

152 *Staunton Spectator,* March 11, 1862, p. 1, column 4.

153 *Staunton Spectator,* February 25, 1862, p. 1, column 6.

154 Letter from Adam W. Kersh to George P. Kersh, dated January 29, 1862.

155 This account is drawn from Woodward, *Defender of the Valley*, pp. 50–52.

156 Col. John Imboden to G. W. Randolph, June 23, 1862, *OR*, Series 1, vol. 51, Serial 108, ch. 63.

157 Diary of Jacob Hildebrand, entry dated April 11, 1862, in John R. Hildebrand, ed., *A Mennonite Journal, 1862–1865: A Father's Account of the Civil War in the Shenandoah Valley* (Shippensburg, Pa.: Byrd Street Press, 1996).

158 The following account is drawn from Samuel L. Horst, *Mennonites in the Confederacy: A Study of Civil War Pacifism* (Scottsdale, Pa.: Herald Press, 1967), pp. 15–17.

159 *Staunton Spectator,* March 25, 1862, p. 1, column 2.

160 Horst, *Mennonites*, pp. 49–56.

161 Diary of Jacob R. Hildebrand, entry dated March 14, 1862.

162 Diary of Jacob Hildebrand, entry dated March 17, 1862.

163 Diary of Jacob Hildebrand, entries dated March 19 and March 20, 1862.

164 Diary of Jacob Hildebrand, entries dated, March 26, March 27, and April 6, 1862.

165 Alexander H. H. Stuart to George W. Randolph, April 29, 1862, Stuart Family Papers, University of Virginia.

166 Quoted in James I. Robertson, *Stonewall Jackson: The Man, the Soldier, the Legend* (New York: Macmillan, 1997), p. 330.

167 Quoted ibid, p. 421.

168 Letter from Jedediah Hotchkiss to Sara Hotchkiss, dated March 25, 1862.

169 Diary of Joseph Waddell, entry dated March 21, 1862.

170 Ibid., March 23, 1862.

171 Ibid., March 27, 1862.

172 Ibid., April 17, 1862.

173 Ibid., April 17, 1862.

174 Diary of Jacob Hildebrand, entry dated April 19, 1862.

175 Ibid., May 2, 1862.

176 Letter from William Smith Hanger Baylor to Mary Baylor, dated April 22, 1862, William S. H. Baylor Letters, Virginia Polytechnic Institute and State University.

177 Ibid.

178 Ibid.

179 Hotchkiss quoted in Miller, *Mapping for Stonewall*, p. 47.

180 Letter from William Smith Hanger Baylor to Mary Baylor, dated April 22, 1862.

181 Diary of Joseph Waddell, entry dated May 3, 1862.

182 Ibid., May 4, 1862.

183 Ibid.

184 Ibid.

185 Diary of Jacob Hildebrand, entry dated May 5, 1862.

186 Robertson, *Stonewall Jackson*, pp. 363–72.

187 Diary of Joseph Waddell, entry dated May 7, 1862.

188 Diary of Jacob Hildebrand, entries dated May 7 and May 8, 1862.

189 Diary of Jacob Hildebrand, entry dated May 9, 1862.

190 Quoted in Archie McDonald, ed., *Make Me a Map of the Valley: The Civil War Journal of Stonewall Jackson's Topographer* (Dallas: Southern Methodist University Press, 1973), p. 40.

191 Letter from Jedediah Hotchkiss to Sara Hotchkiss, dated May 9, 1862.

192 Letter from Jedediah Hotchkiss to Sara Hotchkiss, dated May 10, 1862.

193 Diary of Jacob Hildebrand, entry dated May 10, 1862.

194 Diary of Joseph Waddell, entry dated May 10, 1862.

195 Diary of Jacob Hildebrand, entry dated May 11, 1862.

196 McDonald, ed., *Make Me a Map*, pp. 42–46.

197 Diary of Joseph Waddell, entry dated May 14, 1862.

198 Diary of Jacob Hildebrand, entry dated May 16, 1862.

199 Ibid., May 18, 1862.

200 Ibid., May 20, 1862.

201 Letter from Jedediah Hotchkiss to Sara Hotchkiss, dated May 25, 1862.

202 Ibid., May 26, 1862. The following account is drawn from this letter.

203 Robertson, *Stonewall Jackson*, pp. 411, 413.

204 Diary of Joseph Waddell, entry dated May 28, 1862.

205 Diary of Harvey Bear, May 29, 1862.

206 Diary of Jacob Hildebrand, entries dated May 28 and May 30, 1862.

207 Diary of Joseph Waddell, entry dated June 2, 1862.

208 Ibid., May 29 and May 30, 1862.

209 Ibid., June 1, 1862.

210 Ibid., June 6, 1862.

211 Diary of Jacob Hildebrand, entries dated June 10 and June 11, 1862.

212 Diary of Joseph Waddell, entry dated June 17, 1862.

213 *Valley Spirit*, May 28, 1862, p. 5, column 1.

214 Ibid.

215 *Valley Spirit*, June 11, 1862, p. 5, column 1.

216 *Valley Spirit*, May 28, 1862, p. 4, column 1.

217 Ibid.

218 Ibid.

219 Letter from Christian Geisel to his sister, dated April 22, 1862.

220 Letter from Nathaniel Dunn to his brother, dated May 4, 1862.

221 Letter from Bob Taggart to John Taggart, dated May 30, 1862.

222 *Semi-Weekly Dispatch*, May 6, 1862, p. 2, column 1 and May 2, 1862, p. 3, column 2.

223 *Valley Spirit*, June 18, 1862, p. 3, column 1.

224 Ibid.

225 Ibid., p. 5, column 1.

226 McPherson, *Battle Cry of Freedom*, p. 858.

227 Stephen Jay Gould, *Wonderful Life: The Burgess Shale and the Nature of History* (New York: W. W. Norton & Company, 1989), pp. 283–85.

228 For a fascinating counterfactual essay, see William W. Freehling, "'Absurd' Issues and the Causes of the Civil War: Colonization as a Test Case," in Freehling, *The Reintegration of American History: Slavery and the Civil War* (New York: Oxford University Press, 1994), pp. 138–57.

Part Four: The Presence of Mine Enemies

1 James McPherson, *Battle Cry of Freedom: The Civil War Era* (New York: Oxford University Press, 1988), p. 462.

2 Diary of Joseph Waddell, entry dated June 17, 1862, Joseph Addison Waddell Diary, University of Virginia.

3 Ibid., June 19,1862.

4 Letter from Thomas Smiley to Mary Smiley, dated June 9, 1862, Smiley Family Papers, University of Virginia.

5 Diary of Joseph Waddell, entry dated June 27, 1862.

6 Ibid., July 4, 1862.

7 Report of Col. William S. H. Baylor, July 9, 1862, *OR,* Series 1, vol. 11, Serial 13, ch. 23.

8 Report of Brig. Gen. Charles S. Winder, C.S. Army, commanding 1st Brigade, 2d Division, of the Battles of Gaines' Mill and Malvern Hill. *OR,* Series 1, vol. 11, Serial 13. For an overview of the battles of 1862, see James I. Robertson, *Stonewall Jackson: The Man, the Soldier, the Legend* (New York: Macmillan, 1997).

9 Diary of Joseph Waddell, entries dated July 7, 1862.

10 McPherson, *Battle Cry of Freedom*, p. 471.

11 Diary of Joseph Waddell, entry dated July 8, 1862.

12 Letter from James Gabbert to Mary Baylor, dated July 24, 1862, William Smith Hanger Baylor Papers, Virginia Polytechnic Institute and State University.

13 Diary of Joseph Waddell, entry dated June 14, 1862.

14 Diary of Nancy Emerson, entries dated July 4, 1862, and Tuesday, no date, 1862, Nancy Emerson Diary, University of Virginia.

15 Ibid., Wednesday, no date, 1862.

16 Ibid., Thursday, no date, 1862.

17 Ibid., July 4, 1862.

18 Ibid.

19 *Valley Spirit*, June 25, 1862, p. 5, column 1.

20 *Valley Spirit*, July 9, 1862, p. 5, column 1.

21 *Valley Spirit*, July 2, 1862, p. 4, column 3.

22 Ibid.

23 *Valley Spirit*, July 16, 1862, p. 5, column 1.

24 Alexander K. McClure, *Old Time Notes of Pennsylvania,* pp. 538, 540.

25 *Valley Spirit*, July 30, 1862, p. 5, column 1.

26 Letter from James A. Carman to his father, dated July 18, 1862, James Carman Papers, U.S. Military History Institute.

27 *A Sketch of the 126th Regiment of Pennsylvania Volunteers, Prepared by an Officer, and Sold for the Benefit of the Franklin County Soldiers' Monumental Association* (Chambersburg, Pa.: Cook and Hays, 1869), pp. 6–7.

28 *Valley Spirit*, August 6, 1862, p. 5, column 1.

29 *Valley Spirit*, August 20, 1862, p. 1, column 1.

30 Ibid.

31 Ibid., p. 4, column 4.

32 For comparisons, see Maris Vinovskis, "Have Social Historians Lost the Civil War? Some Preliminary Demographic Speculations," in Maris A. Vinovskis, ed., *Toward a Social History of the American Civil War: Exploratory Essays* (Cambridge: Cambridge University Press, 1990), p. 14, and in the same volume, Thomas R. Kemp, "Community and War: The Civil War Experience of Two New Hampshire Towns," p. 59.

33 *Valley Spirit*, July 23, 1862, p. 5, column 4. See Mark Grimsley, *The Hard Hand of War: Union Military Policy toward Southern Civilians, 1861–1865* (New York: Cambridge University Press, 1995).

34 Letter from James A. Carman to his father, dated July 18, 1862.

35 Quoted in McPherson, *Battle Cry of Freedom*, p. 524. On Imboden, see John J. Hennessey, *Return to Bull Run: The Campaign and Battle of Second Manassas* (Norman: University of Oklahoma Press, 1993), p. 15.

36 Letter from William Kindig to Henry Bitner, dated July 21, 1862, Henry A. Bitner Letters, University of Virginia.

37 Letter from J. B. Sweigert to his cousin, dated July 24, 1862. On the effect of Pope's orders, see Hennessy, *Return to Bull Run*, p. 18.

38 *Valley Spirit*, August 6, 1862, p. 8, column 2.

39 Ibid.

40 Ibid.

41 Letter from Bob Taggart to John Taggart, dated August 12, 1862, John Taggart Papers, Pennsylvania Historical and Museum Commission.

42 *Valley Spirit*, August 27, 1862, p. 1, column 1. Letter by unidentified correspondent to the *Valley Spirit*, dated August 22, 1862.

43 Hennessy, *Return to Bull Run*, pp. 21–22.

44 Letter from Thomas Smiley to Mary Smiley, dated July 31, 1862, Smiley Family Papers, University of Virginia.

45 Letter from John Wise to Mary Wise, dated August 17, 1862, Michael G. Wise Papers, University of Virginia.

46 Letter from Jedediah Hotchkiss to Sara Hotchkiss, dated July 22, 1862, Hotchkiss Papers, Library of Congress.

47 Letter from John Wise to Mary Wise, dated August 17, 1862.

48 Letter from Jedediah Hotchkiss to Sara Hotchkiss, dated July 18, 1862.

49 Diary of Joseph Waddell, entry dated July 29, 1862.

50 Ibid.

51 Ibid., August 1, 1862.

52 Ibid., August 11, 1862.

53 Letter from Jedediah Hotchkiss to Sara Hotchkiss, dated August 3, 1862.

54 Robert K. Krick, *Stonewall Jackson at Cedar Mountain* (Chapel Hill: University of North Carolina Press, 1990), pp. 242–46.

55 Letter from Jedediah Hotchkiss to Sara Hotchkiss, dated August 9, 1862.

56 Diary of Joseph Waddell, entry dated August 13, 1862.

57 Letter from Jedediah Hotchkiss to Sara Hotchkiss, dated August 16, 1862.

58 Letter from Jedediah Hotchkiss to Sara Hotchkiss, dated August 16, 1862.

59 Ibid., August 28, 1862.

60 Diary of James E. Beard, entry dated August 27, 1862, James Beard Diary, Fredericksburg and Spotsylvania National Battlefield Park.

61 Letter from William Smith Hanger Baylor to Mary Baylor, dated August 18, 1862.

62 Quoted in Hennessy, *Return to Bull Run*, p. 175.

63 This and the following account are drawn from Lee A. Wallace, *5th Virginia Infantry*, 2d ed. (Lynchburg, Va.: H. E. Howard, 1988), pp. 39–40.

64 This account is drawn from Hennessy, *Return to Bull Run*, p. 348, including the quotes.

65 Diary of Joseph Waddell, entry dated September 23, 1862.

66 Letter from Jedediah Hotchkiss to Sara Hotchkiss, dated September 21, 1862.

67 Letter from Edward P. Walton to Mary Baylor, dated October 1, 1862.

68 Ibid.

69 Ibid.

70 Letter from Jedediah Hotchkiss to Sara Hotchkiss, dated September 1, 1862.

71 Diary of Joseph Waddell, dated September 10, 1862.

72 *Valley Spirit*, September 3, 1862, p. 4, column 1.

73 *Valley Spirit*, September 10, 1862, p. 1, column 1.

74 Ibid. Letter originally written by unknown correspondent to the *Valley Spirit* using initials D. A. N., dated September 3, 1862.

75 Ibid., p. 4, column 1.

76 Ibid.

77 *Valley Spirit*, September 3, 1862, p. 4, column 1.

78 Ibid.

79 Ibid.

80 *Valley Spirit*, September 24, 1862, p. 1, column 1. Letter originally from Kennedy to *Valley Spirit* dated September 12, 1862.

81 Diary of Samuel Cormany, entry dated August 17, 1862. James A. Mohr, ed., *The Cormany Diaries: A Northern Family in the Civil War* (Pittsburgh: University of Pittsburgh Press, 1982).

82 Diary of Samuel Cormany, entry dated August 19 1862, ibid.

83 Diary of Samuel Cormany, entry dated September 9, 1862, ibid.

84 Diary of Samuel Cormany, entries dated September 12 and September 13, 1862, ibid.

85 *Valley Spirit*, September 24, 1862, p. 1, column 1. Letter originally from Kennedy to *Valley Spirit*, dated September 12, 1862.

86 George McClellan to Governor Andrew G. Curtin, September 10, 1862, *OR*, Series 1, vol. 19, Serial 28, ch. 31.

87 D. H. Hastings, Capt. 1st Cavalry, Cmdg. to Gen. Lorenzo Thomas, September 12, 1862, *OR*, Series 1, vol. 19, Serial 28, ch. 31.

88 Diary of Joseph Waddell, entry dated September 10, 1862.

89 Ibid., September 11, 1862.

90 Letter from Jedediah Hotchkiss to Sara Hotchkiss, dated September 8, 1862.

91 Ibid.

92 Ibid., September 8, 1862.

93 Ibid., September 17, 1862.

94 Ibid., September 21, 1862.

95 Ibid.

96 Diary of Joseph Waddell, entry dated September 22, 1862.

97 Ibid., September 24, 1862.

98 Letter from Thomas Garber to Addie Garber, dated September 17, 1862, Garber Family Papers, Augusta County Historical Society.

99 Diary of Joseph Waddell, entry dated September 24, 1862; September 27, 1862.

100 Ibid., October 1, 1862; October 2, 1862.

101 *Valley Spirit*, September 24, 1862, p. 4, column 1.

102 Ibid.

103 George B. McClellan to Maj. Gen. H. W. Halleck, Gen.-in-Chief: September 14, 1862, *OR*, Series 1, vol. 19, Serial 28, ch. 31.

104 George B. McClellan to Maj. Gen. H. W. Hallack, Gen.-in-Chief: September 17, 1862, *OR*, Series 1, vol. 19, Serial 28, ch. 31.

105 Report of Captain James MacThompson, Antietam,107th Pennsylvania Infantry, October 7, 1862, *OR*, Series 1, vol. 19, Serial 27, ch. 31.

106 *Valley Spirit*, October 1, 1862, p. 4, column 1. James M. McPherson, *Crossroads of Freedom: Antietam* (New York: Oxford University Press, 2002). For a countervailing argument, focusing on the Southern response to the battle, see Gary W. Gallagher, "The Net Result of the Campaign Was in Our Favor: Confederate Reaction to the Maryland Campaign," in Gallagher, ed., *The Antietam Campaign* (Chapel Hill: University of North Carolina Press, 1999), pp. 3–43.

107 *Valley Spirit*, October 8, 1862, p. 4, column 2.

108 *Valley Spirit*, October 15, 1862, p. 1, column 1.

109 Diary of William Heyser, entry dated October 4, 1862, Kittochtinny Historical Society.

110 Ibid., November 4, 1862.

111 *Valley Spirit*, October 15, 1862, p. 5, column 1.

112 Diary of William Heyser, entry dated October 10, 1862.

113 Ibid., October 11, 1862.

114 Ibid.

115 Ibid., October 15, 1862.

116 McClure, *Old Time Notes of Pennsylvania*, pp. 582–83.

117 Ibid., pp. 579–87. The following account is drawn from these pages.

118 *Valley Spirit*, October 22, 1862, p. 4, column 5.

119 Letter from Samuel North to his brother, dated October 14, 1862, Samuel W. North Papers, U.S. Army Military History Institute.

120 *Valley Spirit*, November 5, 1862, p. 1, column 3.

121 Ibid.

122 *Valley Spirit*, October 22, 1862, p. 5, column 4.

123 Ibid., p. 4, column 1.

124 Ibid., column 4.

125 Ibid., column 1.

126 McClure, *Old Time Notes of Pennsylvania*, pp. 557–59.

127 *Valley Spirit*, October 22, 1862, p. 4, column 1.

128 *Valley Spirit*, November 5, 1862, p. 4, column 1.
129 Diary of William Heyser, entry dated October 29, 1862.
130 Ibid., November 11, 1862.
131 Ibid., November 20, 1862.
132 *Valley Spirit*, October 22, 1862, p. 6, column 1.
133 *Valley Spirit*, November 12, 1862, p. 1, column 5.
134 Ibid.
135 Ibid.
136 Diary of William Heyser, entry dated November 27, 1862.
137 *Valley Spirit*, December 3, 1862, p. 5, column 2.
138 *Valley Spirit*, November 19, 1862, p. 5, column 4.
139 Letter from Peter Boyer, Jr., to Peter Boyer, Sr., dated November 20, 1862, Peter Boyer Papers, U.S. Army Military History Institute.
140 *Staunton Spectator*, October 7, 1862, p. 2, column 1.
141 Diary of Joseph Waddell, entry dated October 22, 1862.
142 *Staunton Spectator*, October 21, 1862, p. 2, column 2.
143 Ibid.
144 *Staunton Spectator*, November 4, 1862, p. 2, column 1.
145 Diary of Joseph Waddell, entry dated October 18, 1862. On the ways that Virginia communities dealt with such problems, see William Blair, *Virginia's Private War: Feeding Body and Soul in the Confederacy, 1861–1865* (New York: Oxford University Press, 1998).
146 Ibid., November 29, 1862.
147 Ibid., October 22, 1862.
148 *Staunton Spectator*, December 9, 1862, p. 1, column 7.
149 *Staunton Spectator*, December 2, 1862, p. 2, column 3.
150 Ibid.
151 *Staunton Spectator*, October 28, 1862, p. 1, column 1.
152 *Staunton Spectator*, December 2, 1862, p. 2, column 4.
153 *Staunton Spectator*, November 4, 1862, p. 2, column 1.
154 Diary of Joseph Waddell, entry dated October 22, 1862.
155 Report forwarded from General Franz Sigel to Major General Ambrose Burnside, December 3, 1862, *OR*, Series 1, vol. 21, Serial 31, ch. 31.
156 *Staunton Spectator*, October 14, 1862, p. 2, column 6.
157 Letter from Kent Langhorne to his mother, dated November 16, 1862, Jacob Kent Langhorne Papers, Virginia Military Institute.
158 Letter from A. W. Kersh to his brother George Kersh, dated October 14, 1862, A. W. Kersh Letters, Fredericksburg and Spotsylvania National Battlefield Park.
159 Ibid., November 22, 1862.
160 *Staunton Spectator*, December 9, 1862, p. 2, column 4.
161 *Staunton Spectator*, December 16, 1862, p. 1, column 6.
162 Ibid.
163 *Staunton Spectator*, December 30, 1862, p. 2, column 1.
164 *Staunton Spectator*, December 16, 1862, p. 1, column 6.
165 Letter from Jedediah Hotchkiss to his wife, Sara, dated January 2, 1863.

166 *Valley Spirit*, December 10, 1862, p. 4, column 5.
167 Ibid. For a full account, see George C. Rable, *Fredericksburg! Fredericksburg!* (Chapel Hill: University of North Carolina Press, 2002).
168 *Valley Spirit*, December 17, 1862, p. 4, column 5.
169 Letter from Samuel North to his brother, dated December 18, 1862.
170 *Valley Spirit*, December 24, 1862, p. 4, column 5.
171 *Sketch of the 126th Regiment*, pp.17–21.
172 Letter from Samuel North to his brother, dated December 18, 1862.
173 Letter from James Carman to his father, dated December 17, 1862.
174 *Valley Spirit*, December 24, 1862, p. 1, column 6.
175 Ibid., p. 4, column 5.
176 Ibid., column 1.
177 Letter from James Carman to his father, dated December 17, 1862.
178 *Valley Spirit*, December 31, 1862, p. 2, column 4.
179 Ibid.
180 Letter from Christian Geisel to his sister, dated January 17, 1863, Pennsylvania Historical and Museum Commission.
181 Diary of Samuel Cormany, entries dated January 3 and 4, 1863.
182 Diary of Rachel Cormany, entry dated January 9, 1863.
183 *Valley Spirit*, January 21, 1863, p. 2, column 6.
184 Letter from Thad Donely to Henry Bitner, dated January 20, 1863.
185 *Sketch of the 126th Regiment*, pp. 25–27.
186 Ibid.
187 *Valley Spirit*, February 4, 1863, p. 2, column 3.
188 *Valley Spirit*, February 11, 1863, p. 2, column 2.
189 *Valley Spirit*, October 22, 1862, p. 5, column 1.
190 *Valley Spirit*, December 10, 1862, p. 5, column 1.
191 Diary of Samuel Cormany, entries dated February 9 and 10, 1863.
192 Diary of William Heyser, entries dated January 7, January 10, January 28, and February 21, 1863.
193 Letter from Jedediah Hotchkiss to his wife, Sara, dated January 11, 1863.
194 Ibid., January 21, 1863.
195 Letter from Jedediah Hotchkiss to Nelly Hotchkiss, dated December 17, 1862.
196 Letter from Jedediah Hotchkiss to his wife, Sara, January 21, 1863.
197 *Staunton Spectator*, January 6, 1863, p. 2, column 3.
198 Diary of Joseph Waddell, entry dated January 4, 1863.
199 Ibid., January 12 and 13, 1863. The following account is drawn from these pages.
200 *Staunton Vindicator*, February 20, 1863, p. 1, column 5.
201 Letter from Jedediah Hotchkiss to his wife, Sara, dated January 25, 1863.
202 Ibid., March 27, 1863.
203 Ibid., January 25, 1863.
204 *Staunton Spectator*, January 27, 1863, p. 2, column 5.
205 Diary of Nancy Emerson, entry dated January 8, 1863.
206 Diary of Joseph Waddell, entry dated January 7, 1863.
207 Diary of Jedediah Hotchkiss, entry dated January 7, 1863, in Archie P. McDonald,

ed., *Make Me a Map of the Valley: The Civil War Journal of Stonewall Jackson's Topographer—Jed Hotchkiss* (Dallas: Southern Methodist University Press, 1973), p. 107.

208 *Staunton Spectator*, January 6, 1863, p. 2, column 2.

209 Diary of Joseph Waddell, entry dated January 1, 1863.

210 *Staunton Spectator*, January 20, 1863, p. 2, column 2.

211 *Staunton Spectator*, February 3, 1863, p. 2, column 1.

212 Jedediah Hotchkiss, March 8, 1863, in McDonald, ed., *Make Me a Map of the Valley*, p. 119.

213 Letters from Jedediah Hotchkiss to his wife, Sara, dated January 21, January 25, April 13, and April 24, 1863.

214 *Staunton Spectator*, January 27, 1863, p. 2, column 1.

215 *Staunton Spectator*, February 3, 1863, p. 2, column 2.

216 Diary of Joseph Waddell, entry dated February 12, 1863.

217 Letter from Thomas M. Smiley to his sister, dated January 4, 1863.

218 Letter from Adam W. Kersh to his brother, George Kersh, dated January 1, 1863.

219 Ibid., January 27, 1863.

220 *Staunton Vindicator*, February 20, 1863, p. 2, column 7. On this pattern of desertion elsewhere, see Kevin Conley Ruffner, "Civil War Desertion from a Black Belt Regiment: An Examination of the 44th Infantry," in Edward L. Ayers and John C. Willis, eds., *The Edge of the South: Life in Nineteenth-Century Virginia* (Charlottesville: University Press of Virginia, 1991).

221 *Staunton Spectator*, December 16, 1862, p. 2, column 6.

222 Letter from Joseph A. Wilson to Henry Hamilton, dated January 11, 1863, private collection on the Valley of the Shadow website.

223 Letter from Joseph A. Wilson to Henry Hamilton, dated February 17, 1863.

224 Letter from Thomas Garber to his sister, Addie Garber, dated April 15, 1863.

225 Letters from Jesse Rolston to his wife, Mary, dated March 15 and April 3, 1863, reprinted in Joyce DeBolt Miller, ed., *"Until Seperated by Death": Lives and Civil War Letters of Jesse Rolston, Jr., and Mary Catharine Cromer* (Bridgewater, Va.: Good Printers, Inc., 1994), pp. 27–29.

226 Letter from Jedediah Hotchkiss to wife, Sara, dated March 1, 1863.

227 Letter from Jesse Rolston to his wife, Mary, dated April 3, 1863, in Miller, *"Until Seperated."*

228 Diary of Joseph Waddell, entry dated March 7, 1863.

229 Diary of William Heyser, entry dated January 1, 1863.

230 *Valley Spirit*, January 7, 1863, p. 2, column 1.

231 Hans L. Trefousse, *Thaddeus Stevens: Nineteenth-Century Egalitarian* (Chapel Hill: University of North Carolina Press, 1997), pp. 130–31.

232 *Valley Spirit*, February 11, 1863, p. 2, column 3.

233 *Valley Spirit*, March 4, 1863, p. 2, column 1.

234 Letter from William Barnitz, dated March 27, 1863. Letter printed in *Pennsylvania Daily Telegraph*. The issue of the *Transcript* in which this letter was reprinted is no longer extant.

235 Ibid.

236 Ibid.

237 *Valley Spirit*, April 15, 1863, p. 2, column 2. Reprinted from the *Franklin Repository and Transcript*, no date.

238 Ibid.

239 Ibid.

240 *Valley Spirit*, March 25, 1863, p. 2, column 1.

241 *Valley Spirit*, April 1, 1863, p. 2, column 6.

242 *Valley Spirit*, March 25, 1863, p. 2, column 5.

243 *Valley Spirit*, April 1, 1863, p. 2, column 1.

244 *Valley Spirit*, May 6, 1863, p. 2, column 1.

245 Russell Duncan, *Where Death and Glory Meet: Colonel Robert Gould Shaw and the 54th Massachusetts Infantry* (Athens: University of Georgia Press, 1997), p. 63; Joseph T. Glatthaar, *Forged in Battle: The Civil War Alliance of Black Soldiers and White Officers* (New York: Macmillan, 1990).

246 *Valley Spirit*, March 18, 1863, p. 1, column 7.

247 *Valley Spirit*, March 25, 1863, p. 3, column 1.

248 *Valley Spirit*, April 29, 1863, p. 3, column 2.

249 Edwin Redkey, "Brave Black Volunteers: A Profile of the Fifty-fourth Massachusetts Regiment," in *Hope and Glory: Essays on the Legacy of the Fifty-fourth Massachusetts Regiment*, ed. Martin H. Blatt, Thomas J. Brown, and Donald Yacovone (Amherst: University of Massachusetts in association with the Massachusetts Historical Society, 2001), p. 22.

250 Redkey, "Brave Black Volunteers," p. 27.

251 Letter from Jacob Christy to his sister, May 1863. All the letters from the Christys and Demus are in the pension file of Wesley Krunkleton, 54th Massachusetts, Pension Files, RG 105, National Archives. I am grateful to Edwin Redkey for calling my attention to these wonderful letters.

252 Letter from Jacob Christy to his sister, Mary Jane, May 1863.

253 Letter from David Demus to his wife, Mary Jane, dated May 8, 1863.

254 Letter from Samuel Christy to his sister, Mary Jane, dated May 9, 1863.

255 Ibid., June 19, 1863.

256 Ibid.

257 Letter from David Demus to his wife, Mary Jane, dated June 18, 1863.

258 Luis F. Emilio, *A Brave Black Regiment: History of the Fifty-fourth Regiment of Massachusetts Volunteer Infantry, 1863–1865,* 3d ed. (Salem, Mass: N. W. Ayer and Company, 1990), pp. 40–43; Duncan, *Hope and Glory,* pp. 90–91.

259 Duncan, *Hope and Glory,* pp. 90–93.

260 *Staunton Spectator*, February 10, 1863, p. 2, column 1.

261 *Staunton Spectator*, January 20, 1863, p. 2, column 4.

262 Ibid.

263 *Staunton Spectator*, January 27, 1863, p. 2, column 2.

264 *Staunton Spectator*, February 17, 1863, p. 2, column 1.

265 *Staunton Spectator*, March 3, 1863, p. 1, column 5.

266 *Staunton Vindicator*, March 13, 1863, p. 1, column 6.

267 *Staunton Vindicator*, March 6, 1863, p. 2, column 2.

268 *Staunton Spectator*, March 24, 1863, p. 2, column 6.

269 *Staunton Vindicator*, February 20, 1863, p. 2, column 6.
270 *Staunton Vindicator*, April 3, 1863, p. 2, column 5.
271 *Staunton Vindicator*, April 17, 1863, p. 2, column 5.
272 *Staunton Vindicator*, April 24, 1863, p. 2, column 4.
273 *Staunton Vindicator*, May 22, 1863, p. 2, column 5.
274 *Staunton Vindicator*, March 27, 1863, p. 1, column 2. Reprints of letter from James Baldwin to James A. Seddon, dated January 28, 1863, and from James A. Campbell, acting for Seddon, to James Baldwin, dated January 31, 1863.
275 *Staunton Vindicator*, March 27, 1863, p. 1, column 2.
276 Diary of Joseph Waddell, entry dated April 3, 1863.
277 *Staunton Vindicator*, April 10, 1863, p. 2, column 3.
278 *Staunton Spectator*, April 7, 1863, p. 2, column 1. For a helpful overview, see Michael Chesson, "Harlots or Heroines? A New Look at the Richmond Bread Riot," *Virginia Magazine of History and Biography*, vol. 92 (1984), pp. 131–75.
279 *Staunton Spectator*, April 7, 1863, p. 2, column 5.
280 For a superb overview, see Stephen W. Sears, *Chancellorsville* (Boston: Houghton Mifflin, 1996); quote from Hooker on p. 192.
281 Quoted ibid., p. 110.
282 Letter from Jedediah Hotchkiss to his wife, Sara, dated April 29, 1863.
283 Ibid., May 6, 1863.
284 Ibid., May 10, 1863.
285 Letter from Adam W. Kersh to his brother, George, dated May 15, 1863.
286 Ibid., May 8, 1863.
287 Ibid., May 15, 1863.
288 Letter from Thomas Smiley to his sister, dated May 9, 1863.
289 This account is related in Sears, *Chancellorsville*, pp. 329–31.
290 Letter from Thomas Smiley to his aunt, dated May 12, 1863.
291 Letter from Jesse Rolston to his wife, Mary, dated May 9, 1863.
292 Letter from Henry Dedrick to his father, dated May 10, 1863.
293 *Staunton Spectator*, May 19, 1863, p. 2, column 4.
294 Ibid.
295 Letter from Adam W. Kersh to his brother, George, dated May 8, 1863.
296 Letter from Henry H. Dedrick to his father-in-law, dated May 10, 1863, Dedrick Family Papers, Virginia Military Institute.
297 Letter from Adam W. Kersh to George B. Kersh, dated May 15, 1863.
298 Letter from Jedediah Hotchkiss to his wife, Sara, dated May 10, 1863.
299 Diary of Joseph Waddell, entry dated May 11, 1863.
300 Ibid., May 13, 1863.
301 Letter from Jedediah Hotchkiss to his wife, Sara, dated May 19, 1863.
302 Ibid.
303 Ibid., June 6, 1863.
304 Letter from Adam Kersh to his brother, dated May 24, 1863.
305 Hotchkiss, February 23, 1863, in McDonald, ed., *Make Me a Map of the Valley*, p. 116.
306 *Valley Spirit*, May 13, 1863, p. 2, column 5.
307 Ibid., column 1.

308 *Sketch of the 126th Pennsylvania Regiment,* pp. 36–37.
309 Letter from Samuel W. North to his father, dated May 7, 1863.
310 Diary of Samuel Cormany, entries from May 5, 8, and 9, 1863.
311 *Valley Spirit,* May 13, 1863, p. 3, column 1.
312 Ibid.
313 *Sketch of the 126th Pennsylvania Regiment,* pp. 37–38.
314 *Valley Spirit,* May 20, 1863, p. 3, column 1.
315 *Valley Spirit,* May 27, 1863, p. 2, column 2.
316 Ibid., p. 3, column 1.
317 My emphasis on the relative strength of white Virginians' devotion to the Confederacy draws on Gary W. Gallagher, *The Confederate War* (Cambridge: Harvard University Press, 1997). My emphasis on the divisions in the North builds upon that of historians of labor and race, most prominently Iver Bernstein, *The New York City Draft Riots: Their Significance in American Society and Politics in the Age of the Civil War* (New York: Oxford University Press, 1990), and Mark E. Neely, Jr., *The Union Divided: Party Conflict in the Civil War North* (Cambridge, Mass.: Harvard University Press, 2002).
318 *Staunton Spectator,* June 2, 1863, p. 2, column 5.
319 Ibid.
320 Diary of Nancy Emerson, entry dated March 6, 1863.
321 Letter from Henry Dedrick to his wife, dated June 14, 1863.
322 Letter from Jedediah Hotchkiss to his wife, Sara, dated June 15, 1863.
323 Diary of Joseph Waddell, entry dated June 19, 1863.
324 Ibid.
325 Ibid., June 16 and 17, 1863.
326 Diary of William Heyser, entry dated June 14, 1863.
327 Alexander K. McClure to Eli Slifer, June 9, 1863, Slifer-Dill Collection, Dickinson College Library.
328 Diary of Philip Schaff, entries dated June 19, 22, and 23, 1863, in *Old Mercersburg,* Woman's Club of Mercersburg, Pa. (Williamsport, Pa.: Grit Publishing, 1949), pp. 167–71. The following account draws from these pages.
329 Diary of Philip Schaff, entry dated June 18, 1863; Jacob Hoke, *The Great Invasion of 1863* (Dayton, Ohio: W. J. Shuey, 1887), pp. 95–96.
330 Diary of Philip Schaff, entry dated June 27, 1863.
331 Diary of William Heyser, entry dated June 14, 1863.
332 *Franklin Repository and Transcript,* July 8, 1863, p. 1, column 1.
333 Diary of Rachel Cormany, entry dated June 15, 1863.
334 Hoke, *Great Invasion,* pp. 98–99.
335 Letter from L. M. Blackford to his father, June 28, 1863, Blackford Family Papers, University of Virginia.
336 Roger U. Delauter, Jr., *McNeill's Rangers* (Lynchburg, Va.: H. E. Howard, 1986), p. 47.
337 Letter from L. M. Blackford to his father, June 28, 1863.
338 Diary of Joseph Waddell, entry dated June 22, 1863.
339 Ibid.
340 Ibid., July 2, 1863.

341 Letter from Jedediah Hotchkiss to his wife, Sara, dated June 24, 1863.
342 *Staunton Vindicator*, July 3, 1863, p. 2, column 2.
343 Ibid.
344 Letter from Jedediah Hotchkiss to his wife, Sara, dated June 24, 1863.
345 Letter from L. M. Blackford to his father, June 28, 1863.
346 Letter from Jedediah Hotchkiss to his wife, Sara, dated June 24, 1863.
347 Letter from L. M. Blackford to his father, June 28, 1863.
348 Diary of Joseph Waddell, entry dated July 4, 1863.
349 Ibid., July 7, 1863.
350 *Franklin Repository and Transcript*, July 8, 1863, p. 1, column 1.
351 Ibid.
352 Ibid.
353 Hoke, *Great Invasion*, pp. 133–34, June 23, 1863.
354 Ibid., pp. 109–10.
355 Ibid., p. 111.
356 Ibid.
357 Diary of Rachel Cormany, entry dated June 16, 1863.
358 Hoke, *Great Invasion*, pp. 107–08.
359 The quotations on this episode from Schneck, Cree, and Heyser appear in Ted Alexander, "A Regular Slave Hunt: The Army of Northern Virginia and Black Civilians in the Gettysburg Campaign," *North and South* (September 2001), pp. 82–89.
360 Diary of Amos Stouffer, June 19, 1863, private collection on the Valley of the Shadow website.
361 Alexander, "Regular Slave Hunt," pp. 86–87.
362 Diary of Rachel Cormany, entry dated June 17, 1863.
363 Michael Hege, "God's Help in Trouble," translated by Peter Hoover, 1998, Michael Hege Collection, Mennonite Historical Association of the Cumberland Valley, Chambersburg, Pennsylvania.
364 Diary of Rachel Cormany, entry dated June 24, 1863.
365 Ibid., June 30, 1863.
366 Ibid., June 27, 1863.
367 Hoke, *Great Invasion*, pp. 215–26.
368 Telegram from Alexander K. McClure to Abraham Lincoln, June 30, 1863, Abraham Lincoln Papers, Library of Congress.
369 Lincoln quoted in Library of Congress note to telegram from Alexander K. McClure to Abraham Lincoln, June 30, 1863, LC; Letter from Alexander K. McClure to Abraham Lincoln, July 1, 1863, LC.
370 Diary of Jacob Stouffer, entry dated July 2, 1863.
371 Diary of Philip Schaff, entry dated June 30, 1863.
372 Ibid.
373 Diary of William Heyser, entry dated July 2, 1863.

ACKNOWLEDGMENTS

Far more than most books, this one is a collaborative effort, growing from the work of dozens of people in the Valley of the Shadow Project at the University of Virginia. The Valley of the Shadow began as one of the two founding projects at the Institute for Advanced Technology in the Humanities in 1991. It benefited early on from the imagination and dedication of Ross Wayland and Thornton Staples, gifted programmers willing to see what humanists might be able to do with powerful computers. In those early days too the support of William Wulf, Alan Batson, Jerry McGann, and John Unsworth was crucial.

The Valley Project has required more work and attention than we could have imagined at the outset. Anne Sarah Rubin, then a doctoral student at Virginia, signed on early as the project manager and oversaw the creation of the first versions of the effort. She managed the other graduate students we brought on board, coordinating their research and assuring the quality of their contributions. Anne's contribution to the entire project is immense—and deeply appreciated. A full acknowledgment of the people who have made the Valley Project is posted on the website, but I should like to mention the following people here for their particular contributions: Alice Carter, Andrew Chancey, Scot French, Charles Irons, Peter Kastor, Benjamin Knowles, Jeff McClurken, Gregg Michel, Amy Minton, Josh Rothman, Philip Troutman, and Drew VandeCreek.

Helpful individuals have generously contributed materials or called our attention to important collections or documents we would have missed. I particularly thank Edsel Burge, Jr., Noel Harrison, and Edwin

Redkey. I am grateful, too, for the early support of the Virginia Foundation for the Humanities, the Woodrow Wilson Birthplace, the Augusta County Historical Society, the Kittochtinny Historical Society, and the Mennonite Historical Society of the Cumberland Valley.

The Valley Project made a leap forward in 1996, when it received a grant from the National Endowment for the Humanities. I thank the NEH, a valuable contributor to American culture, for this support. We have also received crucial support from several private donors, including Dixon Brooke, Richard Coin, John Nau, Roby Robinson, and Jim Stephens. Their help has made it possible to complete the project.

John Casteen, Melvyn Leffler, and Peter Low, leaders at the University of Virginia, supported this effort at critical times, as have friends in the library community in Charlottesville, especially Karin Wittenborg, Michael Plunkett, Kendon Stubbs, and David Seaman.

In 1996, William G. Thomas III took over leadership of the Valley Project from Anne, who went on to finish her dissertation and begin her career as a professor. Will, a gifted teacher and writer, has given the project the benefit of his enormous energies, his wide-ranging knowledge of the Civil War, and his mastery of complex and continually changing technologies. A widely admired member of the university and our local community, Will has directed the Virginia Center for Digital History since its creation in 1999. The Valley Project has flourished because of him. My respect for and gratitude to him are great.

I met Steve Forman of W. W. Norton early in the life of the Valley Project. From the outset, Steve has expressed faith that this effort would succeed and by his patience and skill has made it possible for that faith to be fulfilled. When the CD-ROM we built faced delay and unanticipated challenges, other editors might have washed their hands of the strange enterprise. But Steve never abandoned us and saw the CD through to completion, even to awards and warm reviews. His insightful advice and his careful reading of this book have improved it greatly. Steve is a brilliant editor and a warm friend.

All along, as the website grew and the CD emerged, I dreamed of writing this book. I finally had a chance to begin it during an idyllic year at the Center for Advanced Study for the Behavioral Sciences in Palo Alto, California, in 1999–2000. Sitting at a bare desk with only a laptop computer and unfamiliar hours of quiet before me, I wove stories from the pages of the Web site back in Virginia. I could not have asked for a better place to experiment with voice, organization, and pace. Lynn Gale helped me with statistical work and instructed this unpracticed Easterner in the rudiments of volleyball. Kathleen Much read my early drafts and suggested, helpfully, that I focus the story on major characters. I learned a great deal from the other fellows, especially Carol Gluck, Michael Johnson, Anne Stoler, Richard Stern, Arthur Lupia, Gil Noam, and Larry Cuban.

Upon returning home to Virginia I found myself appointed dean of arts and sciences. Honored, I nevertheless worried about finishing this book as the considerable duties of the new job descended on me. My friends in the dean's office have helped make it possible for me to push ahead thanks to their remarkable energy, professionalism, and goodwill. Heidi Winter and Adam Daniel, in particular, have proved wonderful friends and allies.

Even as I have worked on this manuscript, we have continued to add to the Valley of the Shadow Project, taking it through emancipation and into the memories of war in the Gilded Age. That work, as well as patient responses to countless E-mails about one aspect or another of the Valley, has been provided by talented graduate students. Among those colleagues and friends are Amy Murrell, who served as interim associate director of the Virginia Center for Digital History, Watson Jennison, and John Riedl. I have relied especially heavily on Susanna Lee, expert in letters and diaries, and Aaron Sheehan-Dean, expert in statistics and mapping, as I have labored to drive this book to completion. Kim Tryka, associate director of VCDH, has brought her remarkable skills to bear on our digital work, as has Jennifer Muter.

I have shared drafts of this book with friends and colleagues in Virginia's History Department, a place I have been proud to call home throughout my career. I thank Brian Balogh, Gary Gallagher, Grace Hale, Michael Holt, Peter Onuf, and Will Thomas for their insightful and generous readings, as well as Steve Cushman and Franny Nudelman of our English Department. Several graduate students, especially Andrew Torget, Wayne Hsieh, Ted Hutchinson, and John Mooney, have provided useful comments. Katherine Pierce pored over the notes, checking them against the original sources and offering helpful advice on the manuscript itself. As much help as I have had, the mistakes that surely remain are my responsibility.

Finally, and above all, I thank my family, for Abby, Hannah, and Nate have given me the priceless gifts of their love, laughter, and courage.

INDEX

Page numbers in *italics* refer to illustrations.

ABOUT THE AUTHOR

EDWARD L. AYERS is Hugh P. Kelly Professor of History at the University of Virginia. His first major book, *The Promise of the New South*, was a finalist for the Pulitzer Prize and the National Book Award. In 1991 he originated the Valley of the Shadow Project, a vast digital archive of primary-source materials on the Civil War in the Great Valley. These materials are housed on an award-winning website and CD-ROM. He is currently drawing on this archive to write the next installment of the Valley story, which continues through emancipation, the end of the war, and into Reconstruction. An East Tennessee native, Ayers lives with his wife, Abby, and their children, Hannah and Nate, at the foot of Dudley Mountain outside of Charlottesville, Virginia.